Making states work: State failure and the crisis of governance

Edited by Simon Chesterman, Michael Ignatieff and Ramesh Thakur

United Nations University Press

TOKYO · NEW YORK · PARIS

The views expressed in this publication are those of the authors and do not necessarily reflect the views of the United Nations University.

United Nations University Press
United Nations University, 53-70, Jingumae 5-chome,
Shibuya-ku, Tokyo, 150-8925, Japan
Tel: +81-3-3499-2811   Fax: +81-3-3406-7345
E-mail: sales@hq.unu.edu
General enquiries: press@hq.unu.edu
http://www.unu.edu

United Nations University Office in North America
2 United Nations Plaza, Room DC2-2062, New York, NY 10017, USA
Tel: +1-212-963-6387   Fax: +1-212-371-9454
E-mail: unuona@ony.unu.edu

United Nations University Press is the publishing division of the United Nations University.

Cover design by Sese-Paul Design
Cover photograph© Getty Images/AFLO FOTO AGENCY

Printed in the United States of America

UNUP-1107
ISBN 92-808-1107-X

Library of Congress Cataloging-in-Publication Data

Making states work : state failure and the crisis of governance / edited by Simon Chesterman, Michael Ignatieff, and Ramesh Thakur.
      p.   cm.
   Includes bibliographical references and index.
   ISBN 928081107X (pbk.)
   1. Political stability. 2. Legitimacy of governments. 3. Social contract. I. Chesterman, Simon. II. Ignatieff, Michael. III. Thakur, Ramesh Chandra, 1948–
JC330.2.M355   2004
320′.01′1—dc22   2004025266

Contents

v

Figures and tables

Contributors

Samina Ahmed is Project Director for South Asia at the International Crisis Group. Educated in Pakistan and Australia, she worked previously as a research fellow at the Belfer Center for Science and International Affairs at the John F. Kennedy School of Government, Harvard University, the Institute of Regional Studies, Islamabad, and the Pakistan Institute of International Affairs, Karachi. Her publications include "The Fragile Base of Democracy in Pakistan" in A. Shastri and A. J. Wilson, *The Post-Colonial States of South Asia: Democracy, Identity, Development and Security* (Curzon, Surrey, 2001) and contributions to the journal *International Security*.

Andrea Armstrong is a Research Associate at the International Center for Transitional Justice (ICTJ), focusing on the design of reparations programmes. Prior to joining the ICTJ, she researched regional conflict dynamics in Central Africa and Central Asia at the Center on International Cooperation at New York University. Ms Armstrong has also conducted research on conflict prevention for the United Nations, the protection of refugees for the International Rescue Committee, and the denial of citizenship for the Commission on Human Security. Ms Armstrong holds a master's degree in Public Affairs from the Woodrow Wilson School at Princeton University.

Stephen Baranyi is the Principal Researcher on Conflict Prevention at the North-South Institute (NSI). At NSI he is leading a multi-country study on the challenges of long-term postwar peace-building and developing new research on land policies and conflict prevention. He has also worked with or advised Canada's International

Development Research Centre, Department of Foreign Affairs and International Trade, and the Canadian International Development Agency, as well as NGO networks in Canada, Europe and Latin America. Dr Baranyi has published widely on the role of multilateral organizations, civil society and Canada in various peace processes.

Alex Boraine founded the International Center for Transitional Justice and served as president for three years before becoming chairperson of the Center's board. He has taught at New York University since 1998 and is currently a Senior Research Fellow at its Global Law School. Dr Boraine is a long-time advocate of social justice, both in his native South Africa – where he worked to end apartheid and address its legacy – and around the world. In 1995, he was appointed deputy chairperson by President Nelson Mandela of the South Africa Truth and Reconciliation Commission, serving under chairman Archbishop Desmond Tutu. Dr Boraine is the author of *A Country Unmasked* (Oxford University Press, 2001).

Michel Cahen, a historian, is a Researcher at the Centre National de la Recherche Scientifique in France. He is deputy-director of Centre d'étude d'Afrique noire of Sciences Po Bordeaux, France. His main fields of investigation are contemporary Portuguese-speaking Africa and political ethnicity. His books include *Les Bandits: Un historien au Mozambique, 1994* (Centre Culturel Calouste

Gulbenkian, 2002). He is the founder of *Lusotopie*, a French-based trilingual (French, English and Portuguese) journal devoted to the political analysis of Portuguese-speaking spaces and communities.

Simon Chesterman is Executive Director of the Institute for International Law and Justice at New York University School of Law. Educated in Melbourne, Beijing, Amsterdam and Oxford, he has written widely on international institutions, international criminal law, human rights, the use of force and post-conflict reconstruction. Dr Chesterman is the author of *You, The People: The United Nations, Transitional Administration, and State-Building* (Oxford University Press, 2004) and *Just War or Just Peace? Humanitarian Intervention and International Law* (Oxford University Press, 2001). He is the editor of *Civilians in War* (Lynne Rienner, 2001).

Sebastian von Einsiedel is a Researcher with the UN Secretary-General's High-Level Panel on Threats, Challenges, and Change. From 2002 to 2004 he served as Senior Program Officer at the International Peace Academy, working on its State-Building Program as well as on Security Council issues. He holds a master's degree in International Affairs from Columbia University's School of International and Public Affairs (SIPA). Prior to going to the United States, Mr von Einsiedel worked as a research assistant at the NATO Parliamentary Assembly in Brussels and as a member of the security policy advisory staff in the German parliament.

Peter J. Hoffman is a Research Associate at the Ralph Bunche Institute for International Studies, and from 2003 to 2005 is Mellon Senior Research Fellow in Security and Humanitarian Action. He has written on the dynamics of war and international responses, including contributions to International Commission on Intervention and State Sovereignty, *The Responsibility to Protect: Research, Bibliography, and Background* (International Development Research Centre, 2001) and the journal *Ethics & International Affairs*. He is a doctoral candidate in political science at the Graduate Center of the City University of New York, where he is writing a dissertation on the use of private military companies by the United Nations and humanitarian non-governmental organizations.

Michael Ignatieff, Carr Professor of Human Rights Practice at Harvard's Kennedy School of Government, is the Director of the Carr Center of Human Rights Policy. His academic publications include *The Needs of Strangers: An Essay on the Philosophy of Human Needs* (Viking, 1985); *The Warrior's Honor: Ethnic War and the Modern Conscience* (Metropolitan Books, 1998); *Virtual War: Kosovo and Beyond* (Chatto & Windus, 2000); *The Rights Revolution* (Anansi Press, 2000); *Human Rights as Politics and Idolatry* (Princeton University Press, 2001); *Isaiah Berlin: A Life* (Henry Holt and Co., 1998); *Empire Lite: Nation Building in Bosnia, Kosovo, and Afghanistan* (Vintage, 2003); and *The Lesser Evil: Political Ethics in an Age of*

Terror (Princeton University Press, 2004). He holds a doctorate in history from Harvard University.

Paul Kenny used to teach literature at London University, and now writes it in Mexico City. He is currently completing his second novel, *The Philosopher of the Kidnap*.

James Mayall is Director of the Centre of International Studies at Cambridge University. He worked for a period as a National Service Officer in West Africa and for six years in the British Civil Service, including time in the British High Commission in New Delhi. Professor Mayall has written and published widely on the international relations of African states, North–South relations, international theory and the impact of nationalism on international relations. His books include *Nationalism and International Society* (Cambridge University Press, 1990); *The New Interventionism 1991–1994: United Nations Experience in Cambodia, former Yugoslavia and Somalia* (Cambridge University Press, 1996); and *World Politics: Progress and Its Limits* (Polity Press, 2000).

Abelardo Morales-Gamboa is the Academic Coordinator of the Facultad Latinoamericana de Ciencias Sociales (FLACSO), Costa Rica. As a researcher with FLACSO since 1989, he has published extensively on labour migration, civil society and political processes in the Central American region. During this period he has also been a visiting professor in universities across the region, and has been a consultant on social development issues to various international agencies. In his current capacity he coordinates a research programme on labour migration in Central America and other studies on strengthening civil society, political development, social policy and poverty reduction.

Benjamin Reilly is a Senior Lecturer in the Asia Pacific School of Economics and Government at the Australian National University. His work focuses on political institutions, democratization and conflict management, and he has advised numerous governments and international organizations on these issues. He has previously been a Democratic Governance Advisor with the United Nations Development Programme in New York and a Senior Programme Officer at the International Institute for Democracy and Electoral Assistance in Stockholm. He is the author of *Democracy in Divided Societies: Electoral Engineering for Conflict Management* (Cambridge University Press, 2001) and of three other books on related subjects. He is currently working on a book on democracy, ethnicity and governance in the Asia-Pacific region.

Barnett R. Rubin is Director of Studies and Senior Fellow at the Center on International Cooperation in New York. In November–December 2001 he served as special advisor to the UN Special Representative of the Secretary-General for Afghanistan, Lakhdar Brahimi, during the negotiations that produced the Bonn Agreement. Dr Rubin's books include *Blood on the Doorstep: the Politics of Preventing Violent Conflict* (The Century Foundation and the Council on Foreign Relations, 2002); *The Fragmentation of Afghanistan: State Formation and Collapse in the International System* (2nd edn, Yale University Press, 2002); *Stabilizing Nigeria: Sanctions, Incentives, and Support for Civil Society* (The Century Foundation and the Council on Foreign Relations, 1998); *Post-Soviet Political Order: Conflict and State Building* (edited with Jack Snyder; Routledge, 1998); and *The Search for Peace in Afghanistan: From Buffer State to Failed State* (Yale University Press, 1995).

Amin Saikal is Professor of Political Science and Director of the Center for Arab and Islamic Studies (the Middle East and Central Asia) at Australian National University. He has been a visiting fellow at Princeton University, Cambridge University and the Institute of Development Studies (University of Sussex), as well as a Rockefeller Foundation Fellow in international relations (1983–1988). He is the author of numerous works on the Middle East, Central Asia and Russia, including *Islam and the West: Conflict or Cooperation?* (Palgrave-Macmillan, 2003) and *Modern Afghanistan: A History of Struggle and Survival* (I. B. Tauris, 2004).

Mónica Serrano is a professor of politics at El Colegio de México and a Research Associate at the Centre for International Studies, Oxford. She has written extensively on the politics and the international relations of Latin America. Recent publications include "Bordering on the Impossible: US–Mexico Security Cooperation after 9-11", in P. Andreas and T. Bierstecker, eds, *The Re-Bordering of North America* (Routledge, 2003) and "The Political Economy of Terrorism", in J. Boulden and T. Weiss, eds, *Terrorism and the UN* (Indiana, 2004). She is the co-editor of two forthcoming volumes, *Managing Unequal Power: Regionalism and Governance in the Americas* and *America and the Andes: Intervention in Crisis.*

Hazel Smith is Professor of International Relations at the University of Warwick. She received her doctorate from the London School of Economics in 1992 and was a Fulbright scholar and visiting fellow at Stanford University in 1994/95. Between 2000 and 2002 Dr Smith was on research leave: from 2000 to 2001 she was located in North Korea, working for the UN World Food Programme, and from 2001 to 2002 she was based in Washington, DC, as Jennings Randolph Visiting Senior Fellow at the United States Institute of Peace.

Patricia Shu Ming Tan directs the COMO Foundation, a non-profit organization that builds markets for goods produced by women in developing countries. A graduate of Stanford University, she completed her doctorate at Oxford, writing on the postwar reconstruction of Germany. Dr Tan has previously worked for the Singaporean embassy in Washington, DC, for the Asia-Europe Foundation, and for Interbrand, a branding consultancy.

Her recent publications include articles on the brand identity of non-profit organizations and attempts to market the United States to the Islamic world.

Simon S. C. Tay teaches international law at the National University of Singapore. He is concurrently chairman of the Singapore Institute of International Affairs, a non-governmental think tank. Since July 2002, he has been chairman of the National Environment Agency, the country's major agency for environmental protection and public health. In 2003, he was appointed a visiting professor at the Harvard Law School and the Fletcher School of International Law and Diplomacy. His work on international law and policy focuses on sustainable development, peace and governance, especially in Asia and ASEAN.

Ramesh Thakur is Senior Vice-Rector of United Nations University and Assistant Secretary-General of the United Nations. Educated in India and Canada, he has held full-time academic appointments in Fiji, New Zealand and Australia. He has served on advisory bodies on peace and disarmament to the governments of Australia and New Zealand, was Senior Advisor on Reforms and Principal Writer of the UN Secretary-General's second reform report, and currently serves on the advisory boards of several research institutions in Africa, Asia, Europe and North America. He is the author/editor of some 20 books and 200 journal articles and book chapters; he also writes regularly for the national and international quality press.

Elsina Wainwright directs the Strategy and International Program at the Australian Strategic Policy Institute (ASPI). Prior to joining ASPI, she was an Associate with the management consulting firm McKinsey & Company. She also worked as a consultant political analyst for the International Crisis Group in Bosnia. Dr Wainwright completed both her master's degree and her doctorate in International Relations at Oxford University. While at Oxford, she was a Stipendiary Lecturer in Politics at Oriel College and a tutor in Politics at Christ Church. After finishing her law degree at the University of Queensland, she was Associate to Mr Justice Mackenzie of the Queensland Supreme Court.

Thomas G. Weiss is Presidential Professor of Political Science at the Graduate Center of the City University of New York and Director of the Ralph Bunche Institute for International Studies, where he is also co-director of the United Nations Intellectual History Project and editor of *Global Governance*. He served as research director of the International Commission on Intervention and State Sovereignty and continues to work on follow-up. His recent authored books include *Ahead of the Curve? UN Ideas and Global Challenges* (with Louis Emmerij and Richard Jolly; Indiana University Press, 2001); *The United Nations and Changing World Politics* (with David P. Forsythe and Roger A. Coate; 4th edn, Westview, 2004); and *Military–Civilian Interactions: Intervening in Humanitarian Crises* (2nd edn, Rowman & Littlefield, 2004).

I. William Zartman is the Jacob Blaustein Professor of International Organization and Conflict Resolution and Director of the African Studies and Conflict Management programs at the Johns Hopkins University's Paul H. Nitze School of Advanced International Studies in Washington, DC. He has held previous faculty positions at the University of South Carolina and New York University and has served as Olin Professor at the US Naval Academy, Halevy Professor at the Institute of Political Studies in Paris and visiting professor at the American University in Paris. His recent books include *Preventive Negotiations* (Rowman & Littlefield, 2001) and (edited with Bertram Spector) *Getting It Done: Post-Agreement Negotiations and International Regimes* (United States Institute of Peace, 2003).

Foreword

This timely volume represents the culmination of efforts by three institutions and many individuals to advance thinking about why states fail and why they succeed.

Two of the editors, Michael Ignatieff and Ramesh Thakur, served as commissioners of the International Commission on Intervention and State Sovereignty. Its landmark report *The Responsibility to Protect* transformed the debate over humanitarian intervention and what role the "international community" should play and what responsibilities it bears when facing states that are unable or unwilling to protect their populations. That report and a launching event convened in New York by the International Peace Academy (IPA) in February 2002 provided the intellectual foundation of the project that has produced this volume.

At roughly the same time, Simon Chesterman was leading a project at IPA on the transitional administration of countries and regions in crisis. This and other research at IPA had shown that the role of the state had been somewhat neglected in earlier literature on post-conflict reconstruction. Indeed, humanitarian and human rights constituencies often saw the state mainly as the perpetrator of oppression and mismanagement.

Through the 1990s, human rights activists in particular began to recognize that states might well be major violators of rights – but they were also the only vehicle through which rights could be guaranteed. This insight was recognized in *The Responsibility to Protect*, but it was only after the 11 September 2001 terrorist attacks in New York and Washington,

DC, that the prevention of state failure and "nation-building" moved front and square onto the international agenda.

"Lessons learned" are rarely truly absorbed in capitals or within large international intergovernmental or non-profit bureaucracies. This is demonstrated painfully by the case of Haiti. Ten years after international intervention restored democratically elected President Jean-Bertrand Aristide to power, the country was plunged into chaos and despair in early 2004 as this volume was being completed. Haiti's problems demonstrate that cookie-cutter strategies are easily undermined by the specificity of local circumstances, the interests and actions of local actors and the painfully short attention span of major capitals. Those setting out to renew international efforts to assist Haitians in their quest for a capable, democratic state would do well to scan these pages, not least on the importance (but also the frequent contrariness) of local actors.

Institutions such as the three represented here – the Carr Center for Human Rights Policy, the International Peace Academy and the United Nations University – exist at the intersection of the research and practitioner communities, and can often most usefully focus on gaps in either research or policy development that urgently need to be addressed by decision makers. In a variety of ways, by focusing on state capacities and capability rather than on state failure, this is what the authors and editors seek to do here.

Because such projects tend to arise serendipitously, often as undeveloped ideas first generated in other circumstances, they are hard to plan for. We are thus doubly grateful to those funders who, through their flexibility and foresight, made it possible for us, on short notice, to meet and work together at the Pocantico Conference Center and elsewhere. Direct support for this project came from the Government of Australia, the Government of Germany, the Government of Sweden and the Rockefeller Brothers Fund. Additional support for IPA's work in this area was provided by Carnegie Corporation of New York and the John D. and Catherine T. MacArthur Foundation. The commitment of these governments and foundations to strengthening the capacity of the research community to contribute effectively to policy development is impressive. It has been rewarded here, not least in the volume's conclusions.

For me personally, it has been a privilege occasionally to join in the consultations among authors and editors. Their conclusions will greatly influence my own work in the months and years ahead as I return to the practitioner world to grapple with the challenges they discuss here with such skill, elegance and insight.

David M. Malone
President
International Peace Academy

Acknowledgements

This book has its origins in the work of the International Commission on Intervention and State Sovereignty. Two of the editors, Michael Ignatieff and Ramesh Thakur, were ICISS Commissioners. The International Peace Academy, the third institutional partner in this enterprise, hosted information and dissemination seminars to discuss the ICISS report *The Responsibility to Protect*. In its introductory chapter setting out the policy challenge, *The Responsibility to Protect* remarked that:

It is strongly arguable that effective and legitimate states remain the best way to ensure that the benefits of the internationalization of trade, investment, technology and communication will be equitably shared. Those states which can call upon strong regional alliances, internal peace, and a strong and independent civil society, seem clearly best placed to benefit from globalization. They will also be likely to be those most respectful of human rights. And in security terms, a cohesive and peaceful international system is far more likely to be achieved through the cooperation of effective states, confident of their place in the world, than in an environment of fragile, collapsed, fragmenting or generally chaotic state entities.[1]

That statement, emphasizing the link between international peace and strong states respectful of human rights and robust civil societies, provided the point of departure for a project convened by the International Peace Academy, the Carr Center for Human Rights Policy at Harvard University, and the United Nations University. The three partners would like to record their deepest thanks to the Government of Australia, the Government of Germany, the Government of Sweden and the Rockefeller Brothers Fund for the generous support provided to make the project possible. Naturally, the views expressed here are those of the individual authors and may not reflect those of the funders.

After discussion among the editors on the broad outlines of the project, two meetings were convened to provide the shape and context of the volume. The first, held at the Pocantico Conference Center of the Rockefeller Brothers Fund in Tarrytown, New York, took place in November 2002. This brought authors together with key representatives of and ambassadors to the United Nations. Together, they examined the contemporary phenomenon of state failure and its implications. In particular, the meeting focused on advancing research and policy development on different forms of engagement with weak states that become the subject of international concern. From this initial meeting, the editors commissioned original work from the authors that would speak to this problem and to the other chapters. A second meeting was then convened of the authors only at the United Nations University in Tokyo in May 2003. This provided an opportunity for authors to review each other's work and for the editors to draw together themes that are now elaborated in the concluding chapter.

Special thanks go to Sebastian von Einsiedel at the International Peace Academy and Yoshie Sawada at United Nations University for work above and beyond the call of duty in the course of the project.

Note

1. International Commission on Intervention and State Sovereignty, *The Responsibility to Protect*, Ottawa: International Development Research Centre, December 2001, available at ⟨http://www.iciss.gc.ca⟩, para. 1.34.

Introduction: Making states work

Simon Chesterman, Michael Ignatieff and Ramesh Thakur

[Globalization and interdependence compel us to] think afresh about how we manage our joint activities and shared interests, for many challenges that we confront today are beyond the reach of any one state to meet on its own. At the national level we must govern better; and at the international level we must govern better together. Effective states are essential to both tasks. (Kofi A. Annan, *"We the Peoples"*[1])

In the wealth of literature on state failure, curiously little attention has been paid to the question of what constitutes state success and what enables a state to succeed. This book seeks to fill that gap through examining the strategies and tactics of international actors, local political elites and civil society groups to build or rebuild public institutions before they reach the point of failure – to make the state work.

It is frequently assumed that the collapse of state structures, whether through defeat by an external power or as a result of internal chaos, leads to a vacuum of political power. This is rarely the case. The mechanisms through which political power are exercised may be less formalized or consistent, but basic questions of how best to ensure the physical and economic security of oneself and one's dependants do not simply disappear when the institutions of the state break down. Non-state actors in such situations may exercise varying degrees of political power over local populations, at times providing basic social services from education to medical care. Even where non-state actors exist as parasites on local populations, political life goes on.

1

How to engage in such an environment is a particular problem for policy makers in intergovernmental organizations and donor governments. But it poses far greater difficulties for the embattled state institutions and the populations of such territories. The present volume examines how these various actors have responded to crises in the legitimacy and viability of state institutions, with a particular emphasis on those situations in which the state has been salvaged or at least kept afloat.

Basic concepts of political philosophy in this area remain contested, including sovereignty, power, authority and legitimacy. As Sebastian von Einsiedel's chapter demonstrates, there are wide variations in the definitions not merely of "state failure" but of the very idea of the state itself. For present purposes, the state is considered to be an abstract yet powerful notion that embraces a network of authoritative institutions that make and enforce top-level decisions throughout a territorially defined political entity. The modern state is a manifestation of political power that has been progressively depersonalized, formalized and rationalized; the state is the medium through which political power is integrated into a comprehensive social order. In idealized form, the state embodies the political mission of a society; its institutions and officials express the proper array of techniques that are used in efforts to accomplish that mission. When those institutions and officials cease to function, this abstract idea of the state collapses and the political power that had been channelled through such structures finds alternative, less ordered, means of expression.

State failure is not, therefore, a static concept. Rather, it denotes a continuum of circumstances afflicting states with weak institutions; this continuum extends from states that do not or cannot provide basic public goods through to Somalia-style collapse of governance.

Definitions are important politically as well as analytically. The institution of the modern state and much of the theoretical literature about it originated in Europe; so too did nationalism as it is presently understood. Yet the relationship between "nation" and "state" is historically contingent rather than logically necessary. In particular, in many "post-colonial" states, wars of national liberation and state formation have been followed by even more destructive wars of national debilitation and secession, as James Mayall's chapter demonstrates. The difficulty for most post-colonial societies was that state-building and nation-building (as well as economic development) had to be pursued simultaneously: at times they worked against one another, leading to crises of state legitimacy and the weakening of state institutions.

One of the most important requirements for making states work, therefore, is the creation of apolitical bureaucratic structures (civil service, judiciary, police, army) supported by an ideology that legitimates the role of neutral state authority in maintaining social order through prescribed procedures and the rule of law. This is a theme that runs through the volume – especially the "successes" described in part IV – and is revisited by the editors in the concluding chapter.

The book is organized in five parts. The first two parts outline the major issues confronting international engagement in this area and the regional dynamics that create "bad neighbourhoods" and cultivate dysfunctional states. The third and fourth parts turn to case-studies of states on the edge of failure that have yet to tumble over the precipice and of states that have returned from the brink to achieve varying degrees of success. The final part examines specific policy options available to international actors.

The choice of cases – including the Solomon Islands instead of Somalia, Singapore instead of Sierra Leone – intentionally runs counter to the accepted wisdom in the discourse of state failure. Whereas most accounts of state failure tend to undertake autopsies of states that have failed or collapsed, the interest here is in building or rebuilding institutions before they reach that point. This requires a broader frame of reference than is typically used in the literature, but the lessons of Singapore in the 1960s or the Solomon Islands today have important implications for efforts to establish functioning states or simply generate the political will to try.

Part I provides the intellectual, historical and political context of contemporary engagement to support states with weak institutions. In the first chapter, Sebastian von Einsiedel presents an overview of current policy and analytical approaches to state failure. The 11 September 2001 attacks on the United States transformed the security environment within which such questions are considered, epitomized in the bald statement in the 2002 US *National Security Strategy* that "America is now threatened less by conquering states than we are by failing ones".[2] Seeking to make states work in the interests of national security, however, both understates the nature of the problem posed by weak institutions and overstates the capacity of intervention to resolve it. Einsiedel examines theories of the state and its collapse, emphasizing the need to tailor international responses to the specific circumstances of a case. As always, prevention is preferable to cure. But it is hard to generate the political will to justify concerted action to respond to the causes of state failure rather than merely to protect oneself from its consequences.

James Mayall's chapter examines the legacy of colonialism – a common (and commonly misunderstood) factor in the history of states that develop weak institutions. Colonial structures did not merely define the boundaries of many states but also reified internal divisions along ethnic or religious lines. Nevertheless, the most lasting impact of a colonial past may well be the form of political struggle that was required to end it.

Anti-colonial nationalism provided a potent rallying cry for overthrowing foreign institutions, but it did not provide an ongoing social basis for organizing political activity and structures in the post-colonial state. How this tension was resolved in each case depended largely upon local factors, in particular the political culture and social structures in place before, during and after the period of colonial rule.

In chapter 3, Michael Ignatieff examines the ways in which human rights have been used to justify regime change, "nation-building" and military intervention for human protection purposes – three methods used by intervening powers to make recalcitrant states "work". His chapter focuses in particular on how human rights have figured in the exercise and rationalization of US power, with the 2003 intervention in Iraq providing a troubling bookend to his narrative. If human rights are invoked opportunistically to justify convenient foreign policy choices, and if the outcomes are testimony to the low ranking that human rights assume in those foreign policy priorities, does this mean that such interventions should be abandoned in future? Not entirely, he argues, but the failure of such "nation-building" projects to live up to the rhetoric should make us sceptical as to our capacity to make states work from the outside.

Part II examines the regional context of states with weak institutions. Even so-called intra-state wars are typically transnational in character, involving the dark side of globalization or elements of uncivil society (arms flows, refugees or illicit commodity flows such as drugs and diamonds, for example).[3] These three chapters consider overlapping factors that can influence – both positively and negatively – government capacity, such as regional conflicts, transborder criminal networks, porous borders and economic instability. The regional context may also determine the international response to these situations, ranging from the greater engagement with Central Asia after 11 September 2001 to the relative lack of interest in the South Pacific.

In chapter 4, Barnett Rubin and Andrea Armstrong provide an analytical framework within which to examine these factors: regional conflict formation. Regional competition for political and economic influence may lead to the establishment of networks that are more significant than weak state institutions. By examining how these dynamics played out in two otherwise very different regions – the Great Lakes region of Africa and South Central Asia – Rubin and Armstrong put the conflicts in the Democratic Republic of Congo and in Afghanistan into a regional context. This context is important not merely in understanding how the descent into conflict took place; it provides some suggestions as to how regional approaches can be an important part of conflict management and post-conflict reconstruction. Importantly, the authors warn against an agenda that focuses only on state-building of the weak state in question. It is not the simple lack of a state that undermines human security in these regions, but the incentives that dictate how power is wielded and to what ends. Shaping these incentives may demand an approach that adapts to existing networks and that supports institutions not just in one state but in other key states in a given region.

Regional dynamics played a more subtle role in the phenomenon of weak states in Latin America. Using Colombia as a departure point, Mónica Serrano and Paul Kenny argue in chapter 5 that Latin American states have traditionally enjoyed at best a tenuous monopoly of violence. In such an environment, the legitimacy of the state as the primary provider of security is called into question. Rather than berating the weak state and seeking to bolster its capacity to respond to alternative sources of violence, however, Serrano and Kenny argue for a "critical weak state perspective", focusing on realistic goals for the state in question. Such a perspective would challenge utopian visions of radical reform in short order, but also undermine opportunistic military support from outsiders in furtherance of a domestic political agenda – most notably US support for the counter-narcotic Plan Colombia.

In chapter 6, Benjamin Reilly and Elsina Wainwright examine a different form of regional dynamic among the troubled island states of the South Pacific. Until recently seen as comprising relatively prosperous and stable countries, this region is now termed an "arc of instability". The region suffers from factors common to other regions with weak states – ethnic divisions, unequal distribution of resources, civil–military tensions, proliferation of small arms – but these are compounded by questions of viability. For some island states, rising sea levels make this question a physical one; for others, their small size and dispersed populations challenge conventional forms of governance. Central to international involvement in the South Pacific is the role of Australia, though until recently it has been reluctant to engage deeply in the region. The possibility of terrorist activity in failed states has contributed to a policy shift, but the key problems confronting the South Pacific are not military. Rather, police support and further economic integration are needed to address the more systemic problems confronting the island states. This demands a long-term commitment from Australia, for there is no viable exit strategy from one's own region.

Part III looks at marginal cases: states with weak institutions that have either not failed or have fared better than expected. Pakistan, with a history of conflict, Islamic extremism and nuclear weapons, is too important to allow it to fail and it has been the recipient of extensive external support, most importantly from the United States. As Samina Ahmed argues in chapter 7, however, this support for the status quo, in particular the military's monopoly over power, is itself largely responsible for

Pakistan's crisis in state legitimacy. Challenging the authoritarianism and centralization that have undermined the state will require concerted international support for new, representative institutions. As long as the United States, among others, supports direct military rule, meaningful change in Pakistan will be impossible. But, as long as the military remains unaccountable to political processes, the state will continue to lose the allegiance of its citizens, incrementally eroding its stability and thus escalating the risk that Pakistan poses to the international community.

The Democratic People's Republic of Korea (DPRK) – more commonly known as North Korea – is generally viewed as bad, mad or sad, or all three. In chapter 8, Hazel Smith provides a more nuanced account of the DPRK as a state that was never intended to "work" in the way that the liberal model of institutions distinct from governing political authority suggests. Instead, the DPRK was established as a fusion of party and society permanently mobilized for self-defence activities. When this party/society complex began to disintegrate during the food shortages of the mid-1990s, it became possible that a state in its modern sense could emerge, but the contours of foreign engagement with the DPRK must be mapped by reference to this unusual political heritage.

Afghanistan is suggestive of the opportunities and dangers of modern state-building – and of the importance of seizing opportunities for meaningful change when they arise. As Amin Saikal shows in chapter 9, despite the challenges to Afghanistan as a state since the late 1970s, Afghans still demonstrate a strong sense of society. Remarkably, despite a generation of almost unceasing conflict, there is no serious secessionist movement. Instead, Afghanistan is dominated by a web of overlapping micro-societies, whose personalized power structures long undermined the formation of coherent state institutions, ultimately creating the political space for extremist unifying forces such as the Taliban. The 11 September 2001 attacks on the United States thrust Afghanistan onto the international agenda, but efforts to secure a lasting peace were soon overtaken by the crisis in Iraq. Plans to create a strong centralized state in Afghanistan are intended to overcome divisions between the micro-societies, but they run the risk of merely papering over the political dynamics that these micro-societies represent. The only way to secure a stable political environment is to embrace those dynamics and design political structures around them accordingly, but international actors appear to be more focused on exit deadlines – exit without a strategy.

Part IV turns to three states that are now broadly considered successful but that experienced a basic crisis in their legitimacy or effectiveness, or had to establish themselves against a backdrop of deep initial scepticism, and it examines how that crisis and scepticism were overcome.

Mozambique is frequently touted as a relatively successful case of international intervention to turn a state from war to relative stability. As Michel Cahen argues in chapter 10, however, the conclusion of war is far from identical with the achievement of peace. In examining whether Mozambique actually "works", he suggests that early assumptions that the conflict was driven by external factors – most importantly South Africa's policy of destabilization – are mirrored in present assessments of Mozambique's relative economic success based on models advocated by the international financial institutions. Just as the causes of what was ultimately an internal conflict were overlooked for many years, so today the economic figures mask a fragile social and political balance. Cahen's central argument is that building up institutions of the state has, for too long, overshadowed the need for engagement at the level of the nation.

Costa Rica, discussed in chapter 11, has achieved a remarkable level of stability in a notoriously bad neighbourhood. As Abelardo Morales-Gamboa and Stephen Baranyi explain, this exceptionalism has historical roots in the relatively marginal role that colonialism played in the country's early development. Stable political parties and a culture of tolerance laid the foundations for the present pillars of Costa Rican democracy, consolidated after a brief civil war in 1948: political institutions based on inclusive liberal democracy, demilitarization, a mixed economy, a welfare state and a strong sense of nationhood. These factors and enlightened leadership enabled Costa Rica to escape the civil wars and foreign intervention experienced by its neighbours in the 1980s, but more recent drives for further economic liberalization have challenged the consensus that lies at the heart of Costa Rican politics.

Singapore, with a stable government and a gross domestic product per capita that rivals that of Britain, is today an unambiguous success. But the strength of today's city-state belies its fragile beginnings and concerns for its future. A number of chapters in the present volume discuss international intervention, but less has been said about the implications of foreign withdrawal. Chapter 12, by Patricia Shu Ming Tan and Simon Tay, examines how Singapore managed the withdrawal of British troops from the former colony soon after its unexpected separation from Malaysia. Preparations for the departure of an external actor served in themselves as an important state-building exercise. Importantly, Singapore fought to manage its own timetable and development plans, drawing upon foreign expertise but always under local leadership. The security threat posed by the British withdrawal was also used as a springboard for nation-building, with compulsory National Service together with housing and education programmes designed as pan-ethnic institutions to encourage Singaporeans to identify Singapore as state, nation and home. Thus, Tan and Tay argue, Singapore may not have assumed a strictly liberal democratic form but it is nonetheless a stakeholder society that works.

Part V turns to forms of engagement available to interested outsiders, with four chapters examining distinct trends in recent international practice: prevention, humanitarian action, transitional justice and international administration.[4]

Chapter 13, by I. William Zartman, outlines the web of policy options confronting international actors seeking to prevent the downward spiral of dysfunctional states. Each stage has its own difficulties, from diagnosis of the problem and the mandate to intervene before things get too late, to the question of what one does when the political will to act exists. Political will lies at the heart of the problem: early warnings are plentiful, but this does not always lead to early awareness or early determination to act. Various regimes governing non-military forms of early intervention have emerged in recent years, ranging from human rights and democratization to anti-corruption and fiscal responsibility. All too often, however, it is only the final phase of failure that draws international attention, by which time more intrusive measures may be required.

Whether or not strategies are in place to address the political consequences of weakened state institutions, vulnerable populations require humanitarian assistance. Those providing such relief, however, are frequently confronted by an array of overlapping and conflicting political authorities in the recipient state. As Thomas Weiss and Peter Hoffman argue in chapter 14, humanitarian actors must therefore become more flexible in dealing with a wider variety of actors – a challenge that presents both doctrinal and political challenges. Non-state actors may impede access to populations at risk or distort the provision of assistance through their economic interests, but they may also provide the seeds of future peace-building networks. A central dilemma for humanitarians, then, is to distinguish between spoilers and civil society, as well as dealing with those non-state actors that embody qualities of both. Responding to this challenge demands a better understanding of non-state actors ("humanitarian intelligence") and operating strategies better tailored to the environment within which humanitarians now find themselves. In this way, it may be possible to make humanitarianism "work".

Getting the state itself to work is another question. Although the forms that state failure assumes vary widely, it is almost always characterized by weak judicial institutions. Building or rebuilding institutions demands a reckoning with past injustices that were perpetrated in the absence or with the connivance of those institutions. In chapter 15, Alex Boraine examines the transitional justice options available to states emerging from violent conflict. How that transition comes about has important ramifications for the appropriateness of different judicial and non-judicial mechanisms. This is, however, only one aspect of the need to tailor such mechanisms to local requirements: unless transitional justice mechanisms are seen as enjoying local legitimacy, the outcomes themselves may be called into question. This demands flexibility on the part of international actors, including on the controversial question of amnesties.

Chapter 16, by Simon Chesterman, examines the most extensive form of intervention in the service of making a state or territory work: international administration. Is it possible to establish the basis for legitimate and sustainable self-rule through a period of benevolent autocracy? Focusing on the experiments conducted by the United Nations in the 1990s, and those pursued by the United States in the name of its war on terror, there are reasons to be modest. Transitional administration combines an unusual mix of idealism and realism: the idealist project that people can be saved from themselves through education, economic incentives and the space to develop mature political institutions; together with the realist basis for that project in what is ultimately military occupation. In this way, the international community is exposed at its most hypocritical: the means are inconsistent with the ends, they are frequently inadequate for those ends, and in many situations the means are simply inappropriate for the ends.

The final chapter, by the editors, brings together the policy implications of the earlier chapters. Not surprisingly, the key insight is that states cannot be made to work from the outside. As the cases examined in this volume show, success in maintaining the viability and legitimacy of a state requires enlightened local leadership, coherent institutional coordination and international assistance – including simply providing the necessary space – for consolidating a national response. For international actors, this is a humbling conclusion: assistance is often a necessary but never a sufficient factor in achieving success. But for local actors this should be seen as an opportunity to seize responsibility – "ownership" in the present jargon – and use the brief window of international interest to foster conversation among the population about what sort of state it wants.

Notes

1. Kofi A. Annan, *"We the Peoples": The Role of the United Nations in the 21st Century*, New York: United Nations, Department of Public Information, 2000, p. 7.
2. *The National Security Strategy of the United States of America*, Washington, DC: President of the United States, September 2002, available at ⟨http://www.whitehouse.gov/nsc/nss.html⟩, p. iv.
3. *Report of the Panel on United Nations Peace Operations*, UN Doc. A/55/305-S/2000/809, 21 August 2000, para. 18.
4. The list is not exhaustive – notably, different forms of economic engagement are not considered in the present volume. See, for example, Mats R. Berdal and David M. Malone,

eds, *Greed and Grievance: Economic Agendas in Civil Wars*, Boulder, CO: Lynne Rienner, 2000; Hernando de Soto, *The Mystery of Capital: Why Capitalism Triumphs in the West and Fails Everywhere Else*, New York: Basic Books, 2000; Paul Collier, *Breaking the Conflict Trap: Civil War and Development Policy*, New York: Oxford University Press, 2003; Karen Ballentine and Jake Sherman, eds, *The Political Economy of Armed Conflict: Beyond Greed and Grievance*, Boulder, CO: Lynne Rienner, 2003; Michael Pugh and Neil Cooper, *War Economies in a Regional Context: The Challenge of Transformation*, Boulder, CO: Lynne Rienner, 2004.

Part I
Issues

1

Policy responses to state failure

Sebastian von Einsiedel

After years of relative neglect, the events of 11 September 2001 put the issue of failed states firmly at the centre of international attention. The danger of terrorists using failed states as a safe haven from which to operate internationally has become a commonplace of media analysis. After the fall of Afghanistan's Taliban regime at the hands of the United States, it was initially not Iraq but Somalia, without a central government since 1991, that appeared to be next on the US list of terrorist-harbouring countries. This strategic outlook appeared to be supported by the 2002 US *National Security Strategy*, which bluntly stated that "America is now threatened less by conquering states than we are by failing ones".[1] A growing body of literature identifies state failure as a national security threat rather than simply a humanitarian issue.[2]

Without dismissing the terrorist danger emanating from failed states situations, focusing on this one element of state collapse is too narrow. Terrorists have proven their capacity to operate undetected anywhere from Faisalabad to Florida and from Hamburg to Hebron. Failed states should be of concern to the international community – and the UN community in particular – for reasons beyond al Qaeda. As the cases of Angola, Somalia, Liberia, the Democratic Republic of Congo, Sierra Leone, Lebanon, Afghanistan, Tajikistan and others show, failing and failed states often lead to humanitarian disasters, endemic civil war, immense flows of refugees and internally displaced persons, and international trade in illicit drugs and weapons. The chapters in this volume on South

13

Central Asia and the Great Lakes region, the South Pacific, and the Andean region demonstrate that failed states create "bad neighbourhoods", drawing whole regions into a quagmire (this can also be seen in the South Balkans, the South Caucasus and West and East Africa).[3]

Apart from regional destabilization and threats to international security, it is the human suffering engendered by state failure that merits the greatest concern. Michael Ignatieff goes so far as to say that "The human rights dilemmas of the twenty-first century derive more from anarchy than tyranny".[4] The International Commission on Intervention and State Sovereignty in its report *The Responsibility to Protect* put great emphasis on failed states, stating that they "are quite likely to generate situations which the international community simply cannot ignore".[5] Indeed, during the past decade, the United Nations had ample opportunity to experience first-hand the challenge posed by violent conflict in failed states. James Fearon and David Laitin have made the point that, whereas the United Nations has been extremely reluctant to intervene in anti-colonial wars and – with a few exceptions – in separatist conflicts, it has dispatched over a dozen UN peacekeeping operations into "wars for capture of the centre by rebel armies in weak states".[6]

Given the grave consequences of state collapse, the international community has a considerable interest in preventing the collapse of states in the first place. Strengthening weak states against failure is, in theory, far easier than reviving them after collapse. This underlines the importance of exploring the causes of state failure, developing methods of risk assessment and early warning, and devising strategies to strengthen the capacities of weak and failing states. This chapter offers a review of recent literature addressing these issues by way of introduction to the examination of issues and cases in the chapters that follow.

The first section looks at the problem of defining the term "failed state", highlighting the interrelationship of state failure and civil war and presenting different theories on the causes of collapse. The second section then surveys different attempts to develop early warning indicators, most notably the results of the State Failure Task Force, and outlines what preventive and non-military reactive tools the international community has at hand to face the challenge of failing states.

The problem

What are failed states?

Before one attempts to define the term "failed state", it is helpful to consider different approaches to defining what a state is. At a very basic level, there are three dominant conceptions of the state. The first views the state as a social contract in the tradition of Hobbes, Rousseau and Locke.[7] From this viewpoint, the authority of the state rests upon an agreement among the members of a society to acknowledge the authority of a set of rules or a political regime. This puts special emphasis on the relation between state and society, implying not only the submission of all members of society to the state, but also a responsibility by the state to deliver services, most notably security but also – according to more recent contract theory – social justice.[8] The second approach, identified with German sociologist Max Weber, defines the state as a corporate group that claims to monopolize the legitimate use of force over a territory.[9] This tends to emphasize a state's means, rather than its ends. A third approach focuses not on the de facto attributes of the state but on juridical statehood. According to the 1933 Montevideo Convention, a state has the following characteristics: (1) a defined territory, (2) a permanent population, (3) an effective government, and (4) the capacity to enter into formal relations with other states.[10]

There is no agreement in the scholarly literature on the definition of a failed state, but the various definitions that are in use may be contrasted to these different conceptions of the state. The most often cited is the definition based on the social contract used by I. William Zartman, for whom collapse means "that the basic functions of the state are no longer performed".[11] A collapsing state is therefore one that maintains few or no functioning state institutions, has lost its power to confer identity, can no longer assure security and has lost its legitimacy. Ignatieff uses a broader, "Weberian" definition of failed states, which for him are characterized by an "inability to maintain a monopoly of the internal means of violence". As a consequence, his list of failed states would include countries, such as Sri Lanka and Colombia, that are "capable states" but are nevertheless "fighting a losing battle against insurgents".[12]

An even more inclusive definition has been chosen by the State Failure Task Force (discussed in greater detail below), sponsored by the US government, which equates state failure with civil war.[13] This empties the concept of much of its meaning, however, and Peter Wallensteen is right to point out that "state failure can take place without civil war, and there can be civil war without state failure".[14] Albania in 1997 is an example of the former constellation, contemporary Colombia arguably an example of the latter.

There is no doubt, of course, that state failure dramatically increases the likelihood of civil war, so it is worth looking briefly at the interrelationship of the two phenomena. The weakening of state institutions increases the likelihood of violent conflict in several ways. First, the erosion of state authorities sharpens the security dilemma for minority groups within a state. Second, Jack Snyder has argued that in weak states ethnic concepts of nationalism or other exclusionary ideologies such as religious fundamentalism are more likely to prevail than are civic concepts of nationalism – with the former being more conflict prone than the latter.[15] The strong currents of ethnic nationalism in parts of the Balkans, East Central Europe and the former Soviet Union are examples of this.[16] Third, the weaker the state, the greater the incentives for regional leaders to exploit the power vacuum. This may take the form of outright warlordism, as seen in Afghanistan prior to the Taliban and in Somalia today. Nevertheless, state weakness should be treated as a permissive or structural cause of violent conflict, rather than as a consequence or the equivalent of conflict.

In addition to such studies of failed states within political science, there is a separate economic literature on state failure, focusing less on the violent conflicts that may accompany the breakdown of state institutions than on factors such as economic growth, governance and development. The economists' underlying definition of the term "failed state" differs significantly from how it is understood in political science. According to one economist, "persistent shortfalls in growth rates compared to comparable countries provides prima facie evidence of state failure and its severity".[17] As a consequence, the economists' list of failed states includes countries such as Argentina in the aftermath of its economic breakdown in 2001–2002.[18] Cross-fertilization between the two disciplines is mostly absent, which is unfortunate in that some of the economists' findings and conclusions might be of relevance to political scientists.

For present purposes, no attempt will be made at a final definition of the term "failed state". Much ink has been spilled on developing typologies of the forms of state failure, using either the degree of failure or its cause as a criterion (then distinguishing between weak, endemically weak, aborted, fragile, ungovernable, shadow, failing, failed, anarchic, phantom, anaemic or collapsed states).[19] Instead, this volume treats state failure as a continuum of circumstances that afflict states with weak institutions – ranging from states in which basic public services are neglected to the total collapse of governance, exemplified by the "ideal-type" of Somalia.

Why do states fail?

Ignatieff has assembled a list of causes of state collapse:

Sometimes the cause is colonial legacy; sometimes it is maladministration by an indigenous elite; sometimes, failure is a legacy first of interference by outside powers, and then abandonment.... [M]ost important, many failed and failing states are poor and have suffered from the steadily more adverse terms of trade in a globalized economy.[20]

The list suggests that causes of state failure may be located at many levels: the system level, the state level and the level of individual leaders. These various explanations of the root causes of state failure are not mutually exclusive, but should be seen as complementary explanatory models.

Among the most often mentioned root causes of state collapse is the legacy of colonialism, an issue that is explored in depth in the chapter by James Mayall in this volume.[21] Apart from colonial borders creating unviable entities prone to ethnic conflict, the imposition of colonial rule frequently saw the destruction of traditional social structures without re-placing them with Western constitutional and institutional structures.[22]

Pointing to the wave of state failure in Africa in the 1990s, several authors go further and argue that the European model of the nation-state is simply the wrong institution for that continent.[23] They claim that Africa's demography (sparse population in rural areas),[24] geography (poor communication lines and trade routes),[25] political culture and her-itage (characterized by political control over people rather than land and by multiple layers of sovereignty)[26] and social structure (built around family relationships and spiritual authority)[27] are incompatible with the state model imposed by the European colonizers. According to Jeffrey Herbst, the etiquette of sovereignty that newly independent African states were granted was nothing but a "legal fiction". The sanctity of boundaries that came with the grant of sovereignty removed the threat of secession and with it incentives for leaders to reach accommodation with disaffected populations.[28] Arguing along the same lines, Christo-pher Clapham differentiates between African countries with a tradition of pre-colonial statehood (such as southern Uganda, Ethiopia, Eritrea, southern Ghana and Rwanda) and those without (such as Somalia, north-ern Uganda, southern Sudan, Liberia and Sierra Leone), arguing that the former "are far better able to survive (and even learn from) the experi-ence of bad government". Furthermore, insurgent movements within the first group of countries have been more likely to set up effective political structures after the successful overthrow of governments than have those within the second group.[29]

Although accepting the importance of the colonialist experience for the understanding of Africa's ongoing malaise, Zartman and others reject the argument that the state is simply the wrong institution for Africa.[30] Zartman argues that "no common theme or characteristic runs through the cases of collapse that would indicate that collapse was the result either of the same 'Western-style' malfunction in the state or of particularly badly adapted Western institutions". Zartman affirms that "there is no typical 'African state' especially adapted to African circumstances, or specifically derived from a precolonial protoinstitution; rather is there a set of functions that need to be performed for the coherence and the effectiveness of the polity – *anywhere*".[31] Liberia could serve as an interesting case-study in this respect. It has a long history of independence and did not experience typical foreign colonial rule, yet it was one of the most extreme cases of state collapse in the 1990s.

An important tool in understanding how state legitimacy and bureaucratic (that is, based on the rule of law) state institutions may be hollowed out from within is provided by the concept of the "shadow state". As proposed by William Reno, the shadow state is "the product of personal rule, usually constructed behind the façade of *de jure* state sovereignty".[32] Protected by the sanctity of borders, propped up during the Cold War by a superpower patron or profiting from natural resource extraction, rulers had no interest in nurturing taxable autonomous groups of internal producers. This situation allowed them instead to impose heavy demands for resources on their own population. Reno writes,

In these circumstances, rulers had little prospect of attracting popular legitimacy, or even compliance with their directives. Thus, many rulers preferred to conserve resources that otherwise would be spent for services, devoting them instead to payouts to key strongmen in return for obedience and support.[33]

Reno argues that this privatization of state assets and prerogatives created a framework of rule outside formal state institutions, a shadow of state bureaucratic agencies based on personal ties. The states that Reno lists as falling within this category read like a "who's who" of failed states: Zaire under Mobutu, Albania in the 1990s, Liberia under Samuel Doe, and Somalia under Siad Barre. An important element of Reno's analysis is that rulers, from their own perspective, have a vital interest in making the lives of their populations less secure and more materially impoverished, since this encourages individuals to seek the ruler's personal favour to secure exemption from these conditions.

Reno's analysis is consistent with the view of those authors who view the present incidence of state collapse as largely a function of the major powers' withdrawal of interest and resources from weak states after the end of the Cold War.[34] This sudden ending of outside support, which took place against the background of a structural economic crisis in the developing world starting in the early 1980s, left the leaders of many shadow states without resources to distribute to their followers and to maintain a strong, functioning army. Increasingly, this meant that states lost the monopoly over violence.[35]

State failure did, of course, occur prior to the end of the Cold War. Leaving aside Congo's collapse in 1960–1961, Zartman suggests that state collapse in Africa occurred in two waves.[36] He locates the first wave in the late 1970s and early 1980s, when established but poorly functioning regimes of the original nationalist generation were overthrown, carrying the whole state structure with them into a vacuum. Examples of this wave are Uganda and Chad. The second wave, according to Zartman, occurred in the late 1980s and has continued since. This wave, like the first one, was characterized by authoritarian rulers who were overthrown by new "successor regimes that could destroy but not replace", with the case of Somalia serving as the prime example.

Before turning to efforts by international actors to prevent and respond to state failure, it is instructive to turn the question of state failure on its head – as this volume attempts. Why do some states not fail? Robert Rotberg, for example, asks why Sri Lanka, in spite of its 19-year civil war, Indonesia, in spite of its separatist wars, and Colombia, in spite of its decades-old insurgency and widespread insecurity, have not joined the ranks of failed states. His tentative answer seems to be that the relative legitimacy of the state or the government and its ability to deliver basic functions account for the continued survival of states that would have otherwise collapsed under the weight of circumstances.[37] To say that a state has not failed because it continues to deliver some basic functions seems to be a circular argument, however, and equivalent to saying that a state has not failed because it has not failed. This book is in part an effort to break out of that circle.

The issue of legitimacy in particular merits further exploration. One must be careful not to conflate the legitimacy of a state, of a regime and of a government, because these are different units of analysis. A government can lose its legitimacy while the old regime and the state remain unscathed (such as the Nixon administration in the United States in 1974) and a regime can lose its legitimacy while the state retains its own (such as the PRI government in Mexico in 2001 or the Argentinian military regime in 1982). Arguably, a state might slide into failure while the regime stays in power – at least temporarily, before it is eventually swept away when the state finally collapses (for example, the Mobutu regime during the last two decades of its existence).

What are the necessary ingredients for a state to be legitimate? For the classic definition one has to turn, once again, to Weber, who identifies three pure types of legitimate authority: legal authority, traditional authority and charismatic authority.[38] The main characteristic of legal authority is that the subjects and their officials owe obedience to the legally established impersonal order. Within a "legal authority with a bureaucratic administrative staff", a subcategory into which the modern nation-state falls, trained and specialized officials receive a fixed salary and are organized in a hierarchy. Advancement in this hierarchy is based on merit, and members of the official staff are separated from ownership of the means of production or administration.[39] Weber concludes that this type of authority is capable of attaining the highest degree of efficiency and is "the most crucial phenomenon of the Western state".[40]

By contrast, the governance of many states that are today considered to be failed or failing bears the characteristics of traditional authority, where the obedience of a population is owed not to enacted rules but to the person who occupies a position by authority, a concept that re-sembles Reno's shadow state.[41] Even though characterized as one ideal-type of legitimate authority by Weber, modern states that operate this way are simply too inefficient and mostly too corrupt to master the challenges of complex public administration successfully.

As Samina Ahmed's chapter on Pakistan in this volume shows,[42] the Weberian bureaucracy-based understanding of legitimacy competes with a more modern concept of state legitimacy centred on the principle of democracy and respect for human rights. Successive authoritarian, dictatorial or military governments that are unresponsive to their populations' needs and wishes – or hijack state structures to pursue their limited parochial interests – risk alienating and destroying the civil society that every state needs to thrive. However, as the case of contemporary China demonstrates, an order can be viewed as legitimate even if it is not based on democratic principles. At least for now, the regime in Beijing rather successfully manages to make up for the lack of democratic legitimacy with a Weberian legitimacy based on economic growth made possible through an efficient state administration.

Against this background, the crucial question for outside actors then becomes how they can contribute to a state's legitimacy – bearing in mind Wallensteen's warning that a state "should be strong enough to protect its citizens and their collective assets, but not too strong, so as to threaten the inhabitants it is to serve".[43]

International responses

As outlined in the Introduction to this volume, the international community has a vital interest in developing instruments and strategies to prevent state collapse. As in the broader field of conflict prevention, there are substantial challenges to this endeavour – most obviously the principle of state sovereignty, but also the general lack of political will on the part of other states to act early. The recent linkage of state failure to terrorism may help overcome some of these obstacles, but it addresses only one aspect of the phenomenon of state failure.

Article 2(7) of the UN Charter states that the United Nations shall not intervene in "matters, which are essentially within the domestic jurisdiction of any state". Chapter VII of the Charter provides for the exception to this general principle of non-interference, allowing for coercive measures including military intervention where the Security Council determines the existence of a threat to international peace and security. More than 10 years ago, Gerald Helman and Steven Ratner argued that "[n]ot all failing states pose true dangers to the peace" and that therefore "[t]he UN's responsibility for international peace and security is not ... a sufficient basis for its action to resurrect all failed states".[44] Since then, the Security Council has proved that it is willing to interpret dangers to international peace and security more broadly, involving cases that pose an indirect threat if any. For example, the Security Council invoked Chapter VII in 1992–1993 when it was faced with a humanitarian catastrophe in Somalia, in 1994 when a military junta deposed democratically elected President Aristide in Haiti and in 1997 when the Albanian state dissolved into chaos after the collapse of a popular pyramid scheme.

The events of 11 September 2001 have created a situation in which the international community in general and the Security Council in particular are even more likely to support interventions in failed or failing states. Even prior to the 11 September attacks, there had been a growing tendency to promote an international oversight responsibility and even a right to intervene militarily for certain cases of state failure. The *Responsibility to Protect* report interprets sovereignty not just as a shield against outside interference but also as an obligation that states have vis-à-vis their respective populations. It concludes that military intervention with Security Council authorization would be justified in "situations of state collapse and the resultant exposure of the population to mass starvation and/or civil war".[45] This view has been at least rhetorically acknowledged by many policy makers, as exemplified by former President Clinton's speech at the UN Millennium summit in which he stressed the need to "find ways to protect *people* as well as *borders*".[46] Unfortunately, the willingness of the Security Council to bypass the principle of non-intervention and mandate any form of intervention materializes only in cases of near or total state collapse. Moreover, as Susan Woodward has pointed out, the international community has tended to respond to state failure in humanitarian rather than political terms, "treating the matter as an emergency to be ended quickly, not a political collapse to be reversed let alone prevented".[47] In the wake of the US-led action in Afghanistan, it is possible that subsequent interventions may add a military dimension – though it is unclear that this will be accompanied by a political strategy sufficient for the task of building or rebuilding sustainable institutions after the military objective has been completed. The major challenge facing the international community is how to intervene at an early stage in order to prevent the worst from happening.

There are impediments to preventive or pre-emptive action beyond the principles of sovereignty and non-intervention. Among these is, first, the difficulty of predicting state failure. Dozens of states in the current international system are endemically weak, yet only a handful slide into total collapse. Given the scarce resources available for preventive measures, reliable tools of analysis enabling us to make predictions that are as precise as possible are a basic requirement for an active prevention policy. The United Nations is highly dependent on input from its member states, academia and non-governmental organizations (NGOs) in this respect, since it does not have and is unlikely to acquire in the future a well-funded and centralized bureau for the collection and analysis of information capable of providing early warning assessments. Massive preventive efforts and investments are also hard to mobilize in the early stages of state weakness – that is, at a point when it is not yet clear whether or not a state is going to collapse completely.

Second, the more state institutions have eroded and the more a state is overwhelmed by chaos, the less the outside world can intervene effectively. Although a situation of state failure may facilitate humanitarian action – witness the cases of Afghanistan, Sudan and Somalia – diplomatic or economic pressure is difficult to apply when local interlocutors and institutions are simply absent.[48]

Third, it has been argued that the international institutional architecture devised in the wake of the Second World War is simply unsuited to dealing with the challenge of state failure. While the United Nations seems to be badly equipped to deal with the political and military consequences of state failure, the Bretton Woods institutions seem to be equally overburdened by the economic consequences. As Jean-Germain Gross writes: "Indeed, the problem with failed states is not that there is too much state, which the World Bank and the IMF, mainly through privatization and state personnel attrition, know how to reduce, but rather too little, which they are ideologically ill-disposed to help enlarge."[49]

Early warning and evaluation

Zartman writes that state collapse is not a short-term phenomenon but a "long-term degenerative disease".[50] If this is true, it is good news for those who want to intervene preventively and cure the disease, since there may be plenty of time for diagnosis. A major challenge is to develop early warning indicators of a high likelihood of state collapse.[51]

Political scientists in the past have identified certain factors associated with the phenomenon of state failure (which may or may not be interpreted as causes) based on more or less casual observation and logic rather than on systematic statistical analysis. Thus Jean-Germain Gross, for example, writes that five factors appear to correlate strongly with the implosion of failed states: poor economic performance; lack of social synergy; authoritarianism; militarism; and environmental degradation caused by rampant population growth.[52] The problem with this analysis is that these factors are often present for many decades and are therefore not particularly helpful as early warning indicators. For Wallensteen, the best indicator of collapse is how well a government is able to deliver services such as law, order, taxation and social services. Wallensteen notes that the breakdown of these services "normally can be observed long before a crisis, whether in the declining quality of the services or in the reduced territorial penetration of the government".[53]

In order to remedy a perceived lack of systematic analysis of state failure, in 1994 the US government, at the behest of then Vice-President Al Gore, established and funded the State Failure Task Force, the most ambitious and broadly conceived empirical effort to develop early warning indicators. The Task Force consists of a panel of distinguished academic social scientists, experts in data collection and consultants in statistical methods. Its objective was to "develop a methodology to identify key factors and critical thresholds signalling a high risk of political crisis in countries some two years in advance".[54] Although the Task Force identified only 12 cases of complete collapse of state authority during the past 40 years, it enlarged the data set to include almost all revolutionary wars, ethnic wars, genocides and politicides, and adverse or disruptive regime transitions between 1955 and 1994 – a total of 127 cases. These events were what the Task Force considered to be extreme crises of governance. On the basis of this data set, the Task Force tested a large number of possible independent variables comprising demographic, societal, economic, environmental and political indicators. Multivariate analysis yielded a "single best model" for predicting state failure with three variables: openness to international trade; infant mortality; and democracy. According to this model, states with low openness to international trade, above-median infant mortality and a low level of competitive political participation and institutionalized checks on executive power have a high risk of failure. However, the Task Force confirmed earlier studies that had also found that partial democracies are more vulnerable to state failure than are either autocracies or democracies.[55] These empirical findings are consistent with several theoretical explanations of state failure. The model's predictive power for regime crisis is 80 per cent for any given year. More focused models of sub-Saharan Africa, Muslim countries and ethnic war are even more accurate.

Although these are interesting results, a word of caution is nevertheless in order. First, as pointed out by the Task Force itself, most variables in the model refer to background or structural conditions that are relatively slow to change so "the models are (at best) suitable for long-term risk assessment" and "must be complemented by the analysis of potential accelerators and triggers". Knowledge about these triggers is scant and more research is clearly needed. Second, the choice of the data set, which results from an underlying definition that equates state failure with internal war, empties the concept of state failure of much of its content. For example, the data set contains the Rwandan genocide of 1994, although it has been rightly pointed out that the genocide was far from the result of failed state institutions; on the contrary, the killings were overwhelmingly carried out by disciplined forces under the control of the state.[56] The Task Force's defenders counter that a state turned by its agents into an instrument to harm society is, by definition, a failed state.[57] Policy makers still face the very difficult challenge of strengthening states to prevent them from failing and at the same time making them immune to capture by state agents attempting to make use of state institutions to pursue a distorted or parochial agenda.

What role for the international community?

Before looking at the array of means available to the international community to avert state failure, it is useful to consider the more basic question of whether putting failed states back together again is a worthwhile goal. Clapham and Herbst have argued independently that alternatives to insisting on statehood should be devised. In Clapham's view, states are no precondition for social order, and much of social and economic life is capable of sustaining itself in the absence of states: "In parts of Africa, indeed, states are more of a hindrance than a help." He notes that statehood brings not only benefits but also immense costs: social costs (the sacrifice of identities and social structures that are inimical to the hierarchies of control that states seek to impose); economic costs (a vast military and bureaucratic apparatus and the need for illegitimate leaders to buy political allegiances); and political costs (the bad governance of many African rulers). He therefore concludes that the "project of attempting to restore universal statehood appears to me to be chimerical".[58] Focusing primarily on Africa, and basing his arguments on the assumption quoted earlier that Africa's political culture is not suited to the nation-state model, Herbst urges the international community to take a more flexible and favourable stance towards secession and the changing of borders and even to look for alternatives to the nation-state – emphasizing that any proposed alternatives should come from Africans themselves.[59]

Herbst's position runs counter to the well-established international law doctrine of *uti possidetis*, which provides that states emerging from decolonization shall presumptively inherit the colonial administrative borders that they held at the time of independence.[60] Yet even eminent international lawyers have criticized *uti possidetis* for its rigidity, arguing that it leads to "genuine injustices and instability".[61] A more serious criticism was levelled at Herbst by Richard Joseph, who accuses him of cooking up "a virtual recipe for more catastrophes".[62] Herbst himself acknowledges that his recommendations might initiate a process that involves "full-fledged civil wars", but sees this as a necessary evil in the creation of viable political entities. According to Joseph, Herbst fails to take sufficiently into account "the devastating effects that the resort to violence by both state and non-state actors is having not only on economic and other material infrastructure but also on the very moral character of African societies".[63]

Writing before Herbst's and Clapham's articles appeared, Zartman pre-empted their reasoning by making the case for a reconstruction of the sovereign state. He argued that, today, "more is expected from the state than ever before" and that "such universal expectations cannot be met by a weakened institution".[64] Indeed, it is not clear what kind of institution or authority could substitute for the state's functions of maintaining internal and external security and of generating revenue. Speaking from a human rights vantage point, Ignatieff argues that "the chief prerequisite for the creation of a basic rights regime for ordinary people is the recreation of a stable national state capable of giving orders and seeing them carried out throughout the territory, a state with a classic Weberian monopoly on the legitimate means of force. Without the basic institutions of a state, no basic human rights protection is possible."[65]

If the reconstitution of states is indeed necessary, what can the international community and in particular the United Nations do to strengthen the state? What strategies and instruments exist and what proposals have been made to help ailing states to develop functioning and legitimate institutions, and what are their advantages and disadvantages?

One of the basic questions that international actors face – conceptually and politically – is whether to direct state-building efforts primarily at strengthening the central institutions of the state and its leaders (a top–down approach) or at fostering a functioning civil society (a bottom–up approach). The Cold War saw the most drastic kind of top–down approach, with friendly authoritarian rulers being propped up by both superpowers. In some cases, such "strongmen" did indeed play a successful role in reviving state legitimacy and in keeping disintegrating states together, at least temporarily. Robert Mugabe in Zimbabwe in the 1980s, Mobutu Sese Seko in Zaire in the 1960s, and Yoweri Museveni in Uganda in the late 1980s and early 1990s are examples of the useful role strongmen can play. However, most of these so-called strongmen eventually become so attached to power that they install increasingly dictatorial regimes built around their personal rule, thereby creating weak and hollow states. Thus, as the later years of Mugabe and Mobutu illustrate, strongmen are as much the cause of state failure as they may sometimes be the solution.[66]

Pursuing a bottom–up approach with the aim of assisting in the development of democratic civic rule by strengthening non-governmental actors is naturally a more ambitious and time-consuming task. In failing or failed states civil society is notoriously weak, and reviving it involves profound reforms in the public sphere, such as education and creating space for political participation. If successful, however, this may lead to more sustainable outcomes.

The debate over whether to strengthen the central government or non-governmental, private and community-based organizations has been particularly acute in the field of economic assistance. Given the capacities of corrupt governments in weak or failing states to let aid money disappear into their own corrupt pockets, there has been a tendency since the end of the Cold War to channel some aid and investment money around governments. The recent US initiative of creating a Millennium Challenge Corporation to promote private sector investment, as well as the World Bank's recent plans to give grants to private companies instead of to the public sector, suggests that this trend is increasing.[67]

The bulk of foreign aid, however, is still aimed at governments. Yet aid can accomplish something only in states where the government is broadly committed to development. Therefore there are good reasons to be sceptical about whether simply increasing foreign aid will be an adequate policy response, even though poverty and a scarcity of resources have been identified as one structural cause of state collapse.[68] Bosnia and Herzegovina, for example, has received more per capita assistance than Western Europe did under the Marshall Plan, yet is still a highly fragile entity.[69] This situation has been linked to the failure to establish basic institutions of the rule of law. Rotberg might therefore be right that foreign aid can achieve a lot if "outside support [is] conditional on monetary and fiscal streamlining, renewed attention to good governance, reforms of land tenure systems, and strict adherence to the rule of law".[70]

But promotion of "good governance" is easier said than done.[71] Every donor agency now echoes the mantra of good governance and insists on the need for countries to strengthen their laws, institutions and enforcement, to fight corruption, to ensure transparency, and to promote public access to information, decision-making and justice. Yet countries often prove unwilling to allow outsiders an intrusive oversight role to monitor aid recipients' performance. Helman and Ratner's proposition to get "the UN [to] assign personnel to work directly with governmental officials on the country's most pressing needs" and to allow "UN personnel [to] help administer the state"[72] seems highly unpopular in large parts of the globe. A case in point is the New Partnership for Africa's Development (NEPAD), a recent African initiative to promote good governance and encourage investment and aid flows into Africa. NEPAD distinguishes itself from past development plans through its explicit emphasis on African ownership of ideas and its pledge to uphold norms of democratic governance and market policies in exchange for a partnership with the Group of Eight (G-8) and other donors.[73] Ownership translates also into a reluctance to be judged by non-African countries or institutions, and NEPAD countries have proposed a "Peer Review Mechanism", allowing African countries to judge themselves.[74]

In a recommendation closely linked to the concept of good governance, several authors have stressed the importance of democratic reforms and have promoted a possible role for the United Nations in fostering democratic institutions.[75] In doing so, however, it is crucial not to focus simply on the holding of elections and to neglect other elements such as the rule of law.[76] There is also the danger of the West promoting a one-size-fits-all model of democracy, ignoring local politico-cultural traditions.[77] In any case, democratization should not be presumed to be a panacea. Snyder and Mansfield have presented evidence that democratic transitions are often accompanied by violent conflict.[78] Focusing more specifically on Africa, Ali Mazrui claims that, "when defined as unregulated multiparty pluralism, democracy in Africa can even be disastrous". He further points out that, "[i]n the first quarter-century of Africa's independence, the longest surviving civilian administrations were single-party regimes. These included Côte d'Ivoire, Zambia, Tanzania, Malawi, Kenya, and Guinea under Sekou Touré. In contrast, multiparty politics in Sudan, Ghana, and Nigeria repeatedly precipitated military interventions." Nevertheless, Mazrui admits himself that "prolonged denial of democracy and social justice can precipitate rebellion and demonstrations, if not revolution".[79]

A highly ambitious and encompassing goal for the international community to save states from failing is the concept of nation-building. Sometimes identified in the United States with elite soldiers accompanying children to kindergarten or conflated with state-building, nation-building more properly means building a common identity of a society within a state and thereby strengthening its fabric. The Subaltern Studies movement in India is one of the better-known examples of this.[80] Even in the early 1970s, however, some authors argued that nation-building should be regarded as obsolete in the view of "ethnic persistence".[81] Pointing to social science literature of the last decade, Lothar Brock counters that identities constituting difference are not fixed but always evolving and that "ethnicity can be deconstructed and reconstructed to meet the basic functional requirements of social life". Although Brock cautions that "nation-building cannot be achieved by the international community", he provides reason for hope by arguing that it can "try to deal with 'ethnic conflict' in a way that is conducive to the pursuit of common political projects".[82] Brock points out that the notion of nation-building in the 1950s and 1960s viewed ethnic difference as pre-modern patterns of social differentiation that needed to be overcome. He argues that the nation-building efforts of that period fostered developmental nationalism, ethnic clientelism and institutionalized ethnic rule in multi-ethnic states. In this respect, nation-building was also detrimental to the practice of self-determination.[83] Recent nation-building efforts in the Balkans and Afghanistan suggest an effort to avoid this pattern, with the fostering of a national identity that is distinct from ethnic identities. Examples include issuing national rather than entity licence plates in Bosnia and the establishment of a national army in Afghanistan.[84]

Moving from carrots to sticks, sanctions are one of the most common tools used to pressure rulers into responsible behaviour (and thus contributing to state legitimacy). But Reno's analysis, described earlier, of the incentives for leaders to undermine the functioning of state institutions suggests that sanctions might in fact have a negative impact. Sanctions expert George Lopez also concludes that "[s]anctions do little to deter or halt ... breakdown when it is in the offing or already occurring".[85] Whereas sanctions to compel corrupt leaders into good behaviour might be ineffective, sanctions aimed at denying them arms and money have had more impact. Lopez therefore is optimistic that smart sanctions – including targeted financial measures, arms embargoes and restrictive international travel and participation bans – could be further developed so that coercive measures would "contribute more to state capacity than detract from it".[86]

In advanced stages of state failure, when neither compulsion nor denial will have any hope of achieving much, the imposition of direct rule has been put forward as an alternative. In an influential 1993 article in *Foreign Policy*, Helman and Ratner argued that the UN community should revive the concept of trusteeship as a way to resuscitate failed states.[87] Trusteeship as a model was raised more recently in the *Responsibility to*

Protect report. Zartman dismisses such solutions, arguing that its promoters "err in the arrogant presumption that only the West can govern and in the ignorant fallacy that a 190-member bureaucracy that cannot pay for its emergency interventions is suited to exercising or supervising colonial-like rule".[88] Robert Jackson objects to trusteeship on ethical grounds, maintaining that, "[i]n an international society based on non-intervention, the domestic good life is something for which the governments and citizens of those states are primarily responsible". Jackson concludes that, "whatever it may be termed, trusteeship is normatively at odds with the ethos of equality of cultures, civilizations, races, etc. that [rightly] entered into international society, during the course of de-colonization after centuries of inequality and discrimination".[89] Apart from these ethical questions, the problem of feasibility looms large. The *Responsibility to Protect* report, for instance, notes the low probability that the international community would provide the resources necessary for such trusteeship operations.[90]

The closest that the international community has come to embracing such an approach has been in the very limited number of transitional administrations established by the United Nations. Though these assumed their most advanced form in Kosovo and East Timor, Simon Chesterman in chapter 16 of this volume shows that these may be seen as part of a series of operations in which the United Nations has exercised some or all government powers on a temporary basis. This has been undertaken in the context of decolonization (Namibia, East Timor), as part of a transfer of territory from one power to another (West Papua/Irian Jaya, Western Sahara, Eastern Slavonia), in order to hold elections (Cambodia), as part of an open-ended peace process (Bosnia and Herzegovina, Kosovo, Afghanistan), and through mission creep in areas lacking governmental institutions (Congo, Somalia, Sierra Leone). It remains a controversial form of operation, a point made clear in the oblique reference to such operations in the Brahimi Report on UN Peace Operations[91] and on the very different form of operation deployed in Afghanistan.

The imposition of a US military occupation over Iraq following the ousting of the Saddam Hussein regime in April 2003 raises the question of whether the unilateral intervention of a big power in the internal affairs of the weak state might be an alternative to imposition of UN rule via trusteeships over failed countries. Stephen Mallaby, for example, has called for a US neo-imperialism to address the failed state issue.[92] This, however, is clearly not the dominant trend in US strategic thinking. Despite the fact that the *National Security Strategy* places failed states at the centre of its threat assessment, the strategy that is put forward to meet this challenge is rather limited in nature, focusing on strengthening border security, law enforcement and intelligence infrastructure to deny havens for terrorism.[93] But the United States is not the only potential agent of imperial solutions to state reconstruction. The examples of Syria's ongoing involvement in Lebanon and Tanzania's unilateral intervention in Uganda in 1979 suggest that unilateral interference of an outside power can be a key element for recovery from state failure.[94] Although Wallensteen is right that "in general there are no internationally acceptable actors to pursue an intrusive, sustained, and constructive role of state recovery",[95] it is worth noting that the United States was often criticized for having abandoned Afghanistan after the withdrawal of the Soviet Union, at a time when it could have arguably played a quasi-imperial role.

Conclusion

This chapter on the causes of and remedies for state failure yields three broad conclusions. First, and most obviously, the institution of the state remains the primary vehicle for providing important functions for any given population – in particular, security and order. Although human rights activists have long been suspicious of the arrogation of power by states, a failing or failed state is, arguably, as dangerous to its citizens and neighbours as a tyrannical or aggressive state. Proposals to tackle the problem of state failure by looking for alternatives to statehood should be considered with caution.

Second, given the dangers that emerge from failed states, the international community should increase its efforts to strengthen weak states prone to failure. Structural obstacles make such prevention difficult. Among these obstacles are the ongoing importance of sovereignty as the organizing principle of international society and the lack of political will on the part of the international community to act on early warning signs. The 11 September 2001 attacks and the response in Afghanistan suggest that the international community – or a particular state or states – may be more willing to intervene in failed states. Nevertheless, the explicit linkage to security interests makes such intervention coincident, at best, with the humanitarian interest in preventing or redressing state failure. In addition, such military and humanitarian responses to the symptoms of state failure may fail to provide a necessarily political cure.

Third, providing such a cure is neither easy nor consistent across the range of cases and the various stages of declining state institutions. Forgiving debt, increasing development assistance and fostering democratization remain controversial and difficult to justify at the early stages in which they may be most effective. Sanctions, unless they are well targeted, are ineffective or counter-productive. More intrusive strategies, such as trusteeships, transitional administrations and neo-imperialism, are still more controversial – and far from certain to provide sustainable outcomes.

The challenge of "making states work" therefore remains. Improving the international community's response to state failure will be an incremental process. It will require deepening our understanding of the causes and dynamics of state failure, improving early warning mechanisms, and further developing institutional capabilities aimed at addressing this problem. It will also require marshalling sufficient political will to ensure that action to deal with state failure is not simply justified through protecting ourselves from its consequences.

Acknowledgements

I am most grateful to Karen Ballentine, Simon Chesterman, Heiko Nitzschke and I. William Zartman for their helpful comments on an earlier draft of this chapter.

Notes

1. *The National Security Strategy of the United States of America*, Washington, DC: President of the United States, September 2002, available at ⟨http://www.whitehouse.gov/nsc/nss.html⟩, p. iv.
2. Robin Dorff, "Responding to the Failed State: What to Do and What to Expect", paper presented at the Conference on Failed States, Florence: Purdue University, April 8–11, 1999; Michael Ignatieff, "Intervention and State Failure", *Dissent*, Vol. 49, No. 1, Winter 2002, pp. 114–123; Sebastian Mallaby, "The Reluctant Imperialist: Terrorism, Failed States, and the Case for American Empire", *Foreign Affairs*, Vol. 81, No. 2, March/April 2002.
3. See part II of the present volume.
4. See Ignatieff, "Intervention and State Failure", p. 117.
5. International Commission on Intervention and State Sovereignty, *The Responsibility to Protect*, Ottawa: International Development Research Centre, 2001, para. 5.24.
6. James Fearon and David Laitin, *International Institutions and Civil War*, draft report, Stanford, CA: Department of Political Science at Stanford University, 2002, pp. 6–7. Fearon and Laitin's list includes: Afghanistan, Angola, Cambodia, Central African Republic, Democratic Republic of Congo, Dominican Republic, El Salvador, Guatemala, Haiti, Lebanon, Liberia, Mozambique, Rwanda, Sierra Leone, Somalia, and Tajikistan.
7. Thomas Hobbes, *Leviathan*, edited with an introduction by C. B. Macpherson, London: Penguin, 1982; John Locke, *Two Treatises of Government*, edited by Peter Laslett, Cambridge: Cambridge University Press, 1988; Jean-Jacques Rousseau, *The Social Contract*, translated by Maurice Cranston, London: Penguin, 1968.
8. John Rawls, *A Theory of Justice*, Cambridge, MA: Belknap Press, 1971.

9. Max Weber, *The Theory of Social Economic Organization*, edited with an introduction by Talcott Parsons, New York: The Free Press, 1964, pp. 154–156.

10. *Convention on Rights and Duties of States*, signed at Montevideo on 26 December 1933, available at ⟨http://www.yale.edu/lawweb/avalon/intdip/interam/intam03.htm⟩.

11. William Zartman, "Introduction: Posing the Problem of State Collapse", in William Zartman, ed., *Collapsed States: The Disintegration and Restoration of Legitimate Authority*, Boulder, CO: Lynne Rienner, 1995, p. 5.

12. Ignatieff, "Intervention and State Failure", p. 117.

13. Daniel C. Esty, Jack A. Goldstone, Ted Robert Gurr, Pamela T. Surko and Alan N. Unger, *State Failure Task Force Report: Phase II Findings*, McLean: Science Application International Application, 31 July 1998.

14. Peter Wallensteen, "Beyond State Failure: On Internal and External Ways of Ending State Failure", paper presented at the Conference on Failed States, Purdue University, Florence, 7–10 April 2000, p. 1.

15. Cited in Michael E. Brown, "The Causes of Internal Conflict", in Michael E. Brown et al., eds, *Nationalism and Ethnic Conflict: An International Security Reader*, Cambridge, MA: MIT Press, 1997, pp. 8–9.

16. Brown, "The Causes of Internal Conflict", p. 9.

17. Mushtaq Khan, "State Failure in Developing Countries and Strategies of Institutional Reform", draft paper for the Annual Bank Conference on Development Economics, Oslo, 24–26 June 2002, p. 2.

18. Ronald E. Berenbeim, "The Role of Business in Zones of Crisis", *Executive Action*, No. 16, February 2002. The question of whether the IMF should adopt sovereign bankruptcy provisions (comparable to US bankruptcy protection under Chapter 11) remains an open one. See "Battling over the Bankrupt", *The Economist*, 3 October 2002.

19. For such an attempt, see Jean-Germain Gross, "Towards a Taxonomy of Failed States in the New World Order: Decaying Somalia, Liberia, Rwanda, and Haiti", *Third World Quarterly*, Vol. 17, No. 3, 1996, pp. 458–460.

20. Ignatieff, "Intervention and State Failure", p. 118.

21. See chapter 2 by James Mayall in the present volume.

22. Daniel Thürer, "The 'Failed State' and International Law", *International Review of the Red Cross*, No. 836, December 1999, p. 3.

23. See, for example, Jeffrey Herbst, "Responding to State Failure in Africa", in Brown et al., eds, *Nationalism and Ethnic Conflict*. See also Christopher Clapham, "Failed States and Non States in the International Order", paper presented at the Conference on Failed States, Purdue University, Florence, 7–10 April 2000.

24. Clapham, "Failed States".

25. Ibid.

26. Herbst, "Responding to State Failure", pp. 381–382.

27. Clapham, "Failed States".

28. Herbst, "Responding to State Failure", pp. 384–386.

29. Clapham, "Failed States".

30. See, for example, Georg Sørensen, "War and State Making – Why Doesn't It Work in the Third World?", paper presented at the Conference on Failed States, Purdue University, Florence, 11–14 April 2001, p. 5.

31. Zartman, "Introduction", pp. 6–7.

32. William Reno, "Shadow States and the Political Economy of War", in Mats Berdal and David Malone, eds, *Greed and Grievance: Economic Agendas in Civil Wars*, Boulder, CO: Lynne Rienner, 1999, p. 45.

33. Ibid., p. 46.

34. Mohammed Ayoob, "State-Making, State-Breaking and State Failure: Explaining the

Roots of Third World Insecurity", in Luc Van de Goor, Kumar Rupesinghe and Paul Sciarone, eds, *Between Development and Destruction: An Enquiry into the Causes of Conflict in Post-Colonial States*, London: Macmillan, 1996. Also Susan Woodward, *Failed States: Warlordism and 'Tribal' Warfare*, 1998, available at ⟨http://www.nwc. navy.mil/press/Review/1999/spring/art2-sp9.htm⟩.

35. Herbst, "Responding to State Failure", p. 377.
36. Zartman, "Introduction", pp. 5–6.
37. Robert Rotberg, "The New Nature of Nation-State Failure", *Washington Quarterly*, Vol. 25, No. 3, Summer 2002, pp. 91–2.
38. Weber, *The Theory of Social Economic Organization*, pp. 328–392.
39. Ibid., pp. 329–341.
40. Ibid., p. 337.
41. Ibid., pp. 341–358.
42. Chapter 7 in this volume.
43. Wallensteen, "Beyond State Failure", p. 2.
44. Gerald Helman and Steven Ratner, "Saving Failed States", *Foreign Policy*, No. 89, Winter 1992–93, pp. 8–9.
45. ICISS, *The Responsibility to Protect*, para. 4.20.
46. Speech on 6 September 2000, available at ⟨http://www.un.org/millenium/webcast/ statements/usa.htm⟩.
47. Woodward, "Failed States".
48. Thürer, "The Failed State", p. 2.
49. Gross, "Towards a Taxonomy", p. 496.
50. Zartman, "Introduction", p. 8.
51. I would like to thank Dr Monty Marshall for comments on an earlier draft of this section.
52. Gross, "Towards a Taxonomy", p. 462.
53. Wallensteen, "Beyond State Failure", p. 2.
54. Esty et al., *State Failure Task Force Report: Phase II Findings*, p. 1.
55. Jack Snyder and Edward Mansfield, "Democratization and the Danger of War", *International Security*, Vol. 20, No. 1, Summer 1995.
56. Clapham, "Failed States".
57. For this view, see, for example, Peter Wallensteen, "State Failure, Ethnocracy and Armed Conflict: Towards New Conceptions of Governance", paper presented at the Conference on Failed States, Purdue University, Florence, 8–11 April 1999, p. 2.
58. Clapham, "Failed States".
59. Herbst, "Responding to State Failure", pp. 394.
60. *Uti possidetis* already governed the shape of borders during the decolonization of Latin America, European Africa and South East Asia, and most recently during the dissolution of the Soviet Union. Steven Ratner, "Drawing a Better Line: *Uti Possidetis* and the Borders of New States", *American Journal of International Law*, Vol. 90, 1996, pp. 590–624.
61. Ibid., pp. 590–591.
62. Jeffrey Herbst and Richard Joseph, "Correspondence: Responding to State Failure in Africa", *International Security*, Vol. 22, No. 2, Fall 1997, p. 178.
63. Ibid., p. 179.
64. I. William Zartman, "Putting Things Back Together", in Zartman, ed., *Collapsed States*, p. 267.
65. Ignatieff, "Intervention and State Failure", p. 119.
66. On "strongmen", see also Njuguna Ng'ethe, "Strongmen, State Formation, Collapse, and Reconstruction in Africa", in Zartman, ed., *Collapsed States*.

67. Alan Beattie, "World Bank: Shift in Culture Promises Funds for Companies in Africa", *Financial Times*, 25 June 2003; James Lamont, "Good Governance: Annual Programme to Reward Emerging Markets", *Financial Times*, 11 December 2002.
68. See, for example, Dorff, "Responding to the Failed State", p. 11.
69. Jacques Klein, "What Does It Take to Make UN Peacekeeping Operations Succeed? Reflections from the Field", speech given at IPA/UNDPKO seminar marking the 10th anniversary of the UN Department of Peacekeeping Operations, 29 October 2002, available at ⟨http://www.unmibh.org/stories/view.asp?StoryID=226⟩.
70. Rotberg, "The New Nature of Nation-State Failure", p. 95.
71. The concept of governance suffers from the fact that it lacks an agreed upon definition. The authoritative World Bank understanding of governance ("the exercise of political, administrative and economic authority to manage a nation's affairs"), encompassing "every institution and organization in society, from the family to the state", has been criticized for making reference to all things political. A further disagreement on the concept is whether to emphasize public sector management or democracy. Hydén has provided a useful alternative to the World Bank definition, describing governance as "those measures that involve setting the rules for the exercise of power and settling conflicts over such rules". On a practical level, he explains, "[s]uch rules translate into constitutions, laws, customs, administrative regulations, and international agreements". See Göran Hydén, "Governance and the Reconstitution of Political Order", in Richard Joseph, ed., *State, Conflict and Democracy in Africa*, London: Lynne Rienner, 1999, p. 185.
72. Helman and Ratner, "Saving Failed States", p. 13.
73. Dorina Bekoe and Chris Landsberg, "NEPAD: African Initiative, New Partnership", International Peace Academy Workshop Report, New York: IPA, 16 July 2002, p. 2.
74. Johannes Lamont, "UN Trusts in Africa to Judge Its Own Record", *Financial Times*, 19 October 2002.
75. Helman and Ratner, "Saving Failed States", p. 14.
76. Fareed Zakaria, "The Rise of Illiberal Democracy", *Foreign Affairs*, Vol. 76, No. 6, Winter 1997; Marina Ottaway, "Democratization in Collapsed States", in Zartman, ed., *Collapsed States*.
77. Ali Mazrui, "The Failed State and Political Collapse in Africa", in Olara A. Otunnu and Michael W. Doyle, eds, *Peacemaking and Peacekeeping for the New Century*, Lanham, MD: Rowman & Littlefield, 1998, p. 237; Hydén, "Governance", pp. 187–9.
78. Snyder and Mansfield, "Democratization".
79. Mazrui, "The Failed State", p. 235.
80. Ranajit Guha, ed., *A Subaltern Studies Reader: 1986–1995*, Minneapolis: University of Minnesota Press, 1998.
81. See Lothar Brock, "Nation-Building: Prelude or Belated Solution to the Failing of States?", paper presented at the Conference on Failed States, Purdue University, Florence, 11–14 April 2001, p. 1.
82. Ibid., p. 3.
83. Ibid., p. 8.
84. See chapter 9 by Amin Saikal in this volume.
85. George Lopez, "Economic Sanctions and Failed States: Too Little, Too Late, and Sometimes Too Much?", paper presented at the Conference on Failed States, Purdue University, Florence, 8–11 April 1999, p. 2.
86. Ibid., p. 9.
87. Helman and Ratner, "Saving Failed States".
88. Zartman, *Collapsed States*, p. 272.
89. Robert Jackson, "Surrogate Sovereignty: Great Power Responsibility and Failed

States", paper presented at the Conference on Failed States, Purdue University, Florence, 8–11 April 1999, p. 12.
90. ICISS, *The Responsibility to Protect*, para. 5.24.
91. *Report of the Panel on United Nations Peace Operations* (Brahimi Report), UN Doc. A/55/305-S/2000/809, New York, 21 August 2000.
92. Mallaby, "The Reluctant Imperialist".
93. *National Security Strategy*, pp. 10–11.
94. Wallensteen, "Beyond State Failure"; Mazrui, "The Failed State", p. 241.
95. Wallensteen, "Beyond State Failure", p. 6.

2

The legacy of colonialism

James Mayall

It was, surprisingly, Winston Churchill who most accurately foresaw the transformation of the imperial idea in the second half of the twentieth century: "The empires of the future", he told a Harvard audience in 1943, "will be empires of the mind."[1] The transfer of power by the European imperial powers, between 1947 and the mid-1960s, was carried through against the background of a struggle to define the shape and structure of the modern world. Both the competing ideologies – liberal capitalist and socialist – claimed to be universal, democratic and secular. In this sense, their ambitions may justly be called imperial.

They also shared two other features that distinguished them from all previous imperial ideologies. First, they offered a blueprint for a future that would be different from – and much better than – the past. Second, the new order would eventually be self-policing, resting not on the projection of power from a distant and alien metropole but on the self-determination of peoples. It is true that by establishing the United Nations Security Council, with its five permanent veto-wielding powers, the international community appeared to place more faith in traditional power politics than in political visions; however, at the time of the 1945 San Francisco Conference, the incompatibility between the world views of the emerging superpowers was not yet fully realized. Since the fascist and Nazi axis had been defeated by a grand coalition, it seemed sensible to make provision for the same coalition to preside over the orderly transition from the old world of competing empires to the new one of cooperating states.

Both the United States and the Soviet Union claimed to be anti-imperial states, and it was ultimately their global competition – and the instruments they used to pursue their objectives – that created the environment in which the successor states to the European empires achieved independence. When the Europeans left, however, they did not simply disappear in the manner of earlier empires, which collapsed as the result of conquest or internal decay. Compared with the states that they left behind, the ex-colonial countries remained both influential and powerful, with Britain and France occupying permanent seats on the Security Council. Unsurprisingly, the colonial elites who took over used these countries both as models to emulate – they were, after all, ready to hand – and as scapegoats when things went wrong. In the context of the Cold War, scapegoating dominated the public discourse of the former colonial states at the United Nations and at other international gatherings. After the end of the Cold War, a few leaders, such as Zimbabwe's Robert Mugabe, continued to blame the former colonial powers for their troubles, but most abandoned the habit.

Nevertheless, if we are to understand the problem of contemporary state failure, we must necessarily start by trying to understand the contribution of the colonial legacy. This is because, at the most general level, the concept of the state itself was a colonial export. Modern international society is essentially a Western creation. Its foundational principles of sovereignty, territorial integrity and non-interference in the domestic affairs of other states emerged simultaneously with the rise of the centralized state in Europe. These values – and the practices that typically embodied them such as the state monopoly on the legitimate use of force and legal jurisdiction – were subsequently spread around the world by imperial conquest. Because sovereignty can be reduced to a principle of political sovereignty, it can be represented as a universal rather than a culturally specific concept. For this reason, rulers everywhere are attracted to it.

At the same time, as the case-studies in this volume illustrate, the concept of the state was grafted onto a wide variety of pre-existing forms of government and social organization. In some cases, the state was even superimposed where order had traditionally been maintained without central institutions of any kind. No wonder, therefore, that the shadow cast by the European state and state-system has had different consequences, for good and ill, in different parts of the world. Where the graft did not take, or produced an unforeseen mutation, the post-colonial state failed to provide the most basic public goods of law, order and minimal welfare. In extreme cases it collapsed altogether.

It seems important to begin by stating the obvious, however, namely that, in the majority of cases, the transfer of power did not lead to state collapse. It is true that very few states achieved the social, political and economic transformation that their leaders promised during the anti-colonial struggle. There is little surprise in that: democratic politicians everywhere promise more than they can deliver. It is often claimed that the authoritarian character of East Asian societies and states played a part in their political stability and economic success – the twin ingredients of the Asian miracle. Perhaps they did; but, given the number of unstable and economically unsuccessful authoritarian states, the case is hardly proved. As Amartya Sen has also demonstrated, in the handling of famine the relatively open Indian state had the advantage over the closed state of China for reasons that directly relate to democratic freedoms.[2] There seems no obvious reason why what holds for famine should not apply to other areas of administration and government. But, whether they built on the authoritarian structures inherited from the colonial powers or opted for an open system of government, very few states disintegrated to a point where – in a ghastly mirror image of Hobbesian theory – their governments became the main source of human insecurity and misery. Some did, however. Why?

Other chapters in this volume deal with the immediate causes and consequences of state disintegration. Many of these derive from the Cold War and the impact of globalization rather than from colonialism. At first sight, the emergence of the regions of conflict discussed in Barnett Rubin and Andrea Armstrong's chapter (chapter 4) cannot be blamed on colonialism. These are fuelled by the ready availability of small arms and financed by the sale of high-value commodities such as diamonds or narcotics on a deregulated world market. A search for causes, however, opens up a potentially infinite regress. Colonial borders that bisected historical communities remained highly porous and, in that sense, paved the way for the more recent spillover of ethnic conflict across international borders.

This chapter, therefore, takes a longer view. It considers four aspects of the colonial legacy that may help us to unravel the puzzle of state failure. None is a sufficient explanation in its own right, but taken together they may help us to establish criteria for identifying those countries most at risk. The first section examines the nature of anti-colonial nationalism, in particular the emphasis that was placed on state capture rather than on the social basis of legitimacy in the post-colonial state. The second section considers the political implications of accepting the colonial political map in territories where society was deeply divided along ethnic or religious lines. One of the unforeseen consequences – the tendency for economic development policies to reinforce these divisions rather than resolve them – is discussed in the third section. Since the state did not fail everywhere, even in divided societies, the fourth section discusses the impact of empire on different kinds of pre-colonial social structures and state formations. In a final section I shall attempt to derive some implications from these observations for the policy debate on reconstruction in ex-colonial failed and failing states.

Anti-colonial nationalism

Most European nationalists – particularly but not exclusively those east of Vienna – grounded their nationalism in a formula that Ernest Gellner represented as "one culture, one state", by which he meant one *ethnic* culture, one state. Nationalism, he believed, arose not because its ideas were inherently appealing but because a national culture was a necessary accompaniment of the transition from agricultural to modern society. This was largely because the division of labour on which industrialism depends, and the competition to which it leads, require occupational mobility and therefore a literate and trainable labour force. Peasants who mainly stay in one place do not need to read and write in order to function, and they tend to regard whoever governs them with deep suspicion. Modern states, on the other hand, require educated (or at least semi-educated) citizens whose loyalty they can command.[3] To explain why citizens identify with the state, Benedict Anderson traced the rise of the nation to the development of print capitalism. Traditional cultures in which priests had a near monopoly on literacy were well served by sacred languages and the beautifully crafted manuscripts in which the scriptures were recorded and to which only the priests had access. By contrast, the manufacture of printed books was driven by the profit motive and required a market of readers. This in turn put a premium on the production of literary works in the vernacular and facilitated the emergence of an *imagined community* of people who did not know one another directly.[4]

These accounts are suggestive – they can be adapted quite successfully to account for post-Meiji Japan, for Attaturk's revolution in post-Ottoman Turkey and for the successor states to the Spanish empire. But in relatively few of the territories ruled by the West European powers did nationalism take this form. At the time of decolonization, Sukarno and his followers insisted that they were taking over the Dutch East Indies in a deliberate act of self-creation. Ethnic criteria were wheeled in only after 1974 in an attempt to justify the annexation of East Timor for geopolitical reasons.[5]

In India, vaguely civilizational reasons were offered to justify the incorporation of Hyderabad and later Goa, but the main justification was again political and geopolitical. In Africa, the language of nationalism was pan-African, the reality territorial. Before independence there was much talk of the need to put right the evils of "Balkanization"; afterwards this version of African unity was widely regarded as a threat to existing leaders and, after a period of internecine political warfare, was quietly pocketed.[6] Leaders of mass parties sometimes had an ethnic base – as they did in Nigeria – but sometimes also rose to the top precisely because they lacked one – as in Zambia or Tanganyika.

With a few obvious exceptions, such as Pakistan, anti-colonial nationalism was overwhelmingly a political rather than a cultural, ethnic or religious phenomenon. Even in Pakistan, as we shall see in Samina Ahmed's chapter (chapter 7), religion, the ostensible basis of the new state, was unable to hold its disparate parts together. By contrast, opposition to alien rule had wide appeal, with the result that ethnic or religious antagonisms could be conveniently masked. These antagonisms emerged fairly soon after the transfer of power, but by then the "nationalists" – those who inherited the state – not only were recognized internationally as the legitimate governors of the former colonies, but had a virtual monopoly over the production and use of national symbols. At the United Nations, self-determination came to be understood as tied in time and space to the act of decolonization. The United Nations provided the theatre in which nationalist leaders from what came to be called the third world could pursue the anti-colonial struggle by other means.

In many parts of the former colonial world, society is still predominantly rural. Peasants far outnumber urban workers, and the transition from agricultural to modern society has barely begun. This does not mean that a Gellnerian or Andersonian analysis has no relevance for an understanding of anti-colonial nationalism. The number of nationalists – those who aspire to establish modern nation-states – has always exceeded the number of societies that can meet the preconditions for a successful national project. The power of demonstration effects should never be underestimated, particularly at a time when formal empire has been proscribed and suzerain and tribute relationships are widely regarded as anachronistic. The nation-state is the benchmark at which all political societies must aim. Successful modernization, in other words, is not the only evidence for the existence of national sentiment.

Three other features of the post-colonial situation serve to keep nationalism alive. First, over the past half-century, cities have grown at an exponential rate in most parts of the post-colonial world. Enclaves and ghettoes are features of all such urban explosions, but in the end a process of cultural homogenization is to be expected. Second, as a result, the formation of something like Anderson's *imagined community* can be observed in many countries, although linguistic fragmentation and the fact that the language of government and higher education is frequently English or French are complicating factors. Third, although literacy levels lag far behind those in the industrial world, they are sufficient to create a significant national community. Indeed, the small size of the modern sector in most countries means that there is a large population of un-employed and underemployed people capable of being mobilized by or against the government depending on circumstances. The tragic case of Rwanda, where the unleashing of the genocide by ultra-nationalist Hutu in 1994 was followed by the state being recaptured by the minority Tutsi, is the most dramatic illustration of the continuing power of nationalism in post-colonial societies. The policy implications of these developments will be considered in the final section of this chapter.

The territorial settlement

The system into which the former colonies were fitted was essentially a real estate system. Until the twentieth century, borders had changed at regular intervals, either on the battlefield or as a result of dynastic marriage settlements, or occasionally as the result of a commercial trans-action (for example, the Louisiana purchase, Oregon, and Alaska). The worldwide expansion of Europe had started during a period when terri-tory was regarded as a legitimate prize of war, and the loyalties – let alone the preferences – of the population were not a material consider-ation. Even in Europe, not much changed before the end of the First World War, although the population exchanges between France and Germany in Alsace Lorraine after the Franco-Prussian war provided a foretaste of the new attitude towards territory that was rapidly emerging. Outside Europe, during the final imperial enclosures of the nineteenth century, the concern was less the proper relationship of people to their homelands than the need to provide a justification for alien rule. Ideas such as the standard of civilization and the division of the world into three categories – civilized, barbarian and savage – provided the Euro-pean imperial powers with a convenient justification for their activities.

When imperial competition threatened to destabilize relations amongst the European powers, they generally reached pragmatic agreements about the division of the spoils amongst themselves. At the 1884 Con-gress of Berlin, they established the principle of effective control as a means of introducing an element of order into the previously unregulated scramble for Africa. Notoriously, this produced a new political map of Africa in which the frontiers between territories – mostly straight lines drawn across largely uninhabited territory – paid scant attention to cul-tural, historical or ethnic criteria. So long as the empires lasted, such car-tographical carelessness did not seriously affect the way people lived their lives. In India, as Ramesh Thakur reports, a post-independence survey to establish what villagers thought of the changes in government since the end of British rule in 1947 had to be abandoned when it was discovered that the majority of peasants were unaware that the British had ever been there.[7] In Africa, lines of communication and trade mostly ran from the mines and plantations of the interior to the coastal ports, so that inland boundaries were porous, as for the most part they remain.

Nonetheless, as in Europe, the rise of nationalism challenged the right of conquest as a legitimate means of acquiring legal title. The principle of national self-determination undermined the time-honoured way in which a human wrong – the use of force for aggressive rather than defensive purposes – could be translated into a political and legal right. Whether or not one accepts the argument that nationalism is a form of secular religion, there is little doubt that everywhere one of its consequences was the sacralization of territory. In the international system of nation-states, land grabs may be accepted temporally as a *force majeure*, but the underlying political dispute is seldom if ever resolved by such action. The strategic reasons for Israel's occupation of the Golan Heights or Turkey's of northern Cyprus may be understood, but in neither case has the file been closed or the political legitimacy of the occupation recognized. Because many former colonial states were socially heterogeneous – more like mini Habsburg empires than like the politically centralized imperial democracies of Britain and France – the territorial aspects of the colonial legacy potentially presented a major obstacle to their future political development and stability.

At one level, secessionist and irredentist threats have been fairly successfully contained within international society. In Asia, some territorial consolidation and fragmentation took place in the immediate aftermath of decolonization. For example, India successfully faced down international criticism over its "police actions" in support of those in Hyderabad and Goa who wanted to express their right of self-determination by joining the Union, in the first case against the wishes of the local ruler, in the second against those of the Portuguese colonial authorities. Fifty years on, there is little visible evidence of the conflict that accompanied these actions.

The same cannot be said of Kashmir, whose Hindu ruler's decision to join India triggered a conflict with Pakistan that continues today. As Samina Ahmed argues in chapter 7, the Kashmir dispute has not only reinforced the Pakistan military's distrust of India but also contributed to the prolonged legitimacy crisis in Pakistan, since the army uses the dispute to justify its hold on power. Whether this crippling legacy can be overcome remains to be seen. So far, India has stuck to its view that any concessions would undermine the secular credentials of the state, whereas Pakistan continues to believe that considerations of natural justice should have consigned the Muslim majority state to Pakistan. In Malaysia, by contrast, Singapore agreed to a peaceful (if acrimonious) secession rather than mount an ethnic challenge to the majority Malay community, a decision that neither state has had any reason to regret.[8]

By the time Indonesia attempted to absorb the former Portuguese colony of East Timor in 1974, the conventional interpretation of self-determination as decolonization within the frontiers established by the colonial power had taken shape at the United Nations. It was not until 1999 that Indonesia was persuaded to concede that the East Timorese might decide their own future in a referendum. But Indonesia's failure to establish the international legality of the annexation – Australia's *de jure* recognition was the most notable exception – was largely a consequence of events in Africa rather than in Asia. It was in Africa that the threat of territorial disintegration seemed most pressing, if only because there were so few African states with a pre-colonial past that could be used to legitimize existing boundaries.

After a period of uncertainty in the early 1960s, the Organization of African Unity revived the principle of *uti possidetis juris* (what you have, you hold), which had been developed in nineteenth-century South America to minimize territorial conflicts after the withdrawal of Spain and Portugal. Steven Ratner is no doubt right to argue that "decolonization did not have to entail adoption of *uti possidetis*", but he is wrong when he states that it was adopted to satisfy the Western powers "because it kept decolonization – a development regarded almost universally as imperative – orderly".[9] *Uti possidetis* was widely endorsed by the international community for this reason, but its revival was the work of post-colonial states attempting to deal collectively and responsibly with one of the potentially most explosive aspects of the colonial legacy.

On another level, the success of *uti possidetis* in containing secession and irredentism has had more ambiguous consequences. It attempts to use law to combine state and nation, concepts that are mutually dependent but nonetheless analytically distinct. Two arguments can be offered in its support. The first is that, in the absence of any generally agreed objective definition of the nation and as a result of the historical mingling of populations, there is ultimately no non-arbitrary way of settling where international boundaries should be drawn. Where contingency rules, there is much to be said for allowing each state to keep what it already possesses. Historically, most modern nations were established by conquest and then maintained by force on the part of the rulers and by familiar habit on the part of the ruled. National cultures are thus mostly the product of assimilation and accommodation between groups that had no option but to live side by side. Whatever nationalists believe to the contrary, nations do not have a pre-existing natural identity independent of political structures.

The second argument is that secession very seldom, if ever, settles such arguments. The reason is that within the larger separatist population there is invariably a trapped smaller minority for whom the *status quo ante* was preferable to life within the secessionist state. But although the principle can be generally accepted as a useful instrument for conflict management, if it is regarded as an absolute and therefore non-negotiable principle, it may cease to operate as a solution to rational problem-solving and serve instead to legitimize savagery and the militarization of society to a point where the cure is often worse than the disease.

The political role of economic development

After the transfer of power, the new rulers faced the oldest question in politics: by what right were they to rule? The answer that they gave was almost everywhere the same, namely that a nationalist government was better placed to modernize society and transform the state than were alien rulers who could not share their interests. At first sight, it may seem odd to claim the policies of developmental nationalism as a co-lonial legacy. These were adopted, after all, in a self-conscious attempt to break with the colonial past. But it is evident not only that the ground for these policies was prepared during the final years of colonial rule, but also that in many cases the inability of post-colonial governments to bring about the transformation to which they aspired had imperial roots. The idea of a managed economy pre-dated independence: the development of commodity-marketing schemes and various kinds of public–private partnerships grew out of the ad hoc efforts of the colonial authorities to contain the worldwide spread of the Great Depression. At the same time, the capacity of the successor states to undertake a programme of mod-ernization varied greatly. The Congo, which achieved independence with just a handful of secondary school graduates, was only the most extreme example. In 1960, the UN General Assembly passed Resolution 1514, which, amongst other stipulations, ruled that lack of preparation for inde-pendence could not be used as a reason for delaying it.

Such grand political ideas resonated in a world in which macroeco-nomic thinking had become dominant and when it was easier than it later became to ignore the capacity problems resulting from underinvestment in human capital during the colonial period. After the Second World War, considerations of economic welfare and security increasingly came to dominate the political agenda everywhere. Western governments be-lieved that Keynesian economics had given them the instruments with which to prevent any repetition of the Great Depression of the 1930s, which had been widely blamed for the rise of fascism and the subsequent drift to war. From this point of view, the preoccupation of post-colonial governments with economic development was the equivalent of the preoccupation in the industrial world with economic welfare and full employment. Although the debate was largely conducted by professional economists, often in highly technical language, in both cases it was initially driven forward by political rather than economic considerations.

A few traditional rulers such as the Sultan of Brunei or the kings of Morocco and Jordan survived the transfer of power, but for the most part colonialism had undermined the prescriptive right to rule as surely as revolution, nationalism and war had previously undermined it in Europe. Nationalist leaders who took over from the departing imperialists enjoyed a honeymoon period when their status as the founding fathers of the nation provided them with all the legitimacy they needed. But it soon ended once the physical presence of alien rule was no longer available as a focus for national mobilization. In Europe after 1945, those who had been required to risk their lives for their country now demanded welfare and employment in return. In Asia, Africa, the Caribbean and Oceania, those who had been drawn into the international system to serve imperial interests looked to the system for a share of its benefits. At both ends of the imperial spectrum, governments that could no longer fall back on the hereditary or some other customary principle needed programmes and structures to legitimize their hold on power.

Three other factors led post-colonial leaders to adopt an economic approach to nation-building. The first was that colonial economies had produced modernized enclaves but most people were left living traditional lives mired in poverty. Their primary purpose was to supply raw materials to metropolitan industries and agricultural commodities that could not be produced in temperate climates. There were exceptions, such as the entrepôt cities of Hong Kong and Singapore and the indigenous industries developed by the Birlas, Tatas and others for the Indian market. More commonly, development was confined to coastal cities and to the margins of the rivers and railways that linked them to the mines and plantations of the interior. If post-colonial governments were to make good on their claim of bringing the benefits of modernity to the population as a whole, they needed to diversify the economy both geographically and in terms of industrial production.

Second, the international environment seemed favourable to this project. The majority of former colonies opted for non-alignment in the Cold War. This in turn allowed them to accept economic and technical assistance from both sides, without compromising their independence. For opposing reasons, both the Soviet Union and the United States had supported the anti-colonial struggle, and from the early 1960s their competition for influence was conducted mainly by economic means – except in the Middle East and South East Asia, where economic diplomacy was reinforced by the projection of military power and the maintenance of spheres of influence.

Finally, the United Nations and Bretton Woods institutions provided a theatre in which the strategy of continuing the anti-colonial struggle by other means could be staged. The Keynesian emphasis on macroeconomic management provided the vehicle. Political independence, so the argument ran, would be complete only if it was complemented by economic independence; in an interdependent world, economic interdependence in turn required the rules of the capitalist world economy to be changed to help the developing countries to close the widening gap in living standards with the industrial countries. The Soviet Union and its allies supported this campaign politically, but the northern part of the North–South dialogue, as it was called, was dominated by the West.

As a political strategy, national modernization had a respectable ancestry. It was more or less the justification offered by the Japanese nationalists after the Meiji restoration and by Attaturk after the fall of the Ottoman empire. The Japanese and the Turks had two advantages – a relatively homogeneous population and a pre-existing high culture on which to base a modernizing nationalism. Some former European colonies, particularly in South East and, to a lesser extent, South Asia, enjoyed a similar inheritance. But many did not. In Africa, where several states descended into chaos in the 1990s, living standards, infant mortality rates and life expectancy all deteriorated following independence. A similar fate now threatens some of the island states of the South Pacific. There, as in Africa, a lack of capacity does not necessarily correlate with poverty. The Solomons may have failed because of a lack of revenue to cover the basic cost of administration, but Nauru has failed because of an inability to handle riches.[10]

In deeply divided societies, reliance on economic development as an instrument of nation-building was always liable to have perverse effects. In theory, economic patronage would transfer loyalty from local and regional communities to the centre. In practice, it more often resulted in the re-tribalization of politics as the anti-colonial alliances disintegrated and control of the state became a prize in a ferocious competition between ethnic groups. The search for a "quick fix" in former colonies that lacked an indigenous entrepreneurial class also led to the overdevelopment of the state and para-statal sectors. Moreover, among those who controlled access to hard currency, it led to massive corruption.[11] The result was the creation of a class of quasi-states, to use Robert Jackson's term, that enjoyed juridical sovereignty and international recognition but could not enforce their writ throughout the territory over which they claimed jurisdiction.[12] In extreme cases, such as Liberia, Sierra Leone and Zaire, even juridical sovereignty provided little protection. Massive and sustained corruption led to the collapse of the state or its capture, criminalization and plunder by a victorious warlord or the incumbent strongman and his immediate henchmen.

The new Washington consensus, which replaced global Keynesianism with a more intrusive set of conditionalities in the early 1980s, weakened the hold of quasi-state authorities still further. It is true that bureaucracies had become swollen, corrupt and inefficient in many post-colonial countries, but it did not follow that the problem could be solved by the simple expedient of structural adjustment. The original intention was to reduce the need for financial support. The package included devaluation, the removal of urban food subsidies, the winding up of commodity marketing boards and rationing by price rather than by import licensing. If implemented properly, structural adjustment was intended to allow the recapture of the peasantry, who would be attracted back to the market by the prospect of being able to earn a profit for their produce; at the same time, it was to allow a downsizing of the state.

Although structural adjustment programmes have been improved and tailored more closely to local conditions since they were first introduced, they are still fundamentally driven by economic analysis and have difficulty in factoring in their impact on political stability and development. This weakness of the international financial institutions is particularly problematic where the state has failed to strike deep roots. In such cases, rolling back the state may threaten to roll it out of existence. It is difficult to overestimate the enduring importance of patronage networks in societies that are still largely organized within ethnic communities and along kinship lines. As chapter 4 powerfully argues, where political offices can no longer be farmed out, the political class may simply choose to do without the state and to profit from a war economy instead.

The policy implications of these observations will be discussed in the final section of this chapter. The point to note here is that not all deeply divided post-colonial states have collapsed, or appear to be in imminent danger of collapsing, even though a majority of them have been hit by shrinking aid flows and subjected to structural adjustment programmes. The withdrawal of international support from these states may be a necessary component of state failure, but it is clearly not sufficient. The group of chronically dysfunctional states, it seems, is smaller than Robert Jackson's analysis of the post-colonial situation might suggest. To understand the colonial contribution to state failure, therefore, we need to look also at social structure and the colonial impact on different forms of precolonial political systems.

Social structure and political development

As a chaotic but nonetheless reasonably functioning democracy, India was often viewed as a model post-colonial state. As Thakur has pointed out, even the Indian Civil Service, perhaps the key institution on which the new Indian state depended, was better suited to the maintenance of law and order and tax collection than to the active promotion of economic development. Still, the contrast he draws between India and other post-colonial societies is largely accurate. In India, the authoritarianism of both pre-colonial government and the Raj itself had been softened by the gradual introduction of representative institutions. Elsewhere, pre-colonial political systems "were usually authoritarian; loyalties were concentrated within clans and kinship groups; and systems of peaceful succession had not yet evolved. As the British progressively withdrew from former colonies, the political and economic institutions that they had established were in most cases managed in ways that were a throwback to the earlier social patterns: authoritarian, clique-ridden, and corrupt."[13]

Why were some of these throwbacks more destructive than others? This is a complex issue, but three sets of considerations may help to explain why the colonial legacy was more problematic for some states than for others. The first concerns the creation of state structures to govern populations not merely that had not previously been united politically – that after all was true of India – but for whom the state itself was an exotic import.

Somalia is the most spectacular example. Only a few years before Somalia disintegrated in the late 1980s, it was commonly represented as one of the few genuine nations in Africa: all Somalis share a language and culture and virtually all are Muslim. Indeed, the strength of Somali nationalism was viewed with alarm by other African states. It had been strong enough in 1960 to forge a union between the former Italian trust territory and the British protectorate, but Somalis also refused to accept the *uti possidetis* principle and at independence claimed the adjoining Somali-occupied territories of north-east Kenya, the Ogaden in Ethiopia and Djibouti. Despite urbanization and some settlement, the majority of Somalis are still pastoral nomads, a fact that continued to obstruct the process of reconstruction 10 years after the departure of UN peacekeepers.[14]

Pastoralists notoriously make bad citizens because they cannot easily be disarmed. Their way of life involves the accumulation and protection of flocks and herds from predatory neighbours. Since it also involves predation as a means of accumulating stock, the local political system adheres quite closely to the ancient maxim that "the enemy of my enemy is my friend". Furthermore, pastoralists make enthusiastic but unreliable nationalists, because, although they can unite at any level from the sub-clan to the people as a whole in the face of a common enemy, they are so fiercely egalitarian that they will not long submit to a central authority.

With hindsight, it seems clear that the state never really functioned as an effective national administration in Somalia. After the military coup in 1969, Siad Barre concentrated power in his own hands to an extent unprecedented in Somali history. He did so in a traditionally Somali fashion by building an alliance from his own clan and that of his mother-in-law. As long as the irredentist option remained, he was able to contain the centrifugal forces inherent in the clan system by concentrating on pan-Somali goals; once the 1979 incursion into the Ogaden had been defeated by a Russian- and Cuban-led force, this safety valve no longer existed and the society imploded into full-scale civil war. Long before the American-led intervention in 1991, all administrative state institutions had collapsed. The civil servants, judges and police had disappeared back to their rival clan organizations because there was no central revenue to pay them. Except in the north-west and north-east, where a measure of stabilization has been achieved (without significant international involvement), whatever order is to be found is still mostly provided within informal clan structures.[15]

Analogous considerations may limit the prospect of good governance, at least in the conventional sense of this term, amongst two other groups that have recently received considerable international attention: the Kurds and the Afghans. In both northern Iraq and Afghanistan, clan loyalties and rivalries remain much stronger than state institutions or any sentiment of national solidarity. Indeed, both the Kurdish and the Afghan problems can be classed amongst the unfinished business of the imperial age. The Kurds, the largest stateless national population in the world, constitute sizeable minorities in three countries – Turkey, Iran and Iraq – and are spread more thinly in Syria and other parts of the Middle East and the Caucasus. Recognized as a nation with a right to self-determination in 1919, the Kurds were never been able to build a united resistance once this recognition was withdrawn following Attaturk's revolution, although on occasions they have united on a territorial basis to resist control from the centre in all three major countries of settlement. Afghanistan was never subdued for long by an imperial power – and in the nineteenth century maintained a precarious independence as a buffer state in the great game of imperial rivalries between Britain and Russia – but its central government seldom controlled the entire territory, let alone succeeded in disarming its population.

Pastoral, nomadic or semi-nomadic clan societies such as these were certainly not without their own systems of governance and mechanisms for maintaining order. Still, pre-colonial forms of governance that were hostile to the state were often viewed as backward by nineteenth-century thinkers. Even Hegel employed a surprisingly materialist distinction between hunter-gatherers, pastoralists and agriculturalists to account for the progress of civilization and the march of the world spirit.[16]

Teleology is not very helpful in explaining state failure, however. Apart from the fact that pastoralists tend to look down on agriculturalists, it ignores the fact that certain clan-based societies have no difficulty in accommodating to the modern world on their own terms. The survival – and even relative prosperity – of the Somali diaspora provides ample evidence of the adaptability of their culture. But it is true that what Richard Burton described in the nineteenth century as their fierce and anarchic brand of republican democracy would not easily evolve into its twentieth-century institutionalized and representative form. This was concealed by colonialism because the minimal government employed by the British left Somali social structures largely untouched. At present, the self-styled Somaliland Republic is the only part of the country that has something approaching a functioning state, notwithstanding the refusal of the international community to recognize it. This achievement provides powerful support to the lasting impact of colonial frontiers – the borders of Somaliland are congruent with those of the former British protectorate – but is also fortuitous since the Isaq clan family was united by its experience as Siad Barre's major target in the civil war and is able to dominate the region more or less to the exclusion of other clans.

The second set of considerations that may help to identify the causes of state failure concerns the differential impact of colonialism on neighbouring communities within the same territory. The European empires were much less coherent than they sometimes appear in retrospect, or even as they were presented at the time by theorists of imperialism such as Hobson and Lenin. There were many different kinds of colonial possessions or protectorates, and within some of them the colonial powers did not conceal their preferences. Thus, certain groups such as the Sikhs in India were identified as "martial", and others, already dominant, such as the Tutsi in Rwanda and Burundi, were deliberately used as tools of colonial administration. If certain groups received special treatment under colonial rule, it is not surprising that this cast a shadow over political development and stability after the transfer of power.[17]

There is no shortage of examples. The imperial powers frequently co-opted minorities to help them run the colonial state. In part, the long Tamil insurgency in Sri Lanka had its origin in Tamil overrepresentation in the civil service prior to independence. Similarly, Western-educated Ibos spread all over Nigeria and made themselves a target of resentment by the northern, primarily Hausa Fulani, majority prior to the civil war in

1967. In Rwanda, the Belgians reinforced – and rendered much more rigid – the pre-colonial Tutsi dominance over the Hutu majority, setting the stage for a series of massacres that culminated in the 1994 genocide. In Sierra Leone – and even more so in Liberia, which was established as an independent state for the descendants of slaves from the United States – the Creole minority formed a local aristocracy whose influence was disproportionate to its numbers. It is noteworthy that in all these cases it was the introduction of formal democracy, in situations in which there was neither a human rights culture nor in many cases a properly independent judiciary, that fanned the flames of post-colonial conflict.

Divide and rule is one of the oldest principles of imperial statecraft, but it was not always deliberate. Indeed, in some cases it was an unintended consequence of a desire to protect weaker communities from those who had historically preyed on them. In others, it was a consequence of a reluctance to meddle with established religion.

In Sudan, both these legacies contributed to the post-colonial catastrophe. From the 1920s, the British in effect partitioned the country into its African and Arab parts. Enthusiastic European imperialists believed that civilization, commerce and Christianity formed an irresistible trinity, but in practice, whenever the British subdued Muslim peoples, they not only co-opted their leaders in accordance with the policy of indirect rule but did their best to prevent the Christian missions from proselytizing. In Sudan, this policy involved respecting the power and authority of the Mahdi's family while simultaneously keeping the Arabs from extending their influence into the African south, where they had traditionally gone in search of slaves. In the south, the Christian missions were allowed free rein and it was they who provided the limited modern education to which the new post-colonial elite were exposed. Christian missionaries were concerned to save souls, not to create secular nationalists. While the colonial authorities policed the border between the two Sudans – even preventing Arab traders from operating in the south without a pass – the missions set about translating the Bible into the many different southern languages.

In 1956, the British handed over control to an Arab-dominated government, which then set about the Arabization and Islamization of the south, with predictable results. All attempts to broker a power-sharing deal between the two sides have foundered, not only as a result of northern intransigence but also because of southern disunity.[18]

The third set of considerations concerns the impact of indirect rule. This was the system under which the British allowed traditional rulers to continue in authority, although in an ultimately subordinate relationship to the colonial power. The system allowed the British simultaneously to show a measure of respect for local custom and to run an empire on the cheap. Indirect rule cannot itself be blamed for state failure, since in parts of the world it smoothed the way to independent statehood. But in other areas, particularly in Africa, the co-option of local chiefs – or their creation where such institutions did not exist – undermined the political legitimacy of the traditional ruling class in the eyes of the nationalists.

The manner in which Europeans exercised their dominion over the Islamic world may also have contributed to state failure. Conservative Muslim rulers – whether in the Gulf, northern Nigeria, Malaya or elsewhere – had little difficulty in supporting the British empire, since it buttressed their rule and privileges while insulating them from grassroots challenges, whether of a radical nationalist or a religious fundamentalist variety. It is the latter challenge that is currently most feared, partly because it threatens to take over the state (or so it is feared in the West) by democratic means but for anti-democratic or theocratic purposes, as in Algeria. It is also feared because it feeds on the strain of Islamic political thought that denies the primacy of political over religious legitimacy on which the current world order is based.

The pattern under which Muslim dynastic governments were periodically destroyed by religious zealots from the desert was analysed long ago by Ibn Khaldun.[19] Until recently, the survival of religious fundamentalism as a political strategy was taken more seriously by Muslim governments than by others. Since the 11 September 2001 attacks in the United States, the fear that Islamic fundamentalists may strike at what they regard as a corrupt Saudi government tainted by its alliance with the United States suggests that the sins of the colonial fathers may yet be visited on their post-colonial children, in ways that could not possibly have been predicted.

Policy implications

What implications for policy can we draw from these reflections on the colonial legacy? Perhaps the main one is that we must be wary of drawing the wrong lessons from history. The desire to discover a single strategic doctrine that, properly applied, will produce the desired results everywhere is not new. If the grand schemes of the European imperialists – assimilation in the French case, indirect rule in the British – produced wildly divergent results in terms of the political stability and legitimacy of the successor states, the contemporary internationalist formula, with its emphasis on democratization, the empowerment of civil society and human rights, is likely to meet the same uncertain and inconsistent fate. Respect for the law of unintended consequences requires that those involved in post-conflict reconstruction should pay close attention to the particular cultural and historical conditions of the societies in which they operate.

Against this general background, this section considers the policy implications of the four aspects of the colonial legacy discussed in this chapter.

Anti-colonial nationalism

Forty or fifty years after the transfer of power, little remains of the popular enthusiasm that the nationalist parties were able to generate around the political goal of independence. The cocktail of developmental optimism and anti-Western sentiment has lost much of its appeal. The wave of popular protest against authoritarian third world governments that erupted after the collapse of communism in Europe was usually genuine enough. There was real anger that governments had usurped the symbols of nationalism for themselves and had frequently used their monopoly of state power to enrich themselves at the people's expense. When it was announced in 2000, the New Partnership for Africa's Development (NEPAD) was widely welcomed in the West as evidence that Africa had finally escaped from the straightjacket of anti-colonialism. Under NEPAD, African governments agreed that, in seeking assistance from the Group of Eight (G-8), they would take responsibility for their own problems rather than seeking reparations for damage inflicted by colonialism, as in the past. In a deliberate echo of the procedure agreed by the Organisation for European Economic Co-operation (OEEC) under the Marshall Plan, they even agreed to set up a system of peer review to monitor their progress in entrenching democratic government, the rule of law and efficient administration.

Desirable as this change of direction may seem, it does not follow that the new order can be legitimated without the creation of a more broadly based national sentiment. Fascism had discredited nationalism, but after 1945 European states and European nations remained sufficiently coherent for reconstruction to be a practical project. As Alan Milward has argued, cooperation was a way of rehabilitating European states not, despite the rhetoric that suggested otherwise, a strategy for transcending them.[20] In Africa, the situation is different: the states are not just disgraced, they are frequently radically dysfunctional. Indeed, in many cases state-wide national identities have failed to replace (or, sometimes, even to compete with) parochial loyalties, whether of an ethnic, religious or clan-based kind. But nor does it follow that the politics of envy – and consequently a latent anti-Western sentiment – has been (or, indeed, can easily be) eradicated from post-colonial societies. Modern communications, which project Western lifestyles and values into the remotest parts of the world, will pose particular problems for the new elite, on whom reconstruction depends. Not only will it be difficult to attract qualified people back from exile, as is proving to be the case in Sierra Leone, but many of the most able people may still wish to seek their fortunes abroad. The wry observation of a US-based Indian from the subcontinent about the attitude of his fellow Indians towards the United States – "Yankee go home, and take me with you!" – applies to many parts of the post-colonial world. It is not obvious how this problem should be addressed in the reconstruction of failed states. That it is a problem, however, certainly needs to be recognized.

The territorial settlement

The adoption of the principle of *uti possidetis juris* was a sensible post-colonial response to the cavalier and potentially disastrous European approach to imperial borders. It was revived – in the first instance by the Organization of African Unity – because African leaders feared opening a Pandora's box of secessionist and irredentist claims. By adopting the principle, the international community also recognized the reality that secession is more likely to deepen the conflict than to resolve it, because of the trapped minority problem. On the other hand, whether a failed state can be successfully reconstructed within its original borders will depend on circumstances. Opportunity costs have to be considered. Partition may be a second-best solution, but there may be times when that is the price of progress. In 1969, Julius Nyerere lost the argument that Nigeria had forfeited its right to represent the Ibos because they had come to believe that the state was threatening their existence.[21] Federal Nigeria's victory helped to entrench *uti possidetis* as non-negotiable, yet the principle was successfully breached after the Cold War by Eritrea and it is at least doubtful whether a long-term solution of either the Somali or the Sudanese conflicts can be secured without further breaches.

The subsequent history of Ethiopian–Eritrean relations – within three years the two countries were locked in a ferocious border conflict – suggests that if such partitions are to be stabilized they may need the help of third-party mediators. The Kashmir and Cyprus conflicts should warn us against undue optimism that this can be achieved quickly.

Economic development

The globalization of the world economy creates opportunities for the reconstruction of failed states but also places formidable obstacles in their way. Even when the colonial powers pursued liberal economic policies, metropolitan and colonial economies were linked in what was in effect a single preferential area. When the effects of the Great Depression spread to the colonial world, these arrangements were institutionalized, but after independence most post-colonial states pursued economic nationalist policies. Although they protested against the subsequent dismantling of imperial preferences (and their French equivalent), these preferential arrangements could not protect the import substitution industries on which it was believed economic diversification depended.

National economic protection was used by all industrial latecomers as a strategy of modernization. It was the policy pursued by the United States, Germany and Japan in the nineteenth and early twentieth centuries and by the East Asian tiger economies after the Second World War. However, it no longer seems to offer a viable alternative to the open market regime, which is underpinned by the World Trade Organization. The standard advice to small countries is to develop niche markets, and for some this response to global markets may indeed work. Yet it is difficult to see how countries that have been racked by civil conflict can quickly develop the tourist or offshore financial services sectors, two of the most favoured niche markets. By contrast, the disintegration of several of these states was encouraged by the relative ease with which, in a deregulated globalized economy, warlords and rebel leaders could finance their activities through the sale of such commodities as diamonds or timber on world markets. Reconstruction will need not merely to cut off these sources of income from those who profit from war – as has now been substantially achieved in Sierra Leone – but to develop mechanisms that will ensure that the proceeds from such sales are ploughed back into economic and social development. Since many of the conditions that led to the inflation and corruption of the state sector have not changed, including the virtual absence of an independent entrepreneurial class in many failed states, this remains a formidable challenge.

Political culture and social structure

The European empires had one advantage over the recent experiments in international administration that have been cobbled together to cope with the aftermath of state collapse. Although the colonies were intended to serve the interests of the metropolitan power, colonial government necessarily involved the development of a class of officials with an understanding of local languages, political cultures and social customs and taboos. The cosmopolitan group of conflict management experts who move around from crisis to crisis are unlikely – except here and there and fortuitously – to be able to draw on a similar set of skills. There will always be a danger, therefore, of the transition being hijacked by those in the society with a particular rather than a general interest to pursue. To some extent this happened in Cambodia, where the jurisdiction of the international authority exceeded its capacity and created a vacuum that could be filled only by those who already ran the system. The genocide in Rwanda was precipitated by an international peace process that was stronger on conflict management theory than on local knowledge. The process included everyone except the one group who stood to lose by the deal and retained the capacity to sabotage it.[22]

Two other aspects of the international response to state failure deserve some comment. The first concerns the role of civil society, the second the development of a democratic culture. To the extent that the problem is seen as resulting from tyranny, the international prescription is generally to encourage democratization and the empowerment of civil society, often with the help of international non-governmental organizations (NGOs). In many failing states, the problem is not that civil society does not exist but that it is the wrong kind, at least from the point of view of the international community. What is wanted is private organizations that mobilize people on a country-wide level but across ethnic and sectarian lines. The model is provided by South Africa during the last years of apartheid. More typical are strong tribal or regional organizations, often with their roots in traditional society. NGOs, which are unaccountable, may find themselves unwittingly reinforcing the fault lines in divided societies rather than overcoming them. In many post-colonial societies, politics remains essentially a winner-takes-all game. Under democratization, the temptation will be for the losers to regroup within civil society and under the protection and patronage of NGOs.

If secession seldom solves the problem of state failure, nor does democratization – unless it can accommodate the complexity of the peoples who have to share the same political space. One of the more unfortunate colonial legacies is that the democratic constitutions that were grafted on to the colonial state prior to independence were usually modelled on the constitution of the metropolitan power, rather than being tailored to the needs of the successor state. If self-determination disputes cannot be resolved through partition however, it may be possible to redesign a constitution to allow for more appropriate forms of power-sharing. But since it remains extraordinarily difficult to persuade those in power to share it on a temporary, let alone a permanent, basis, it would be wrong to see this as a panacea.

Conclusion

Will the legacies discussed in this chapter continue to cast a long shadow over the development of former colonies? There can be no simple answer to this question. Nor is the answer likely to be the same everywhere. As the colonial period recedes beyond the memory of the citizens of the successor states, it will no doubt be used less and less by political leaders as a reference point, either for defining the problems they face or for mobilizing the population. But it would be wrong to assume that the past will therefore cease to be relevant for an understanding of their predicament. On the contrary, it will continue to constrain and shape developments, sometimes in ways that may not be immediately recognizable to the actors themselves. In most parts of the world, language, law, religion and cultural pursuits and pastimes – all those aspects of a nation's life that seem most home-grown and constitutive of a people's identity – will on closer inspection reveal traces of old conquests and long-forgotten foreign influences.

There is a limit to what can be done by social engineering to channel this process of evolution and indigenization. It seems clear, however, that, if troubled post-colonial states are to be helped in their efforts to create working and viable polities, close attention will need to be paid to the way that the four legacies discussed in this chapter interact in different contexts. It will be necessary to focus simultaneously on those forces that reinforce the positive aspects of nationalism (that is, those that encourage the emergence of a state-wide national community) and the ways these are strengthened or weakened by existing international frontiers. Economic development must also be geared to the way the society is structured and functions economically, rather than to conformity with a general macroeconomic theory. And constitutional arrangements will need to be tailored to fit the social reality of divided societies rather than ignoring them. All this may seem a tall order. It is certainly true that a one-size-fits-all approach is cheaper, but the record since the end of the Cold War does not suggest that it is effective.

Notes

1. Winston Churchill, "The Price of Greatness Is Responsibility", speech delivered at Harvard University, Cambridge, MA, 6 September 1943, available at ⟨www.winstonchurchill.org/speeches/responsibility.htm⟩.
2. J. P. Dreze and A. K. Sen, *Hunger and Public Action*, Oxford: Clarendon, 1989.
3. See Ernest Gellner, *Nations and Nationalism*, Oxford: Blackwell, 1983, and *Nationalism*, London: Weidenfeld & Nicolson, 1997.
4. Benedict Anderson, *Imagined Communities: Reflections on the Origins and Spread of Nationalism*, London: Verso, 1983, pp. 60–65.
5. James Mayall, "Nationalism and the International Order, the Asian Experience", in Michael Liefer, ed., *Asian Nationalism*, London: Routledge, 2001, p. 193.
6. Kwami Nkrumah, the first prime minister of the Gold Coast and president of Ghana, was widely regarded as the source of this threat. His exhortation "Seek ye first the

political kingdom" was one to which other African leaders could respond; but most believed that his campaign to establish a United States of Africa was merely a cover for his own imperial ambitions.

7. Ramesh Thakur, *The Government and Politics of India*, London: Macmillan, 1995, p. 39.
8. See the discussion of this issue in chapter 12 by Patricia Shu Ming Tan and Simon S. C. Tay in this volume.
9. Steven R. Ratner, "Drawing a Better Line: *Uti Possidetis* and the Borders of New States", *American Journal of International Law*, Vol. 90, 1996, p. 610.
10. See chapter 6 by Benjamin Reilly and Elsina Wainwright in this volume.
11. For a fuller version of this argument, see James Mayall, "The Dream of a 'Quick-Fix': The Commonwealth Third World in the International Economy", in James Mayall and Anthony Payne, eds, *The Fallacies of Hope: The Post-Colonial Record of the Commonwealth Third World*, Manchester: Manchester University Press, 1991, pp. 161–190.
12. Robert Jackson, *Quasi-States: Sovereignty, International Relations, and the Third World*, Cambridge: Cambridge University Press, 1990, pp. 18–21.
13. Thakur, *The Government and Politics of India*, p. 38.
14. For background, see I. M. Lewis and James Mayall, "Somalia", in James Mayall, ed., *The New Interventionism: UN Experience in Cambodia, Former Yugoslavia, and Somalia, 1991–1994*, Cambridge: Cambridge University Press, 1996, pp. 94–124.
15. The Isaq-dominated Somaliland Republic in the north-west coincides with the former British protectorate. It declared itself independent in May 1991 but has not so far been formally recognized by any other state or international organization. Puntland in the north-east is an autonomous region with its own constitution. The region was previously part of Italian Somaliland and has not so far declared itself to be independent. Its relative stability, like that of Somaliland, is helped by the fact that the territory is largely occupied by a single family clan, the Darod.
16. G. W. F. Hegel, *Philosophy of Right*, translated by T. M. Knox, Oxford: Oxford University Press, 1979, Part 3: Ethical Life, (iii) The State, (c) World History.
17. The consequences were not always entirely negative. The overrepresentation of the Sikhs in the Indian armed forces, and in the public service more generally, was certainly a factor in the Punjab crisis of the late 1980s; but in the longer term it equally helped to resolve the crisis since the Sikh professional class was identified too closely with the Government of India for it to be able to afford to sever the link.
18. These include, at the time of writing, one sponsored by the United Nations and the African Union.
19. Ernest Gellner, *Moslem Society*, Cambridge: Cambridge University Press, 1981, pp. 1–85.
20. A. S. Milward, *The European Rescue of the Nation State*, London: Routledge, 1993.
21. "Tanzania's Memorandum on Biafra's case", in A. H. M. Kirk-Greene, ed., *Crisis and Conflict in Nigeria: A Documentary Source Book, Vol. 2, July 1967–January 1970*, Oxford: Oxford University Press, 1971, pp. 429–439.
22. See Bruce Jones, *Peacemaking in Rwanda: The Dynamics of Failure*, Boulder, CO: Lynne Rienner Publishers, 2001.

3

Human rights, power and the state

Michael Ignatieff

On the eve of the Iraq war, when UK Prime Minister Tony Blair was facing resignations from his cabinet and stubborn resistance to his policy from the British voters, he remarked to a journalist, "What amazes me is how many people are happy for Saddam to stay. They ask why we don't get rid of Mugabe, why not the Burmese lot. Yes, let's get rid of them all. I don't because I can't, but when you can, you should."[1]

This remark is a revealing way to begin an examination of human rights arguments for coercive regime change in the modern era. Blair was always in favour of regime change on human rights grounds alone and unhappy about any resolution of the Iraq crisis that would have left Saddam Hussein in power, even if he had fully complied with UN weapons inspections. But Blair knew that this position had no support at the Security Council. No state actually endorses the proposition that tyranny alone could justify military intervention. Although both Blair and US President George W. Bush made much of Saddam's human rights abuses, neither argued that these alone justified regime change. The reason for this is obvious enough. There are many tyrannies in the world; some may be odious but pose no threat to powerful states, whereas others, although also odious, are allied to powerful states. The Mugabes or the "Burmese lot" are safe from intervention because their abysmal human rights behaviour posed no threat to Washington or London; others, such as Egypt or Uzbekistan, also with dreadful human rights records, are exempt too because they were useful allies of the leading

59

interventionists. Saddam did not benefit from either exemption. He was a tyrant in a strategically critical region, with a record of provoking the world's major power and with the resources – oil – to keep doing so in perpetuity. These factors, rather than mere tyranny, made him a target for intervention.

Yet Blair was insisting that tyranny does legitimize regime change, even if regime change in this instance could not meet standards of moral consistency. The anti-war faction in his own party kept arguing that intervention was morally acceptable only if applied universally, to all tyrants and human rights abusers, not just to those who happen to oppose the interests of powerful states. Blair objected not only to the lack of realism in this standard of consistency but also to its covert cynicism. Perfect consistency is a test of legitimacy that political action can never meet, and hence the prerequisite of consistency serves (even if it does not intend to do so) either as a justification for doing nothing or as a condemnation of any intervention actually undertaken.

But even this partial analysis does not exhaust the implications of Blair's remark. As his critics would have replied, his vexation was insincere: his support of the American project of regime change was not driven fundamentally by human rights at all. He supported the American project because he wished to increase his own, and his nation's, power by aligning UK foreign policy with American imperial designs in the Middle East. Were these designs motivated by human rights, the United States would be overturning rights-violating regimes from Morocco to Egypt. The real driver for regime change in Iraq was traditional state interest – the US desire to consolidate control over Gulf oil supplies by establishing a friendly regime in Iraq. In the wake of the attacks of 11 September 2001, the Bush administration had concluded that its Middle East policy, built on the relation with the Saudis, had brought it nothing but trouble. Many of the terrorists of 11 September were of Saudi origin, and Osama bin Laden's apparent *casus belli* had been American military presence in the Holy Places in Saudi Arabia. The rationale for US troop presence in Saudi Arabia had been the hostile regime next door. By overthrowing Saddam, the United States would, at a stroke, reduce its vulnerability in Saudi, eliminate Israel's major security threat, consolidate its grip on the Persian Gulf and create, in a democratic Iraq, a new anchor for the prosecution of its interests in the region.

The point of beginning here – with one prime minister's vexation about human rights – is not to present an analysis of what actually motivated the project of regime change in Iraq or explain why Blair took the strategic gamble of aligning, more or less alone, with the American superpower. With regime change ongoing as I write this, any analysis of what really drove intervention policy in Washington and London would be premature and, for the purposes of this book, beside the point. My point in beginning with Blair is that even this brief analysis indicates that human rights arguments are intensely problematic ways to rationalize regime change, nation-building and humanitarian intervention – three ways in which powers have intervened in order to "make states work". Yet using human rights arguments to rationalize intervention is unavoidable. They lend moral allure to the more naked aspects of state interest, and one abiding test of whether such interventions have worked, over the long term, is whether they do produce rights-respecting states.

The problem with using human rights arguments, however, is that it turns out to be impossible to reconcile the consistency requirements of human rights language with the prudential requirements of *raison d'Etat*. These consistency requirements arise because human rights doctrine is universalist: the rights of the Burmese, the Zimbabweans and the Iraqis are equally important. But only a consistently universalist foreign policy could adequately serve universalist moral principle, and no foreign policy can afford to be so ecumenical. No state has the resources for it and no state has an interest in being universally consistent. Sometimes states must turn a blind eye to the crimes of their friends, or even the abuses of their enemies. Hence human rights always has a destabilizing effect on the arguments that leaders use to defend their decisions to intervene. When leaders make a human rights case, hoping to capture the higher moral ground, the resulting justifications for the use of force, far from commanding general assent among states, divide as much as they unite. Every state supports human rights only up to the point at which its own prerogatives of sovereignty are cast into doubt. This essentially is what the Iraq debate showed. Furthermore, no amount of high moral argument could convince America's allies that it was engaged in anything other than a war of conquest.

The purpose of this chapter is to elucidate these complexities, to lay out where international opinion and international law now stand on when human rights justifies intervention in sovereign states and to suggest some clarification of how the emerging clash between human rights and state sovereignty might be better regulated, so that human rights does not become simply a callow accomplice of imperial state interest on the one hand, or an empty form of rhetorical moral perfectionism on the other.

Human rights and intervention

This is not the place to account for the moral and political ascendancy of human rights as a global movement, as a body of international law and as a set of moral arguments for intervention (I have done this elsewhere[2]). What needs emphasis here is that the rise of human rights has coincided historically with the emergence of US military and strategic predominance, and the global ascendancy of human rights is impossible to understand without recognizing its relation to US power. This is more than just the fact that the two Roosevelts, Franklin and Eleanor, were the founders of postwar international human rights – one bequeathing the UN Charter, the other serving as the drafting chairperson of the Universal Declaration of Human Rights.[3] Beyond this founding role, American leadership in the postwar world used international human rights to internationalize its claim about the political and moral superiority of liberal freedom in the battle with communism.

Throughout the Cold War, but with decreasing conviction, the Soviet bloc contested the American version of human rights, claiming that the communist emphasis on social and economic development, instead of political freedom, offered an alternative and superior account of the human good. With the Helsinki Final Act in 1975, however, the Soviets admitted the right of their own peoples to form human rights organizations and, in doing so, conceded, perhaps inadvertently at first, the hegemony of the American version of liberal freedom as the single, guiding account of human rights in the modern world.[4] From then until the collapse of the Soviet regime, Eastern dissidents used human rights claims to call for free trade union rights in Poland, glasnost in Russia and freedom of political expression everywhere in the Soviet bloc, and finally, after 1989, multi-party elections. The collapse of the Soviet Union in 1991 represents the historical apogee of human rights as a movement and as an ideology of freedom. The moment also coincided with the apogee of American power and influence.

Since 1991, the relation between the human rights movement and American power has become much more complex and adversarial. The collapse of the Soviet Union removed a structural obstacle to the exercise of US military force abroad, as well as seeming to demonstrate the superiority of the American political, social, cultural and military model. The effect of historical success was to exacerbate long-standing American tendencies towards the unilateral use of force, rather than following the competing US tradition, epitomized by the Roosevelts, of achieving US goals through multilateral institutions such as the United Nations. Human rights played a complex role in these developments. First, the US administration became increasingly resistant to scrutiny of its own human rights record at home and abroad and has taken the United States out of human rights conventions and bodies that apply such standards to American performance.[5] Second, this unilateralist turn has been accompanied, paradoxically, by an ever more strident use of human rights arguments, couched as the advancement of human freedom, as justification for the coercive use of US military force.[6] This more than anything else has put the international human rights movement and US power on a collision course.

This clash did not come all at once. In the immediate aftermath of the end of the Cold War, the first Bush administration was notably dubious about whether human rights language had any place in a foreign policy properly directed by realist, national interest concerns. Thus, the goal of the first Iraq war was neither regime change nor humanitarian intervention to rescue the Kurds and the Shia, but a classic exercise in reversing territorial aggression. As such it enjoyed nearly unanimous support from the international community. Human rights activists, however, were appalled that President Bush, having appealed in an imprudent moment for the Kurds and Shia to rise up, then refused to allow US troops to aid the uprisings, which were put down, often in sight of the US military, with horrible brutality. Yet this refusal to allow an intervention to embrace a human rights objective was entirely consistent with the design of the war itself and of the coalition that supported it.

The same resistance to human rights arguments can be detected in Secretary of State James Baker's famous remark in 1991, as the Balkan wars erupted, that the United States had "no dog in the fight".[7] The remark shocked human rights advocates at the time because, even as he made the remark, civilians were already being killed, large numbers of refugees were on the roads and the prospect of ethnic cleansing and massacre was already evident. For more than four years, however, the Bush and Clinton administrations concluded that the humanitarian distress in the Balkans, awful though it was, did not justify the risks of military intervention.

The first sign in the post–Cold War era that an American administration might be sympathetic to what has become known as humanitarian intervention was the operation, launched in the waning days of the Bush senior administration, to respond to the Somali famine. The operation began well with US Marines delivering food supplies to famine areas. When US forces allowed themselves to be drawn into factional fighting between clans in Mogadishu and engaged the strongest of these clans with military force, disaster ensued; 18 US forces were killed, the largest death toll in combat since Viet Nam. After that, the military were precipitously withdrawn and the folly of intervention in the name of "nation-building" became a cliché for both Republicans and Democrats.

So what made the Americans cross the "Mogadishu line", the supposed distinction between the use of military power for humanitarian relief and its use for nation-building and later regime change? A small domestic US lobby of human rights activists and liberal internationalists (not necessarily the same thing) kept up a strong political clamour for intervention during the first Clinton administration, but their arguments – that humanitarian catastrophe in itself mandated action – did not gain traction with the administration until they began to make the argument that the Balkans posed a national security challenge. War on Western Europe's doorstep was dividing Europe and America in an increasingly bitter war of words over whose responsibility it was to stop the carnage. The NATO alliance was being damaged by the disagreement. Eventually, Clinton intervened in Bosnia with military force in 1995, partly because the Srebrenica massacre exposed him to accusations of a lack of leadership, and partly because serious divisions within the NATO alliance called for the reimposition of American leadership.[8] In other words, human rights abuse in Bosnia – massacre, ethnic cleansing – was only a subsidiary cause of intervention. What actually triggered presidential action, and the subsequent commitment to make Bosnia work as a state, was the conviction that a national interest was at stake.

Since Bosnia, the United States has led or backed humanitarian intervention in Kosovo and East Timor, and the claim that serious human rights abuses justify coercive use of force has gained some ground throughout the international community. The International Commission on Intervention and State Sovereignty (ICISS), sponsored by the Canadian government, sought to capture this new consensus in its report *The Responsibility to Protect*, released in December 2001.[9] The report defined two instances of human rights abuse that would justify coercive use of military force under UN authorization: actual or apprehended genocidal massacre or massive ethnic cleansing. Significantly, the report did not believe coercive military force was justifiable in the case of tyranny involving serial forms of human rights abuse below the level of massacre or ethnic cleansing. Nor did it endorse coercive regime change in the case of military overthrow of democratic civilian government. As an attempt to capture and define a new international consensus, the report sought to strike a conservative balance, going less far than many human rights activists would have liked but somewhat further than most states in the developing world, suspicious of humanitarian intervention as a cover for imperial aggression, were prepared to accept.

Two additional remarks about the ICISS report are worth making. The first is that the report's attempt at establishing a new international consensus has not yet succeeded. Most non-European states in the UN system remain dubious about any intervention standard that goes beyond the UN Charter's unequivocal endorsement of state sovereignty. Whereas NATO states support humanitarian intervention in some circumstances, most other UN states remain doubtful. Within the UN system, in other words, it is questionable whether there is any evolving common law standard in favour of intervention in sovereign states. The only cases that command universal assent in the UN system would be territorial aggression. Abominable internal behaviour remains a contested trigger for coercive military force.

The second remark about the ICISS would be that it was published on the eve of September 11. After September 11, the intervention question changed decisively. Self-defence, the sole legitimate use of force allowed under the UN Charter, returned as the legitimating grounds for the US attack on Afghanistan. Since then, pre-emptive interventions to prevent states from acquiring weapons of mass destruction or from becoming terrorist bases have also been justified on self-defence grounds. The chief consequence of the self-defence argument, when used by the United States, has been to make the US administration deny any obligation to seek UN approval for its military operations. The United States did go to the United Nations to seek legitimacy for action over Iraq, but always argued that it did not need UN approval, since self-defence provided it with all the justification it needed.[10]

Iraq ushered in an era in which regime change has become the key external instrument used by the United States to make less powerful states work, or at least to work in its interest. It is vital to notice this distinction – between states that work in the Weberian sense of enjoying a monopoly over the means of violence within their borders and states that work to the satisfaction of their larger and more powerful neighbours. Neither of the states attacked in the Kosovo intervention of 1999 or the Iraq intervention of 2003 were failures in the Weberian sense. Both Serbia and Iraq deployed a repressive apparatus and efficient instruments of central authority. Both enjoyed a Weberian monopoly over the means of force, even though the Kosovars were contesting this monopoly. They were failures in two other dimensions, first as defenders of the human rights of all of their people and second because they were led by figures who opposed key strategic objectives of the United States.

Failed and failing states, where government does not control national territory or is incapable of supplying services to the whole population, have turned out to be less of a focus for intervention, in other words, than authoritarian regimes whose leaders pursue policies that simultaneously damage their own population and antagonize the vital interests of Washington and London. Humanitarian intervention in places such as Sierra Leone or Liberia belongs in a category of optional intervention cases, where action will be taken if human suffering allows an intervening state, such as the United Kingdom and the United States, to do good while also demonstrating its military and political capacity for action and leadership. Human rights suffering alone does not trigger intervention, as we can judge from the total inaction of the great powers in relation to the ongoing war in the Democratic Republic of Congo, which has resulted in the death of several million people, or the equal inaction that has attended the ongoing war between northern and southern Sudan. Failing states or failed ones that pose no security challenge to vital interests are unlikely to be the target of coercive intervention, even when the human suffering inside them cries out for action.

A further corollary is that intervention or coercive regime change is never going to occur where a state possesses the means to resist intervention effectively. The Russian state is doing considerable harm to the Chechen population and the human rights abuses that have accompanied its war of re-conquest in Chechnya are well documented. Yet Vladimir Putin is unlikely to meet the fate of Slobodan Milosevic. He is too important an ally and potentially too dangerous a foe.

Raison d'Etat, in other words, effectively rations coercive regime change, nation-building and humanitarian intervention to states that (a) abuse their populations, (b) while posing a threat to US and British interests, yet (c) lack the capacity to repel external attack. Yet although *raison d'Etat* predominates – and does so because interventions are politically risky and because military commanders rightly expect their political leaders to give them national interest rationales for putting soldiers in harm's way – human rights abuses, and the claim they make upon the conscience of media-sensitized electorates and political leaders, are also significant factors in determining when and where interventions happen. A rights-respecting Iraqi regime, even one seeking weapons of mass destruction, would have been difficult for the United States to attack. The fact that Iran, another possible target for intervention, allows a degree of political freedom makes it a difficult object for the use of force, because peaceful regime change from within remains possible. If peaceful regime change from within remains even a possibility, coercive external pressure is less likely. The legitimacy of coercive regime change, therefore, is irrevocably tied to the human rights character of the regime. Saddam made the mistake of both antagonizing the United States and then, through his human rights abuses, providing grounds to justify the use of force.

Yet these mixed motives for interventions truly satisfy no one. Those who favour a stricter rationing of force by national interest and realpolitik criteria – a Kissingerian view, for example – are unhappy that messy moral platitudes such as human rights are allowed to influence political decisions in Washington and London.[11] The problem with this realist position is that human rights cannot be dismissed as sentimental moralizing. The human rights character of a regime is a very good predictor of its long-term internal stability as well as of its external dangerousness. The fundamental weakness of the supposed realists who ran American foreign policy in the Gulf region – and this included Kissinger – was the failure to realize in time that a dictator who gasses his own population is bound to become a menace to his neighbours. Many countries possess weapons of mass destruction or the research capability to develop them. The only ones that pose any danger are those that abuse their own populations in order to maintain power and have strategic designs on other people's populations. So, in the end, even a realist must concede the relevance of human rights as an indicator of the risks that regimes pose to vital interests.

Human rights activists are unhappy about the salience of human rights in intervention decisions, but for different reasons. Some take the view that human rights is essentially a pacifist doctrine, mandating protest at human rights conditions but forbidding human rights organizations from endorsing intervention by states, since intervention will necessarily entail loss of life and other human rights costs. Others do not object to the use of force in principle but argue that those who intervene should be more consistent. They are the ones who ask: If Iraq, why not Mugabe or the Burmese junta? If Kosovo, why not Chechnya? Some merely register their discontent about this inconsistency, but others go further, refusing to support interventions that lack this element of consistency. They do so out of a genuine fear that they will be lending moral support to interventions that are actually driven not by moral principle but by imperial interest.

Human rights organizations have good reasons to stay clear of any position that appears to endorse the power interests of major states. They have built their legitimacy by defending their independence. All this is as it should be. A professional, impartial human rights movement that refuses to bow to power and insists on its own standards of assessment is essential to effective human rights protection. This means that human rights organizations should not take active public positions on whether interventions are advisable or justified on human rights grounds. This is certainly how Human Rights Watch operates: it documented abuses in Iraq for 20 years but took no position on the legitimacy of intervention in Iraq.[12] Other organizations, such as Amnesty, although purporting to be neutral on intervention, actually seemed to be swayed, as membership organizations, by their members' visceral suspicion of American motives and intentions, and so their neutrality was something of a fiction.[13]

Human rights believers, as opposed to organizations, have no necessary obligation to stay neutral in these debates, and for them the intervention question has become the most difficult aspect of human rights belief. Pacifists who oppose the use of military force in defence of human rights have an easy time of it, since pacifism cuts through all difficulties. But pacifism does leave those who suffer tyranny, massacre and genocide without an effective remedy. Non-pacifists who can support military action in defence of human rights have their problems too, chief of which is whether to lend support to force when it is obvious that remedying human rights abuses is only a subsidiary reason for the action. They must then assess the likely consequences of intervention independently of the intentions of the interveners. These intentions are never going to be pure. But the human rights of ordinary people might well be improved by those with impure intentions. If the human rights benefits of a use of force seem large, and the human rights costs of intervening seem low, then on balance it seems justifiable to support the use of force. An argument focused on consequences, such as this one, would not insist overmuch on consistency. The fact that you cannot intervene everywhere is not an argument for not intervening when and where you actually can.

But this argument – think of the consequences, ignore the intentions – will only take you so far. For there is a further problem: insincere intentions may prevent good consequences from occurring. If the United States and the United Kingdom actually do not much care about human rights in Iraq, then they are unlikely to do very much to improve them once they occupy the country. At some point, and it is not possible to know in advance when this point is reached, doubts about the sincerity of interveners will begin to trump hopeful expectations of consequences. In short, it is difficult to support coercive use of force if you believe that you are being lied to.

Human rights and state-building

If we turn now from the role of human rights in decisions to intervene to the role of human rights in re-making states once intervention has taken place, the same complex interplay of high principle and state interest can be seen at work. Human rights has become a signal indicator of whether states are working in post-conflict or transitional settings. At the same time, this is not a neutral indicator. The power and interest of large states largely determine what most legitimate international advice, whether by academics, human rights professionals, or bilateral and multilateral aid organizations, defines as a state that works.

The word "governance" has become popular because it purports to bring a neutral, technocratic set of criteria to the evaluation of whether states work. It would be nice to believe that states with "good governance" work and that those with "bad governance" do not. In fact, "governance" as a term is an artful illusion. There are no value-neutral or politically neutral definitions of "working", if we mean performing the range of functions that Weber said a state should perform. What the World Bank or the International Money Fund regard as "good governance", what the US government agencies for the promotion of democracy overseas define as good government and what Fidel Castro, or even Saddam Hussein, might regard as "good governance" are very different things. In the consensus favoured by most Western governments, "good governance" essentially means some approximation of liberal democratic government, consisting of free political competition with multi-party elections, an independent judiciary and rule of law, free markets and rights that guarantee juridical equality, property, privacy and freedom of religious belief and political opinion. Even those who admire liberal democracy wonder whether this institutional package in its entirety can be applied in every instance. Sceptics ask whether this model of good governance can possibly work in societies whose per capita income is below a certain figure, usually US$7,000–8,000 per year.[14] Below this level, states have such difficulty maintaining the infrastructure to collect taxes and distribute services that they have very little capacity either to coerce obedience or to conciliate conflict. But if this is so, if the liberal democratic model cannot work in poor states, this would restrict its ambit mightily and would force us to devise other measures for such states.

In the post-colonial period, it was held to be axiomatic that poverty and lack of development justified a larger and necessarily more coercive role of government in production and the distribution of resources. Hence the checks and balances intrinsic to the liberal democratic model were inapplicable in post-colonial contexts. What these states needed was decisive executive power. The effect of putting more power over the economy in the hands of government, however, was simply to increase the opportunities for corruption and the possibilities for economic misrule. After 40 years of post-colonial misrule in sub-Saharan Africa – or, if not always misrule, then rule unequal to the challenges – it is scarcely an exaggeration to say that no one knows, least of all Africans themselves, what "works" in terms of governance in sub-Saharan Africa. A lot has been tried, and most of it has failed, and the countries that have made the best fist of a difficult situation have been countries such as Uganda, which are neither liberal nor democratic but simply have relatively farsighted and honest, if authoritarian, leadership.

If there are doubts about what will "work" in very poor societies, can the model of good governance implied in liberal democracy work in less poor societies with acute religious or ethnic divisions? Many sceptics doubt that it can, since free political competition on the liberal democratic model sometimes has perverse effects: (a) exacerbating ethnic or religious majority tyranny, (b) exacerbating separatist tensions, and (c) fomenting civil wars. This seems to have been the effect of the coming of party pluralism and democracy in the former Yugoslavia.[15] Versions of guided, authoritarian democracy, in which a single leader manipulates ethnic and religious divisions to ensure stability, might "work" better than the free market political competition proposed in the liberal democratic model.

Can liberal democracy, with its long-standing historical commitment to separating religion and politics, work in societies where religion is politics or where the religious tradition, Islam for example, asserts the primacy of religious teaching and religious law in deciding political issues? Can a liberal democratic constitutional model, which asserts the primacy of secular law, work in societies where religious systems of law are predominant, both in the private or family sphere and in the public or political sphere? Attempts to impose secular constitutionalism on Iraq, for example, might not "work" at all, and raise questions about the universality or universal applicability of Western secularism.[16] An Iranian form of religious democracy, if freed from the obscurantist tyranny of the Shia clerics, might serve many Islamic societies better than a Western secular model.

Finally, can the liberal democratic model work in societies with no tradition of a state at all? Since James Mayall has raised this question already in the previous chapter, though in a different form, I shall have little to say about it here, except to say that, in addition to his examples of Somalia and Sudan, Afghanistan would qualify as one of those juridical sovereigns that throughout the twentieth century has rarely been a real and effective sovereign.[17] Its political traditions are tribal and clannish, and though these traditions include valuable forms of popular consultation such as the Loya Jirga, which eager foreigners have seized upon as an indigenous form of democracy, it is not obvious that there is either an institutional structure of state power throughout the territory of Afghanistan or any very deep tradition of political accountability, collective deliberation or local self-rule. Warlords are a problem in Afghanistan, not just because they use violent means, but also because they capitalize upon these enduring weaknesses in the Afghan political tradition. They are not so much excrescences on this tradition as its fullest expression, providing protection while extorting and bullying their people in return. Making a state – with coverage of service and coercion throughout the territory and not just in Kabul – may simply be impossible.

Despite the fact that there are substantial questions about the universal applicability of Western ideas of governance in poor, ethnically divided religious societies and in societies without state traditions, Western nation-building exercises in Afghanistan, Timor, the Balkans and now Iraq have all been driven by the utopia of this liberal democratic model. Applicable or not, the model has the full weight of Western power and Western self-regard behind it, and hence there is really no point pretending that making states work is a value-neutral project. The more relevant issue is whether, in working towards such a utopia, the results will be anything other than delusive.

One response to this problem has been to develop a chopped down version of the project, one supposedly applicable to less favoured societies. Fareed Zakaria has criticized the degree to which exporters of liberal democracy have essentially severed the liberal from the democracy, putting exclusive emphasis on frequent multi-party elections and putting almost no emphasis on the rule of law, development of an independent judiciary and training an honest prosecution service.[18] It is as if exporters were conceding that the whole integrated package of liberal democracy may be too much for developing societies or those exiting from tyranny and that they will have to be satisfied with majority rule and to secure rule of law later, if ever. What makes the challenge of making states work so austere is that the desirable package is not really divisible. In Bosnia, after many elections failed to uproot the entrenched system of local patronage and corruption, European transitional administrators, such as Paddy Ashdown, have come to the reluctant conclusion that regular elections must be supplemented with a determined attempt to implant the rule of law.[19] But if this is so, that is, if the desirable package cannot be reduced to a minimum programme, then the difficulty of introducing it at all becomes all the more salient.

This preliminary analysis suggests one obvious thought: if the applicability of the liberal democratic model is questionable in different contexts, then one way to make it more flexible might be to increase the ability of local actors in these nation-building experiments to inflect and change the Western agenda so that it more nearly reflects local history, tradition and constraints. Making states "work" will have to mean giving power, even in the transitional stages of nation-building exercises, back to local political actors and ensuring that Western administrations, whether they be in Kosovo, Afghanistan or Iraq, seek to do less imposing and more channelling of political competition among local actors, so that they create parties, alliances and structures that will allow them to take responsibility for making their state work. The question, still unanswered, is what the West will be prepared to live with once local ownership of the process runs its course. For example, will we be prepared to accept Shia majority rule in Iraq? Or Kosovar majority rule in Kosovo? Local ownership of the state actually means allowing majority elites to impose majority rule or ethnic, religious or clan forms of dominance. The people who can be expected to lose as local ownership increases are vulnerable minorities. Once Western interveners decide that local ownership must be increased, they will have to decide what diminished version of rights protection they are prepared to accept as a suitable end state and pretext for withdrawal. So the question of how you make states work turns out to pose a prior question: Who do you want to make them work for? Local elites? International civil servants? Or the political leaders in large Western capitals? This issue is covered more fully by Simon Chesterman in chapter 16 of this volume, so I shall not say more about it here.

For my purposes, the key question is what role human rights values and human rights protection can or should play in ideas of how to make states work, once more powerful states begin to intervene. Here what matters is not just the inevitable disjunction between local and international interests but a second disjunction between Western professional human rights activists and the international military personnel and international economists who run new regimes. What a human rights activist, assessing different regimes, might regard as "good governance" – rule of law, due process, rights guarantees as a constraint on administrative and military discretion – would seem like costly luxuries to a military governor interested primarily in security. What an international economic analyst working for the World Bank or the IMF might regard as "good governance" – in terms of debt reduction, fiscal responsibility and so on – might also reduce the revenue necessary for the creation of good government in the human rights sense of the word.

What happens once interventions occur seems to indicate that security soon becomes more important than human rights, and economic development more important than justice. It is a signal fact that, although human rights figured prominently in the rationale for intervening in the first place (in Kosovo and Iraq, for example), human rights protection and monitoring, together with the long-term development of human rights ombudspersons and other mechanisms for redress of abuses, have all tended to get short shrift once interventions occur. Typically, the most under-funded area of a post-intervention presence is the human rights pillar, and, in the priority conflict between order and justice, order usually wins, to the degree that order is possible at all. Thus, in Afghanistan and Iraq, it is unlikely that there will be much of an attempt to prosecute and punish human rights offenders from the previous regime, apart, in the case of Iraq, from the top 50 or so Saddam loyalists. The wider and deeper culpability of thousands in a regime of torture, disappearances and extra-judicial execution will remain unexplored, because to explore it would be to deprive the successor regime of the useful bureaucratic expertise of the culpable but competent survivors of the old regime. However, ending impunity for past human rights crimes is usually regarded as the *sine qua non* for creating a culture of human rights observance in the future. Thus interventions to put an end to lawless states may, without necessarily intending to do so, end up recreating states whose civil service, police and senior bureaucracy are just as lawless, just as rights violating as the old.

Conclusions

Only depressing conclusions seem to follow from this analysis. Human rights is used by powerful states to rationalize interventions conducted essentially for other reasons. Once these interventions occur, the insincerity of the human rights intentions is revealed in the short shrift given to human rights programmes in the reconstruction process. Even if intentions were sincere and programmes well funded, creating states that respect human rights may not even be possible, because we do not actually know how to make states work in societies that are poor, divided on religious or ethnic lines or lacked a substantial state tradition in the first place.

If this is true, why bother? Why not stay at home and try to do something about the substantial injustices still festering in our own societies? Why this compulsion to go abroad and make states work, when our own barely do?

Far from being the counsel of despair, these questions seem entirely apposite, and they do lead to at least one sceptical conclusion: we should be much less confident about what makes states work and more doubtful that interventions are likely to make them work better. Everything in this analysis would underscore prudential doubt about the advisability of interventions. We should indeed stay at home, not just to tend our gardens but to ration our restless impulses more effectively, to think more carefully about what works and to show a great deal more respect for the cultural variation and historical specificity of the societies we think we can change.

It would not follow, however, that, just because some interventions have not made things better, they have always made things worse or they should never have happened in the first place. If there had been no military intervention in Bosnia, even more than a quarter of a million people would have died; and it is possible that they would be dying still. If there had been no intervention in Kosovo, Milosevic would have proceeded to a final solution of the Kosovar problem, which would have led to mass murder and the expulsion of the entire Kosovar population beyond the borders of the province. If there had been no military action over East Timor, Indonesian militias would still be terrorizing the people of Dili. If there had been no intervention to overthrow Saddam Hussein, people in Iraq would be being tortured for political and religious belief and Iraq's oil revenues would be being spent on palaces and weapons programmes rather than on hospitals, roads and schools. Any evaluation of intervention on human rights grounds has to reckon with what would have happened had nothing been done. By this standard, there remain grounds to say that we did the right thing, even if we often did so for the wrong reasons and even if what we have put in its place is only marginally better.

Notes

1. Peter Stothard, *30 Days: A Month at the Heart of Blair's War*, London: HarperCollins, 2003, p. 42.
2. Michael Ignatieff, *Human Rights as Politics and Idolatry*, Princeton, NJ: Princeton University Press, 2001.
3. Mary Ann Glendon, *A World Made New: Eleanor Roosevelt and the Universal Declaration of Human Rights*, New York: Random House, 2001.
4. Daniel C. Thomas, *The Helsinki Effect: International Norms, Human Rights, and the Demise of Communism*, Princeton, NJ: Princeton University Press, 2001.
5. Michael Ignatieff, ed., *American Exceptionalism and Human Rights*, Princeton, NJ: Princeton University Press, 2004; see also Harold Koh, "On American Exceptionalism", *Stanford Law Review*, Vol. 55, 2003, pp. 1479–1527.
6. *The National Security Strategy of the United States of America*, Washington, DC: President of the United States, September 2002, available at ⟨http://www.whitehouse.gov/nsc/nss.html⟩.
7. Richard Holbrooke, *To End a War*, New York: Random House, 1998, p. 27.
8. Ibid.
9. International Commission on Intervention and State Sovereignty, *The Responsibility to Protect*, Ottawa: International Development Research Centre, December 2001, available at ⟨http://www.iciss.gc.ca⟩. I was a member of this commission.
10. See, for example, President Bush's remarks at the UN General Assembly, 12 September 2002: "My nation will work with the U.N. Security Council to meet our common challenge. If Iraq's regime defies us again, the world must move deliberately, decisively to hold Iraq to account. We will work with the U.N. Security Council for the necessary resolutions. But the purposes of the United States should not be doubted. The Security Council resolutions will be enforced – the just demands of peace and security will be met – or action will be unavoidable. And a regime that has lost its legitimacy will also lose its power."
11. Henry Kissinger, *Does America Need a Foreign Policy: Toward a Diplomacy for the 21st Century*, New York: Simon & Schuster, 2001, pp. 253, 258.
12. "Human Rights Watch Policy on Iraq", available at ⟨http://hrw.org/campaigns/iraq/hrwpolicy.htm⟩.
13. Irene Kahn, "Iraq II: Who Cares about the People", *International Herald Tribune*, 25 September 2002; Amnesty International (General Secretariat, New York), "Not in the Name of Human Rights", 12 September 2002.
14. Paul Collier, "The Market for Civil War", *Foreign Policy*, May/June 2003, pp. 38–45.
15. Michael Ignatieff, *The Warrior's Honor: Ethnic War and the Modern Conscience*, New York: Metropolitan, 1995.

16. Noah Feldman, *After Jihad: America and the Struggle for Islamic Democracy*, New York: Farrar, Straus & Giroux, 2003.
17. Barnett R. Rubin, *The Fragmentation of Afghanistan: State Formation and Collapse in the International System*, New Haven, CT: Yale University Press, 1995.
18. Fareed Zakaria, *The Future of Freedom: Illiberal Democracy at Home and Abroad*, New York: W.W. Norton, 2003.
19. Paddy Ashdown, Inaugural Speech of the New High Representative for Bosnia and Herzegovina, 27 May 2002.

Part II
Regions

4

The Great Lakes and South Central Asia

Andrea Armstrong and Barnett R. Rubin

In both southern Central Asia and the Great Lakes region of Central Africa, sets of conflicts and actors in those conflicts have formed networks across borders that create regional conflict formations. The failure of Afghanistan and the Democratic Republic of Congo (DRC) to consolidate power effectively and accountably accelerated corrosive regional dynamics that in turn undermined these states even further. Armed groups, some supported by neighbouring states, exploited the weaknesses of these states by forming networks and alliances on their territory. Regional competition for political and economic influence shattered these weak states, creating strong ties between armed groups and criminalized economic actors in the peripheries of these failed states and their neighbours. To understand these dynamics better, this chapter explores the process of state failure and reconstruction in the Great Lakes region of Africa and South Central Asia.[1]

Regional conflict formations are sets of transnational conflicts that form mutually reinforcing linkages with each other throughout a region, making for more protracted and obdurate conflicts. Both processes that generate conflict and those that can be marshalled for peace-building can be located within the region. Networks of armed groups, traders, leaders and states within a region use violence to achieve political, ideological and economic goals. They often capitalize on social relationships that extend influence across borders and operate within the territory of a failed state without reference to legal authorities. Certain cross-border groups, such as traders engaged in smuggling, in some circumstances facilitate conflict but in others may seek and promote the stability needed for state reconstruction.

The regional dynamics of conflict show strong resemblances in these otherwise dissimilar regions. From the involvement of neighbouring states, to the alliances of armed groups, to the operation of the transnational informal economy, these two regions exhibit phenomena that undermine efforts to make states work and that illustrate the need for regionally focused policies.

The collapse of some states within a region accelerates the regional spread of conflict. Sebastian von Einsiedel's chapter (chapter 1 in this volume) noted that international efforts to "make states work" have largely concentrated on reconstituting the state. Strengthening some states in a conflict-prone region might only shift violence from place to place. If such policies are integrated with region-wide initiatives of the right type, however, they could start to contribute to de-escalating conflict throughout the region by shutting down a principal mechanism through which violence spreads, namely the creation of unpoliced areas in collapsed states.

Competing notions of "region" as well as the conflation of "power" with legitimate authority often block understanding of these situations. Hence we first clarify what these terms mean in this context. Next, we explore regional processes and factors that contribute to state collapse and armed conflict in the Great Lakes region of Africa and South Central Asia. Last, we identify regionally based strategies that official and unofficial policy makers and practitioners could adopt to alleviate the insecurity and violence that result from state failure.

The region and power

The characteristics of a region

Rather than just spilling over from their point of origin, conflicts often involve actors with regional strategies, regional reach and regional identities. These regional linkages are not simply a by-product of conflict. They emerge from social and political ties that pre-date the state borders and institutions instituted by Western colonialism and imperialism. That is not to make a value judgement, as if the regional ties were autochthonous and authentic whereas the national borders are imposed and artificial. Actors can use either for a variety of purposes. Analysis of failed states that focuses solely on the national level will miss important conflict dynamics that result from the historical legacy of the regional construction of systems of states.

A growing body of scholarly evidence affirms that neighbourhood matters, especially if neighbours are at war. In its 2002 annual review of world conflict, the Stockholm International Peace Research Institute found that 11 out of 15 most deadly conflicts "spilled over" into their neighbouring states – thus belonging to "regional conflict complexes".[2] Three out of the four remaining conflicts are on islands and thus face "natural barriers" to spillover. Even if a state avoids military or political entanglement in a neighbouring conflict, it still suffers economically. A study by James Murdoch and Todd Sandler confirms not only that countries are vulnerable to conflict in their region, but that they often suffer the same magnitude of economic impact as those countries actively in conflict.[3] In fact, the longer a state's contiguous border with its neighbours in civil war, the more severe the short-run economic impact. A neighbour in conflict disrupts cross-border trade, deters foreign investment and forces states to shift resources to support refugee populations and strengthen border control.

Accepting the premise of regional impact, however, does not make identifying a "region" any easier. In international law and institutions, a "region" consists of a fixed set of more or less contiguous states with a name (Africa, the Americas, South East Asia, Central Asia), usually with some cultural or linguistic affinity, as well as strategic and economic interests that are closely interrelated, and that may be organized into a regional organization. When the security of states in a region is, in some sense, more dependent on states within that same region than on states outside, the region can become a "security community".[4] Organizations working in international or global affairs, whether foreign ministries or schools of international relations, assign countries to different regional bureaus, departments, institutes or centres, based on such criteria.

In all of these cases, however, the "region" is something different from what we mean by "region" in the concept of regional conflict formation. The regional conflict formation concept defines "region" ex post as the set of territories over which conflict networks are closely linked. Such a region might include entire states or parts of states, and it might not correspond to any named region. We define the "region" empirically as those geographical areas where the networks and linkages are concentrated.

Both conflict formations studied here exemplify the problem. The conflicts in Central Africa were initially focused on Rwanda and Burundi, both of which belong to the region of the Great Lakes as defined geographically or culturally. Southern Uganda, western Tanzania and eastern DRC (ex-Zaire) – all of which belong to the Great Lakes region – were also involved, but most of the DRC and Tanzania were not. As the conflict escalated, however, it came to engulf the whole of the DRC and to include Zimbabwe, Angola, Namibia, Chad and the Congo-Brazzaville. Libya, Zambia and South Africa became more involved trying to influence the outcome of various negotiations that eventually merged into the Lusaka process. The United States, France, Belgium, the European Union and the United Nations also participated. Even if we restrict ourselves to the countries with direct military involvement – Rwanda, Burundi, Uganda, the DRC, Zimbabwe, Angola, Chad and Namibia – it is clear that they do not belong to a recognized "region", certainly not to the Great Lakes region. The regional conflict formation includes countries from Central Africa, East Africa and Southern Africa, according to organizational criteria.

Similarly, Afghanistan sits at the intersection of what are usually defined as three different regions: the Middle or Near East, or West Asia; Central Asia; and South Asia. The regional conflict formation in and around Afghanistan, referred to here as "southern Central Asia", includes Afghanistan, Pakistan, Iran, all of Afghanistan's northern neighbours (Tajikistan, Uzbekistan and Turkmenistan), networks reaching into the Persian Gulf and the conflict in Kashmir, with, therefore, some implications for India as a state. As in the previous case, we define the region where the conflict formation is located as the territories where linked conflict behaviour is most concentrated, not as a static set of states clustered for historical or organizational reasons.

This distinction, which may appear academic, has practical implications. One often hears that, if conflicts are regional, solutions should also be regional, involving regional organizations or regional arrangements. The difficulty is that the "regions" linked together by conflict need not correspond to the "regions" that are units of action. Furthermore, conflicts within an empirically defined region may largely be generated by actors external to the region.

A focus on regional components should not negate but complement analysis of local, national and global arenas for conflict and peace-building. Any level of focus is in a sense arbitrary. A more complete way of describing today's wars might be to use Mark Duffield's term "network wars".[5] These are wars waged and supported by transnational, often non-territorial, networks of people connected through information and exchange. These networks cross borders with increasing ease, as do other networks in the age of globalization. Such networked transactions are on the whole more likely to occur in proximity to the actual locus of violence – that is, in the region – than further away. This is particularly true for transactions of lower value and higher cost per unit, such as the recruitment of soldiers. Other transactions – in diamonds or weapons, for instance – although requiring networks or regional intermediaries, are high-value enough to figure in long-distance conflict transactions. The same is true of the export of a small number of highly trained terrorists able to attack the World Trade Center, the Pentagon and other targets at a cost well under US$1 million.

Global linkages shape regional dynamics. Competition among major powers and the global appetite for natural resources affect local actors' calculations of interest and risk. All of these conflicts are fought with modern weapons, which are not manufactured by the poor societies that fight them. Since weapons have to be purchased, unlike at the height of the Cold War, protagonists need to export some commodity, whether opium, diamonds, emeralds, smuggled consumer goods or coltan.[6] Regionally based businesses and trading networks usually organize the local sales or wholesale purchases, but both the import of weapons and the export of high-value commodities to finance their purchase depend on links between the regions in conflict and the developed capitalist nations, whether through legitimate business ties, personal links or simply corruption.

The global effects of such dynamics should be obvious enough since the attacks of 11 September 2001, but the perception of such acts primarily as affecting "terrorism", without analysis of the contexts that allow organizations such as al Qaeda to organize, has thus far framed the question differently in public debate. The links of al Qaeda to the conflict diamond trade in West Africa, to Somalia and to Albania, as well as to other regions of institutional breakdown, illustrate how regional instability and failed states can feed global networks of violence and power.

The characteristics of power

How we conceptualize power and its relation to state failure has important implications for state-building projects and strategies. If state failure were characterized as the absence of power, then external parties might try to import "power" in the form of foreign armies, interim authorities composed of exiles or a United Nations administration. These external parties might try to eject "thugs" who exploit the power vacuum for their own benefit. Even if such a strategy is successful, these kinds of approaches may still destabilize the region by shifting instability and violence to neighbouring weak states.

More accurately, state failure should be conceptualized as the transformation of public power into privately held and often fragmented power. Sometimes individuals within a regime fragment and disperse power to weaken resistance to their regime and entrench themselves. People still exercise power on the territory of the state; but, unlike more developed states, states in such regions have few assets worth capturing, and administering a territory as a state often entails more costs than profits. Competing armed groups, unable (or unwilling) to capture the state, settle for their secondary objective of consolidating as much power as possible for their personal benefit, without responsibility for a whole territory or population. State collapse allows many power holders to "win" without necessarily gaining authority over population and territory. Hence, state failure is not the replacement of power with chaos, but rather the transformation and transference of power to private actors, who then have an interest in maintaining the status quo.[7] These actors further dismantle state structures, because institutional disintegration expands their private power. Even in anarchy, order and rational choice guide the decisions of the new power holders.

The defeat of the Taliban by the United States significantly altered the interests of provincial warlords in Afghanistan. In an attempt to co-opt local warlords, the central government in Kabul designated these private rulers as military or civilian officials, though their actual power exceeds that derived from such roles. General Abdul Rashid Dostum, a former communist militia leader who later joined the Northern Alliance and controls provinces in the north, is now deputy minister of defence and for a time held the title of the President's Special Representative in Northern Afghanistan. Similarly, General Ismail Khan, a former mujahidin commander in western Afghanistan, now controls territory beyond the Herat Province of which he is officially governor. The divide between publicly and privately held power can be difficult to determine.

Can such local power holders be an ally of state-building projects? Can their interests change so that they become stakeholders in reconstruction? Or must they be defeated in order to reconstitute the state effectively? Answers to these questions shape strategies.

State failure and bad neighbourhoods

Regional security competition

Neighbouring states are complicit in the state failures of the DRC and Afghanistan. Afghanistan's conflict drew in neighbours; the conflict in the eastern DRC was ignited by spillover from Rwanda. Yet regional security competition cannot fully explain the causes of the conflicts in the DRC or Afghanistan. Internal factors still matter, as Amin Saikal's chapter on Afghanistan (chapter 9) illustrates. Regardless of their origin, however, the very existence of these conflicts provided opportunities to state and non-state actors throughout the region to pursue their own objectives. To address regional security externalities and counter perceptions of threats from the region, neighbours trained, supplied and financed armed group operations in the DRC and Afghanistan, using state and proxy forces to achieve their goals. Populations in these weak states have suffered enormously as a result. Between August 1998 and November 2002, the International Rescue Committee reports that 3.3 million people died as a result of the war in the DRC, either directly through violence or indirectly through malnutrition and disease.[8] In Afghanistan, at least 1.7 million people died of violence between 1978 and 1999, according to the International Committee of the Red Cross.[9] Of course, these numbers paint only a partial picture; fully to grasp the impact of these failed states and the regional conflict formations they facilitated, we would need to include conflict-related deaths in Burundi, Rwanda, Kashmir and Pakistan, among others.

In the Great Lakes region, the regime of President Mobutu Sese Seko was increasingly brittle after his refusal to implement democratization reforms and the withdrawal of US support following the Cold War, but Zaire's collapse was hastened by the activities of Rwandan *génocidaires* among the refugee population in the east.[10] Mobutu had increasingly become a regional pariah. In some cases, he provided explicit support for rebel groups from neighbouring states, such as Angola's União Nacional para a Independência Total de Angola (UNITA); in others, he tolerated the operations of rebel groups such as the Ugandan Lord's Resistance Army. Though he gave refuge to those responsible for the 1994 genocide, including the ex-Forces Armées Rwandaises (FAR) and the Interahamwe, he also tried to use his status as host to over 1 million Hutu refugees to rehabilitate himself on the international scene. In an unusual show of regional cooperation, however, a coalition of states, including Rwanda, Uganda, Burundi, Angola and Zimbabwe, contributed either troops or military supplies to the uprising in 1996 by the Alliance des Forces Démocratiques pour la Libération du Congo-Zaïre (AFDL) led by Laurent Kabila, which ended in Mobutu's overthrow in May 1997.

After his success, Laurent Kabila attempted to consolidate power in the renamed Democratic Republic of Congo and build nationalist support for his government by disavowing his ties with neighbouring states and the Banyamulenge (Congolese of Tutsi origin).[11] He replaced ethnic Tutsi advisers with Congolese and expelled Rwandan and Ugandan officers, although he ultimately failed to quell dissent within his military or to pacify eastern DRC. In an abrupt about-face, he even recruited and armed ex-FAR and Interahamwe.[12] In August 1998, armed groups backed by Rwanda and Uganda rebelled in the east, quickly seizing large swathes of DRC territory. Only intervention by Zimbabwe and Angola (plus Chad and Namibia to a lesser extent) halted the rebels' march towards the DRC capital, Kinshasa. In the course of the conflict, former allies Rwanda and Uganda supported competing factions of the Congolese Rally for Democracy (RCD), culminating in armed clashes between the two states in Kisangani. The territory of the DRC was essentially divided into zones of Rwandan and Ugandan occupation in the east, with the DRC controlling the west with the help of Angola and Zimbabwe.

In South Central Asia, the Soviet invasion of Afghanistan led the United States, Pakistan and Saudi Arabia to funnel arms and money to anti-communist Islamic groups in Afghanistan, including current US foe Gulbuddin Hikmatyar. The battles between US-supported fighters on the one side and the Soviet army and its Afghan allies on the other destroyed the country's infrastructure and eliminated most potential leaders (including much of the educated elite). The halt in Soviet aid as the Soviet Union collapsed culminated in the collapse of the Soviet-supported Afghan army in 1992. The territorial administration had already disappeared in much of the country. Pakistan, anxious to avoid the establishment of a hostile government to the north and west, and wanting to increase its regional influence vis-à-vis India and to establish oil, gas and trade corridors to Central Asia, continued to seek ways of influencing Afghan affairs through funding various Pashtun warlords and providing arms and training via the Inter-Services Intelligence Directorate (ISI). Its support for the Taliban, an indigenous Afghan movement, was countered by Russian, Iranian, Indian, Tajik and Uzbek support for various parts of the United Front (or Northern Alliance), a group of militia organizations mostly from northern Afghanistan led by Ahmed Shah Massoud. States in the region developed relationships with individual commanders in Afghanistan, sometimes based on ethnic or religious lines, which succeeded in dividing Afghanistan into spheres of influence.

Parallel economy, transnational informal economy and transit trade

When the official economy crumbles, individuals collaborate in the unofficial provision of goods and services that are legal but beyond the purview of states. These networks can supply basic goods that are diverted because of regional political tensions, or they may simply fill gaps in the market, as when Afghans circumvent restrictions on Pakistan–India trade by using Dubai as a transit centre. Unofficial commerce can involve the diversion of legal trade to avoid customs duties, as when goods imported duty free via Pakistan for re-export to Afghanistan under the Afghan Transit Trade Agreement (ATTA) are later sold in Pakistani bazaars and warehouses. This can be a significant resource to armed groups. The

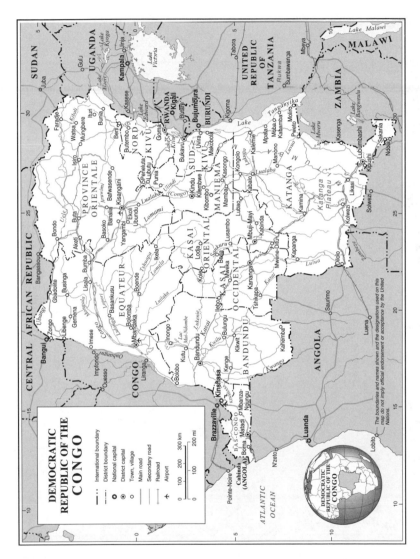

Figure 4.1 Map of the Great Lakes region of Africa (*Source:* United Nations, 2002, reproduced by permission of the United Nations Cartographic Section).

87

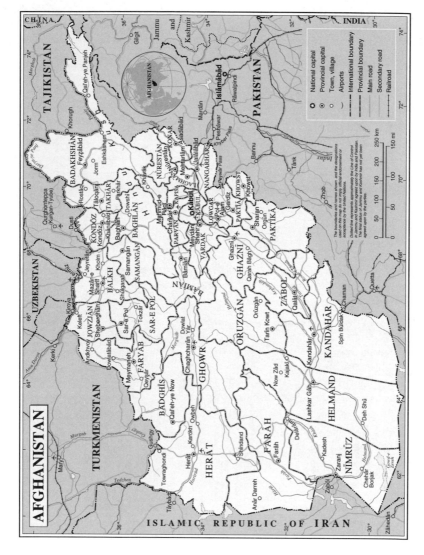

Figure 4.2 Map of South Central Asia (*Source:* United Nations, 2004, reproduced by permission of the United Nations Cartographic Section).

World Bank estimated that the import of goods for re-export to Afghanistan that were illegally sold duty free in Pakistan was worth over US$2 billion a year in the late 1990s.

In Zaire, the informal economy grew as a response to the increasing criminalization of the Mobutu regime. These informal economic survival strategies, which continued and perhaps expanded under Kabila's reign, ranged from smuggling tobacco and spirits across international borders to buying bulk agricultural products to be sold on street corners.[13] The sustained failure of the Zaire/DRC state animated trading linkages among Uganda, Rwanda, the DRC, Burundi, Tanzania and Kenya. Agricultural trade linked Kampala (Uganda) and Bukavu (DRC), and manufactured goods from Bujumbura (Burundi) markets supplied the port town of Uvira (DRC). Coffee, minerals, goods and foreign exchange were traded between the Oriental Province and Kampala, and then beyond to Nairobi and Dubai.[14] The regionally imposed sanctions on Burundi following the coup d'état that returned former military president Buyoya to power in July 1996 increased the profitability of smuggling, strengthening informal trade relationships within the region. The porous borders of Tanzania, Rwanda and the DRC and bribes for border officials facilitated sanctions-busting trade of Burundian tea and coffee for fuel from their neighbours. Rwandan government officials profited from the smuggling of oil into Burundi and used the sanctions to extract Burundian support for the 1998 invasion of the DRC.

In both cases, the weakening of the failed state facilitated the formation of informal trading networks that crisscrossed its territory. These networks may weaken neighbouring states by denying them revenues from customs duties and rewarding government corruption. Neither of these effects, however, can be causally linked to the failure of a state, and some might argue that they actually increase state viability. Such networks threaten security when weapons traffickers, organized crime and armed groups use these trading links to serve criminal or political agendas. The solidarity and habits of cooperation along these informal trade networks constitute a low-cost form of social capital that others can use or appropriate. In different circumstances, actors can use this social capital for different ends – to promote violent conflict or to promote economic recovery.

Transborder social networks

Informal trade networks, because they operate outside of the legal framework (read: protection and taxation) of states, often rely on networks of kinship, belief, history or trust. These social networks, including diaspora groups, refugees, migrants and other cross-border identity groups, can become resources for survival and well-being in times of conflict and predatory or inept governance. Their dispersion across a region, owing to historical migration, colonial border demarcation of labour policies, violent conflict or exclusion by governments, creates a network profitably connecting local traders to individuals conducting business regionally or even globally. A network of ethnic Pashtuns linked smuggling to Pakistan from Dubai via Afghanistan under cover of the ATTA. Dubai has the third-largest urban Pashtun population after Peshawar and Karachi, both important stops on the smugglers' trail. Ethnic Pashtuns, Tajiks, Baluch and Uzbeks have relied on ethnic kin networks to facilitate the opium trade, among other things. In Central Africa, trading networks are often based on linguistic similarities, and business is conducted either in Kinyarwanda or in Kiswahili.

Transborder social networks can also provide the social capital for transnational political movements. Particularly in regions with porous borders and predatory or absent states, rulers may perceive cross-border identity groups as either potential threats or tools of cross-border influence. Pakistan used Pashtun ties to support Taliban efforts to establish a centralized Afghan state in part to counter potential claims for a Pashtun state by Pashtuns on the Pakistan–Afghanistan border. Mobutu, Kabila Sr and Kabila Jr all feared a separatist movement by the Banyarwanda in eastern Congo because it was assumed they were loyal to Kigali and not to Kinshasa. The 1996 rebellion was in part justified by Mobutu's discriminatory treatment of the Congolese Tutsi, whom he had stripped of their citizenship. The treatment of ethnic groups dispersed throughout the region can have ripple effects throughout the neighbourhood. All eyes are watching Burundi to see if the transitional coalition government can stem the violence between Hutu- and Tutsi-led groups.

Transborder groups are inherently neither negative nor positive. They can facilitate cultural or educational exchange or peaceful trade. They often have an interest in order, accountability and security and hence can form an important resource for peace-building. But when transborder groups form the basis of trade that supports violence or form the basis for politically motivated violence, they can become a security concern for an entire region.

Trafficking in narcotics and organized crime

Trafficking in illegal goods, such as narcotics or people, involves many actors: farmers, government officials (including politicians, border guards and soldiers) and unofficial armed groups. People may participate for want of other economic options. In Afghanistan, for instance, futures markets for opium are the main source of rural credit. Although the bulk of the profit from narcotics accrues to traffickers outside the producing country, taxing the drug trade is a profitable protection racket for unaccountable armed groups who provide no services. In Afghanistan, opium farmers earned an average of US$475–750 per year during 1994–2000, often in kind, but still significantly above the average US$360 per year average for unskilled labourers.[15] Afghan traders of opium – networks connected to Afghan warlords – netted between US$720 million and US$1 billion in 2000, after expenses – profits that are expected to increase because opium prices have increased 10-fold since then. The profits increase along each link in the marketing chain: opium trafficking networks in neighbouring countries earned approximately US$4 billion in 2001, and global networks earned at least US$20 billion from the sale of opium and heroin in Western Europe alone.

In 2002, Afghanistan resumed its place as the number one producer of the world's opium. Whereas the opium trade has marginally benefited Afghan farmers and warlords and significantly enriched organized crime syndicates, it has weakened neighbouring states as it transits their territory to primarily European markets. The government of Iran estimates that it now has approximately 2 million opiate consumers, of whom 800,000 to 1.2 million are chronic users. The rate of addiction in Central Asia is increasing: between 1992 and 2000 the number of government-registered drug addicts in the region grew annually by over 16 per cent. Pakistan is home to approximately 800,000 addicts of heroin and opium. Increased rates of HIV/AIDS go along with increased narcotics use throughout the region. In Central Asia alone, between 1994 and 2001 the rate of infection increased 600-fold.[16]

For armed groups, trafficking is often a key source of revenue, at least until they can capture state resources such as customs duties or taxation, and sometimes afterwards as well. In 1998, rebel groups in Central Africa began trafficking in narcotics, a relatively new development for the region. Rwandan ex-FAR and Interahamwe sympathizers in Dar es Salaam (Tanzania) and Mombasa (Kenya) facilitated the shipment of mandrax (also know as Quaaludes) to South Africa and Europe to finance their purchase of arms and ammunition.[17] Drug use is increasing among these groups' soldiers in eastern Congo, usually a "pre-cursor to the establishment of a domestic drug market".[18] Drug trafficking, as well as other forms of looting or exports of natural resources, provides foreign exchange to purchase war matériel (arms, ammunition and fuel) not produced in the region itself.

Natural resources

Various natural resource endowments have different effects. Especially in weak states, guerrilla groups or invaders can readily export easily extracted resources with high unit value (diamonds and coltan in the DRC, emeralds in Afghanistan). Resources that require more investment to extract (oil, copper, iron) may create commercial interests that attract foreign intervention.[19] Rwanda and Uganda both maintained that they intervened in northern and eastern DRC in 1998 to rout out and destroy rebel groups using that territory as a base of operations. They financed their subsequent occupation of entire provinces there, using both their own troops and local proxies, by exploiting Congolese resources. Uganda, which lacks natural gold deposits, became a significant exporter of gold after 1998. The government of Rwanda even established a "Production" section, responsible for exploitation and trade in Congolese resources, as part of the Congo desk in its External Security Organization.[20] Both states, in competition with one another, exploited diamonds, gold, timber and coltan from eastern Congo.

Other neighbours also benefited from alliances with the Kinshasa regime. Angola was granted concessions in the Kasai diamond mines and, with Kinshasa, established a joint petroleum venture in Lower Congo.[21] Zimbabwe used the military assistance it extended to Laurent Kabila to negotiate favourable trading and mining contracts, including the appointment of a key supporter of President Robert Mugabe as chief executive of Gecamines and the establishment of joint mining ventures between the commercial branches of the Zimbabwean Defense Forces and the Congolese Armed Forces.[22] The exploitation of natural resources did not enrich neighbouring states or improve their ability to provide for and protect their populations; instead, the benefits from most of these lucrative ventures personally enriched high-level government officials, depriving government coffers of revenues.

Militarization and arms trafficking

States may provide military assistance to governments, as the United States did to Pakistan and Rwanda, that use it for goals other than those intended. Today, arms supplied to support, or oppose, the Taliban in Afghanistan may instead be used to support militant sectarian violence in Pakistan or Kashmir or regional warlordism in Afghanistan. In addition to accumulating arms, many of which are not regulated by formal institutions, and developing a culture of violence, South Central Asia spends much of its income on the military, largely owing to the tense situations in the contiguous regions of South Asia (competition between Pakistan and India) and the Persian Gulf (affecting Iran). Arms provided by the United States, Saudi Arabia, Russia/Soviet Union, Pakistan and Iran that fuelled the various wars in Afghanistan have been redistributed and used in other conflicts in the region, which nevertheless continues to import weapons and ammunition from elsewhere. Within a year of the US intervention in Afghanistan, states in the region concluded arms sales or military training agreements with no fewer than six countries: China, India, the United Kingdom, Russia, Turkey and the United States, some providing weapons technology at below cost price.[23]

Groups engaged in arms trafficking in one state can contribute to the violent escalation of political conflict in neighbouring states. Like profits from other forms of trafficking, those from arms trading engender incentives to weaken states. Arms trafficking in Central Africa is conducted through networks of rebel groups, "armies of losers", who, in addition to trading weapons amongst themselves, are also supplied by government benefactors in the region. Given the wealth of supply and sanctuary provided by neighbouring states, combatants almost never reach the exhaustion of a "hurting stalemate" that leads to negotiation.

Weak states can become havens for arms trafficking throughout a region. Criminals, who are sometimes as well armed as governments, can challenge the states in the region not only for political reasons but also for economic motives such as securing trade and smuggling routes. The Islamic Movement of Uzbekistan (IMU) – an armed group dedicated to establishing an Islamic Caliphate in Central Asia, beginning with the overthrow of President Karimov of Uzbekistan – was so well armed (and states in the region were so weak) that in 1999 and 2000 it was able to cross Tajik and Kyrgyz territory in its drive to attack Uzbekistan. Some experts allege their incursions were also aimed at establishing key narcotics trafficking routes in the region. In 1999, Uzbekistan responded by bombing Kyrgyz and Tajik territory to rout the IMU fighters, killing civilians and increasing regional fears of Uzbek dominance. Increasing militarization of the borders, including the Uzbek mining of disputed border areas, has resulted in civilian deaths and prompted more rural youth from southern Kyrgyzstan to move to urban areas, increasing Kyrgyzstan's urban unemployment rate and putting pressure on its limited social services.

There is nothing inherently regional, rather than global, about such trafficking. However, the smuggling of large quantities of arms, especially to landlocked countries, normally takes place overland, through neighbouring countries. Moreover, well-armed mobile groups are able to spread violence across borders more easily.

Transborder armed groups

The combination of cross-border social networks with arms trafficking and the start of violent conflict often produces transborder armed groups. In the simplest form these could be refugee warriors based in a neighbouring country who mount raids into their homeland, as did the

Rwandan Patriotic Front, an organization of mainly Tutsi refugees who invaded Rwanda from Uganda in 1990. But more complex variants have developed. The Islamic Movement of Uzbekistan accepted participants from Tajikistan, Afghanistan, Chechnya, the Arab world and elsewhere. It operated in Tajikistan and Kyrgyzstan from bases in Afghanistan in order to fight its way back to Uzbekistan. The Rwandan Interahamwe similarly operated in both Rwanda and Burundi from bases in the DRC and may have recruited or at least allied with Hutus from Burundi. It later fought in support of the Kabila government on fronts far from Rwanda. These groups may be involved in what are usually considered to be several different conflicts at once, though for them it is a common battle. UNITA fought on various sides in the DRC–Rwanda wars, while still battling the ruling Movimento Popular de Libertação de Angola (MPLA) regime and rival warlords in Angola. The Interahamwe battled Rwandan troops alongside Zimbabweans for control of the town of Lubumbashi in the DRC. The IMU fought alongside Pakistani and Arab recruits in defence of the Taliban against the US-led coalition and the United Front. Such groups can forge multifarious alliances and pursue multiple survival strategies, making it harder to integrate them into peace plans and processes.

A common problem in both regions (and others too) is that, confronted with an unfavourable peace process or even a defeat in one theatre, such groups can move across borders and open up hostilities elsewhere. Both the Interahamwe and the Burundian Forces pour la défense de la démocratie (FDD) did this at different times, as did the IMU and Abdul Rashid Dostum's militia, some of whom supported the revolt of Mahmud Khudaiberdiyev in northern Tajikistan. Thus peace processes can sometimes diffuse rather than defuse conflict.

These are the processes through which state failure affects the contiguous region. The spread of cross-border armed groups and trafficking, the political and military mobilization of transborder identity groups, increased drug addiction and HIV/AIDS infection rates, the failure of formal economies, increased mortality as a result of violence and lack of humanitarian access are just some of the implications of state weakness and failure in a bad neighbourhood, but it does not automatically follow that rebuilding the state is the solution to these problems. In fact, focusing *solely* on state-building may contribute to the problem.

The processes, actors and incentives that contribute to the initial failure of states grow out of a post-colonial state-building project that often promotes armed conflict and predatory behaviour. The state becomes an asset to be captured, a form of war booty or spoils. Increasing the value of the spoils does not address the causes of the conflict. Within a failing state, concentrating more and more resources within a central bureaucracy can also promote conflict.

Second, state-building as a solution relies on the premise that the only effective counterweight to warlords' privatization of power is increased state power. It assumes the state to be the saviour of the general public, as an instrument for the public to wield power collectively. More often than not, however, it is not the simple lack of a state that threatens human security, but the incentives that dictate how that power is wielded and to what ends. In that case, state-building as a conflict management response risks exacerbating the problem. The heart of the matter is not who wields power, but how accountable that power is to the people it affects and how incentives for the accountable and positive use of power may be constructed. States can be more accountable than non-territorial networks, but they can also be even more oppressive and predatory.

Statelessness is also no solution. The international system, despite the increasing relevance of non-state actors such as networks of civil society or multinational corporations, is still fundamentally based on states. Access to political and economic forums necessary for development and dialogue is predicated on the representation of people by states.

Regional approaches to state failure

If there is therefore no alternative to state-building, it must go hand-in-hand with strategies to cultivate and support good governance. And, just as state collapse is a result of local, national, regional and international dynamics, so state-building must reflect attention and action at those very same levels. Improving regional and international governance structures, such as formal and informal venues for cooperation and collaboration, can reinforce the emergence of accountable states and a peaceful region. Moreover, as the cases of Singapore and Costa Rica illustrate (chapters 11 and 12 in this volume), regional forums can assist recovering states to address regional security threats that could undermine their transition. Such regional strategies must be complementary to state-building strategies, since formal and informal regional governance mechanisms are effective only insofar as states are capable of utilizing the services they offer.

Understanding the regional linkages that reinforce state failure can lead to concrete policies on issues such as where to house refugees, how to design disarmament, demobilization and reintegration programmes, or where to station military observers. Region-based analysis allows policy officials to understand the flexibility of the networks that undermine states. It could also help humanitarian workers identify appropriate strategies for engaging non-state actors by alleviating the "dearth of solid data" and analysis that, according to Weiss and Hoffman in chapter 14 in this volume, cripples humanitarian efforts.

The literature on conflict prevention and other aspects of conflict management emphasizes that "intervention" is rarely neutral.[24] Intervention is a form of political participation and, like other forms of political action, it is likely to be more effective if it is based on a valid understanding of the strategic choices of other actors. Conflict management in all its aspects will be more effective when actors trying to regulate conflict (or, for that matter, exacerbate or profit from conflict) base their actions on a strategic and integrated analysis that incorporates a regional or transnational understanding. Both Afghanistan and the DRC have frameworks for rebuilding their states, embodied respectively in the Bonn Accords and the Lusaka Agreement. Yet neither agreement sufficiently addresses the complexity of the regional linkages, particularly the political and economic dimensions.[25]

The establishment of regional support offices by intergovernmental organizations, or even by donors, could facilitate the development of such regionally integrated analysis and action using some of the categories outlined in this chapter. The UN Office for the Coordination of Humanitarian Affairs has established a Regional Support Office for Central and Eastern Africa, which produces reports twice a year on political and economic developments having an impact on war-affected populations in the region.[26] Establishing a comparable office for South Central Asia, in addition to the existing Islamabad office of the Integrated Regional Information Network, which provides news reports and analyses, could help alleviate this information gap. Some UN agencies, such as the Office on Drugs and Crime, have adopted a regional approach within their issue areas, but the complexity of the economic, social, political and security linkages is often beyond any particular agency's area of expertise. The establishment of United Nations Regional Support Offices, which are flexible enough to respond to the changing boundaries of certain "neighbourhoods", could provide the necessary coordination to produce thematically integrated reports on regional issues. The potential usefulness of such an endeavour will depend on whether they offer strategic services to existing country officers, or simply create another layer of bureaucracy and obstacles for policy makers.

A more robust approach to state failure in bad neighbourhoods is to focus on improving state capacity for key states within the regional conflict, making them less vulnerable to capture and perhaps providing a stabilizing influence for the region. State-strengthening strategies, ranging from supporting accountability and transparency in government structures to preventive diplomacy and mediation among government and opposition groups, can assist in preventing the outbreak or resurgence of violence. The early and "early late" prevention strategies presented by I. William Zartman in chapter 13 in this volume would be particularly applicable for a "key state" approach to regional conflict formations. Concerted international attention and action in one conflict that has resulted in progress towards peace can be a symbol for others in the region of the potential benefits of peace and the commitment of external states to rebuilding.

Of course, identifying which states are key is no easy task. Statistical studies show simply that the states most affected by neighbouring conflict are those with the longest common border. Others suggest choosing states that are most closely linked to the conflict, states that are perceived as a barometer of the region's tensions and are ripe for assistance. In the Great Lakes region, experts have argued for focusing current state-building efforts on Burundi because of its historical, ethnic and social links with Rwanda, Uganda and eastern Congo. One consequence of the regional conflict formation in Central Africa has been the revival of Hutu–Tutsi animosity and identification on a regional level, not just in Rwanda and Burundi. This identity discourse has even broadened into macro-identities (actually language groups) that have never before been mobilized politically, namely Bantu (incorporating Hutus) and Nilotics (incorporating Tutsis), though both Hutus and Tutsis in Rwanda and Burundi speak the same Bantu languages – Kinyarwanda and Kirundi. Burundi, some argue, is where peace is most likely to be achieved, given the necessary support and attention – and, if peace fails, the ethnic implications would reverberate throughout the region. The Burundi experience of peacefully sharing power has become a test case for coexistence for the region. If it fails there, it fails everywhere.

Regional factors intersect in some geographical areas that abut several countries. In the Great Lakes areas, observers have argued for years that the Kivu provinces of eastern DRC are the incubator for many of the region's problems. They are home to many of the actors in Rwanda's and Burundi's conflicts; they have been barely if at all under the control of the Congolese state; they contain numerous refugees, displaced people and labour migrants; and there are many local disputes over citizenship and property. For years, several actors have argued that an international security presence in the Kivus would have positive repercussions throughout the region.

Central Asian experts make similar arguments, proposing integrated conflict prevention programmes for the Ferghana Valley, which is divided between Uzbekistan, Tajikistan and the Kyrgyz Republic. The US Agency for International Development is attempting such an approach with its Community Action Investment Program (CAIP), targeting, first,

Central Asian areas bordering Afghanistan and, second, the Ferghana Valley with an infusion of development and governance assistance. The Afghanistan–Pakistan border, including the Federally Administered Tribal Areas of Pakistan, is a similar transborder area of problems such as deep poverty, low literacy, few resources and many guns and grievances. Targeted development and security programmes, although politically very sensitive for the states involved, might eventually lower tensions and help stabilize the broader region. The Putumayo region in Colombia, Ecuador, Venezuela and Brazil and the Parrot's Beak, where Liberia, Sierra Leone and Guinea come together, are other such areas.

Some regional networks, sometimes explicitly but often implicitly, facilitate and maintain the failure of states. Identifying and assessing these networks, whether they are networks of traders, farmers or students, is the first step for external actors attempting to intervene. What incentives motivate their participation? Which subgroups within the network have the largest leverage, and thus could effect the most positive change? Are these subgroups beyond the direct control of warlords and strongmen?

For example, the current administration of Afghanistan relies heavily on members of the Afghan diaspora from the West, and donors created programmes to facilitate their short- and long-term participation in rebuilding the Afghan state. Series of questions such as these can inform targeted, transformative strategies while simultaneously building a coalition for peace. In South Central Asia, networks of Pashtun traders from Kabul to Dubai have an interest in road security, minimal duties and profits. For years they supplied Afghans with both necessities and, sometimes, luxuries, because the Taliban provided the necessary security, a one-time transit tax and access to populations willing to pay. Under the current administration, traders are baulking at paying customs duties to each warlord, especially when previously safe roads are now insecure. Strategies to provide these cross-border traders with a cohesive and coherent voice in the region could make a difference. As a group, these traders could be encouraged to communicate common demands to the three capitals (Tehran, Kabul and Islamabad), as well as to the Afghan warlords who also depend on their supplies. Their interest in a centralized customs duty would clearly benefit the cash-strapped central government in Kabul, which currently receives duties as gifts from local warlords.

The most difficult approach of all, but one that nevertheless holds promise, is a comprehensive approach to regional conflict formation. The Esquipulas II Plan, described more fully by Morales-Gamboa and Baranyi in chapter 11 on Costa Rica, set out a multilateral framework and verification process whereby five states agreed to stop supporting insurgencies in neighbouring states and to undertake certain political and economic reforms. A comprehensive approach attempts to address both structural and operational aspects of regional conflict formations through engaging all parties in a single process, but it can be taken hostage by narrow political agendas and recalcitrant states. The planned International Conference on the Great Lakes region of Africa, first suggested to the Security Council in 1994 and now scheduled for 2004, will be an important opportunity for states in the region to demonstrate their commitment to peace both inside and outside their borders.

Conclusion

Analysing the regional dimensions and consequences of state failure is not just a descriptive exercise; it is necessary for designing effective and strategic approaches to state failure and collapse. Since the actors in such states deal with alternatives, opportunities and actors that are not simply local or national but regional and even global, attempts to affect their behaviour based solely on state-centric analysis are likely to fail. For external actors to be effective in their efforts to reconstruct the state, they must incorporate the regional dimension of the conflict into their understanding of the political, economic and social causes of the failure of the state.

Acknowledgements

We thank the Rockefeller Foundation for its support of this research and Gloria Ntegeye for her tireless research assistance and overall substantive contributions to this project.

Notes

1. For more information on regional conflict formations, see the Center on International Cooperation website: ⟨http://www.cic.nyu.edu/conflict/conflict_project1.html⟩.
2. The 11 conflicts belonging to "regional conflict complexes" are: Afghanistan, Angola, Burundi, Colombia, the Democratic Republic of Congo, India (Kashmir), Israel–Palestine, Sierra Leone, Russia (Chechnya), Somalia and Sudan. The remaining four conflicts are Algeria, Philippines, Sri Lanka and Indonesia, three of which are on islands. In fact the conflict in Sri Lanka has interacted strongly with southern India and a global diaspora, and the civil war in Mindanao, Philippines, is increasingly linked to transnational Islamic militancy that is also present in Indonesia. The conflict in Aceh has had an impact on Malaysia as well. See Stockholm International Peace Research Institute, *SIPRI Yearbook 2002: Armaments, Disarmament and International Security*, New York: Oxford University Press, 2002, p. 22.

3. James C. Murdoch and Todd Sandler, "Economic Growth, Civil Wars and Spatial Spillovers", *Journal of Conflict Resolution*, Vol. 46, No. 1, 2002, pp. 91–110.

4. Barry Buzan and Richard Little, *International Systems in World History*, London: Oxford University Press, 2000.

5. Mark Duffield, *Global Governance and the New Wars: The Merging of Development and Security*, London: Zed Books, 2001.

6. Coltan is a metallic ore that is found in large quantities in eastern DRC. When refined into tantalum, it is a key feature in almost all cell phones, laptops, pagers, etc. The technology boom of the 1990s caused coltan prices to skyrocket, averaging US$200 per kilo in late 1999. See United Nations, *Report of the Panel of Experts on the Illegal Exploitation of Natural Resources and Other Forms of Wealth of the Democratic Republic of the Congo*, UN Doc. S/2001/357, 12 April 2001.

7. See Patrick Chabal and Jean-Pascal Daloz, *Africa Works: Disorder as Political Instrument*, Indiana: Indiana University Press, 1999.

8. International Rescue Committee, *Mortality Survey in the Democratic Republic of Congo*, New York: International Rescue Committee, 2003, available online at ⟨http://www.theirc.org⟩. The current population of the DRC is estimated at 55,225,478 (July 2002) by the Central Intelligence Agency, *World Factbook*, Washington, DC: United States Government, 2002.

9. International Committee of the Red Cross, *People on War: Country Report: Afghanistan*, Geneva: International Committee of the Red Cross, 1999, available at ⟨http://www.icrc.org/Web/eng/siteeng0.nsf/htmlall/onwar_reports/$file/afghanistan.pdf⟩.   The current population of Afghanistan is estimated at 27,755,775 (July 2002) by the Central Intelligence Agency, *World Factbook*, 2002.

10. Zaire was later renamed the Democratic Republic of Congo (DRC) after Mobutu's ousting in May 1997. We use "Zaire" to refer to the state under Mobutu's regime and "Democratic Republic of Congo", the state's current name, to refer to successor regimes.

11. Banyamulenge means "people of the Mulenge", which is a mountain range where Tutsi herders settled. Although originally used to refer to a particular geographical place, over time the term has also taken on an ethnic meaning, i.e. Congolese of Tutsi origin.

12. United Nations International Commission of Inquiry, *Final Report of the International Commission of Inquiry*, UN Doc. S/1998/1096, 18 November 1998.

13. Stephen Jackson, "Nos richesses sont pillées: Economies de guerre et rumeurs de crime dans les Kivus, République Démocratique du Congo", *Politique Africaine*, Vol. 84, December 2001.

14. Musifiky Mwanasali, "The View from Below", in Mats Berdal and David Malone, eds, *Greed and Grievance: Economic Agendas in Civil Wars*, Boulder, CO: Lynne Rienner, 2000.

15. UN Office on Drugs and Crime, *The Opium Economy in Afghanistan: An International Problem*, New York: United Nations, 2003, available at ⟨http://www.unodc.org⟩.

16. UN Office on Drugs and Crime, *The Opium Economy in Afghanistan: An International Problem*, New York: United Nations, 2002.

17. UN International Commission of Inquiry, *Final Report of the International Commission of Inquiry*, UN Doc. S/1998/1096, 18 November 1998.

18. Jackson, "Nos richesses sont pillées".

19. For fuller accounts of resource exploitation in the Great Lakes, see the following UN reports: *Report of the Panel of Experts on the Illegal Exploitation of Natural Resources and Other Forms of Wealth of the Democratic Republic of the Congo; Addendum to the Report of the Panel of Experts on the Illegal Exploitation of Natural Resources and Other Forms of Wealth of the Democratic Republic of the Congo*, UN Doc. S/2001/1072, 13 No-

vember 2001; *Final Report of the Panel of Experts on the Illegal Exploitation of Natural Resources and Other Forms of Wealth of the Democratic Republic of the Congo*, UN Doc. S/2002/1146, 16 October 2002.

20. Filip Reyntjens, "Briefing: The Democratic Republic of Congo, from Kabila to Kabila", *African Affairs*, Vol. 100, 2001, pp. 311–317.

21. Herbert Weiss, "War and Peace in the Democratic Republic of the Congo", *American Diplomacy*, Vol. 5, No. 3, 2000, available at ⟨http://www.unc.edu/depts/diplomat/AD_Issues/amdipl_16/weiss/weiss_congo1.html⟩.

22. Michael Nest, "Ambitions, Profits and Loss: Zimbabwean Economic Involvement in the Democratic Republic of Congo", *African Affairs*, Vol. 100, 2001, pp. 469–490.

23. Stephen Blank, "The Arming of Central Asia", *Asia Times Online*, 23 August 2002.

24. Barnett R. Rubin, *Blood on the Doorstep: The Politics of Preventive Action*, New York: Century Foundation Press, 2002.

25. For example, although the Lusaka Agreement provides for the withdrawal of foreign troops and the disarmament of armed groups on DRC territory, it does not address the political issue of citizenship of the Banyarwanda – Congolese of Tutsi (i.e. Banyamulenge), Hutu and Twa origin with real or perceived ties to Rwanda – which was an important factor in unrest in eastern DRC that threatened Kinshasa under Mobutu and Kabila Sr. The issue of Banyarwandan citizenship, though treated as a domestic issue, has become a regional rallying cry pitting Hutus against Tutsis. The Bonn Accord does not specifically address the region at all. Instead it requests the United Nations and the international community to prevent foreign interference in Afghanistan's internal affairs.

26. UN Office for the Coordination of Humanitarian Affairs, *Affected Populations of the Great Lakes Region*, Nairobi, Kenya: United Nations, 31 January 2003, available at ⟨http://www.reliefweb.int/library/documents/2003/ocha-glak-31jan.pdf⟩.

5

Colombia and the Andean crisis

Mónica Serrano and Paul Kenny

Colombia, as Sebastian von Einsiedel has mentioned in chapter 1 in this volume, can be relied upon to feature in most lists of the world's failed states. And the Andes is another region in crisis, not as catastrophic as the Great Lakes, not as globally troubling as South Central Asia, but in deep trouble even so. State failure, regional crisis: for the fighter pilots of the state failure epistemic community, these are tantamount to orders to scramble into action. Something is to be done.

For others, let us say in the world television-viewing community, the question is less likely to echo Lenin's "What is to be done?" than to be "Where did they say this crisis is, exactly?" The images of state failure and regional crisis in the Andes are not as high-impact as those from hotter trouble spots. The cities, where crowds protest against governments here today and gone tomorrow, all look alike – dismal 1960s breeze-blocks with mountains in the background. The remote jungles through which masked "Marxist" guerrillas file in the same old library picture look even more alike. When we hear that the report comes from Putumayo, it might as well be Conrad's Costaguana or Gabriel Márquez's Macondo. This crisis may be real, but it never quite becomes really immediate as we grasp that the turmoil is amorphously indefinite; it never fully crosses the barriers separating us from what, in the title words of an old book on South America by W. H. Hudson, is "far away and long ago".

The specialist and lay international audiences seem themselves far apart. Yet they are coming together too, as regional conflicts have become internationalized by non-governmental organizations (NGOs) as well as by the media, and particularly as the world has adjusted to new forms of international intervention. Intervention, naturally, means different things in different contexts; but it also carries more general metaphorical associations, all the more powerful for their unsurpassed imperialist echoes. Yes, murmur these associations, "we" do have to act and, yes, "we" have to go far to do so, *sending* our humanitarian workers, sending in military aid. Intervention comes from a distance and confirms a distance. As many contributors to this book note, it follows that the question about intervention is most often "When can we get out?"

If the mediatized iconography of the failed state and the region in crisis stresses both remoteness and hazard (these are forbiddingly inaccessible and chaotic places), it also raises an issue that Michael Ignatieff poses in chapter 3: to whom do bad neighbourhoods matter? In a unipolar world, it would seem that that is a question with only one answer: the United States.

Since 2000, the sovereign state of Colombia, with its richly troubled history and territory twice the size of France, has also been a US "plan". After Israel and Egypt, Colombia is the third-largest recipient of US aid. For reasons that this chapter explores, Colombia matters to the United States.

Yet US intervention in Colombia is in competition with other ideas about what intervention should seek to achieve. This chapter is also about these ideas and their sponsors from the European Union and the United Nations. Beyond the struggle of paradigms over Colombia, however, the form of US intervention there raises larger questions about what is to be done with failed states and regions in crisis. For many, the mantra will continue to be constructive engagement, institutional state strengthening, internationalized peace settlements, human rights observance and efforts to prod weak states into a fairer distribution of resources to their populations. These are the concerns that Plan Colombia has side-lined. They are also, though, concerns that do little to address what for another constituency is also a legitimate issue, namely the right of the state to a monopoly of violence over its territory. To the extent that Plan Colombia is an intervention on behalf of a state struggling to regain its monopoly of violence, it serves to open up a discussion that transcends the theme of US strategic interests in bad neighbourhoods. Where does the monopoly of violence fit within the picture of state failure? Currently undergoing an aggressive policy of "democratic security" from its government, Colombia is as good a place as any from which to address that issue. But, as an "ideal type" weak state, Colombia also resists some of the premises of both military and humanitarian intervention. "What is to be done?" too often pushes aside the question of what *can* be done. This chapter ends by suggesting that making weak states work also entails taking a realistically critical perspective upon them.

A region in crisis

The first aspect to note about the Andean crisis is its multi-dimensionality. The chaos has many components. As a result, the crisis means very different things for the very different actors concerned. More than that, though, some of the dimensions weigh so heavily for the different actors that others become invisible to them, while others contest the very terms of the diagnosis, including "crisis".

For humanitarians generally, and the United Nations in particular, the most salient fact about the region is that it is experiencing a refugee crisis on a scale currently exceeded only by the Democratic Republic of Congo and Sudan. With between 1 and 2 million internally displaced people in Colombia, and reports of 250,000 Colombians camped on the border with Ecuador, the regional crisis both is clear and has a clear cause: the conflict in Colombia. Within Colombia, beyond the several thousand people whom the war leaves dead every year (3,000–4,000 of them civilians) and the mass population displacements, there is growing concern over the use of antipersonnel landmines by both guerrillas and paramilitaries. Outside Colombia, the effects of the conflict are spilling across the five adjacent borders. There is social unrest in Ecuador as workers see their wages being undercut by the refugees; rising insecurity along the borders of Ecuador and Venezuela as Colombian guerrillas and paramilitaries extend their practices of criminal extortion there; and increases in arms flows and the violence associated with them, with some reports of trafficking between the FARC (Revolutionary Armed Forces of Colombia) and the Venezuelan army. These are some of the effects that lie behind talk of "Colombianization" in the region – the risk that the region as a whole will be drawn into the Colombian conflict.

Yet for others, not least Colombia's president, Álvaro Uribe, this diagnosis of the regional crisis begins by going wrong: "In Colombia there is neither a conflict nor a war."[1] What there is, instead, is "a terrorist threat, financed by narco trafficking, against a democratic, pluralist state". It follows that there *should* be regionalization of this "conflict".

We shall come to the merits of President Uribe's case below. But his mention of a democratic, pluralist state brings us to another dimension of what for many is the Andean crisis, the political dimension. Here is a region that is a showcase of weak states. In abstract terms, countries such as Bolivia, Ecuador, Peru and Venezuela can be said to be suffering legitimation crises, with poor governance indicators, disastrously low citizen approval of political parties and leaders, and conflicts over scarce resources between central authority and newly decentralized regions.[2] In more compellingly immediate terms, Bolivia saw its president ousted in 2003, Ecuador had coups d'état in 1997 and 2001, Peru was first engulfed in the corruption scandals of the Fujimori regime, then gave 90 per cent disapproval ratings to President Alejandro Toledo, and Venezuela is in the throes of a cycle of attempted coups d'état and mass civilian mobilization. Anti-system protest is a constant across the region's political landscape. It brings us directly to the economic dimension of the crisis.

The Andean region is a case for Sebastian von Einsiedel and Michael Ignatieff's point that state failure ought now to be considered in tandem with globalization. The familiar references are to the increased vulnerability brought by globalization to market falls in prices for key export commodities; mounting unemployment; the burden of interest payment on large foreign debts; and growing fiscal deficits. In fact, though, the region has largely come through fiscal crises of the magnitude of the one that hit Ecuador, for example, in 1998–1999. What it is facing is a *political* fall-out from economic neo-liberalism. The protests that led to the fall of President Sánchez de Lozada in Bolivia started life as opposition to a plan backed by the World Bank to privatize the water supply of the city of Cochambamba in 1999–2000, which then ballooned in 2003 into wider hostility to de Lozada's privatization policy for major state companies as well as to his tax concessions to foreign investors in the hydrocarbons industry.[3] Opposition to state privatization was one of the main planks of Hugh Chávez's campaign for power in Venezuela. Popular as he is, President Uribe's plans to freeze pensions and salaries for two years and cut social spending were rebuffed in a referendum in 2004.

Opposition to neo-liberalism is a rallying call for protest across the Andes. But this dimension of the crisis is about more than public order and the vulnerability of unpopular presidents; it also touches upon the very essence of the region's states. The neo-liberal model for them gained ascendancy on the back of a region-wide rejection of the old stable, inclusive but corrupt corporatist-clientelist model. At the same time, though, the political systems of the countries opened up to new levels of participation. Constitutions were amended, new rights were recognized, decentralization promised more power to regions. The conjunction has proved explosive. On the one hand, there are more actors in the Andes than ever before pressing social demands upon the state; on the other, there is less of a state there to meet and channel them. If neo-liberalism has run its course, does the future lie in going back to the corporatist past? Chávez's Venezuela is not the only quixotic case of an affirmative answer. Even Ecuador, which through dollarization is the region's most globally plugged-in state, in practice relies upon systematic political clientelism to keep political violence at bay. Bolivia is likely to rock between the two models. Region-wide, states are in crisis because neither model promises them a sustainable future.

Underlying both the political and the economic dimensions of the crisis, there is the social dimension. Poverty continues to grow in the region, as does the relative disparity between the incomes of the poor and the wealthy. This reality has been changed by neither structural reform nor state action. For many international agencies and actors, this reality is also the bedrock of the Andean crisis.

Take Colombia. The United Nations Development Programme reported in 2002 that the poorest 20.0 per cent received 3.0 per cent of national income, whereas the richest 20.0 per cent controlled 60.9 per cent. Other statistics abound, from the 60 per cent of Colombia's 44 million population living on US$2 or less a day, to increasing inequity in land distribution, to the notoriously low tax base of the Colombian state.

Yet, if we set Colombia in the context of the above discussion, it also emerges as one of the region's most stable states. Politically, as we shall see, it boasts a well-entrenched system of liberal democracy, one durable enough to survive the major scandal of the presidential campaign funded by drug money in 1994. Economically, its fiscal management has traditionally been prudent, with foreign debt under control and steady if not spectacular growth rates. No military coups, no authoritarian regime, no crowds on the streets – no crisis?

A relativist surveying the Andean crisis would say that different perspectives see different realities. A sceptical realist might say that actors see what they want to see. The conundrum poses a challenge to both the action of international actors and the diagnoses of the state failure community. Certainly, as Armstrong and Rubin argue in chapter 4 in this volume, the collapse of some states within a region accelerates the regional spread of conflict. The trouble in the Andean region, though, is that the state most responsible for conflict, far from collapsing, is by many political and economic criteria stronger than its Andean neighbours. "Failed states", in Sebastian von Einsiedel's words, "create 'bad neighbourhoods'"; but not always. Colombia, after all, has been able to bargain with the actor that counts that it is a state worth defending from its "bad neighbourhood" location. Given the choice between Colombia or its neighbourhood going to hell, the United States has shown little hesitation in making its bet. In so doing, it has taught a hard lesson to some of the received wisdom on state failure generally.

Plan Colombia: *Mi caso es tu caso*

If the argument that failed states create bad neighbourhoods were always true, one would expect Plan Colombia to be an exercise in state strengthening. If the bad neighbourhood were a source of concern to the United States on any of the grounds mentioned in the previous section, one would expect its states not to be further weakened by the synergies of Plan Colombia. If only.

Consider state strengthening first. A report from February 2004 has the following critical things to say about Colombia:

The Government's human rights record remained poor ... Some members of the security forces collaborated with the AUC [United Self-Defense Forces of Colombia] terrorist group that committed serious abuses. Allegations of forced disappearance and kidnappings remained ... Impunity remained at the core of the country's human rights problems. The civilian judiciary was inefficient.[4]

The report is not from Human Rights Watch or Amnesty; it is from the US State Department. Even allowing for the "significant improvements in some areas" clauses, which we have edited out, one might be forgiven for reading it as a damning indictment of state failure (it also includes the obligatory passage on Colombia's "highly skewed" income distribution). Yet the military assistance of Plan Colombia is conditional upon certification of Colombia's human rights compliance. It is not so much that the United States hears no evil, sees no evil, as that its priorities are set. Although it sees much in Colombia that it does not want to see, the United States has for too long now had a vision of the neighbourhood as a source of drugs for millions of its own population. Be they failed or friendly, imploding or exploding, the states in the region are not going to get in the way of that vision.

Take the following rather sad report:

On a visit to the White House last year [2002], President Gonzalo Sánchez de Lozada told President Bush that he would push ahead with a plan to eradicate coca but that he needed more money to ease the impact on farmers. Otherwise, the Bolivian president's advisers recalled him as saying, "I may be back here in a year, this time seeking political asylum." Mr. Bush was amused, Bolivian officials recounted, told his visitor that all heads of state had tough problems and wished him good luck. Now Mr. Sánchez de Lozada, Washington's most stalwart ally in South America, is living in exile in the United States.[5]

This sobering anecdote (which might also be of interest to future presidents of Afghanistan) accounts for much about US involvement in the

Andean region. While humanitarians berate the United States for the collateral damage of Plan Colombia, and while constructive engagers bemoan the US propensity for strategic withdrawal, the United States itself is sitting down comfortably to watch its vision of a promised land where drugs have been eradicated, undistracted by pretty much anything that happens in the region, whether the rise of a mafia state in Fujimori's Peru or the disorderly descent of Chávez's Venezuela. The fact that the Colombia picture shows on only the most expensive pay-to-view channel – costing up to US$3 billion since 2000 – also explains why the viewer has little time for noises off.

The question, then, is less whether the United States gets the picture about the region, than whether the region gets the picture about the United States. One last anecdote may ram home the hardness of the Andean case. Asked how he feels about being posted to an Andean country, a US diplomat replies: "Ah, you know, it's all about drugs and thugs."[6] Bad neighbourhood, bad guys, take them out – does it need to get any more fancy than that?

Limping to the end of his unsuccessful term, with an agonizing peace process in grisly shreds, Colombia's President Andres Pastrana can claim credit for being the first Andean leader really to wise up to the Tarantino-esque US mind-set eloquently summed up by the diplomat. Plan Colombia, which was first proposed to the Clinton administration as a peace plan by Pastrana, has run and run as presidents Uribe and Bush have found new grounds on which to roll narco-traffickers and terrorists together. Re-spinning Colombia's multi-party, decades-long conflict from a symptom of chronic state weakness into a shared security cause with the United States relies too crudely for many Colombia watchers on presenting the bad guys as the worst of all guys. The more significant point, though, is that it works. It may even work too well. The Uribe government's apparent eagerness to do a deal with the paramilitaries, granting them an amnesty from prosecution for everything up to crimes against humanity, is somewhat stymied by the United States' eager addition of the AUC to the list of Colombia's terrorist organizations. It does not help that some of the paramilitary leaders with whom the deal would be done are targets for US extradition on drug-trafficking charges. But, embarrassments aside, for Colombia the essentially blackmailing gambit of Plan Colombia remains unchanged: "help defend us, the good guys here, from becoming more of a threat to you." Of course, President Uribe didn't actually say that in his inauguration speech. What he said was: "Colombia is a more serious menace than Iraq."[7]

Apart from the dream of a Colombia without coca (the plant that seems not to be able to stop itself yielding four to five harvests a year all over the region), and before the nightmare of Iraq, there are other reasons Plan Colombia presented the United States with an invitation to intervene that it could not refuse.[8] Costly as it is, Plan Colombia has the advantages for the United States of a military intervention that, to the chagrin of the country's insurgents, is something of a virtual reality show. In 2003, the number of US military personnel actually in Colombia was 358.[9] Far more visible are the hundreds of US government contractors vying for a slice of the aerial fumigation action. With 11 fatalities since 1998, these semi-private actors are the Americans who bear the costs of being on the front line.

As time has passed, the arm's length militarism of the Plan has become more naked. Originally, there was a fig-leaf in the "social and economic aid" budget of the regional Andean Counter-Drug Initiative (ACI). Read the small print now, and you find that "the ACI funds can be used for counter-narcotics and counter-terrorist operations".[10] From 2002 on, Congressional permission has been given to extend the Plan's military assistance from counter-narcotics to counter-terrorist operations. For those, such as General James T. Hill, head of the US Army's Southern Command, who apparently consider cocaine and heroin to be weapons of mass destruction, this shift may make less difference than it does to others.[11]

Say what you like about Plan Colombia, some might opine, here is a case where the world's superpower has not only noticed a bad neighbourhood but also – bearing in mind Simon Chesterman's observation in chapter 16 that promises of aid tend to be more honoured in the breach than in the observance – put its money where its mouth is. The multilateral lenders who have stumped up an extra US$12 billion in loans for Colombia have clearly been impressed. Shouldn't others be?

As the quasi-legendary figures for Plan Colombia's spending show, money talks. But so too, as Michael Ignatieff suggests, do motives. In the case of Colombia, there is no doubt about the sincerity of the US desire to eradicate a perceived threat, however open to creative representation it is. But that is not the problem. The problem lies in how sincere the US belief is in its avowed auxiliary aims of strengthening Colombian democracy and stabilizing the region. Underlying the diplomatic language in which the protests against Plan Colombia have been couched, what one detects is the suspicion that Plan Colombia was not refused by the United States precisely because it offered the United States an opportunity *not* to engage in either the messy business of state strengthening (the pejorative "nation-building" of yesterday's US discourse) or the larger mess of the region. The militarism of the Plan allows the United States to act like a senior citizen tired of quarrelsome relatives – there, but not all there.

Regionally, the practical consequence of Plan Colombia is a *deepening* of instability. In terms of the war on drugs, eradication produces results not only in Colombia but also in Bolivia and Peru, as drug production and processing hop over there – a simple enough instance of the "balloon effect", but one that seems to leave US agencies baffled. Equally uncomfortably, if less commented upon, a proportion of Colombia's internal refugee crisis – 50,000 in Putumayo in 2002, for example – can be put down to the population dispersal achieved by aerial spraying of *Fusarium oxysporum*, the fungus that has caused irreversible ecological damage in Peru. In terms of the war on terror, Ecuador, Venezuela and Brazil have shown a marked reluctance to respond to overtures inviting them to classify Colombia's insurgents as terrorists, on the grounds that they do not wish to be drawn into the conflict on the United States' terms. Regional states that want to stay out of an intensifying conflict thus risk becoming as much "bad guys" for the United States as the peasant farmers who continue to subsist off coca cultivation because no alternative has been offered to them because they are the bad guys ... Regionally, Plan Colombia is likely to foment anti-Americanism across the Andes, albeit the anti-Americanism of those who would emigrate to the United States tomorrow if they could.[12]

All of this and more, no doubt, the United States can live with. The burning question is how long its Plan can live with Colombia. The United States may not go in for much of the "good governance" talk of the state failure community, but it notices when the general in charge of the Colombian National Police, a key recipient of the Plan's money, has to resign, as he did in 2003, after a corruption scandal. The United States may express only mild disapproval over evidence of collusion between the armed forces and paramilitaries, which does not so much emerge as refuse to go away, but it pays attention when the defence minister who had called for the links to be broken, as well as attempting to establish accountability for US spending, is forced out of her post. Paramilitary infiltration of the Attorney General's Office may lead to paramilitaries receiving advice from the Office on how to dispose of its agents, but, when the deal is near-total amnesty for paramilitary leaders, Senator John Kerry is one who notices.[13]

In the past, such symptoms of chronic state weakness could, perversely, serve as an argument for the United States not to get involved too directly. Making states work is a longer haul than making them work for the United States. But, even without a change of administration in the United States, there are signs of restiveness with Colombia. A Democratic amendment in the House of Representatives to cut military assistance by US$75 million was only narrowly defeated in 2003. Without Plan Colombia, Colombia would have little ground for arguing that it is different from Bolivia, except in its incapacity to resolve its own conflicts.

Colombian administrations may hope, with some reason, that, given the weight of precedent, the United States will remain committed to its counter-narcotics policy even as the policy continues to prove itself a failure. However, there is another dimension of Plan Colombia that merits separate attention in a book on making states work, namely intervention to help a state from failing by helping it win back its monopoly of violence.

The monopoly of violence in Latin America

Colombia has become internationally conspicuous just as analysts hunting for the core of state failure and collapse in the post–Cold War world have revived Max Weber's assertion that the state must "successfully uphold the claim to the monopoly of the legitimate use of physical force in the enforcement of its order".[14] For some people, the question of whether or not Colombia is a failed state begins and ends here. As with Plan Colombia, reciting the facts and figures has become a ritual: FARC's 18,000 armed militants; a state that lost control of 40 per cent of its territory while negotiating with the militants; the 20,000 paramilitaries whom the counter-insurgent state both needs and needs to demobilize; not to mention the world-beating homicide and kidnapping rates. As such facts and figures take on a mythic life of their own (the army, for example, claims to kill over 1,000 FARC militants a year, but still goes on talking of its 18,000 members), the ritual comes to seem like a funeral for the state.

No successful monopoly of violence, no successful state: the Weberian formulation does have a kind of brutal conceptual glamour. A hit in some quarters, it causes malaise in others. Uncontestable in theoretical accounts of modern European state formation, the monopoly of violence also excites something close to anguish in historians of state formation in Latin America.[15] States formed there, but rarely with a successful claim to the monopoly of violence.

Somewhat absurdly, then, the juxtaposition of theory with history yields a "debate" in which the theory would have to deny that modern states formed in Latin America, whereas the historian is left to affirm that they did indeed form, but that the way they formed was disastrous. States in Latin America formed *as* failed states.

Applying the concept of the monopoly of violence to Latin America takes us to a debate that, blocked and rather arcane though it is, is still echoing in hard-headed policy assessments such as the following: "Nearly everyone agreed [in 2001] that the Colombia state had failed – but in truth it had not. It had never succeeded."[16] Maddening though they may be, not only are such judgements of Colombia prevalent, they also tell us why, despite the ritual of state burial with which we started this section, more people in fact believe that Colombia can continue to be a viable failure, even one that can succeed when it should fail.

Colombia's President Uribe is clearly one who would wish to push on with the monopoly of violence, taking it beyond circular debate into the performative realm of state action. His democratic security policy also chimes with the state-supportive championing of the monopoly of violence in which Michael Ignatieff has recently led the way.[17] Summarizing, Ignatieff's case runs like this: when a state loses its monopoly over legitimate force, both personal and regional insecurity ensue; hence intervention that aims at anything less than helping the state win back its monopoly is futile; rather than feel squeamish about this, humanitarians should applaud. Behind the smokescreen of counter-narcotics, is this the real case too for Plan Colombia?

Yes and no. The thing about the monopoly of violence is that, the more it looks like a prescription for state strength, the more debatable it becomes. Brute action is far from enough. In Ignatieff's argument, the crucial premise is that intervention should be on the side of the state because the state should be on the side of its citizens. In Weber's formulation, there is also a crucial premise, albeit one that routinely gets dropped: the state's monopoly of violence must be *legitimate*.[18] Legitimacy is the spirit of the Weberian law. It also hovers in the air above many aspects of the discussion about state failure.

Almost by definition, legitimacy – however we measure it – is in short supply in many weak states. Where it does exist, as it indubitably does in a Colombia that regularly shows only 1–2 per cent public approval for the guerrillas, state legitimacy is a very precious resource. Nor should there be any doubt that the legitimacy of the state in the eyes of its citizens *is* inevitably and rightly bound up with its successful control of the monopoly of violence. The problem in recovering the monopoly of legitimate violence is not foundational; it is pragmatic. Can a state that is legitimate but that has for decades been unable to claim back its monopoly succeed in doing so without squandering legitimacy through the use of illegitimate means such as the clandestine recourse to illegal self-defence groups?

Nebulous as it seems, the question of legitimacy poses pressing dilemmas of pragmatism for weak states. Even with Plan Colombia, the Uribe administration has talked openly of the conflict in Colombia dragging on for years. Sections of the Colombian military hint openly that the paramilitaries are the real weapon by which the war against FARC will be won. The number of paramilitaries during the time of the peace process with the guerrillas was 12,000; now that war is being given a chance, it is 20,000. The state may rightfully claim back control of its territory; but large swathes of that territory have now been violently carved up between narco-traffickers and paramilitaries, in "sales" that the civilian population gets in the way of at its peril. The legitimacy of their status is not an abstract consideration for the paramilitaries. Having recourse to their privatized violence undercuts the effectiveness of the state's claim to the public good of the monopoly of violence. On the one hand, it may well be true that a *legitimate* monopoly of violence in Colombia would have exposed the social isolation and political weakness of the guerrillas.[19] But the practical blurring of already fuzzy lines between legitimate and illegitimate violence is one of the key conditions for extra spirals of violence as increasing numbers of private actors compete for the spoils of unmonopolized violence.[20]

The immediate question, then, may appear to be whether the state will win in the Colombian conflict without unleashing a dirty (or dirtier) war. The deeper question is whether a state as weak as Colombia can pursue a goal as critically legitimate as the monopoly of violence *without losing its own legitimacy*. As we shall see, this is not an abstract consideration under conditions of multiple intervention in the failing state where human rights violations and the plight of the civilian population weigh as heavily as *raison d'Etat*.

From a Latin American perspective, there is a final question about both the Colombian conflict and the monopoly of violence, which takes us back to the malaise inspired by the monopoly of violence. Military rule, the ideology of national security, "states of exception" and dirty wars are all a recent memory in Latin America. That memory stirs up a host of resistances to the already vexed issue of the monopoly of violence's legitimacy. Is it to mean *military solution* all over again? In Colombia itself, the military's overtures for an Argentine-like "national security" solution were accepted by President Julio César Turbay in 1978.[21] The result was both state repression, although not on Argentina's scale of terror, and a proliferation of new insurgent groups (notably M-19) and paramilitaries. Regional states looking now at Colombia's expanded national security legislation, amended constitution and civilian informant programme (which has turned into a programme for private vendettas) can find good reason to stay out of a conflict in which elements of history threaten to repeat themselves. Leftist governments in Brazil and Venezuela – the one cutting back on military spending, the other of a nationalist militaristic hue – have a particularly jaundiced eye to cast upon Colombia's counter-insurgent eradication programme.

From monopoly of violence to "peace laboratory"[22]

The doomsday scenario for Colombia and the Andean region is clear enough: a once legitimate state crippled by a war that not even dirty tactics suffice to win for it; a humanitarian catastrophe of regional proportions. So paralysing is this scenario that, the more its neighbours are threatened by Colombia's conflict, the more they disavow involvement in it. There is no regional plan, merely diplomatic skirmishing, whether over Brazil's bid to lead a regional security community or over that of the president of the Organization of American States (himself a former president of Colombia), César Gaviria, to lend legitimacy to Uribe's negotiations with the paramilitaries. Aside from that, the region is sitting and waiting even as negative internationalization of the conflict mounts.

Clear as the warning signals are, however, there is another constituency for whom disaster prophesying is too easy a game. Led by President Uribe, this constituency includes the overwhelming majority of Colombian citizens now. For them, the legitimacy of the state entitles it to its military means. Their support for the heightening of the state's military action rests upon an overwhelming rejection of a perpetual peace process that saw the conflict's violence only go up. "Peace and all of its horrors" culminated in a guerrilla massacre of 119 civilians at Bojayá in May 2002.[23] For Colombians, it was the epitaph for any immediate attempt by their state to claim the monopoly of violence by peacefully legitimate means. If the peace process saw conflict increase, would not a war process see it decrease?

For the European Union and the United Nations, however, hopes of a comprehensive negotiated peace settlement have died harder. Both staked prestige and some investment upon the peace process, in the hope that it would duplicate the success of the El Salvador settlement a decade earlier. First Plan Colombia, then President Uribe have side-lined this other plan. The de-coupling between the Colombian state and the United States, on the one hand, and the European Union and United Nations, on the other, is in turn now itself an extra dimension of conflict. Indeed, it is hard not to see the rift opened up over Plan Colombia as a diplomatic prequel to the rift over the invasion of Iraq, with Spain's military hardware sales to Colombia making it a notable EU exception in both cases.

Whereas many states where intervention is considered either impossible or undesirable may sink into catastrophic chaos, Colombia presents the interesting case of *over-intervention* in a weak state. It demonstrates that the terms on which failing states should be strengthened are not only wide open but a bone of contention between international actors. And international dissension does not make the life of the weak any easier.

Take the following top items from a shopping list of 24 priorities for Colombia agreed on in a meeting in 2004 between James LeMoyne, the UN Secretary-General's representative, and Chris Patten, the European Union's External Relations Commissioner:

To reinforce democracy; find a negotiated solution to the conflict; deal with the humanitarian crisis and the drama of the internally displaced; improve the Human Rights situation and put into practice the recommendations of the UN's High Commission for Human Rights.[24]

Of drugs and terrorists, not a word. The message is uncoded: Plan Colombia might not exist.

At the same time, 24 priorities are a lot for one meeting. The European Union's humanitarian aid to Colombia comes to US$165 million. Does it do more talking than its money? Human rights, social justice, the reduction of socioeconomic disparities, land reform, better redistribution of wealth and resources, alternative rural development – all, and more, come cascading down upon Colombia from EU and UN recommendations. These recommendations not only quote from the "integral peace" package of the peace process that tried to address *all* the perceived "structural" causes of the conflict; they also quote from some of the guerrillas' programmes. In the words of one European diplomat, "we told Manuel [Marulanda, leader of FARC] that most of the FARC's demands were shared by large sectors of civil society".[25] The European Union has also looked to civil society for an answer to the conflict.

Incautiously enthusiastic as they are, the diplomat's words hit one of the sore spots in the conflict about the Colombian conflict. For actors still committed to a peace settlement, it makes every sense to keep open channels of dialogue with the guerrillas. True, the European Union now classifies FARC and the Army of National Liberation (ELN) as terrorist organizations, but the European Union also set conditionalities upon the insurgents in the Central American peace process. More deeply than this, however, the EU position on Colombia, as it has built up, reaches quite a high pitch of sympathy with the rhetoric, if not the actions, of the insurgents. In the words of one enthusiastically incautious pro-European analyst, "The challenge is to create a new state."[26] FARC could hardly put it better.

These are some of the undercurrents that welled up in President Uribe's intemperate attack in September 2003 on some human rights organizations as defenders of terrorists, "responsible for the social collapse of the nation", in a speech that no doubt hangs on the wall of every NGO office in Colombia. Too much should not be made of one speech; but nor should too little. It expresses the vexation of a president who, even though he is engaged to the United States, still has to court the European Union for aid that is both less than that of the United States and much more tied to compliance with human rights standards set by the United Nations. But it also testifies to the pressures upon the president from the peace missions of the international human rights community. Specifically, their agencies are in Colombia to denounce violations; and this, as others are beginning to note, can become a game in which a legitimate end is also tinged with illegitimate means, such as reporting legally authorized arrests as arbitrary detentions or under-reporting the killings of state functionaries, police as well as judges, in comparison with those of civilians.[27] Non-governmental organizations are in Colombia to see all evil, hear all evil, and, although it would be an exaggeration to say that they have trouble recognizing the word "terrorism" unless it is preceded by "state-sponsored", it is quite plausible that the political agenda of many is to lobby for a reduction of military-security aid to Colombia. Generally, then, the international human rights community is playing a game in which the Colombian state can only be the loser. In this respect, President Uribe was justified in focusing his counter-denunciation upon the unfairness to the state of the rules of the human rights organizations' game. "Other countries with less problems kick them out of their territory," he mused. As indeed did Mexico, while it figured out how to pacify the Zapatista rebellion – small fry compared with FARC – in the mid-1990s, albeit at a subsequent international price.

The Colombian state and the European Union have a problem with each other, a problem that in many ways transcends their different approaches to the conflict. Fundamentally, the issue is what to do with a failed state – and what to do when the state denies its failure. On both counts, the European Union's answer has been to attempt to bypass the state. The counter-argument is that intervention on these terms itself fails the state.

Two dimensions to this disjunction over Colombia are worth noting. Historically, the long peace process generated a rhetoric of state guilt as this Roman Catholic country struggled to find ways of coming to grips with its violence. Just as many Andean politicians live off the discourse of "anti-politics" now so prevalent in the region, so a string of Colombian presidents offered themselves as father confessors of their state's guilt.[28] President Belisario Betancur talked of the "objective" socioeconomic causes of the insurgency; President Gaviria of the need to "pacify and transform Colombia"; President Virgilio Barco of the "altruism" of the M-19 guerrilla movement; and President Pastrana of the guerrillas' pacific vocation.[29] Whereas Uribe's Colombia has turned its back on such not-so-backhanded justifications of the guerrillas, swinging to the opposite extreme of criminalizing them *tout court*, international actors such as the European Union and the United Nations appear still to be listening to the old plainsong.

Theoretically, though, there is a moot point about the degree to which "structural lacks" and a "culture of poverty" count as explanations for state failure as well as conflict.[30] In a range of arguments that echo those anatomized by Michael Ignatieff over regime change, one hears all and any of the following: Colombia is astonishingly poor – but so is Ecuador, which is free of civil conflict; why should Colombia be singled out for aid intervention when there are other deserving cases in the continent? – but shouldn't we start somewhere? Theoreticians of state failure are clear that an equal distribution of "political goods" is a desideratum; they are less clear about how far to include economic criteria of fairness.[31] Many have argued that both conflict and failure should be put down to the syndrome of the absent state; many now argue that the zones of violent conflict in fact correlate with the presence of target-rich state resources and investment.[32]

The upshot of so much conflict over the meaning of peace for Colombia and the failure of its state is mutually reinforcing unhappiness. On the one hand, as it continues to seek maximalist solutions, the European Union's intervention is oddly parallel to its competitor, Plan Colombia. On the other hand, the weak state itself – neither as repressive as it appears, nor yet deserving to be free of suspicion – puts up the plea that maximalist interventions overrun its democratic legitimacy. Caught between arm's length military intervention and gung-ho human rights, Colombia provides a good case for a different perspective upon state failure.

A critical weak state perspective

Democratic or not, the Colombian state is too weak to be strong – and its international donors are divided over what is to be done about this. As they intervene in the cycle of weakness, international actors risk getting sucked into what some have argued is the tautology of the weak state thesis: that the state is too weak to stop disintegrative effects, which then are taken to be the causes of its weakness.[33] In this respect, Colombia's shyly withdrawing regional neighbours may be wiser than the international actors. The key question remains: what does intervention *get into*?

Simplifications as colossal as Plan Colombia's run up against the corruptibility of the "good guys". But there are simplifications too in some of the current images of state failure. For I. William Zartman in chapter 13 in this volume, the image is of a driver passing all the warning lights and crashing the car over the cliff. Yet in cases such as Colombia the image should rather be of a vortex in which crisis-talk is also history-talk. Indeed, the earliest warning of state failure in Latin America was provided in 1815, four years before the creation of Gran Colombia. Its author was Simón Bolívar, the founding father of that collapsed state.[34] Ever since Bolívar, crisis and the state in Latin America have gone hand in drowning hand together. For much of Latin America, the assertion that it is in crisis now is likely to be met by the question: and when have we *not* been?

The cyclical nature of crisis in Latin America makes diagnosing state failure an exercise in contortion. Take one last mind-spinning assessment: "Colombia *has been* a collapsed state, but state-building is still possible."[35] Or, to highlight the non-linearity here, the state has failed already, but even failed states have come to stay. Failed states can be strengthened, as the premise of this volume is right to indicate, but not by fantasies of re-creation. If the United States has played fantasy politics with Colombia, so too has the European Union as it presses for governmental standards of transparency, accountability and efficiency that even a Sweden would be hard put to live up to. From all sides – and one could add the international financial institutions as well as the NGOs – interveners seem to agree only in their reluctance to accept the reality principle of the chronically weak state: *very little works as it ought to.*[36]

A critical weak state perspective would, by contrast, be both supportive of realistically achievable institutional reforms and critical of the unjustifiable defences of weakness. It would, that is, take the side of the state against those who either say it is not working hard enough against the odds or set standards of performance too high for it. Such a perspective would not follow the habit of leaping from a state's weakness to its all-out illegitimacy. But it would be entitled to publicize criticism of defences of weakness that amount to setting a course by failure. President Uribe will have to go on giving as good as he gets on the legitimateness of his means of winning back his state's monopoly of violence.

Finally, however, a critical weak perspective ought also to have a regional dimension. For all the current talk of spillovers from the Colombian conflict, there is an even worse doomsday scenario in Bolívar's dream-turned-nightmare Confederation of the Andes. It is one in which Colombia is in fact a more representatively weak state than many (especially in Latin America) would care to concede. Would it be spillover or "endemic weakness" that would account for drug trafficking and criminal violence taking root in, say, Paraguay or any of the Central American states? Is Colombia now a victim of the weakness of the Peruvian and Bolivian states in the late 1980s? You can, after all, take the state out of the neighbourhood, but not the neighbourhood out of the state.

Notes

1. Álvaro Uribe Vélez, "Colombia; La Reivindicación de la Legitimad", *El País*, 7 February 2004.
2. See Mónica Serrano and Michael Shifter, eds, *The Andean Crisis*, forthcoming.
3. See John Crabtree, "Bolivia: A Crisis of Legitimacy", paper commissioned for the project "Crisis in the Andes", University of Oxford–El Colegio de México, 2003–2004 (forthcoming in Serrano and Shifter, eds, *The Andean Crisis*).
4. US State Department, "Country Reports on Human Rights Practices", 25 February 2004, available at ⟨http://usinfo.state.gov/dhr/human_rights.html⟩.
5. Larry Rother, "Bolivian Leader's Ouster Seen as Warning on U.S. Drug Policy", *New York Times*, 23 October 2003. If one wanted to rub salt into the wound, one might quote the reaction of US Ambassador Greenlee, in the same report, after the coup: "We think on balance that our policies and our emphasis on alternative development, together with Bolivian participation and their own policies regarding drugs, have been positive things for Bolivia. We don't think it's a problem."
6. Jimmy Langman and Joseph Contreras, "Beyond 'Drugs' and 'Thugs'", *Newsweek*, Vol. 143, No. 5, 2 February 2004.
7. Cited in Human Rights Watch, "Human Rights and Counter-Terrorism: Briefing to the 60th Session of the UN Commission on Human Rights", 29 January 2004.
8. An analogous, if more plausibly justified, "intervention by invitation" occurred in 2002 when the United States sent 650 troops to the Philippines, at the request of President Gloria Arroyo, to support the fight against the armed group Abu Sayyaf linked to al Qaeda; US$100 million followed in 2003.
9. This and the following figure come from the Center for International Policy's Colombia Project, ⟨http://www.ciponline.org/facts/co.htm⟩.
10. International Crisis Group, *Colombia: President Uribe's Democratic Security Policy*, Latin American Report No. 6, Bogotá/Brussels, 13 November 2003, p. 12.
11. Human Rights Watch, "Human Rights and Counter-Terrorism".
12. Emigration is an under-observed symptom of the Andean crisis: 500,000 people have left Colombia in recent years; 377,908 have left Ecuador since the early 1990s. See César Montúfar, "Ecuador: Fantasms, Fractures and Opportunities", paper commissioned for the project "Crisis in the Andes", University of Oxford–El Colegio de México, 2003–2004 (forthcoming in Serrano and Shifter, eds, *The Andean Crisis*).
13. Letter from four US Senate Democrats to Secretary of State Colin Powell, 30 September 2003, available at ⟨http://www.ciponline.org/colombia/030930dems.htm⟩.
14. Max Weber, *Economy and Society* [1922–1923], vol. 1, Berkeley, CA: University of California Press, 1978, Vol. 1, p. 56. The provision of basic services to the population often accompanies the successful claiming of the monopoly of violence in contemporary Weberian definitions of what the state must do not to fail.
15. For the theory, see Anthony Giddens, *The Nation-State and Violence*, Cambridge: Polity Press, 1989. For the history, see Miguel Angel Centeno, "The Centre Did Not Hold: War in Latin America and the Monopolization of Violence", in James Dunkerley, ed., *Studies in the Formation of the Nation State in Latin America*, London: University of London, Institute of Latin American Studies, 2002, pp. 54–76.
16. Harvey F. Kline, "Colombia: Lawlessness, Drug Trafficking, and Carving up the State", in Robert I. Rotberg, ed., *State Failure and State Weakness in a Time of Terror*, Washington, DC: Brookings Institution Press, 2003, p. 161. Compare Eduardo Pizarro and Ana María Bejarano, "Colombia a Failing State?", 30 May 2003, available at ⟨http://drclas.fas.harvard.edu/publications/revista/colombia/pizarro.html⟩: "it may be possible that Colombia will, in the mid-term, overcome the partial collapse of its state."

17. See Michael Ignatieff, "Intervention and State Failure", *Dissent*, Winter 2002.
18. The challenge of the Weberian clause is seen, but ducked, by the most influential of the European historical promoters of the monopoly of violence, Charles Tilly. See "War Making and State Making as Organized Crime", in P. Evans, D. Rueschemeyer and T. Skcopol, eds, *Bringing the State Back in*, Cambridge: Cambridge University Press, 1990, p. 186: "The distinction between 'legitimate' and 'illegitimate' force, furthermore, makes no difference to the fact." For a counter-view, see Blondine Kriegel, *The State and the Rule of Law*, Princeton, NJ: Princeton University Press, 1995.
19. This is the argument of Eduardo Pizarro Leongómez, *Insurgencia sin Revolución: La Guerrilla en Colombia en Una Perspectiva Comparada*, Bogotá: Tercer Mundo, 1996, p. 98.
20. See Pizarro, *Insurgencia sin Revolución*, p. 122, on how from the late 1970s governments compensated for the extreme weakness of the Colombian state with systematic use of illegal violence, to the extent of providing constitutional status for self-defence groups, after which today's paramilitaries hanker.
21. Marco Palacios, *Entre la Legitimidad y la Violencia: Colombia 1875–1994*, Bogotá: Grupo Editorial Norma, 1995, pp. 272, 274.
22. Joaquín Roy, *Europe: Neither Plan Colombia, nor Peace Process – From Good Intentions to High Frustration*, The Dante B. Fascell North–South Center Working Paper Series, University of Miami, Florida, January 2003, p. 14, reports that "the EU executive signed on 7 February 2002, the first concrete European Commission-controlled and coordinated project ... to implement the Magdalen Medio Peace Laboratory ... a concrete step in support of a negotiated solution to the Colombian conflict by encouraging the active participation of civil society organizations in the pacification of the country."
23. The phrase is taken from Palacios, *Entre la Legitimidad y la Violencia*, p. 74.
24. Translated from ⟨http://news.bbc.co.uk/hi/spanish/international/newsid_3422000/342043. stm⟩.
25. Adam Isacson, *Was Failure Avoidable? Learning from Colombia's 1998–2002 Peace Process*, The Dante B. Fascell North–South Center Working Paper Series, University of Miami, Florida, March 2003, p. 13.
26. Roy, *Europe*, p. 17.
27. See Mark Falcoff, "Latin American Outlook", Washington, DC, AEI Online, 23 February 2004; Eduardo Posada Carbó, *Guerra Civil? El Lenguaje del Conflicto en Colombia*, Colombia: Alfaomega Colombiana S.A., 2001, pp. 32, 34.
28. See Montúfar, "Ecuador": "In Ecuador politics is practised, elections participated in, public posts taken, all in the name of anti-politics."
29. Harvey F. Kline, *State Building and Conflict Resolution in Colombia, 1986–1994*, Tuscaloosa: University of Alabama Press, 2001, p. 84, for presidents Betancur and Gaviria; Palacios, *Entre la Legitimidad y la Violencia*, p. 289, for President Barco; and Mauricio Rubio, *Crimen e Impunidad. Precisiones sobre la Violencia*, Colombia: Tercer Mundo Editores, 1999, p. 11, for President Pastrana.
30. The phrases come from the trend-setting report of Colombia's National Commission on Violence and Democracy in 1988. Comisión de Estudios sobre la Violencia, *Colombia: Violencia y democracia*, Bogotá: Universidad Nacional, 1988.
31. See, for example, Robert I. Rotberg, "Failed States, Collapsed States, Weak States: Causes and Indicators", in Rotberg, ed., *State Failure and State Weakness*, pp. 3–4.
32. Rubio, *Crimen e Impunidad*, p. 90; Fernando Gaitán Daza, "Una Indagación sobre las Causas de la Violencia en Colombia", in Malcolm Deas and Fernando Gaitán Daza, *Dos Ensayos Especulativos sobre la Violencia en Colombia*, Bogotá: Tercer Mundo, 1995, pp. 253, 401.
33. Pizarro, *Insurgencia sin Revolución*, p. 16.

34. See David Bushnell, "La Independencia de la América del Sur Española", in Leslie Bethell, ed., *Historia de América Latina*, Vol. 5, Barcelona: Editorial Crítica, 1991, pp. 108–109.

35. Kline, *State Building*, p. 83.

36. See, for just one example, P. P. Kuczyniski, "A Year as Finance Minister of Peru", Oxford: Exeter College Association, 2002, pp. 46–47: "Individual measures were promoted by rather colourful MPs: some MPs, for example, were behind on their taxes, and oh surprise!, promoted a costly tax amnesty for their own benefit." Gabriel Marcella, *The United States and Colombia: The Journey from Ambiguity to Strategic Clarity*, The Dante B. Fascell North–South Center Working Paper Series, University of Miami, Florida, March 2003, p. 23, reports ex-US ambassador Curtis Kamman's claim that "two-thirds of Colombia's Congress took bribes or were intimidated in the late 1990s". As for the international financial institutions, these are now worried about the effects of increased military spending on Colombia's budget deficit.

6

The South Pacific

Benjamin Reilly and Elsina Wainwright

The South Pacific is, at first glance, an unlikely setting for a chapter on state failure. The region is home to a dozen states and a similar number of related territories, all but one of which have a population of fewer than 1 million, and several of them have fewer than 20,000. Most of the region comprises small island states interspersed with vast stretches of ocean waters and isolated from the world's power centres. With one exception, there are no land borders. Most of the island states are small in terms of population and land area, but they lay claim to vast maritime resources.

In recent years, however, perceptions of the South Pacific have changed – from an underperforming but basically benign region, to one that is now characterized as an "arc of instability", comprising "weak" and "failing" states. Armed conflicts in Papua New Guinea's eastern island of Bougainville and the neighbouring Solomon Islands have claimed thousands of lives over the past decade. Regional governments – led by Australia, the dominant metropolitan power in the South Pacific – have headed peacemaking interventions into both countries in recent years, with a considerable degree of success. Despite this, the region receives very little attention in the rest of the world and virtually no international media coverage. This chapter therefore begins by introducing the basic facts about the South Pacific, before moving on to a discussion of state failure and recent interventions in the region.

The Pacific Islands are usually thought to comprise three sub-regions – Melanesia, Polynesia and Micronesia – which reflect both cultural and

colonial differences. In the western Pacific, all of New Guinea and its associated islands are part of Melanesia, which contains the overwhelming
majority of the region's population and land area. Papua New Guinea
is the largest country in Melanesia, and has a population of 5.7 million
people – making it larger than all the other Pacific Islands combined.
Papua New Guinea and the other Melanesian states of Fiji (800,000),
the Solomon Islands (520,000) and Vanuatu (200,000) account for over
90 per cent of the population of the entire South Pacific region.

The cultural boundaries of Melanesia also spread further west, into the
Indonesian province of West Papua (formerly Irian Jaya), the majority of
whose people are culturally kin to those in Papua New Guinea rather
than to the rest of Indonesia. The border between the two takes the
form of a straight line down the middle of the island of New Guinea – a
line that also serves as a bizarre division in international politics between
"Asia" and "the Pacific", separating language groups, tribes and sometimes even villages between the two world regions.

Further east, Polynesia contains some of the region's smallest countries
– including the world's tiniest fully independent state, Tuvalu, which has
a population of just 10,000. The two largest states in the region are Samoa (population 170,000) and Tonga (100,000). In part by virtue of their
homogeneous populations and hierarchical traditional social structures,
these countries have exhibited more stable government than the Melanesian countries – although this has come at the cost of also having a more
limited form of democracy, with political office restricted to members of
the traditional aristocracy. New Zealand has traditionally played a major
role in Polynesian affairs, and two of the smallest Polynesian micro-
states, the Cook Islands (15,000) and Niue (1,500), retain constitutional
links with New Zealand as freely associated states.

Finally, in the Central Pacific, Micronesia's links are mainly with the
United States. Three independent states – the Republic of Marshall
Islands, the Federated States of Micronesia and Palau – remain freely
associated with the United States under a "compact relationship" that
gives the United States extensive military concessions in return for generous economic assistance. There are two other independent Micronesian
states: Kiribati (one of the Pacific's poorest states) and Nauru (an island
formerly administered by Australia that once boasted one of the world's
highest per capita GDPs owing to its now exhausted phosphate reserves).

The Pacific also includes the French territories of New Caledonia,
Wallis and Futuna, and French Polynesia; and the American dependen-
cies of American Samoa, Guam and the Northern Mariana Islands. Other
powers have also played a colonial role in the Pacific: before being taken
over by the United States at the end of the Second World War, much of
Micronesia was held by Japan under a League of Nations mandate; simi-

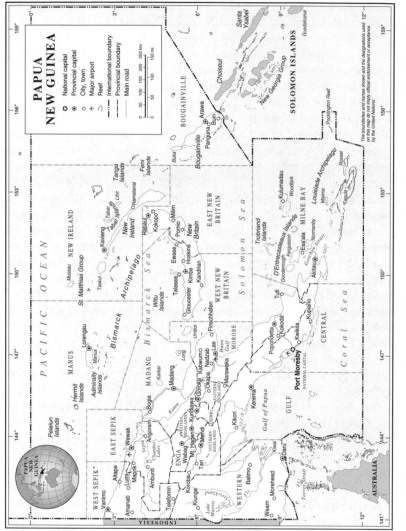

Figure 6.1 Map of Papua New Guinea and the Solomon Islands (*Source:* United Nations, 2004, re-produced by permission of the United Nations Cartographic Section).

124

larly, Australia, New Zealand and the United Kingdom assumed mandate responsibilities originally held by Germany in New Guinea, Samoa and Nauru.

The arc of instability

For most of the past 20 years the South Pacific region has been distinctive not for its failures but for its successes in building apparently stable and democratic post-colonial states. On many comparative rankings of government performance, the South Pacific has ranked amongst the most democratic regions in the world.[1] For example, the US private foundation Freedom House, which publishes a detailed annual ranking of political and civil rights for every country, has routinely placed the entire South Pacific region in the "free" category.[2] Especially in the larger and more populous Melanesian states of Papua New Guinea, the Solomon Islands, Vanuatu and, intermittently, Fiji, freely contested and highly competitive national and local elections have occurred regularly.[3]

Despite this, over the past few years the perception of the South Pacific has changed from an "oasis of democracy" to an "arc of instability".[4] Melanesia in particular has been plagued by violent internal conflict, precipitating an "Africanization" of politics in which democratically elected governments have been deposed through ethnic conflicts.[5] One of the region's most developed states, Fiji, experienced military coups in 1987 and 2000 – both times following the election of governments perceived to be too close to the country's Indo-Fijian community. Papua New Guinea has faced a decade of civil war on its eastern island of Bougainville, which has made claims of affinity with the neighbouring Solomon Islands. In addition, Papua New Guinea, Vanuatu and Fiji have all suffered army mutinies in recent years.

The most dramatic case of state decline in the region is the Solomon Islands. In June 2000 the elected government of the Solomon Islands, one of the Pacific's poorest states, was overthrown after rebels, aided by elements of the police force, seized the capital and forced the resignation of the incumbent prime minister. A peace deal negotiated in the Australian city of Townsville resulted in the distribution of some compensation payments and the holding of elections in December 2001, which saw a new government installed. The country remained in deep difficulty, however, unable to pay public officials such as nurses and teachers or to provide basic government services. Until the Australian-led Regional Assistance Mission to the Solomon Islands commenced in July 2003 (described below), the Solomons was the country most often mentioned in discussions of state failure in the Pacific. The Australian Strategic Policy

Institute called it a "failing state",[6] a term also used by the Australian government, while *The Economist* said that it "faces the prospect of becoming the Pacific's first failed state".[7]

Elsewhere, the tiny island of Nauru (population 11,000) is also approaching "failed state" status, but for very different reasons. Like the Solomon Islands, Nauru is now essentially bankrupt, dependent on laundering money, selling passports and receipts of external aid from Australia (in return for temporarily accepting several hundred unwanted Australian refugee claimants) and China (to which it recently switched allegiance from Taiwan) in order to survive. However, Nauru's trajectory towards a failed state is quite different from that of the Solomon Islands, since it has lost, squandered or spent almost all of a once vast trust fund set up to manage revenues from its now exhausted phosphate resources. As one commentator has noted, "One state has failed because of its poverty, the other because of its inability to handle riches."[8]

The establishment of international shelf banks, shipping flags of convenience and passport sales has also brought the Pacific Islands into contact with a range of shady organizations, including terrorist groups. In early 2003, three vessels flying the Tongan flag were caught in the Mediterranean moving weapons, explosives and men for al Qaeda. In April 2003, US authorities reported that six alleged terrorists, including two alleged al Qaeda operatives, had been arrested in South East Asia carrying Nauruan passports. In 2003, Nauru promised to end its shelf banks and passport sales (which some other Pacific states also use as means of revenue-raising) after the United States proscribed such activities as part of its war on terrorism. It remains to be seen how Nauru will be kept solvent into the future without them.

Indicators of state failure

There is significant variation in the experience of South Pacific countries in building viable states. On the one hand, countries such as Samoa have been relatively successful post-colonial states, providing steady if unspectacular economic growth and stability of government, notwithstanding an ongoing dependence on foreign aid. On the other hand, the Solomon Islands displayed many of the hallmarks of a failing state.

A range of factors contribute to state failure in the region. The colonial legacy left a range of weak and sometimes artificial newly independent countries, some of them barely able to assume even the basic responsibilities of statehood. As a result, poor governance has been a major problem, along with weakened respect for the rule of law and central authority. Over the past decade, corruption has become widespread. Other causes of tension include growing economic inequalities, changing social relations and the challenges to traditional lifestyles and authorities posed by the inexorable forces of modernization and urbanization. Taken together, these factors indicate a growing weakness of state capacity and an increasing likelihood of further troubles in the region in the future.

Many of these factors are common to other "weak state" or "failing state" scenarios. What distinguishes the South Pacific is the concentration of these factors in some of the most ethno-linguistically diverse societies to be found anywhere in the world, creating particular problems of unstable executive government, rent-seeking politics and ethnic conflict. These problems are concentrated in Melanesia, the Pacific's most populous, diverse and impoverished region. Particular phenomena include the increasingly violent manipulation of ethnic identities, disputes over land and natural resources, tensions in civil–military relations, the proliferation of small arms, law and order problems, and deep structural weaknesses of governance. Each of these issues will now be dealt with briefly.

Ethnic divisions

The South Pacific is exceptionally diverse. More languages are spoken in Papua New Guinea alone than in all of Africa. Across Melanesia, over 1,200 indigenous languages (about one-quarter of the world's languages) are spoken by a mere 10 million people, making it easily the most fragmented region in the world in ethno-linguistic terms. Even this figure understates the real level of ethno-political diversity: most linguistic groups are themselves fragmented into dozens of unilateral descent groups known as clans. Regional differences (for example, between coastal dwellers and highlanders in Papua New Guinea, or between east and west coasts in Fiji) are also important, as are tensions between "indigenous" and "settler" communities (such as between indigenous *kanaks* and French-settler *caldoches* in New Caledonia), between different island groups (for example, Malaita versus Guadalcanal in the Solomon Islands), between traditional chiefs and commoners (especially in Polynesia), and ultimately between cultures (for example, ethnic Fijians versus Indo-Fijians in Fiji).

Ethnic divisions are not necessarily negative. One reason that has been advanced for Papua New Guinea's unusual longevity as a democracy is that there are so many groups that none can dominate and thus some kind of power-sharing at the political level is unavoidable.[9] But ethnicity is a fluid phenomenon, and there have been several cases of fragmented social structures being transformed into bipolar, us-versus-them constellations as part of the conflict spiral. This was the case in the long-running Bougainville war and again more recently in the Solomon Islands, where ethnic tensions between different island populations have been exploited in order to challenge the legitimacy of the state itself.

Often ethnicity is used as a way of mobilizing support to achieve economic gains. The centrality of exploitable resources to many apparently "ethnic" conflicts has been an underlying factor driving a number of South Pacific conflicts, most of which are, in reality, power struggles over control of resources and control of the state rather than outbreaks of ancient hatreds. The most obvious manifestation of this resource-driven pattern of conflict is the lucrative tropical timber industry, the exploitation of which has played an important role in contributing to corruption, distortion of the market-place and the resort to violence in countries such as Papua New Guinea, Fiji and the Solomon Islands. In Fiji, where the bicultural ethnic cleavage is most stark, the 2000 coup appears to have been as much about access to mahogany leases and a redistribution of forces within the indigenous Fijian community as it was an attack upon Indo-Fijians.

Land disputes

Across the region, the most precious resource of all is land itself. Land ownership, land redistribution, land reform and land exploitation have been major factors underlying much supposedly ethnic or political conflict. Two main types of conflict over land appear to be at work in the region. In the first type, tensions between indigenous populations and settler groups, each with different approaches to land ownership and exploitation, act as a combustible formula to mobilize deep (but often latent) perceptions of ethnic difference. This has been a recurring pattern in countries with an identifiable indigenous–settler cleavage, such as Fiji and New Caledonia, where disputes over land ownership have been deepened by differences in the skills and livelihoods of the particular ethnic groups. But the second type of conflict is likely to become more common in the future. This is a conflict between established local populations and in-migrants from adjacent islands, as in the Solomon Islands between migrants from Malaita residing on the island of Guadalcanal. In this and a number of other conflicts over land in the region, tensions between traditional forms of title and ownership of private property are increasingly prevalent. In both cases, however, access to land and the perception of group inequality have been readily exploited by ethnic leaders as a potent mobilizing force.

Civil–military relations

Unpredictability in terms of civil–military relations in the region has also been a factor, at least since the first Fijian coups in 1987 carried out by Sitiveni Rabuka and a team of Fijian army officers. Ten years later, in March 1997, came the so-called Sandline affair in Papua New Guinea, when the Papua New Guinea Defence Force refused to accept government attempts to hire a force of largely South African mercenaries for the ongoing secessionist war on Bougainville. The revolt stopped well short of a full-scale attempted coup, but nonetheless forced Prime Minister Julius Chan to stand aside in the lead-up to the 1997 elections, in which he and most of his cabinet lost their seats. The 2000 coup in Fiji led by George Speight was also carried out with the assistance of elements of the Fijian military, particularly the Special Forces, and the aftermath of the coup saw several officers court-marshalled after a bloody shoot-out between different units of the military as traditional power holders re-established control.

Less dramatically, the defence forces of both Vanuatu and Papua New Guinea have been involved in recent years in mutinous industrial protests against government plans for pay-cuts and staff reductions. In both cases, the rebellious units were persuaded to return to barracks after a period of negotiation with the government. The fact that such insurrections occurred at all, however, led governments in both countries to shy away from further attempts at reform, choosing instead to maintain an oversized and underperforming military force. A further problem is that the kinds of security issues countries such as Vanuatu or the Solomon Islands face are internal or transnational, and more suited to a police than a military response. However, indigenous police forces have been poorly equipped to meet these challenges.

Small arms proliferation

Until recently, the South Pacific's geographical isolation helped protect it from the abundant supply of cheap light weapons that have fuelled conflicts in other regions.[10] There is documented evidence, however, of guns being passed from the mainland of Papua New Guinea, through Bougainville, and down to combatants in the Solomon Islands. And small arms and the glamorization of military culture have also spread into other parts of Papua New Guinea – the Southern Highlands province, to give but one example, is plagued by violence.

There are other ways in which guns can be placed in the hands of rebel forces, as was shown by the Fiji coup in May 2000. Utilizing arms stolen from military depots, George Speight and his supporters – including members of the Fijian army's Special Forces Unit – amassed an extraordinary armoury of firepower, taking the government hostage. Two weeks later, in the Solomon Islands, Prime Minister Bartholomew Ulufa'alu was forced to resign at gunpoint after armed rebels from the Malaita Eagle Force seized the capital. In the Solomon Islands it was the police force (whose members are overwhelmingly Malaitan) that supplied the weapons. In each case, the key has been access to weapons, mostly stolen from military or police armouries.

Law and order

Law and order is one of the most serious problems facing states such as Papua New Guinea and the Solomon Islands. Weak governance, a plentiful supply of weapons, the glorification of gun culture and few employment prospects have contributed to an environment of violence.[11] In the Solomon Islands prior to the Australian-led Regional Assistance Mission, for example, the 1998–2000 ethnic conflict shaded into ongoing violence, lawlessness and intimidation.[12] There was a broad pattern of criminality and impunity, as serious crimes such as murder went unpunished. Ex-militants and criminal gangs were involved in extortion and related activities, and regularly intimidated and threatened politicians and public officials.

The Solomon Islands police were themselves a major part of the law and order crisis. Some members of the police force had connections with criminal gangs and ex-militias; most of the rest were powerless to enforce law and order.[13] Those members of the force who were involved in the ethnic conflict on the Malaitan side were allowed back into the police under the Townsville Peace Agreement. Many ex-militants were also appointed as special constables, a move that exacerbated the law and order crisis.

Weak governance

One indicator of state failure is a steady collapse of basic services such as health, education and transport infrastructure. Since governments in some South Pacific countries are nearly bankrupt, there has been insufficient government money to pay healthcare workers or teachers. A youth bulge, poor education and few employment prospects are a dangerous mix: young men look up to those with guns rather than to teachers or other positive role models. In the Solomon Islands, for example, a violent internal ethno-political conflict, amounting to civil war, saw the economy deteriorate sharply: foreign investment plummeted, exports collapsed and the government was bankrupt. The country's GDP had halved since independence. Education was particularly difficult in such conditions, and many primary and secondary schools in the Solomon Islands remained closed for most of 2002.

Governance problems affect different parts of the Pacific in different ways. In Melanesia, problems of governance are endemic and stem in part from the nature of democratic politics. There is an odd mingling of traditional tribal culture with Westminster-style institutions.[14] Political parties are not based around cleavages of class or ideology, and most candidates are not aligned with any party but stand as independents. As a result, executive government tends to be unstable, because without strong parties it is difficult to avoid shifts in support within parliament. No-confidence votes and unstable governments have been ongoing problems in Papua New Guinea, the Solomon Islands and Vanuatu. Most members of parliament lose their seats at each election, meaning there are relatively few politicians who last more than two or three terms. And there are almost no women in parliament. Significantly, in the few cases where there has been a meaningful party system – in Fiji or in Vanuatu, for example – party structures have been formed primarily around identity-based factors, such as the Indian–Fijian split in Fiji or the anglophone–francophone division in Vanuatu. Recently, Papua New Guinea passed an ambitious constitutional reform aimed at building a more coherent and stable political system, although it remains to be seen whether this initiative will have the desired results.[15]

The question of viability

Is there a minimum size of population, economy or territory, or a minimum degree of effectiveness of government, for a successful state? These are questions that should perhaps be asked of the states in the South Pacific. Certainly, there are cases in the region in which the gap between juridical sovereignty and effective statehood is yawningly wide.

Prior to independence there were several proposals to group the states of the South-West Pacific into a Melanesian federation, and similar plans were raised in other parts of the Pacific. But, with one or two exceptions (the Federated States of Micronesia, which was formed by the amalgamation of Yap, Chuuk, Pohnpei and Kosrae in 1986, being the main example), such proposals were never seriously pursued. Indeed, the recent trend in the Pacific has been for even greater fragmentation: Tuvalu was created by its separation from the Gilbert Islands (now Kiribati) in 1978; Bougainville has attempted to secede from Papua New Guinea; and there are persistent "breakaway" movements in other countries, such as the Western Provinces of the Solomon Islands. However, there has recently been a renewed push for the sharing of regional resources. Australia and New Zealand have led this push, and it has received a considerable degree of acceptance throughout the region.

There is a question about the long-term viability of some Pacific Island states, particularly given the effect that global warming and rising sea levels may have on several low-lying atoll states, and other problems such as small populations, lack of employment opportunities, distance from potential markets, unsustainable population growth, the colonial legacy and the difficult overlay of sovereign statehood on to traditional societies that do not cohere with borders. However, it is notable that small size does not appear to be a determinant of state failure. The relative success of the Pacific's (and the world's) smallest state, Tuvalu, has been hailed as proof that "small is viable", whereas the region's most intractable problems have occurred in the larger Melanesian states such as Papua New Guinea and the Solomon Islands.[16]

Part of the problem in these countries is the very "statelessness" of traditional societies. In contrast to the homogeneous and hierarchical Polynesian kingdoms, most of which had well-established statelike forms of social organization prior to European contact, most of Melanesia was essentially stateless, composed of thousands of small acephalous social groups. As a consequence, countries such as the Solomon Islands inherited colonial institutions of statehood that have not properly taken root.[17] The increasing glorification of gun culture in parts of the Solomons and Papua New Guinea is a good demonstration of the vexed question of how modern statehood relates to the pre-existing society. In Papua New Guinea, conflict is part of the traditional social order, and communities had highly ritualized tribal wars. The now-plentiful supply of semi-automatic weaponry, however, has changed the nature of the conflict and made it far more destructive.

International intervention

For most of the world, the Pacific Islands are obscure and unimportant. Conflicts in the region attract little if any international media coverage and have minimal strategic importance for any Western country beyond Australia and New Zealand. This has serious implications for potential international intervention in intra-state conflicts, which are inevitably based on a combination of media coverage and a sober calculation of strategic interest. However, two conflicts in the region, in Bougainville and the Solomon Islands, have recently been the target of international interventions to restore peace.

Bougainville

The most serious security issue in the Pacific Island region in the 1990s centred around the demand by rebel groups for Bougainville's independence, a demand opposed not only by Papua New Guinea but also by many Bougainvilleans. Before the conflict began, Bougainville's substantial contribution to Papua New Guinea's national economy was disproportionate to its small size and population, mainly owing to the enormous open-cut copper, gold and silver mine at Panguna in the central mountains of the main island, which operated from 1972 until the conflict caused its closure in 1989.

A series of increasingly violent clashes between government forces and the various pro- and anti-independence militias came to a head in 1997, when the Papua New Guinea government commissioned an international mercenary service, Executive Outcomes, to attack the rebels. In a surprise move, the Papua New Guinean army's chief commander announced the refusal of his forces to work with the mercenaries, who were ejected from the country. Prime Minister Julius Chan and two key ministers involved in engaging the mercenaries were forced to stand down. These events helped create conditions conducive to the remarkable progress towards conflict resolution that occurred in the latter part of 1997. Taking advantage of that changed position at the national level, rebel forces began to make direct contact with the central government. Further developments resulted in the New Zealand government facilitating talks between the Bougainvillean leaders. These talks resulted in a cease-fire agreement, followed by the deployment on the island of an unarmed Peace Monitoring Group, led by Australia, accompanied by a UN observer team.

Since then, successive agreements – notably the "Loloata Understanding" of March 2000 and the Bougainville Peace Agreement signed at Arawa in August 2001 – have helped sustain peace and have paved the way for a self-determination referendum on Bougainville's political status to be held at some unspecified time in the future, after an extended period of autonomy from the central government. Whether a referendum can actually be conducted in Bougainville, and whether the various disputants will accept the result, remain to be seen. However, the commitment to hold and recognize the results of the referendum has been affirmed by Australia, which previously opposed any such step that could lead to independence.

The Solomon Islands

The slide into civil war in the Solomon Islands, which had been a functioning democracy since its emergence as an independent state in 1978, is a good example of the shifting international interest in conflicts in the South Pacific. When ethnic tension began to escalate in 1998 between residents of Guadalcanal and settlers from the adjacent island of Malaita, the country moved rapidly from a state of ethnic tension to a virtual civil war. In June 2000, Prime Minister Bartholomew Ulufa'alu was taken hostage by Malaitan rebels, who demanded, and received, his resignation. With the capital under the control of a militia force and a democratically elected government deposed by force, the immediate response from the Solomon Islands government, or what was left of it, was to ask for external military assistance to restore peace.

These requests were ignored, both by regional powers such as Australia and New Zealand, but also by the United Nations. Despite the pleas of the Solomon Islands representative in New York, neither the General Assembly nor the Security Council would discuss the crisis – primarily because there was no state willing to raise and sponsor such a discussion. To do so would inevitably have led to the expectation that, if any external assistance were authorized, then Australia and New Zealand – the only developed countries with strategic interests in the islands – would be responsible for any intervention. The governments of both countries had already made it clear that this was not something they were prepared to countenance. So there the matter lapsed, along with the elected government of the Solomon Islands.

However, in October 2000 the Australian and New Zealand governments, with support from the Commonwealth Secretariat, did facilitate a peace process, the Townsville Peace Agreement, which provided a temporary end to hostilities via an unarmed International Peace Monitoring Group composed of officials from Australia and New Zealand and from the police forces of Pacific Islands nations, including Vanuatu, the Cook Islands and Tonga. But the peace deal did not address the underlying issues that had fuelled the conflict, and problems in the Solomons continued to multiply.

In June 2003, in a major policy shift, the Australian government announced its intention to lead a multinational police and military operation into the Solomon Islands in an effort to revive the failing state: over 2,000 personnel from Australia, New Zealand, Papua New Guinea, Fiji, Tonga and other states in the region were deployed in the Regional Assistance Mission to the Solomon Islands, Operation Helpem Fren ("helping a friend" in Pidgin). A civilian Special Coordinator of the mission was also appointed. For its part, Australia deployed 1,500 Australian Defence Force personnel, along with over 200 members of the Australian Federal Police. The first phase of this mission involved the restoration of law and order and the puncturing of the climate of lawlessness and impunity. The deployed police worked alongside members of the Royal Solomon Islands Police – itself in need of substantial reconfiguration – to remove guns from the gangs and ex-militia members and to protect key political figures from intimidation.

Although primarily a policing operation, the mission was initially supported by a sizeable military deployment. This military contingent provided the police with logistical support and protection if required. By the end of 2003, law and order had been significantly restored in the major urban areas, and the bulk of the military contingent withdrew.

The second phase of the assistance mission involves broader statebuilding. A number of civilian officials have been deployed to the Solomon Islands as part of a package of economic, law and justice, and financial assistance. The purpose of this package is to help Solomon Islanders build effective political and security institutions, address their economic and social problems, revive the economy and ensure that government services are again delivered to citizens.[18] The deployed police are helping to conduct criminal investigations and to rebuild the Royal Solomon Islands Police. They will remain on the ground for a number of years. This phase is a long-term commitment, which may last up to 10 years.

The Australian-led Solomon Islands rescue plan received broad support from the region and the endorsement of the Pacific Islands Forum, the multilateral regional organization. Pacific Islands Forum foreign ministers placed the mission within the framework of the Forum's Biketawa Declaration, which provided for a collective response to security threats – this was the first time this declaration had been activated.[19] Neighbouring countries in the South Pacific acknowledged that the Solomon Islands crisis risked destabilizing the rest of the region. Both the UN Secretary-General and the UN Security Council also issued statements after the commencement of the mission welcoming the operation and its regional nature.[20]

The plan also received the support of the Solomon Islands parliament. Indeed, requests from the Solomon Islands Governor General and the prime minister, together with parliament's support and overwhelming popular support, were key factors in this policy shift towards what the Australian government has described as "cooperative intervention".[21] The Solomon Islands' consent to this intrusion on its sovereignty helped to allay regional concerns.

Although the assistance mission has been proceeding well, many challenges still lie ahead. Rebuilding the Solomon Islands' institutions and targeting corruption are long-term and complex endeavours and Solomon Islanders expect continuing improvement. The mission has been based on a minimal derogation of the sovereignty of the Solomon Islands. It is therefore vulnerable to changing political alignments within the parliament. Furthermore, the mission faces the continuing challenge of working in partnership with Solomon Islanders to build up Solomon Islanders' skills, and not to erode them.

Australia's new policy in the South Pacific

Australia's intervention in the Solomon Islands represented a dramatic shift in Australia's policy approach towards the South Pacific. This policy shift stemmed in part from the increasing recognition that Australia's national interests were engaged by the deterioration of some of the states in its neighbourhood.

In general, states determine their level of engagement with a region on the basis of a stark calculation of their national interests. So what are Australia's interests in the South Pacific? As the regional metropole, Australia's interests in the South Pacific arise primarily from geography: the region is on Australia's doorstep, in an arc to its north-east. Australia therefore has enduring strategic interests in the South Pacific. As Australia's *Defence 2000* White Paper makes clear, Australia has a stake in ensuring that the states in its immediate neighbourhood are stable and secure, and not beset by territorial uncertainty or threatened by "major internal challenges".[22] Australia also has an interest in preventing "the positioning in neighbouring states of foreign forces that might be used to attack Australia".[23]

The 11 September 2001 attacks in New York and Washington, DC, and the bombing in Bali on 12 October 2002 – which killed 202 people, 88 of them Australian – also had an impact on Australia's calculation. Policy makers in Australia had a heightened awareness of the security implications of state failure in the region.

Another concern was the potential for transnational crime in the South Pacific. A number of South Pacific states are fast approaching bankruptcy. This makes them vulnerable to influence by both state and non-state actors that might seek to provide money for all sorts of purposes, including the sale of sovereignty.[24] Nauru, Tonga, Samoa and other island states have sold thousands of passports to foreign citizens. Vanuatu has sold shipping flags and, like Nauru, has been a centre of money laundering owing to its weak banking regulations. And the Solomon Islands government has considered receiving aid funding from Taiwan in return for using one of its outer islands as a toxic waste dump, amid other potential sales of its sovereignty.[25]

When states institutions are weak, the shadow state that forms in its stead can become very strong.[26] In Papua New Guinea, networks for drug smuggling are well established. Corruption easily becomes entrenched; often the only way that the state can function (and members of the government get paid) is if shadow state networks and contacts are utilized. In the Solomon Islands, government officials had close contact with former members of the Malaitan Eagle Force and with current criminal gangs.

There are also humanitarian and moral dimensions to any calculation of Australia's interests. Australia has a historical association with the peoples of the South Pacific and has traditionally responded to humanitarian crises in the region. As the major power in the South Pacific, Australia's behaviour in the region affects the way Australia is viewed internationally. In the event of dramatic circumstances – for example, the January 2003 cyclone in the Solomon Islands – there is an expectation, internationally and in the region, that Australia should assist. As the Australian government's 2003 *Defence Update* acknowledges: "The strength of our national interests, and our prominent leadership role in the region, means that Australia could be called upon to provide assistance to the region in times of crisis, and will need to maintain the capability to respond effectively."[27]

Finally, Australia has significant commercial and economic interests in the South Pacific that are damaged by law and order problems, corruption and weak governance. There are also opportunity costs. Moreover, the Australian government has the responsibility to protect the thousands of Australians residing, travelling and conducting business in the South Pacific.

However, Australia had until recently viewed the parlous situation in much of the South Pacific with a relative lack of interest. Australian policy towards the South Pacific countries since their independence had essentially been to provide them with aid but to expect them to solve their own problems and merely to support them in their own efforts. As the decline in the region gathered pace in the 1990s, Australian governments judged that Australia's interests were not sufficiently engaged by the problems in the South Pacific to alter their policy approach; for example, Australia decided not to intervene in the ethnic conflict and de facto coup in the Solomon Islands. Indeed, the objective in the region has been described as being to "cleverly manage trouble".[28]

This policy paradigm towards the South Pacific was underpinned by respect for the status of these countries as sovereign states and by a rejection of colonialism. The Australian government acknowledged in its 2003 Foreign and Trade Policy White Paper: "Australia cannot presume to fix the problems of the South Pacific countries. Australia is not a neo-colonial power. The island countries are independent sovereign states."[29] The policy approach was also based on the assumption that, when these countries became independent, they acquired not only juridical sovereignty but also the capacity to be viable entities in their own right.[30]

Three factors have driven a reassessment of this long-standing policy paradigm. First, there was a growing belief in Australian policy circles that the security challenges posed by state weakness in the South Pacific were such that Australia's level of engagement in the South Pacific should be reassessed. Second, there was growing awareness that the existing policy approach was not working. It was based on the presumption that the island states could solve their own problems, whereas it was increasingly recognized that countries such as the Solomon Islands did not have the capacity adequately to do so. Third, there was a growing consensus that Australia has a responsibility towards the region and is uniquely placed as the region's metropole to assist.

In reality, Australia's choices were relatively constrained. In theory, Australia could cease its assistance to the South Pacific, as some economists had advocated, but in practice this was extremely unlikely.[31] Or Australia could continue its existing policy and keep expecting the countries of the region to solve their own problems. Or Australia could become more engaged. The cautions put forward by exponents of Australia's existing policy paradigm included wariness about raising the spectre of colonialism. The policy challenge for Australia was then to see whether there was a way of constructively engaging the countries of the South Pacific that managed the risks attached to increased engagement.

The Australian-led "cooperative intervention" in the Solomon Islands of July 2003 was therefore a marked departure from the Australian government's previous policy towards the South Pacific. It stemmed in part from a recognition of Australia's responsibility to the region, but also from a calculation of the security implications of regional state failure. Australian Foreign Minister Alexander Downer stated in June 2003 that "we will not sit back and watch while a country slips inexorably into decay and disorder. I say this not just for altruistic reasons. Already the region is troubled by business scams, illegal exploitation of natural resources, crimes such as gun running, and the selling of passports and bank licences to dubious foreign interests."[32]

A greater willingness to intervene on the part of potential interveners such as Australia, as well as acceptance by recipient states such as the Solomon Islands, is likely to lead, over the longer term, to consideration of other consensual intrusions on sovereignty. Indeed, Australia and Papua New Guinea have since agreed to an "Enhanced Cooperation Package", whereby around 300 Australian police and public servants will be deployed to Papua New Guinea to help address governance and law and order problems.

Pacific Island economies are already integrated with Australia and New Zealand through trade, migration, aid, remittances and military security ties. But much more could be done, especially in areas such as trade and labour mobility.[33] This will require more direct engagement on the part of countries such as Australia and New Zealand in relation to secondment of staff, reciprocal placements and training, and service delivery in key areas such as health and education. There are starting to be moves in this direction. Ensuring state viability in the South Pacific will also require closer educational, security and economic integration with neighbours and regional powers, and a more dynamic approach to regionalism from organizations such as the Pacific Islands Forum.

However, there are risks associated with Australia's new policy approach as well. In particular, there are some concerns in the region about Australia's heavy-handedness and its possible motives in seeking greater engagement in the region. To allay these concerns, the Australian government will need to work to build consensus in the region and proceed with due regard for regional sensitivities. Otherwise, there is a risk that worries about Australia's style could scupper the broad agreement on greater Australian engagement and closer regional integration.

Lessons

How then should the international community respond to state failure? From an analysis of the situation in the South Pacific and international interventions in the region, a number of lessons can be drawn for potential interventions in weak and failing states.

First, issues of sovereignty arise as part of any international intervention, and ideally any response should have the consent of the state involved. In the Pacific, this has been less of a problem than in other regions of the world. In fact, there have been complaints from some governments (for example, the Solomon Islands) about the *lack* of forceful and timely intervention from regional powers such as Australia. Consent may allay regional fears of less-than-benign intentions behind the intervention. It also helps to ensure that "intervention" is not understood as merely sending in troops, but focuses on real needs such as the restoration of law and order and restructuring of institutions such as the police.

Second, closer regional cooperation is the key to resurrecting a bad neighbourhood. Regional problems require regional support and a regional response. Wherever possible, such responses should be multinational and draw in interested states from the region and beyond. The broad support of the rest of the South Pacific for the Australian-led involvement in the Solomon Islands, for example, has been a critical feature of the operation. And a multilateral approach helps to deflect accusations of neo-colonialism. Interventions should receive endorsement from a regional multilateral forum and, ideally, from the United Nations.

Third, the new security environment has created opportunities both for regional engagement and regional cooperation. Recent regional cooperation on counter-terrorism and other transnational issues provides a good model, and can be built upon to encourage greater international engagement with the island countries. Note that intervention for peace monitoring does not necessarily mean armed forces. The various international truce and peace monitoring missions in Bougainville and the Solomon Islands succeeded in lowering tensions, in part because of their multinational composition but also because they were unarmed. Indeed, unarmed peace monitors have proven surprisingly good at monitoring shaky peace deals.

Fourth, some of the most serious security problems facing weak and failing states are ones of internal or transnational security, which require a robust policing – as opposed to military – response. Most South Pacific countries do not have a military force at all. Some countries, however, such as Vanuatu, make their police force a branch of the military, complicating relations between the forces. As a result, the division of roles becomes increasingly unclear. Comparative experience suggests that many crisis situations are better suited to a primarily police response than a primarily military intervention.

For example, although the Australian-led deployment to the Solomon Islands initially involved a significant military component to protect the police and to remove illegal weapons, the restoration of security in the Solomon Islands is first and foremost a policing operation. More resources need to be put into building capacity for police responses of this nature. Assistance could involve not only building up indigenous police capacity, but also creating a regional police response capability when crises arise.

Finally, state-building is a long-term process. Supporting weak and failing states requires a sustained and often open-ended commitment. Constructive engagement must directly address weak institution and governance issues and chronic economic and social problems. Efforts should include the creation of robust rule of law (police, corrections and judiciary) and the strengthening of institutions and governance. There should also be increasing moves to deal more directly with grassroots groups and with strong local institutions such as the churches.

For Australia's part, this means an ongoing and increasing commitment to the South Pacific: as one commentator has noted, it makes little sense to devise an exit strategy from your own immediate neighbourhood.[34]

Notes

1. See, for example, Alfred Stepan and Cindy Skach, "Constitutional Frameworks and Democratic Consolidation: Parliamentarism versus Presidentialism", *World Politics*, Vol. 46, No. 1, 1993, pp. 1–22. Stepan and Skach found that, of the 93 countries of the

world that became independent between 1945 and 1979, only 15 were still continuous democracies in 1980–1989 – and one-third of these were in the South Pacific.

2. See Freedom House, *Freedom in the World: The Annual Survey of Political Rights and Civil Liberties*, New York: Freedom House (various editions).

3. Some comparative studies have counted states such as Papua New Guinea amongst the small number of "established democracies" in the developing world. See, for example, Arend Lijphart, *Patterns of Democracy: Government Forms and Performance in Thirty-Six Countries*, New Haven and London: Yale University Press, 1999.

4. This term was brought to prominence by Paul Dibb. See Paul Dibb, "The Strategic Environment in the Asia-Pacific Region", in Robert D. Blackwill and Paul Dibb, eds, *America's Asian Alliances*, Cambridge, MA: MIT Press, 2000.

5. See Ben Reilly, "The Africanisation of the South Pacific", *Australian Journal of International Affairs*, Vol. 54, No. 3, 2000, pp. 261–268.

6. Australian Strategic Policy Institute (ASPI), *Our Failing Neighbour: Australia and the Future of Solomon Islands*, Canberra: ASPI, June 2003.

7. "The Pacific's First Failed State?" *The Economist*, 14 February 2003.

8. Graeme Dobell, "The South Pacific – Policy Taboos, Popular Amnesia and Political Failure", Menzies Research Centre seminar paper, Canberra, 12 February 2003.

9. Benjamin Reilly, "Democracy, Ethnic Fragmentation, and Internal Conflict: Confused Theories, Faulty Data, and the 'Crucial Case' of Papua New Guinea", *International Security*, Vol. 25, No. 3, 2000, pp. 162–185.

10. See Andrea Armstrong and Barnett R. Rubin in chapter 4 in this volume, pp. 92–93.

11. ASPI, *Our Failing Neighbour*.

12. Ibid.

13. Ibid.

14. See James Mayall in chapter 2 in this volume.

15. See Benjamin Reilly, "Political Engineering and Party Politics in Papua New Guinea", *Party Politics*, Vol. 8, No. 6, November 2002, pp. 701–718.

16. See Gerard A. Finin, *Small Is Viable: The Global Ebbs and Flows of a Pacific Atoll State*, Hawaii: East-West Center Working Paper No. 15, 2002.

17. See Michael Ignatieff, chapter 3 in this volume, p. 70, and James Mayall, chapter 2 in this volume, pp. 48–50.

18. Alexander Downer (Australian foreign minister), "Security in an Unstable World", speech at the National Press Club, 26 June 2003; ASPI, *Our Failing Neighbour*; Nick Warner (Special Coordinator of the Regional Assistance Mission to Solomon Islands), "Message to the People of Solomon Islands", 24 July 2003.

19. "Pacific Islands Forum Foreign Affairs Ministers Meeting Outcome Statement", Sydney, 30 June 2003.

20. UN Press Release SG/SM/8811, "Secretary-General Commends Regional Response to Solomon Islands Crisis", 5 August 2003; UN Press Release SC/7853, "Press Statement on Solomon Islands by Security Council President", 26 August 2003.

21. Alexander Downer, launch of ASPI Report, *Our Failing Neighbour*, 10 June 2003.

22. *Defence 2000, Australia's Defence White Paper*, Canberra: Commonwealth of Australia, 2000, para. 4.8.

23. Ibid.

24. ASPI, *Beyond Bali: ASPI's Strategic Assessment 2002*, Canberra: ASPI, 2002, p. 29.

25. See John Henderson and Benjamin Reilly, "Dragon in Paradise: China's Rising Star in Oceania", *The National Interest*, Vol. 72, Summer 2003, pp. 94–104.

26. William Reno, *Warlord Politics and African States*, London: Lynne Rienner, 1998.

27. *Australia's National Security: A Defence Update*, Canberra: Commonwealth of Australia, 2003.

28. Quoted in Dobell, "The South Pacific", p. 2.
29. Australia's Foreign and Trade Policy White Paper, *Advancing the National Interest*, Canberra: Commonwealth of Australia, 2003, p. 93.
30. ASPI, *Our Failing Neighbour*.
31. See Helen Hughes, "Aid Has Failed the Pacific", *Issue Analysis*, No. 33, Sydney: Centre for Independent Studies, 7 May 2003.
32. Downer, "Security in an Unstable World".
33. See Elsina Wainwright, "Transnational Governance for the Pacific: Does Staying out of Hot Water Warrant Dipping into a Pool?" *Australian Financial Review*, 27 July 2003, p. 48.
34. Dobell, "The South Pacific", p. 15.

Part III
Margins

7

Reviving state legitimacy in Pakistan

Samina Ahmed

As Pakistan confronts cyclic political, military and economic crises, there is growing international concern about the stability and even the continuing viability of the state. Although it is one of many weak states in a volatile region that stretches from Central Asia to the Middle East, international concern about Pakistan stems from a number of factors. These include Pakistan's geostrategic location, a history of conflict with Afghanistan and war with neighbouring India, a nuclear weapons capability, and the regional and internal implications of Pakistan-based Islamic extremism. Fearing that Pakistan might move down the stability ladder from weak to failed state, influential external actors, in particular the United States, have opted to support Pakistan's political, structural and institutional status quo. However, this status quo, in particular the military's monopoly of power, is itself largely responsible for the crisis of state legitimacy.

If key elements of state success include the existence of an apolitical bureaucracy, firm civilian control over the military and rule of law, these essential preconditions are notable by their absence in Pakistan. For most of its existence, Pakistan has been ruled by the military, either directly or through military-dominated governments. But the locus of power within the state and the manner in which it is exercised are internally contested. And this basic fault line in the Pakistani state can be traced back to its colonial history. If Costa Rica's success can be explained by a colonial legacy that empowered political parties and encouraged democratic liberal functioning, Pakistan's inheritance included an ex-colonial military, contemptuous of the civilian political elite it had been tasked to control by its British masters, and a civilian political elite, conscious of the benefits of democratic governance in the former metropolis. Ethnic divide- and-rule strategies and centralized structures of governance were also a part of this colonial inheritance.

Retaining this legacy of authoritarianism, centralization and ethnic manipulation, the state's managers oversaw the disintegration of the state. Rejecting authoritarian and centralized control in a multi-ethnic, multi-regional state, the Bengalis of East Pakistan opted for secession after a bloody war of self-determination in 1971. Truncated Pakistan too has experienced chronic crises, emanating from domestic challenges to authoritarian and centralized state structures. While the state's capacity to deliver services to its citizens continues to decline and rule of law is notable by its absence, Pakistan's external directions also undermine its internal stability and contribute to regional tensions.

Domestic challenges to the military's pre-eminence might not threaten the state's sovereignty and control over its territory, but this internal contestation has incrementally eroded the legitimacy of the state and its institutions. The state's managers have thus far successfully warded off internal challenges, but this has been at the cost of state-building and cohesion. Left to themselves, Pakistan's power holders and their domestic challengers might well have reached a *via media* that would then have allowed them to focus their attention on reviving state legitimacy. However, Pakistan's internal dynamics, as in the case of Colombia, have been distorted by external intervention, with the United States playing a major role in influencing the direction of the Pakistani state.

Traditionally an ally, the United States has supported and thus helped to consolidate the Pakistani political status quo in the belief that it best serves US global and regional interests as well as Pakistan's security. But US acceptance of the Pakistani military's political predominance and US disregard for democratic governance in Pakistan have only added fuel to the domestic fire by emboldening the military to retain power. US backing for military or military-controlled state structures has also contributed, albeit indirectly, to regional instability because the military's policy preferences exacerbate tensions with neighbouring India and Afghanistan, helping to sustain a bad neighbourhood and consolidating regional conflict formations. Confident of external support and legitimacy, the Pakistan military continues to pursue domestic and external policies that have rebounded on the legitimacy of the Pakistani state and its institutions.

Focusing on state-building, this chapter examines the internal and external imperatives that have perpetuated the crisis of state legitimacy in

Pakistan. I shall first examine the implications of the domestic distribution of power and the manner in which it is managed, using history to illustrate the contradictions underlying the crisis of the Pakistani state. External factors, in particular the US role in shaping Pakistan's domestic dynamics, will be examined in depth, as will regional imperatives, including Pakistan's relations with Afghanistan and India. Finally, the chapter will identify strategies to contain and reverse Pakistan's crisis of state legitimacy, to promote state cohesion and to avert state failure.

Crisis of state legitimacy

Pakistan presents an intriguing picture of a state that has undergone authoritarian rule for most of its existence but where the military's political dominance is internally contested. Although constitutionalism and the rule of law are the casualties of military intervention and control, the military nonetheless fails to gain domestic legitimacy because it lacks constitutional sanction. Pakistan is a state where an overdeveloped state apparatus is capable, for the most part, of exercising its writ over citizens but fails to subdue a vibrant civil society. Centralized state structures also penetrate and control the periphery, but lack legal and normative sanction and are constantly challenged by a multi-ethnic, multi-regional population.[1]

Because state control and authority are vested in the military and the exercise of that power is absolute and unaccountable (in the absence of representative governance), citizens are denied socioeconomic and political rights at every level – local, regional and national. Neglected or penetrated by the military apparatus, weak and corrupt state institutions have become incapable of delivering basic goods. The state's neglect of the political, social and economic rights of its citizens, the absence of the rule of law, and the military's internal and external directions have collectively contributed to the criminalization of the polity and the economy. As the gap between the rulers and the ruled has grown, domestic divisions have widened and become increasingly violent, since there are no credible and institutionalized participatory mechanisms for articulating internal demands and mediating internal differences.

If authoritarianism and the centralization of power have weakened the Pakistani state, so has an uncertain regional environment, in particular a history of war with India and conflict with Afghanistan. Internal and external factors are, however, closely interlinked. The military's political primacy translates into the formulation and implementation of external policies that are in step with its institutional perceptions and interests. Even when these policies clearly impinge on state security, remedial action is seldom taken or alternative strategies devised – in part owing to the lack of an internal military debate but more importantly owing to the absence of countervailing civil authority.

Just as internal and external imperatives determine Pakistan's security environment, influential external actors – notably the United States – shape its domestic politics and its regional relationships. Since the 1950s, the United States has played and continues to play a significant role in influencing the direction of the Pakistani state.[2] Perceiving the Pakistani military as a regional asset, the United States has tacitly or overtly encouraged military or military-controlled governments to retain power. At the same time, US diplomatic support has conferred the legitimacy that the military cannot obtain domestically. The military also exploits that support to weaken its civilian opposition. For example, US economic and military assistance has helped the Pakistani security apparatus to expand its capabilities at the expense of its domestic counterparts. In the regional context, US support of the political status quo has perpetuated the Pakistan military's control over crucial areas of security policy, often with disastrous results for Pakistani security and regional stability.

Despite chronic instability, Pakistan has yet to reach the point of no return. The crisis of state legitimacy is resolvable and the tasks of state-building and coherence remain well within reach. The state's institutions might have weakened, but they still function. Although the state's control over its territory has eroded, the allegiance of its population remains largely intact. If the state's strategies of power and control were to change, the state and its citizens would both stand to benefit. Democratic governance would help to reorder domestic and external priorities. Constitutionalism and the rule of law would legitimize the state in the eyes of citizens and the presence of representative institutions and regional autonomy would contain and resolve internal strife. Reinvigorated state institutions would then have the capacity to meet the needs and redress the grievances of the citizenry, thereby regaining their allegiance.[3]

Conversely, Pakistan's political fortunes could take a turn for the worse if current structures of state power are not transformed to replace authoritarian control with democratic governance and to replace the centralization of power and authority with tangible political and economic devolution. External factors too will play an important role. If US reliance on the Pakistani political status quo were replaced by support for a representative, pluralistic and hence legitimate political order, US regional and global interests would be better served, as would the security of the Pakistani state and its citizens. However, continued US support for unrepresentative governments, motivated by short-term regional objectives, would inevitably rebound on US interests. Such a policy would also destabilize the Pakistani state and increase the risks of regional conflict.

Power and legitimacy

The Pakistani state has a long and troubled history. Gaining independence in 1947 from British colonial rule on the basis of the "Two Nations" theory – the right of the Muslims of British India to self-determination – 24 years later the state disintegrated. As its Bengali Muslim population opted for self-determination after a bloody civil war and Indian military intervention, the Two Nations theory also lost its relevance.[4] State-building on the basis of religion, in any case, was unlikely to succeed after Pakistan's independence because political Islam had little appeal for a predominantly Sunni and largely secular population.[5] Instead, political bargaining took place along often overlapping regional, linguistic and ethnic lines.[6] The state's managers, however, ignored demands for regional autonomy, instead adopting centralized and authoritarian structures and strategies of control.[7] It was these inappropriate state-building strategies that set the stage for the conflict within.

Pakistan's colonial heritage played a major role in influencing the direction of the state and the manner in which power was acquired and exercised. At Pakistan's independence, the mainly Muhajir leadership of the ruling party, the Muslim League, which was responsible for the state's creation, did not have domestic roots and hence lacked popular support in the new state. On the contrary, the Muslim League soon faced domestic opposition as it rejected demands for democratic, pluralistic governance and institutionalized mechanisms for the devolution of political and economic power.[8] Neglecting the urgent task of framing a constitution for the new state and deliberately postponing national elections, the Muslim League justified its political direction on the grounds of state-building and national security. As their credibility declined and they faced domestic dissent, unrepresentative civilian governments were dependent on an ex-colonial military and civil bureaucracy to retain political power. The political leadership's strategies of state control, however, provided the state apparatus an opportunity to usurp power.[9]

Schooled in colonial traditions, suspicious of politicians and intolerant of political dissent, Pakistan's civil and military bureaucracies reverted to a familiar, colonial mode of governance. The institutional interests of the state apparatus were also best served through the centralization of power and authority. As the servants of the state became its masters, they devised and consolidated authoritarian and centralized state institutions, including dictated constitutions that had as little legitimacy as their creators. Following the example of the British rulers of Imperial India, Pakistan's civil and military bureaucrats also resorted to divide-and-rule strategies to control a restive multi-ethnic and multi-regional population. When their strategies of state control gave rise to domestic resistance, particularly after the military assumed absolute power, all dissent was forcibly curbed, ostensibly in the national interest.[10] Not surprisingly, the end result was political alienation and ethnic conflict – not least because the military was and still is perceived as a partisan ethnic actor.

With no civilian oversight or control, military commanders have perpetuated the recruitment policies of their former colonial masters. The British had created a theory of "martial races" in order to exclude potential regional dissidents from the colonial military's ranks. The Pakistan military is predominantly Punjabi, followed by the Pashtun "martial races". Prior to 1971, the majority Bengali population was largely excluded from the armed forces, and smaller minorities such as the Sindhis and the Baluch are still underrepresented.[11]

If authoritarianism and centralization characterized the Pakistani state even before the first coup d'état, so have popular demands for political pluralism and the devolution of power. Domestic support for democratic governance is amply demonstrated by the military's failure to gain legal sanction for its political role and interventions. Indeed, the 1973 constitution limits the military's role within the state to external defence. Attempts by military rulers to gain legal sanction by distorting that basic law have repeatedly failed.[12]

The legacy of colonialism is partly responsible for this deep-rooted popular support for democratic governance. Denied credible representative institutions and mechanisms by the British, the population was well aware of the benefits of parliamentary democracy in the metropolitan state. Independence from colonial rule thus raised popular expectations of self-rule and participation. Support for self-governance remains an integral part of Pakistan's political dynamics, as does the demand for the devolution of political power and economic resources. The weaknesses of Pakistani civil society have enabled the military to intervene at will, and to retain and expand its control over the state and its institutions. However, that authority has yet to translate into legitimacy. On the contrary, since the 1950s, just years after its independence, Pakistan has witnessed resistance – national or regional, peaceful or violent – to the state's denial of political rights and regional autonomy. In 1971, finally losing all hope that the military-controlled and Punjabi-dominated state would grant them their due political, social and economic rights, the majority Bengali population in East Pakistan opted for secession after a bloody civil war.

In truncated Pakistan, too, political divisions prevail along ethnic, linguistic and territorial fault lines. Sporadically, internal tensions trigger organized, at times violent, resistance to centralization and authoritarianism. But the imperatives of regime survival take precedence over state cohesion for the state's managers. Hence emphasis is placed on strategies of state control even if it is, more often than not, at the cost of state-building. With the vast coercive force at their command, military or military-controlled governments have managed, at least in the short term, to contain or defeat domestic challenges. Successive military or military-controlled governments have also attempted, with differing degrees of success, to coerce and co-opt political parties and other segments of civil society into accepting the state's dictates. Coercion and penetration have weakened the ability of civil society actors to mount effective, organized resistance to the state's directions, but have yet to translate into popular legitimacy for the political status quo.

Since the denial of democratic governance and decentralization lie at the heart of the discord between the state and its citizens, every military or military-controlled government has resorted to the rhetoric of democratic reform and devolution to ensure regime survival. For instance, Pakistan's first military government, led by General Mohammad Ayub Khan, justified its takeover on the grounds of democratic reform, pledging to restore democracy and accusing the political leadership of disregarding democratic norms. The government's rhetoric, however, stood exposed when it imposed curbs on the freedoms of assembly, expression and association, including the exclusion of an entire generation of politicians from participation in governance. The regime's legitimacy eroded further when it moved to centralize power through constitutional mechanisms and a system of local government (the "Basic Democracies"), ostensibly aimed at devolving power, that expanded central control over the periphery.[13] Lacking legitimacy and facing widespread resistance, the Ayub regime fell, only to be replaced by a military successor. Under Pakistan's second military government, headed by General Agha Mohammad Yahya Khan, resistance in East Pakistan transformed into a civil war and ended in secession in 1971.

In truncated Pakistan, the state's military managers were to learn little from their failures at exercising power effectively or indeed from the temporary success in state consolidation during the democratic interlude of the 1970s. Prime Minister Zulfikar Ali Bhutto's propensity to flout democratic norms undermined the democratic transition, giving the military, under Army Chief General Mohammad Zia-ul-Haq, an opportunity to intervene, ousting the elected government in 1977.

However, the presence of an elected government had also given Pakistan its first legitimate constitution. Devised by consensus in parliament, the 1973 constitution creates a federal, parliamentary structure of government. Although the distribution of power still favours the centre, the constitutional formula for the devolution of power was and remains largely acceptable to Pakistan's multiple ethno-regional actors. Because of its democratic and federal framework, the 1973 constitution remains the lodestone of regime legitimacy in Pakistan.[14]

If the 1973 constitution constitutes a major breakthrough in state-building in Pakistan, the Zia interlude demonstrates that constitutionalism and rule of law are no deterrent to military intervention. Although the 1973 constitution contains specific clauses to restrict the military's political role and to de-legitimize military intervention, the military has successfully overridden legal restrictions, imposing its will on the population through brute force. However, regime survival remains uncertain in the absence of constitutional sanction, compounded by performance failures. The policies and performance of the Zia regime best illustrate that state-building in Pakistan is unlikely to succeed without democratic and decentralized institutions of governance. In fact, the negative aftermath of the Zia interregnum is still felt in Pakistan a decade and a half later.

During the 1980s, authoritarianism and centralization adversely affected state-building in a number of ways. Although the Zia regime forcibly curbed political dissent, its strategies of state control contributed to ethnic conflict. In Sindh, for instance, there was widespread resistance because an elected Sindhi prime minister was executed by a Punjabi-dominated military. This distrust of the Punjabi military continues to shape centre–state relations in Pakistan's southern and most conflict-prone province.

To ensure regime survival, General Zia created a system of local government. Ostensibly aimed at devolving power to local levels, these "local bodies" enhanced the centre's ability to penetrate the periphery. The resultant centre–state tensions still prevail in Pakistan, taking the shape of provincial distrust of central authority.[15]

The Zia regime also depoliticized political bargaining through a number of mechanisms to control political parties, including curbs on political freedoms, non-party polls and divide-and-rule tactics. These carrots and sticks succeeded in weakening political parties, which have yet to recover from the military's onslaught. But the military's systematic attempts to undermine political parties also deprived the state of the means to regulate and mediate political divisions. Moreover, the use of Islam as a legitimizing strategy by the Zia regime empowered the Sunni religious right at the cost of moderate, secular political forces, heightening sectarian conflict.[16] A decade and a half later, sectarian divisions and Islamic extremism threaten the security of the Pakistani state and its citizens.

Under the Zia regime, the military also systematically penetrated the civilian institutions of the state. Already weakened by state neglect, they became even less capable of delivering basic services to citizens. Moreover, as in the past, the bulk of the state's resources were earmarked for defence, this diversion of scarce public goods being justified on the grounds of national security. If the failure of state institutions to deliver basic services alienated the citizenry, the military's external preferences threatened their physical security. The military's adventurism in Afghanistan, for instance, created, in Pakistani popular parlance, a "Kalashnikov and heroin culture" in the state.[17] The resultant criminalization of politics and the economy still challenges the state's control of its territory, just as Zia's support for the Afghan jihad has made Pakistan a hotbed of Islamic extremists of every hue.[18] Thus the military's external policies are as responsible as its domestic directions for undermining statebuilding and cohesion in Pakistan.

Regional dynamics

Because the military controls all policy-making, its perceptions and preferences dictate Pakistan's external policies. The military's perceptions of the Indian threat and hostility to India are coloured by Pakistan's territorial dispute over Kashmir and a history of war. Yet the Kashmir dispute is far more a symptom rather than a cause of Pakistani animosity towards India. In the Pakistani military's perceptions, India is bent on destabilizing the Pakistani state, which remains the sole hurdle to India's hegemonic regional designs in South Asia. For the Pakistani military, India is therefore a threat and an adversary; and Pakistan must use all available means to counter that threat and to undermine its adversary.

Colonial legacies are partly responsible for the military's distrust of India and its perceptions of the Indian threat. A hasty partition of its Indian colony by the departing British authority, and the resultant mass exodus of Muslims to Pakistan amid bloody communal rioting, formed the backdrop of Pakistan's relations with India. Subsequent disputes over the distribution of assets of the British Indian empire were to combine with the controversial and disputed inclusion in India of Kashmir, a Muslim-majority princely state that was territorially contiguous to Pakistan. Successive wars and near-war crises have served to reinforce the military's animosity towards and suspicions of India.

A year after its independence, Pakistan fought its first war with India over Kashmir. In 1965, the two states were once again at war, following incursions by Pakistani irregulars and military into Indian Kashmir. In 1971, as a result of Indian military intervention in East Pakistan, Pakistan lost its east wing and more than half of its population. In the past two decades, Pakistan and India have been close to war on several occasions, in 1986–1987, in 1990 and in 2002. In 1999, the two states fought a limited war in Kashmir, following the intrusion of Pakistani-backed insurgents and regular forces in the Kargil and Drass sectors of Indian-administered Kashmir.

The military's emphasis of the Indian threat and the Kashmir dispute, however, is also meant to promote other, primarily domestic objectives. The Indian threat is used to legitimize the military's hold over political power on the grounds of national security. The military's inordinate share of the state's economic resources and its diversion of scarce public goods from development to defence are justified on the grounds of the ever-present Indian threat.[19] The imperatives of national security are used not only to legitimize military coups but also to counter internal dissent. The impact of the military's regional policies on state-building is more than evident.

The centre's appropriation of the surplus extracted from the periphery has exacerbated ethnic divisions. This ethnic divide is further enhanced by the forcible suppression of Sindhi, Baluch or Pashtun dissent by Punjabi-dominated military or military governments, ostensibly on the grounds of national security. As a result, centre–periphery tensions have grown even further. Moreover, the disproportionate emphasis on defence and neglect of the social sector have undermined the state's capacity to deliver basic services and goods. Pakistan's education budget is among the lowest in the developing world, and more than half of the population has little or no access to education; expenditure on health is minimal; and a majority of the population lacks access to potable water. The infrastructure of the state, including roads, communications and electricity grids, is far from adequate. Yet any criticism of the one-line defence budget that is presented to parliament – when indeed there is a functioning parliament – is dismissed as anti-state.

If the state's failure to deliver services undermines the legitimacy of its institutions in the eyes of its citizens, the military's reliance on religious extremists to conduct a proxy war with India undermines their physical security. In the military's perceptions, the use of Islamic extremists across the Line of Control in Kashmir serves many purposes. It raises the political, economic and military costs for India of retaining the disputed territory and undermines India's regional and global standing.[20] Once these combined costs become unbearable, the military believes, India will be forced to negotiate a settlement of the Kashmir dispute on Pakistan's terms. But this use of Islamic extremists in the proxy war in Kashmir has rebounded on Pakistani security. The Pakistani religious right is engaged in both an external (Indian) and an internal (sectarian) jihad. The resultant rise in violent sectarian conflict adds yet another fault line in a deeply divided state and society. Ironically, in a state that was created to protect Muslims, political Islam has become a bone of contention and a source of threat.

The external dimensions of the military–mullah alliance are not restricted to the Indian context. Pakistani military-ruled or military-controlled governments have also used Islamic extremist proxies to promote their perceived interests vis-à-vis Afghanistan. Pakistan's colonial legacy has shaped its uneasy relationship with Afghanistan, at the root of which lies Afghanistan's refusal to accept the legitimacy of the Durand Line, the border drawn by the British and inherited by the Pakistani successor state. The Durand Line divides a common people, the Pashtuns, along Pakistan's southern and eastern borders with Afghanistan. Irredentist Afghan claims on Pakistani territory and attempts to subvert Pakistan's Pashtun population have motivated a Pakistani backlash.[21] Rejecting diplomatic means of resolving its dispute with Afghanistan, the Pakistani military has attempted to pay the Afghans back in their own coin, using Afghan proxies to undermine Afghan interests. Conscious that Afghan nationalist dissidents would support the reunion of Pakistani Pashtuns with the Afghan motherland, Pakistan's military planners have chosen to back Afghan Islamic extremists, fighting for an elusive and unachievable goal – the unity of the Islamic *ummah* (nation).[22]

Pakistan's proxy war in Afghanistan has had an even more detrimental effect on the Pakistani state than its interventionist policies in Indian-controlled Kashmir. The reasons are obvious. Unlike India, Afghanistan is itself a weak state, incapable of controlling its borders. State incapacity, internal incoherence and porous borders have facilitated cross-border smuggling in licit and illicit goods to all its neighbours. In the Pakistani context, deliberate Pakistani policies of encouraging cross-border militancy in Afghanistan have resulted in the flow of narcotics and arms trade into Pakistan itself.[23] The result is the criminalization of the Pakistani economy. As the "black" or informal economy challenges the formal economy, it weakens the Pakistani state. And easy access to arms from Afghanistan enables Pakistani Islamic extremists to challenge the Pakistani state's monopoly over violence.

Dating back to Pakistan's involvement in the Soviet–Afghan war of the 1980s, drug trafficking and use and all their attendant ills are undermining Pakistan's security, as is violent ethnic and sectarian violence.[24] The state's capacity to deal with these threats, however, is hampered by the reluctance of its power holders to reverse their policy directions. On the contrary, dictating the course of Afghan policy even during elected governments, the Pakistan military has yet to reassess the costs and benefits of intervening in Afghanistan.

Although Pakistan has consistently supported Afghan Islamic dissidents since the 1970s, its choice of Afghan allies has shifted in accordance with their perceived political and military utility. In the 1990s, the Taliban – the Pashtun Islamic militia controlling all but a sliver of Afghan territory – were Pakistan's chosen partners. Changed US policies, however, dictated a reversal of that support as Pakistan collaborated with the United States in its military operations in Afghanistan in the aftermath of the 11 September 2001 attacks. The policies of the new Afghan government, dominated by the anti-Pakistan and pro-Indian Northern Alliance, appear to have resulted in revived Pakistani support for Kabul's key foes, the Taliban, in Afghanistan. Yet General Pervez Musharraf's government is likely to refrain from all-out intervention in Afghanistan so long as there is a US military presence there. Just as Pakistani concerns about US preferences are influencing its Afghan policy, US policies have influenced Pakistan's internal dynamics.

Foreign assistance

Although the United States formulates its policy towards Pakistan to advance perceived regional and global interests, the Pakistani military has been the main beneficiary of that policy. Successive US administrations have supported Pakistani military governments for a number of reasons. Because the military controls power and dictates Pakistan's domestic and foreign policies, US policy makers believe that it alone can deliver the goods. Uneasy with the political pluralism that accompanies democratic bargaining within and outside government, US administrations prefer to deal with a Pakistani military establishment that is used to giving and having its orders obeyed. Because the United States has worked closely with successive generations of Pakistani military officers, familiar friends are also preferable to unknown civilian partners. Pakistani military leaders, in turn, exploit their links, professional and personal, with branches of the US government.

The extent to which the Pakistani military influences US perceptions and preferences is reflected in the manner in which US policy makers internalize and accept the military's distrust of Pakistani political leaders and the military's self-serving dismissal of elected governments and distortion of democratic processes and institutions. Although US relations with Pakistan have witnessed their ups and down, the United States accepts and hence acquiesces in Pakistan's political status quo, supporting every Pakistani military regime and failing to condone the military's derailing of Pakistan's brief democratic transitions.

In Pakistan, it is said that the survival of any government depends on the three "As": Allah, the Army and America. US diplomatic recognition gives Pakistan's military rulers the international legitimacy they lack in the domestic context. The Pakistani military also uses the United States' tacit or overt approval to weaken its domestic opponents. There is little doubt that US support for the Pakistani military has strengthened the institution through access to US economic and military largesse. The military's backing by a powerful external ally also deprives pro-democracy segments of Pakistani civil society, including political parties, of opportunities to gain international support for democratic functioning.

The Pakistani military first forged ties with the United States in the 1950s, when an ambitious Army Chief, General Mohammad Ayub Khan, was instrumental (in a supposedly parliamentary system) in ensuring Pakistan's entry into US Cold War alliances.[25] Exploiting US concerns about communism and Pakistan's strategic location, the military depicted itself as a valuable regional ally, providing the United States with bases and facilities to monitor the Soviet Union. Benefiting from the resultant US military and economic assistance, the military expanded its infrastructure and gained in power and authority at the cost of its civilian opponents. In 1958, the military took over the reins of the state. Although the détente of the 1960s changed US regional and global priorities, and regardless of irritants such as the imposition of US military sanctions caused by the use of US weapons in the 1965 India–Pakistan war, US administrations retained close ties with the Pakistani military.

That the US alliance with the Pakistani military remained intact was amply demonstrated when the United States extended its support to Ayub's military successor, General Mohammad Yahya Khan. Although the military takeover had resulted in widespread resistance, particularly in the east wing, the United States remained largely aloof from the tussle between the authoritarian regime and pro-democracy forces in Pakistan. On the contrary, the Pakistan military's perceived utility, which included its role of go-between in the normalization of US–China relations, dictated US policy. The United States continued to work with the Yahya regime even after the military used indiscriminate force against the Bengalis in the east wing in the ensuing civil war.

During the brief democratic transition of the 1970s, however, US relations with Prime Minister Zulfikar Ali Bhutto were far from perfect. In fact, Bhutto was to accuse the United States of complicity in the coup that ousted his government in 1977. Despite General Zia-ul-Haq's execution of an elected prime minister and widespread domestic rejection of his military coup, US administrations soon revived their traditional alliance with the Pakistani military, dictated by the compulsions of a resumed Cold War with the Soviet Union.

During the Zia regime, considered the most brutal in the country's history even by Pakistan's lax human rights standards, US administrations worked closely with the Pakistani military in the Soviet–Afghan war. This collaboration took place at a time when, in Pakistan itself, the Zia regime banned political parties and imprisoned hundreds of thousands of political dissidents, subjecting many, including journalists, to corporal punishments such as public lashings. Ironically, this systematic onslaught against Pakistani citizens took place at a time when the Zia regime was working alongside its US partners to free the Afghans from Soviet military occupation. Pakistan, however, had another more pressing objective: to undermine Pashtun nationalism by promoting Pashtun Islamic extremism. Pakistani support for Pashtun Islamic extremists, the Afghan mujahidin, many of whom were to form the core of the Taliban militia, continues to undermine Pakistan's internal stability, Afghan security and US regional interests.[26]

Although US–Pakistani military intervention in Afghanistan destabilized the Pakistani state, with the blowback including the flow of drugs and arms into Pakistan along with the extremist philosophy of the Afghan holy warriors, the Pakistani military's institutional interests were well served. Benefiting from billions of dollars of US military and economic assistance, as well as US diplomatic support, the Zia regime successfully warded off its civilian contenders for 11 long years. Zia's death in July 1988 finally resulted in a shaky democratic transition, owing to the military's awareness that direct rule would face domestic resistance.

The United States welcomed the restoration of democracy in Pakistan. The Cold War was over and US relations with Pakistan were strained over its nuclear weapons programme. However, the United States remained as averse as in the past to pressuring the Pakistani military not to destabilize the democratic process. When four consecutive elected governments were dismissed at the military's instigation or even directly, the United States largely remained a spectator. In October 1999, when General Pervez Musharraf's coup put an end to the democratic transition, the Clinton administration at first condemned the coup and urged a return to democracy. But US opposition to military rule was abandoned in the light of changed priorities after 11 September.

Throwing its weight behind General Musharraf's regime, the United States believes that the Pakistani military alone can meet US goals of countering regional terrorism, particularly threats posed by the presence of al Qaeda operatives in Pakistan and Afghanistan. Since the Bush administration has accepted the military's monopoly over power, bestowing international legitimacy and economic rewards on the Musharraf regime,[27] the United States is perceived as a partisan actor within Pakistan. Emboldened by US support, General Musharraf refuses to transfer power to civil hands. The military government implies, perhaps with good reason, that the United States will continue to back Musharraf's retention of absolute power until such time that US objectives in Afghanistan are achieved. The prolongation of military rule in Pakistan will, however, undermine Pakistani state-building as well as US long-term regional goals.

Reviving state legitimacy

After the breakup of Pakistan, civilian politicians had joined forces to revive state legitimacy, concerned that the secession of the east wing might be replicated in the remaining territory of the state. There was sufficient reason for their concern. In truncated Pakistan, segments of the Sindhi and Baluch political elite, alienated by their exclusion from power and disenchanted with state institutions that were incapable of delivering basic services, had begun to demand self-determination, some of them voicing support for secession from the federation.[28] But extremist demands did not gain popular support because ethnic and regional alienation was redressed by the democratic transition of the 1970s. The presence of a representative government and participatory avenues for articulating regional demands succeeded in reviving the legitimacy of a state that, for all practical purposes, appeared to have failed.

In particular, the federal parliamentary structure of the 1973 constitution – incorporating popular demands for participatory, pluralistic governance and regional autonomy – played a crucial role in restoring the confidence of citizens in the institutions of the state. In contrast, following Zia's coup, the return to authoritarianism and centralization once again exacerbated internal divisions and fuelled regional and sectarian conflict.

After General Zia's military regime came to an abrupt end in July 1988, the military had two options: to retain direct power or to transfer it to civilian hands. Having calculated that the domestic and external costs of direct military rule would adversely affect their institutional interests, the high command, represented by Chief of Army Staff General Aslam Beg, opted for a tactical withdrawal by transferring power to an elected government. But the manner in which the democratic transition occurred undermined civilian control over the military.

The military's retention of crucial areas of policy-making, internal and external, hindered democratic functioning and undermined the credibility of democratic institutions.[29] The internal clout and ambitions of an interventionist military were also strengthened by the failure of political leaders and elected governments to respect democratic norms and to provide democratic governance. In the absence of a civilian consensus on institutionalizing democratic functioning, the political elite became increasingly vulnerable to the military's divide-and-rule strategies. When the military chose, for instance, repeatedly to dismiss elected governments, the political opposition was more than willing to collaborate with the high command, hoping to gain the military's patronage and hence access, no matter how limited, to the spoils of power. As a result, the military soon regained its monopoly over power, to the cost of its civilian adversaries.

Yet the presence of even inept but elected governments did help to ameliorate domestic dissent since civilian institutions, though weak, provided mechanisms for political bargaining and avenues for articulating political grievances. Moreover, the decade-long democratic interlude also further de-legitimized the military's claims to a political role. As a result, ever since the October 1999 coup, Pakistan's current military rulers have been hard-pressed to justify direct military rule and their refusal to resume the democratic transition.

Not surprisingly, like his military predecessors, General Pervez Musharraf has had to place regime survival and consolidation above state-building and cohesion. Having disrupted the democratic transition, Musharraf, like other military rulers, is aware of his lack of legitimacy and hopes to acquire it through democratic rhetoric. Justifying the October 1999 coup, for instance, General Musharraf denounced elected civilian leaders for undermining democratic functioning and norms, and he pledged the restoration of true democracy and the devolution of political, social and economic authority.[30]

Musharraf's strategies of state control are no different from those of other military regimes. Musharraf hopes to concentrate all powers in his institution by assuming the post of president, and then extending his presidential term through a rigged referendum, by retaining the post of Army Chief, and by distorting the parliamentary and federal structure of the 1973 constitution. Musharraf's constitutional distortions include a bid to gain constitutional sanction for the political role for the military.[31] A district government scheme, ostensibly aimed at devolving political, social and economic power and authority to local levels, has also been devised to centralize power over the periphery at the cost of federal administrative structures.

Musharraf's years in power have also witnessed a systematic campaign to weaken and/or eliminate civilian opponents. This included a selective process of fiscal accountability and electoral rules that disqualified almost half of all former parliamentarians from participating in the October 2002 national elections. Relying on divide-and-rule strategies, the military regime has created divisions in the ranks of its main civilian opponents, the moderate, secular mainstream national parties, and also weakened them by empowering religious right-wing parties.[32] Although the military's political machinations have helped to neutralize civilian threats to regime survival, legitimacy continues to elude the military.

Musharraf's civilian opponents in and outside parliament refuse to accept the constitutional legality of Musharraf's Legal Framework Order, incorporated in the constitution through the 17th amendment. This has tilted the balance of power from the prime minister (the head of government) to the president (the head of state), rendered parliament vulnerable to the president's authority, and legalized the military's political role. The military's "devolution" scheme is also rejected by all shades of political opinion, except, of course, the regime's chosen civilian partners.

Musharraf's external allies, the United States in particular, appear willing to accept his indefinite extension of power. The United States lauded the deeply flawed October 2002 national elections as a meaningful step towards the restoration of a functional democracy, and the military's institutional distortions of federal structures, such as the devolution scheme, have benefited from the financial backing of Western donors and international financial institutions. Clearly, the Bush administration still believes that military rule in Pakistan will serve US goals since the military alone can deliver the anti-terrorist goods. It is this continued US support, as well as the military's confidence in its ability to suppress domestic dissent, that is encouraging Musharraf to reject popular demands for a democratic transition.

The United States' priorities since 11 September might emphasize the dangers posed to its national security by failing or failed states. But, in the Pakistani case, US policy is weakening an already fragile state. Should the United States revise its policy towards Pakistan, opting instead for constructive engagement to promote democratic governance and the decentralization of power, this would serve the interests of both the United States and Pakistan.

Much like Afghanistan, where ethnic divisions play a major role in undermining state stability, ethnic conflict remains a major threat to state security and consolidation in Pakistan. In fact, ethnic fissures pose a far greater danger to Pakistan, with its legacy of a successful secessionist movement, than to Afghanistan, where ethnic contenders have historically contested power to capture the state, not to leave it. So long as the Punjabi-dominated military continues to retain absolute power, ethnic tensions will increase even further, destabilizing an already weak state. In Sindh, in Baluchistan and even in the Northwest Frontier Province, the military's manipulation of the 2002 elections and the subsequent process of government formation have increased centre–periphery tensions. In the centre, the military's political structures are far too fragile to survive. However, the longer they survive, the greater the damage to state-building and cohesion.

Should the military's American allies continue to accept military rule under civilian guise, domestic resentment will also translate into anti-American sentiment. The Bush administration might believe that this is a cost worth paying because the returns are sufficiently high in terms of the Pakistan military's cooperation in the fight against terrorism. It is time that the United States rethought the risks involved both to US regional interests and to Pakistani state security.

Because the Pakistani military remains in absolute control of all aspects of policy, internal and external, Pakistan continues to use Islamic proxies to destabilize Indian-administered Kashmir. Irked by the pro-Indian sympathies of the Kabul administration, the Pakistani military has also begun to pursue a dangerous course in Afghanistan. The military regime is either turning a blind eye or providing quiet support to Islamic Afghan and Pakistani Pashtun insurgents using Pakistani sanctuaries, as in the Soviet–Afghan war, to conduct attacks across the Pakistan/Afghanistan border. Convinced that the United States will continue to back them, Musharraf and his generals have paid little heed thus far to US pressure and persuasion to end the cross-border militancy in India and to curb the incursion of Afghan extremists across the Pakistan/Afghanistan border. To ensure US support, the military government keeps on adding to the tally of captured al Qaeda operatives in Pakistan. But Musharraf's policies will rebound on Pakistani stability and US security. The blowback for Pakistan includes the continued criminalization of the economy and the polity through the cross-border trade in drugs and arms, which translates within the Pakistani context, as it does in the Colombian, into endemic sub-state conflict, undermining the state's monopoly of violence. In the US case, the blowback is equally dire. The resurgence of the Taliban in the southern and eastern Afghan provinces bordering on Pakistan is already taking its toll on the US-led coalition and its Afghan allies. The Pakistan military's use of Islamic proxies to promote regional goals has also emboldened anti-US Islamic extremists, with roots in Pakistan itself.

If the military's grip over security policy were eased, which will happen only when the balance of power in the state shifts from military to civil authority, Pakistan would be more than likely to replace its present interventionist policies in Afghanistan and India with constructive engagement. The normalization of Pakistan's relations with India and Afghanistan is hampered by Indian and Afghan distrust of the Pakistani military. If past voting patterns are any indication of Pakistani popular preferences, free and fair elections would result in mainstream moderate political parties forming government and also dominating the parliamentary opposition. When in power, the centre–left Pakistan People's Party and the centre–right Pakistan Muslim League had abandoned confrontation for a peaceful resolution of Pakistan's relations with India, overtures that received a positive Indian response. During the 2002 national elections, all major mainstream parties supported the normalization of relations with India and Afghanistan. Although the October 1999 coup and the military's continued hold over power have deprived these moderate voices of a role in policy-making, the restoration of civil power would create the necessary climate for a meaningful dialogue on contentious issues such as the Durand Line and the Kashmir conflict. Regional approaches to resolving conflict could then be adopted and Pakistan could play a significant role in helping consolidate the peace in neighbouring Afghanistan, with India's support and participation.[33]

Resuming the democratic transition in Pakistan obviously requires far more than just international support and guidance. As in the past, the military high command's policy choices will depend on an assessment of both the domestic and external costs of retaining direct power. In the domestic context, with the coercive power it has at its disposal, the military can easily continue to counter any civilian resistance. However, the continued civil–military stalemate, which hinges on acceptance of the military's unilateral constitutional amendments, is raising the military's domestic costs. As Musharraf, who represents the institution in his capacity of Army Chief, fasts loses all domestic credibility, the corps commanders and principal staff officers might find it expedient to replace him with someone else, once again using democratic rhetoric to regain domestic legitimacy. But the military's external cost–benefit analysis will continue to play a vital role in determining its policy options. So long as the high command assumes that the United States will continue to back direct military rule, it is unlikely to change its domestic course. Should the policy of influential international actors, particularly the United States, change, the military would be far more likely to opt for another democratic transition. However, the success of that transition would depend on the political elite's ability to ensure that the bargaining process involves a tangible shift from military to civil hands.

External factors too will play an important role, as in the past. Influential members of the international community, particularly the United States, could help the Pakistani state once again to become truly functional, but only if they rethink their current policies. If international approval for military rule were replaced by international pressure for the revival of the democratic process, the Pakistani state would stand to gain. It goes without saying that emulating the Costa Rican model would serve Pakistan far better than going down the Colombian route: participatory liberal democracy would enable the state and its institutions to regain popular legitimacy and ease domestic alienation; reinvigorated political parties would help to ensure good governance in power and play a watchdog role in opposition; and regional autonomy would provide the domestic stability that is needed to enhance the prospects of economic development. Constitutionalism and the rule of law would reinvigorate state institutions, and democratic freedoms and institutions would allow a long-overdue debate on the current directions of both domestic and external policies. If the political status quo remains unchanged, however, the state might incrementally lose the allegiance of its citizens, with dire consequences for regional stability and for international security.

Notes

1. Omar Noman, *Pakistan: Political and Economic History since 1947*, London: Kegan Paul, 1988, p. 21.
2. Saeed Shafqat, *Civil–Military Relations in Pakistan: From Zulfikar Ali Bhutto to Benazir Bhutto*, Boulder, CO: Westview Press, 1997, p. 7.
3. "The relevant issue is not whether the state will continue to exist, but how it can be controlled such that its coercive powers are minimized while its capacity for reform is utilised," says Noman. "Thus a central component of the popular demand for constitutional, democratic government in Pakistan consists of an appeal for the replacement of arbitrary and capricious use of state power by a systematic set of regulations" (Noman, *Pakistan*, p. 210).
4. Bengalis in Pakistan's east wing comprised 54.2 per cent of the population.
5. Iran's Shia majority is more inclined to accept the authority of religious leaders who derive their legitimacy from Shia religious centres and schools. Religion has thus become an important tool of political mobilization. In contrast, Pakistan's predominantly Sunni population is internally divided, identifying with multiple and competing Sunni sects and sub-sects. It is this absence of coherent religious authority, combined with long-standing support for moderate and secular political parties, that prevents religion from becoming a primary source of national identity and restricts the political space of the religious right during democratic interludes. Conversely, the mullahs have historically stood to gain from the marginalization of moderate secular and mainstream political parties by authoritarian rulers, often accompanied by a mullah–military partnership. Islamic extremists have also gained internal clout as a result of the military's security preferences, particularly the use of the jihad to conduct proxy wars against perceived external adversaries.
6. East Pakistan (now Bangladesh), which is largely Bengali, was separated from the west wing by a thousand miles of Indian territory. In the west wing, Baluchistan had 40 per cent of the land area and the smallest share of the total population (3 per cent), divided into Baluch and Pashtu speakers. The mainly Pashtun Northwest Frontier Province had 16 per cent of the population. Sindh had 22 per cent of the population, with its urban areas being dominated by Urdu-speaking Muhajirs (migrants or their descendants from India) and its rural countryside by Sindhis. Punjabis in the Punjab constituted the majority population of the west wing (56 per cent).
7. Dietrich Reetz, "National Consolidation or Fragmentation of Pakistan: The Dilemma of

General Zia-ul-Haq", in Dietrich Reetz, ed., *Nationalism, Ethnicity, and Political Development: South Asian Perspectives*, New Delhi: Manohar, 1991, p. 18.

8. Noman, *Pakistan*, pp. 12–13.

9. Lawrence Ziring, *Pakistan in the Twentieth Century: A Political History*, Oxford: Oxford University Press, pp. 21, 228.

10. Army Chief General Ayub Khan imposed military rule in October 1958. But he had first joined government as early as 1954 after the Constituent Assembly (the central legislature), which was also responsible for framing the constitution, was dissolved at the behest of the civil–military bureaucracies.

11. Samina Ahmed, "The Military and Ethnic Politics", in Charles H. Kennedy and Rasul Bakhsh Rais, eds, *Pakistan 1995–96*, Boulder, CO: Westview Press, 1996, p. 18.

12. Pakistani constitutions include the 1956 constitution, enacted by President Iskander Mirza, General Ayub Khan's 1962 constitution, and the 1973 constitution, which was validated by an elected parliament. Military rulers have enacted far-ranging changes within the 1973 constitution – General Zia-ul-Haq in 1985 and General Pervez Musharraf in 2002 – only to face political resistance.

13. Ayub's 1965 constitution created an all-powerful president, Ayub himself, a rubber-stamp parliament and a subordinate judiciary. Formally a federation, the constitution vested all powers, political and economic, in the central government.

14. Hamid Khan, *Constitutional and Political History of Pakistan*, Oxford: Oxford University Press, 2001, p. 486.

15. Noman, *Pakistan*, pp. 193–194.

16. Religious parties were included in Zia's cabinet and a body of Islamic legislation was introduced, which remains in place today, that undermines fundamental constitutional freedoms.

17. Khan, *Constitutional and Political History*, p. 683.

18. Shahid Javid Burki, "The Management of Crises", in William E. James and Subroto Roy, eds, *Foundations of Pakistan's Political Economy: Towards an Agenda for the 1990s*, New Delhi: Sage, 1992, pp. 127–128.

19. Although most of the national budget goes on debt servicing, this debt and interests on loans are directly linked to an ever-increasing defence budget.

20. Robert G. Wirsing, "Kashmir Conflict: The New Phase", in Charles H. Kennedy, ed., *Pakistan: 1992*, Boulder, CO: Westview Press, 1993, p. 149.

21. Afghanistan claims Pakistan's Pashtun territories as its own, and Afghan governments have also supported secessionist movements within Pakistan's Pashtun population, including the demand for "Pashtunistan", the land of the Pashtuns.

22. Frederic Grare, *Pakistan and the Afghanistan Conflict, 1979–1985*, Oxford: Oxford University Press, 2003, pp. 89, 194.

23. Noman, *Pakistan*, p. 20.

24. Mumtaz Ahmad, "Revivalism, Islamization, Sectarianism and Violence in Pakistan", in Craig Baxter and Charles Kennedy, eds, *Pakistan 1997*, Boulder, CO: Westview Press, 1998, pp. 114–115.

25. Pakistan joined the Southeast Asia Treaty Organization and the Central Treaty Organization.

26. Partly in reaction to Pakistan's continued intervention and partly motivated by domestic considerations, influential Afghan politicians within and outside the Karzai government have upped their anti-Pakistani rhetoric and have once again begun openly to question the legitimacy of the Durand Line.

27. Samina Ahmed, "The United States and Terrorism in Southwest Asia: September 11 and Beyond", *International Security*, Vol. 26, No. 3, Winter 2001–2002, p. 85.

28. Some Sindhi nationalists supported the creation of a "Sindhu Desh" (land of the

Sindhis) and segments of the Baluch political elite advocated a "Greater Baluchistan", an independent state that would incorporate Baluch-majority regions of neighbouring Afghanistan and Iran.

29. Shafqat, *Civil–Military Relations in Pakistan*, p. 251.
30. Zahid Hussain and Farah Durrani, "Interview with General Musharraf", *Newsline*, November 1999, p. 26.
31. Musharraf's Legal Framework Order, now embedded in the constitution through the 17th amendment of December 2003, contained 29 constitutional amendments. In April 2004, the military ruler succeeded in gaining parliamentary approval for the formation of a military-dominated National Security Council that will oversee all policy and state functioning, internal and external.
32. See *Pakistan: Mullahs and the Military*, ICG Asia Report No. 49, 20 March 2003.
33. In the context of Afghanistan, for instance, tensions over the Durand Line would ease as Pakistan normalized economic relations with its land-locked neighbour. Enhanced economic stakes in relations with Pakistan would encourage Afghan officials to downplay the Durand Line. However, in both the Afghan and the Indian context, tensions would ease only if Pakistani political leaders were willing to translate into practice their pledges of non-intervention within Afghanistan and in Indian-administered Kashmir.

8

Disintegration and reconstitution in the Democratic People's Republic of Korea

Hazel Smith

The Democratic People's Republic of Korea (DPRK) – more commonly known as North Korea – is generally considered either "bad, mad, or sad".[1] According to the conventional approach, it is a rogue state that is so completely lacking in transparency as to be unknown, impossible to understand and therefore irrational. Its irrationality means it is unpredictable, threatening and dangerous – its very existence contributing to the dangerous levels of tension that threaten war on the peninsula and chaos in North East Asia. This chapter, however, takes a different tack. The premise is that the DPRK is understandable, predictable and – if rationality implies choosing appropriate means to reach desired ends – eminently rational. This does not mean that the government always makes prudent, efficient or ethical decisions. It does mean that the DPRK can be understood and analysed using conventional social science methodologies, concepts and theories.

Like others in this book, this chapter uses a Weberian frame of reference to trace the peculiar institutionalization of the North Korean state as a specific rejection of the Weberian model and the conscious adoption of the concept and practice of the state as a party/military/society complex. The chapter shows how the system of state created under the aegis of Kim Il Sung was that of a "permanent campaigning political movement". It identifies the inbuilt fissures and flaws of the system that in the end meant that the system could not withstand the economic and food crises of the 1990s and onwards. The chapter traces the disintegration

167

and reconstitution of the Korean state from the late 1990s onwards. The chapter concludes by demonstrating how outside actors contributed to the changed socioeconomic landscape after the crisis of the mid-1990s and also suggests appropriate policy options for key external actors. Normative as well as technical criteria are adopted in that I suggest that, for a state to "work", it must deliver on human security in the political as well as the economic arenas. It must provide for the conditions of human freedom as well as human survival.

In terms of the three-part typology offered by Sebastian von Einsiedel, the DPRK has never been a state based on liberal contract theory (first type), but it has most certainly controlled the means of violence (second type) and it also has the characteristics of juridical statehood (third type).[2] The second type of state, derived as von Einsiedel points out from Weberian analysis, is not entirely viable in modern times through only its control of the security apparatus (the police and the military). It must also be legitimate, and in Weberian terms legitimacy comes about from the nature of authority, whether "legal", "traditional" or "charismatic". Kim Jong Il did not inherit the charismatic authority of his father Kim Il Sung. His dilemma is to develop and impose "legal" authority. Domestically, a reconstituted state cannot flourish economically without the implementation of an efficient modern bureaucracy. Internationally, powerful political adversaries show no sign of mitigating hostility unless the DPRK becomes more transparent and its legal system less arbitrary – concomitants of the legal state.

The state as permanent campaigning political movement

The conventional idea of the state draws on a sociological tradition associated most closely with the work of Max Weber and summarized by Fred Halliday as "a specific set of coercive and administrative institutions, distinct from the broader political, social and national context in which it finds itself".[3] The Weberian state, with, at its heart, an independent bureaucracy and national military overseen by a central government machinery, had never existed in the north of the Korean peninsula.[4] Prior to partition, the colonial state machinery had centred around the capital, Seoul, and the northern provincial administrative centres were cut off from the capital and each other by the mountainous and forested terrain, poor physical communication, lack of efficient transport systems and, with the exception of the city of Pyongyang and the main port cities of Wonsan and Nampo, the general priority given to the relatively more accessible southern part of the peninsula.[5]

Kim Il Sung chose not to create modern state structures after he consolidated political control over the northern half of the peninsula; instead he deliberately set about creating a state that can be best understood as a permanent campaigning political movement rather than a set of semi-independent institutions through which the population was governed.[6] A bureaucratic structure and a military and security apparatus existed in the DPRK, but these were constituted quite differently from the analogous institutions in liberal capitalist societies. In the latter, the bureaucracy and the military are characterized by a measure of organizational autonomy, although subordinated to the will of a political party that rules through these institutions.[7] The institutions of the DPRK state were also constituted differently from those of communist states of the Soviet type. In the Soviet model, historically constituted bureaucracies existed that were not synonymous with the party, even if their technical independence was sharply constrained by party dictates. The military in the Soviet Union, although also closely overseen by the party, was an institutionally separate organ of the state from the party.[8] In the DPRK, by contrast, the party directly constituted the bureaucracy, most visibly at county and district level – the lowest level of political administration, where party and governmental officials were often one and the same person.[9] The military in the DPRK also historically evolved as an institution of the party from which any separation was inconceivable, even though, under Kim Il Sung's rule, the role of the military in domestic politics was subordinated to that of the party.[10]

Institutionalizing the new state

The coercive institutions of the state – the military and security apparatus – were vast, inclusive and fluid.[11] Both contained a core of long-term cadres, but the structure of the military, on which, inevitably, more data are available than on the semi-clandestine security apparatus, was designed to encourage integration of the entire adult population and youth into military, militia and self-defence activities. This was neither a professional army on the US or British model, in which volunteers sign up for a career post, nor a full-scale conscript army. Instead, volunteers signed up for terms of service of 3–10 years, and at the same time the population as a whole was continuously organized so that it could be mobilized for self-defence activities.[12]

The effect was to create a population used to administration by hierarchy.[13] Social and public organization reproduced military-style patterns of working. The population became used to taking orders, however apparently illogical, and to operating within hierarchical patterns in which questioning of orders was punished and, eventually, seen as antinationalist and anti-patriotic. Individual (as opposed to collective) initiative was not encouraged and it was sometimes penalized. Horizontal communication across societal units, such as workplaces or neighbourhoods, was structurally discouraged in that strategic decision-making could take place only through vertical authority channels – much the same as horizontal communication does not take place across military units in other societies other than at the most trivial or informal level.[14]

The DPRK military heritage was of clandestine guerrilla warfare that had operated on a "need to know" basis in order to protect the physical security of combatants.[15] The incorporation of military mores in DPRK society therefore included much more extreme values than simply the restriction on public information common to most militaries; it involved, in addition, a sense of the virtues and efficacy of secrecy as a standard operating procedure. The population became socialized within a culture of secrecy as the norm, as "common sense".

The spread of militarized patterns of social organization through the larger society was facilitated by the weakness of putative alternative institutional patterns. The administrative institution of the state – the bureaucracy – was so closely integrated within party imperatives that it could not meaningfully be understood as merely subordinated to party dictates; rather it was constituted by those party imperatives and ideology.[16] Officials owed prior loyalties to the party rather than to their technical function – in health, education, industry or government, for example. Official or bureaucratic duties incorporated serving the party as co-equal to carrying out functional tasks. Social practice in technical sectors, such as health and education, institutionalized the permanent campaign as the dominant method of public organization.[17] Every year, students from the cities were mobilized to the countryside to help in the labour-intensive tasks of transplanting and harvesting. They were also expected to participate regularly and intensively in party-directed "voluntary" activities such as mass games or physically exhausting tasks such as road-building.

A bureaucracy as a rules-based permanent agency with "methodical provision ... made for the regular and continuous fulfilment of ... [specified] duties and the exercise of the corresponding rights" was antithetical to DPRK political philosophy.[18] Indeed, a systematic and continuous "anti-bureaucratization" campaign was waged by the party to prevent such a development.[19] This campaign was conducted throughout the mechanisms of the network of party/society organizations that constituted the core of the state apparatus as permanent campaigning political movement – thus actively preventing the creation of a Weberian bureaucracy that might have adopted an independent role vis-à-vis the party.

The state structure and pattern of social organization were kept in place by rewards allocated through the public distribution system, which, prior to the crisis of the 1990s, distributed food and goods to the entire popula-

tion on the basis of a national work points allocation system.[20] Contrary
to unsupported assertions made by CIA analysts, there is no substan-
tiated evidence that parts of the population had food withheld on the
basis of their loyalty to the party.[21] On the other hand, as in all societies,
those with highly valued work were rewarded proportionately. Non-
tangible rewards, such as fame, status or privilege, were also possible
only through state allocation mechanisms. No private markets in goods
or media existed in this tightly controlled state, so that no alternative
form of incentives could be offered or gained other than through the
state distribution system.[22]

The state model was also sustained by astute political management, in
that Kim Il Sung made concerted efforts to balance and meet the interests of what could have been competing social groups – rural and urban
workers, provincial populations as well as those based in the capital city,
students and workers, and women as well as men. A human security
trade-off guaranteed freedom from want in return for a lack of freedom
from fear.[23] For a generation that had known only an extremely brutal
colonialism and that for the most part saw genuine benefits in a nation-
building project, this trade-off was probably bearable as long as the state
continued to provide rewards for most.

Mass mobilization, based on guerrilla-type military organization,
underpinned by institutions that had no existence except through
their constitution as instruments of the party, was the social paradigm
adopted and rewarded by the state. National mythologies glorified the
anti-Japanese guerrilla struggle, with monuments, media, school textbooks and political campaigns constantly reinforcing and legitimizing the
creation of the new state.[24] The permanent campaigning political movement was institutionalized in the DPRK as the legitimate social order, in
that, in Weberian terms, the state was "valid" for its members – including
those who disagreed with its precepts – and was thus far more stable than
one constituted through either expediency or customary practice.[25]

Potential fissures

There were shortcomings to the model from the beginning, most overtly
in the lack of political freedom in every sphere – freedom of assembly, of
the press, of association and of thought.[26] The state thus created also had
less visible deficiencies. The impressive mobilization capacity of the state
– for military and militia service, civil defence exercises, mass gymnastics,
immunization campaigns and welcoming demonstrations for foreign
dignitaries – served to mask the inability of the state form to deliver efficient, regular and economically rational public administration.[27] Disincentives to individual initiative encouraged inertia and apathy in the
workplace and avoidance of complex tasks that would have involved the

risk of taking decisions outside often very vaguely defined policy parameters.[28] Mobilization capacity, in other words, substituted for organizational efficiency.

The DPRK was not a historical *tabula rasa*, and historical social practices both facilitated the creation of this new state organization and constrained the assimilation of all social sectors into the dominant mode of
public organization. Some sectors, for instance the industrial workers
newly liberated from the brutality of Japanese colonialist practices in
the chemical, steel and heavy industries of the north-east, were easier to
incorporate into the new state practice, lacking as they did a prior stable
pattern of functional, social or political organization. Other social sectors,
most notably in agriculture and the rural communities, were incorporated
into the state as permanent mobilization campaign, but at the same time
continued to organize themselves around very old social structures inherited from pre-colonial Korea.

Fragile stability

The system worked – for a time. It delivered economic growth until
at least the late 1970s, significant gains in agricultural production, the installation of an enormous heavy industrial capacity, an extensive chemicals and fertilizer sector, a nationwide, comprehensive education capacity
from nursery up to and including a large tertiary education capacity, and
an almost 100 per cent literacy rate.[29] It also instituted, for the first time
in northern Korea's history, a nationwide medical and health care service
such that, according to DPRK sources, life expectancy nearly doubled
from 38 to 74 between the late 1930s and 1986.[30]

The manifest flaws in the new system did not threaten the stability of
the new state largely because support from outside actors ensured that
the DPRK could continue to enjoy economic growth and development.
The Soviet Union, Eastern Europe and China provided unconditional
aid in the form of military help (in the Korean War), economic support
(in the form of concessional trade), technology transfers and energy inputs (cheap oil).[31] During the Cold War, characterized as it was by the
suborning of client states for both sides, a relatively small outlay for
China and the Soviet Union brought a fairly large thorn in the side for
the United States, Japan and the Republic of Korea.

Disintegration and reconstitution

The state as permanent campaigning organization lost its major prop in
the late 1980s with the advent in the Soviet Union of President Gorba-

chev and his increasing reluctance to subsidize the DPRK economy, followed by President Yeltsin's outright hostility, which resulted in the end of concessional and barter trade and the cessation of preferential access to technology transfers, spare parts for industrial infrastructure from the USSR or the Eastern bloc, and cheap oil.[32] China also undermined its erstwhile ally – from 1993 demanding market prices for trade goods, including oil.[33] The DPRK could not obtain credit from Western banks because it still owed money from the 1970s after it had ceased debt repayments on funds borrowed to pay for imported technology. Neither could it obtain loans from the international financial institutions, given that US sanctions policies in effect precluded the DPRK from membership and thus eligibility for funds. By the early 1990s the DPRK was appealing to its citizens to curb food intake in the "eat two meals a day" campaign – a response to the increasing food shortages owing to lack of chemicals, fertilizer, electricity for irrigation, spare parts for agricultural machinery and transport, and petrol.

In 1995, floods "of biblical proportions" hit the country, destroying food harvests as well as up to 3 million tonnes of emergency grain reserves, which had been stored in tunnels – over half a year's food supply for the entire population.[34] Coal mines, which produced the majority of the country's electricity supply, necessary for agriculture as well as industry, railway transport as well as residential lighting, in addition to providing the most important fuel for heating, were flooded throughout the country. A country that was already in emergency mode simply had no safety net – either domestic or external – upon which to fall.

The acute crisis of 1995 meant the state was no longer able to deliver regular supplies of food and other basic goods, including fuel and clothing, to most of the population. Many cooperative farmers had seen their harvest destroyed and so could not feed themselves, and the majority of the population who were non-cooperative farm members and who had always therefore had to depend upon the state public distribution mechanism for literal survival had no alternative source of supplies.[35] The state could no longer perform the basic function of ensuring human survival and, furthermore, there were no alternative private or civic channels to which the population might have recourse. Severe malnutrition and famine were the consequence – bringing an eventual total of over 600,000 "excess deaths" between 1995 and 1998, the worst years of crisis, and leaving a brutal legacy of chronic malnutrition among the country's children and women.[36]

The state, in the classical, Weberian sense, did not fail in the DPRK. Indeed it could not, because it did not exist as a set of interlinked but separate semi-autonomous institutions. One consequence of the absence of a modern state bureaucracy was that blame for the crisis could not be shifted in its direction. The bureaucracy was the party, which constituted in a very real sense the organs of the state. When Kim Il Sungism no longer delivered even the basic part of the human security trade-off – the guarantee of physical survival – there was no place to allocate blame other than in the system of state itself.

Individual responses

Individuals responded to this wholly new social crisis through intra-country population movements to stay with relatives who might have access to food, through expanding urban agriculture (that is, growing food and keeping livestock on every patch of space – on roofs, balconies, roads), through barter and swapping, through deforestation and growing food on marginal lands, and through developing legal and illegal trade with China.[37] Some also migrated to China, many for recurrent short-term visits to obtain food and goods and to bring these back for relatives before going back into China when food ran out.[38] The DPRK became a country of individual entrepreneurship, with a population physically and constantly on the move.

Individuals bartered, borrowed and grew what they could as the state literally could no longer provide the means to keep them alive.[39] The almost worthless local currency, the DPRK *won*, became a currency of last resort and individuals attempted to obtain dollars – or Japanese yen and Chinese yuan – and from late 1998 used foreign currency throughout the country.[40] Prior to the mid-1990s the security apparatus would have arrested poor lower social class individuals caught handling dollars, but by the late 1990s the entire population, including party members and members of the security forces, were trying to obtain hard currency, by definition through illegal means because only the *won* was legal tender in the DPRK. Dollars were obtained through contact with foreigners in the capital city, Pyongyang, and in port towns such as Nampo and Wonsan, through contact with Chinese traders in the north-east or through border-crossing into China. Hard currency was obtained through gift-giving, trade and also corruption, as bribes or "inducements" for commercial and sometimes non-commercial transactions. Not all Koreans operated in this manner and many were scrupulously ethical and unselfish – prioritizing the recovery of the country above self-interest.[41]

Societal responses

Rural communities in the breadbasket areas were initially some of those hardest hit by the natural disasters of the mid-1990s, but they also proved to be the most resilient in responding to crisis.[42] As cooperative farms recovered productive capacity in the late 1990s, they extended their autonomy, under-declaring yields and selling as much as they were able on the burgeoning private markets.[43] Cooperative farms, home to just under one-third of the population, had never been recipients of state food distribution and had achieved a degree of independence from the party in the management of agricultural activities. Historically constituted ties of community solidarity sustained social stability and provided organizational structures and social practices around which rural communities found ways to survive the worst of the food shortages. These tight-knit social interconnections continued to provide a culture of sharing and community support long after Kim Il Sungism had lost its legitimacy.

In the medium to long term, it was industrial workers, a hitherto privileged social group in a social system that had prioritized heavy industry as the central plank of "socialist reconstruction", who were worst hit by the continuing food and economic crisis of the mid-1990s onwards.[44] Many lived in crowded, dilapidated tenement buildings in the northeastern cities of Chongjin, Kimchaek and Hamhung in the provinces of North and South Hamgyong, the former bordering the far eastern regions of China and Russia. They had been economically important, providing the workforce for the network of chemical, steel and fertilizer factories that had sustained the country's model of agro-industrial development in former days. They had also been a politically significant force – constituting the mass base for the North and South Hamgyong sections of the Korean Workers' Party, which was disproportionately represented in central party and government decision-making bodies. Within the space of a few years these formerly privileged workers lost regular access to food, income and basic goods.

Industrial workers responded by migrating to China or securing food from relatives in China or elsewhere if any or either of these options were open to them. Lacking access to good arable land or farming experience, some turned to petty trade, bartering and selling any assets they had accumulated from more prosperous times. Others were forced into destitution – with family members, usually the women, scavenging for food and, when none was available, forced into eating "alternative" foods as stomach-fillers, despite a paucity of nutritional value, simply to stave off hunger pangs.[45] Women, who in the Korean tradition eat last, ate tree bark, a wholly non-nutritious commodity, in an effort to stave off hunger – sometimes resulting in death or permanent chronic digestive problems.[46]

The relentless socialization process glorifying and reaffirming the legitimacy and "naturalness" of Kim Il Sungism as a political system could no longer be sustained as the human security trade-off upon which it had depended collapsed. Many schools and educational institutions were no longer physically fully operable owing to lack of transport, food, electricity, heating and staff, who spent their days literally looking for food.[47] The state could not continue to satisfy basic needs, let alone reward the population – with goods or meaningful status – for participation in the system. In addition, the contrast between the continuing desperate physical conditions of most of the population and the ever-optimistic government rhetoric of the "arduous march" and later the "forced march" towards reconstruction generated a reconsideration for most of the population of the large gap between government propaganda and the actual day-to-day misery of existence for most.[48] The de-legitimization of the regime was most dramatically demonstrated in the 1999 uprising in Onsong, a mining and factory county in the remote northern province of North Hamgyong.[49] The Onsong uprising was physically suppressed by the army, with an unknown number of deaths and casualties.

Local government responses

Local officials were tasked by central government with meeting the food needs of their local population, because from the mid-1990s the state could no longer guarantee supply.[50] These officials had a history of decentralized local food production to draw on, although hitherto the state had managed to maintain strategic control over what had been considered ancillary food production. Many county officials, particularly in areas more remote from Pyongyang, responded with imaginative mechanisms – ranging from engaging in semi-licit trade with China, condoning and sometimes encouraging short-term population movement in-country and across the China border, developing unofficial swapping mechanisms with other counties, farms and enterprises, and, most of all, tolerating and encouraging the development of what were supposed to be limited private or "farmers'" markets. Non-state solutions to the food crisis became legitimate, if not fully legal.

In lieu of an independent bureaucratic structure of local government, local party officials functioned as civil servants, and vice versa. Party officials were accountable to their local constituencies in that, although not elected through competitive elections, they for the most part lived and worked in the factories, farms, apartment blocks and neighbourhoods of the people they represented. In the rural and semi-urban areas, party officials would very likely be members of extended families and/or very long-standing, historically constituted social networks. In addition, the Korean Workers' Party was a mass party, as opposed to a vanguard elitist party, that included in its ranks almost all adult males and many women. The thousands of county and local officials, at least at these lowest levels of government and party administration, did not have a separation of life and living standards from the people they represented. Hunger affected local party officials and their families as much as their neighbours – propelling local party members into supporting and encouraging coping solutions about which central government and party officials were much more ambivalent.

Government responses

The government was initially paralysed in that it could not find measures to feed the population through any of the policy instruments it had available to it or experience of. The methods first used in wartime and in the creation of the state – the intensification of physical labour to try to substitute for a lack of manufactured inputs – were wholly useless given the scale of the food gap, which required an input of some 1 million tonnes of grain in order to meet only basic needs.[51] In 1995, in a second year of flood damage, in an act of desperation the government made an unprecedented appeal for food assistance to adversaries such as the United States government. It also requested assistance from UN humanitarian organizations, including UNICEF and the UN World Food Programme, and from non-governmental organizations (NGOs), which it had minimal contact with or experience of prior to the crisis.[52]

The government's greatest domestic policy change, coincident with if not consequent on this huge social and economic crisis, was to strengthen the role of the military in the country's domestic affairs, making the National Defence Council, of which the "paramount leader" Kim Jong Il was chairman, the central decision-making body in domestic politics.[53] This was a major change because Kim Jong Il's father and predecessor, Kim Il Sung, as was the practice in the former Soviet Union, had subordinated the military to civilian rule through dominant and effectively single-party rule. The positioning of the military at the centre of DPRK domestic politics may have reflected a recognition by Kim Jong Il that the social and institutional structures developed in previous decades and their attendant patterns of legitimation could no longer be sustained during the extreme crisis of the 1990s. Reinforcing the coercive apparatus of the state and integrating the leadership's role and functions with the army, so that one constituted the other in a symbiotic relationship, provided an insurance policy against any popular uprising or other source of opposition to regime policies.

Unlike the government of Kim Il Sung, the government of Kim Jong Il did not demonstrate effective political management strategies in respect of the interests of different social sectors. The farming and agriculture sector was given clear priority as a response to the massive food emergency. Apart from the fact that the government still attempted some redistribution of basic grain from food-surplus to food-deficit areas, industrial workers, coal miners, service workers and many local officials were left to fend for themselves. Inequalities in food distribution grew as self-help became the new norm.[54]

These ambivalent socioeconomic policies were reflected within the agricultural sector as the government channelled aid to both rich and poor farmers in support of innovative agricultural policy development such as double-cropping initiatives and seed and crop diversification – in close cooperation with international agencies.[55] The government maintained a basic food safety net, which provided significant improvements in the nutritional levels of young children by 2002 compared with the period of famine of 1995–1997.[56] On the other hand, the government increasingly tolerated participation by farmers in private markets, despite sporadic attempts to regulate their activities and control prices. Markets provided freedom of choice but also helped to institutionalize growing inequality, because only those with independent purchasing power could afford to buy food and goods. Those who could not afford to buy were doubly handicapped in that, from the late 1990s, there was little of a social safety net to fall back on. During the worst of the crisis in the mid-1990s, public goods had been so scarce as to be unobtainable for almost the entire population. By the late 1990s, welfare goods, for instance medicines, had become available again but through retail outlets such as shops and markets as much as through regular distribution to hospitals and clinics. Purchasing power rather than equity had become one of the new determinants of physical survival.

Having secured the integrity of the regime through strengthening the coercive apparatus, some sections of the government sought, eventually unsuccessfully, to reconstitute the system along old lines. As late as 1998, DPRK representatives were denouncing reform in other socialist countries such as Viet Nam as "Americanization".[57] The July 2002 announcement of economic reforms, including partial freeing of price and wage controls, signalled the end of the debate within the DPRK about the possibilities of retrieving old state forms.[58] Government policy was not yet, however, decisively changed towards the reconstitution of the state such as to implement politically liberal reforms and institutions.

The role of outside actors – positive and negative

Prior to 1995, DPRK contact with the outside world had been characterized by formal, diplomatic intergovernmental exchange with the Soviet Union and China (its two primary allies), with the Non-Aligned Movement, in which it was active, and with other countries in Africa,

Asia, Latin America and Eastern Europe.[59] Although trade, aid (which it gave to some African states) and scientific interchange took place, visitors did not engage in substantial interaction with DPRK institutions. By contrast, in the aftermath of the acute food crisis of the mid-1990s and the advent of resident and non-resident humanitarian organizations, significant intercourse developed between DPRK officials and international workers at the local level throughout most of the country.

From 1995 onwards, hundreds of humanitarian officials, donor representatives, foreign faith-based groupings, diplomats, agronomists, engineers and business representatives visited, travelled, worked and lived in the DPRK. Many individuals worked for periods of three or four years with the same hospitals, farms, schools, nurseries and orphanages, building professional relationships with their counterparts that reinforced new operating principles of transparency, efficiency and, most importantly, accountability. The most senior county officials in those counties and districts accessible to the humanitarian community (162 out of 206, representing 85 per cent of the population) had continuous access to and negotiating relationships with humanitarian organizations, in the process absorbing the basic conventions of humanitarian assistance transfers.[60] This does not mean to say that all county officials adopted principles of openness and accountability in their daily practice. But it does mean that local officials were systematically exposed to alternative methods of social organization to the one that they were used to – permanent mobilization.

Interaction with external actors also brought exposure to less positive social practices. The primitive banking system and lack of a developed mechanism of non-cash transfers, combined with the non-transparency of the entire state system, facilitated the spread of a practice of doing business with foreigners in which it became the norm, rather than the exception, for hard currency cash to be transferred in ways that made it difficult to account for or trace all expenditure. Corruption was the inevitable outcome of these circumstances, in which poverty was widespread and hard currency was one of the few guarantees of delivering families from the continuing overhanging threat of starvation.

The unintended consequences of the crisis

The coping reactions to crisis of individuals, families and communities – combined with the activities of outside actors – caused an unanticipated reconstitution of the state/society system. Political change did not occur, but the ways in which individuals, households and communities organized their daily life changed dramatically because the state could no longer provide the incentives and penalties required to keep the old state/ society system in place.

The unintended result of the extension of farmers' autonomy and the inability of the government effectively to develop and implement social and economic policy management was the institutionalization of an inchoate but vital market economy.[61] Price was no longer determined by government but resulted from the relationship between supply and demand; those who could afford to buy benefited, whereas those who could not were no longer adequately protected by state subventions. Where it could, the population sought help from outside – either in China or from visiting foreigners – so the country became dollarized because of the population's de facto use of hard currencies, especially dollars, as a means of exchange, store of value and mechanism of accounting. Although hard currency did not become available to the majority of the population, the mechanisms associated with its use and its preference as a functioning currency rapidly dominated socioeconomic interchange. Individual action – in saving, budget planning and expenditure – became a more rational choice than the previously dominant collective mode of economic activity. Contact with foreigners and the use of hard currencies were both cause and consequence of the dollarization of the economy; as these social phenomena swept the country at the end of the 1990s, so easier interchange with the outside world became not just desirable for individuals but necessary for the whole socio-economy to survive.

As the party withdrew from direct economic management and recognized for the first time a separation of economics from politics, so the possibility opened up of the establishment of a bureaucracy based on "experts" who could help build the foundations for a modern state. The government's new interest in the opportunities offered by foreign interlocutors for "capacity-building" – often a euphemism for training in Western concepts of accountability, efficiency, profitability and transparency – is some indication of a shift in this direction. The rapid rise of the real money economy, with the dollarization of the DPRK since the crisis, also provided opportunities for bureaucrats and workers to be paid in a real money system that could start to replace the system of rewards and penalties hitherto provided by party dictates.[62] Such rewards, combined with the acceptance that it is legitimate and legal for individuals to accumulate private wealth, could also herald a real incentive system, thus helping to inject more dynamism into economic processes.

The "legitimate social order" was undermined from within and without through the introduction into the DPRK of alternative social practices in which thousands of local officials, along with central government representatives, were implicated. Officials were forced into a degree of transparency over food supplies and agricultural production as they provided detailed quantitative and qualitative information (on average every two months) through their interaction with humanitarian and other international agencies. It was county officials who hosted foreign business representatives, on a continuing and intensifying basis from 1995 onwards, providing information on everything from mining output to the state of repair of local power stations. The larger humanitarian organizations also routinely and systematically insisted on accountability for health, agriculture and food assistance. Some transactions with foreigners were accompanied by corrupt transfers of money and goods – an inevitable accompaniment of an unregulated yet marketized economy.

These alternative social practices were not always welcomed by local and central government officials, for diverse reasons. Some objected to the corruption that accompanied foreign links. Some regretted the moves away from egalitarian principles and towards the introduction of structural, market-based inequalities. Others resented the loss of independence and status that accountability mechanisms implied. Others simply were hostile to the weakening of the old system of a tightly controlled and hierarchical polity and economy.

Not all elements of the egalitarian social practice and principles that legitimated collective action and social solidarity disappeared from the system. The government maintained redistribution of a basic ration when there was food in the system, and county officials attempted to ensure that local populations received enough to prevent starvation. Local communities shared food between themselves.[63] Children receiving international food aid shared with brothers or sisters or other relatives who were not so fortunate. Social egalitarian principles were challenged, however, not just by new modes of economic action stressing individual self-help but also by diverging community priorities. Given an absolute limit on food availability, county officials were sometimes forced to decide between allocating available food to hungry children, to the hungry elderly or to key workers. Coal miners, for instance, were engaged in arduous physical activity without real income other than the more or less worthless *won* and they needed food in order to be able physically to carry out the necessary work of providing coal for community and national electricity supplies. Coal miners were not recipients of international food aid, which was allocated almost entirely to children and pregnant and nursing women, and they were unlikely to have either assets to barter or contact with foreigners through which they could secure hard currency. Deciding whether to feed a hungry working coal miner or a sick elderly person, also unlikely to be in receipt of international food aid, would be a typical and common dilemma for county officials.

The government's foreign policy increasingly focused on encouraging business, trade and investment links with foreign, liberal and capitalist actors; in tandem with the effective institutionalization of a market economy, this militated against the reconstitution of the state along old lines. By 2003, the dominant model was discredited by its inability to lift most of the population out of a semi-permanent state of poverty and hunger. Alternative social practices to the state as permanent campaigning political movement, based around the individual as the unit of ethical value as opposed to the collective, were established, thus also helping to undermine the legitimacy of the previous model as the only possible state form. These social changes did not by themselves herald the introduction of liberal state forms. It was neither automatic nor "functionally necessary" for new state forms along the Weberian model to emerge out of the withering away of the old.

Rebuilding or reconstituting the state?

As long as diplomatic and economic resources could be secured from the Soviet Union and China to help maintain distributive rewards and as long as the population could continue to be mobilized around a never-ending nation-building project – always in the context of an immediate and ever-present threat of invasion or war – the incapacity of the state to carry out modern state-like functions had been masked. When the crisis of the mid-1990s arrived, there was no longer any support from abroad, the population was too hungry and exhausted to participate in collective mobilizations, and the nation-building project was visibly threadbare. The state as permanent campaigner could not deliver food or support for the basic survival of the population. The state as constituted in liberal states, where it is expected to administer welfare and justice efficiently and impartially, did not exist.

The state as permanent campaigning movement was not wholly delegitimized, although its discrediting allowed for the emergence of an alternative model of state with the possibility of the creation of independent political institutions. By definition and in practice, capitalist democracy is structurally impossible when the institutions of the state are constituted by a singular political party machinery. Intrinsic to the concept of capitalist democracy is the idea that technical or neutral institutions must exist prior to the activity of political parties, which contend over which will control or direct these institutions of the state. These neutral institutions include a functioning, technically independent bureaucracy, a professional military and an independent judiciary. The evolution of a liberal or republican state marked by a separation of powers requires the prior existence of Weberian institutions. In the DPRK, however, the inchoate possibilities for new state forms provided necessary but not sufficient conditions for capitalist democracy.

Policy options

Domestic and external actors, as agents of change, can make choices about which alternative models of the state to support and foster. Non-decision, through either ignorance or apathy, allows for the negative aspects of social change in the DPRK, such as the growth of corruption, to run rampant. As borders become more porous, this involves risks for the economic security of the whole of North East Asia.

Government options

By 2003, the government was left with at least two competing options for state rebuilding. The first was to consolidate an authoritarian military as the dominant institution in what, given the disintegration of the popular legitimacy of the old state system, would probably become an increasingly physically repressive society. This would be an inherently unstable dual society, with economic freedoms generated by liberal market-led mechanisms (of mobility, personal choice, association) conflicting with a political authoritarianism that would be driven to the Sisyphean role of attempting to prevent those new freedoms from entering the political sphere (freedoms of political association and political choice). Another option for the DPRK was to build a modern state with a semi-independent bureaucracy, separated from a judiciary and government, which would allow a range of political freedoms for individuals within specified political parameters – broadly the Chinese model. The latter model would be more likely to bring foreign investment and provide a base for transition to integration with the Republic of Korea. By 2000/2001 there were some indications that this model was gaining favour with the government.[64] However, in the aftermath of President Bush's "axis of evil" speech of January 2002 and the US and UK invasion of Iraq in March 2003, the DPRK government retrenched, and official pronouncements stressed consolidation of a military deterrent over and above economic opening.[65] The government considered the promotion of more openness to the outside world to be tantamount to providing useful intelligence to an enemy whose only interest was searching for the DPRK's vulnerabilities prior to launching a military attack.

External actor options

External actors are already involved with the DPRK, and humanitarian agencies in particular have acted and can continue to act as transmission belts for DPRK negotiators to learn about Western norms, practices and expectations. It is foreign governments, however, that are the key agents for change, either positive or negative, in the DPRK.

External actors bring change to the DPRK in a number of ways. They may make decisions to effect or support change based on an analysis of DPRK society that indicates where the pressure points lie. If external actors choose to work to encourage change in the direction of a liberal and free capitalist state, they could identify changes already taking place in the society and sustain and encourage them. An inadequate response, by contrast, would be to act on the basis of ignorance and stereotyping. To assume, for instance, that the DPRK is a monolithic actor intent on irrational, unpredictable acts and has no domestic imperatives pushing its foreign policy agenda leads only to either paralysis – the DPRK cannot be reasoned with – or aggression – the only way to deal with this mad and dangerous actor is through the use of force.[66]

Alternatively, external actors may opt for non-decision-making and non-intervention – allowing the unintended consequences of domestic socioeconomic change to end as they will. This last option risks the evolution of the DPRK as a zone of uncontrolled and unregulated criminal capitalism that would likely become controlled by a hybrid mix of corrupt state bureaucrats and criminal external actors. The internationalization of gangster-type organized crime would be inevitable because porous northern borders and an unregulated domestic economy provide enabling conditions for criminal elements to join forces with the "snakeheads" of bordering China, the Russian "mafia" fringes of nearby Vladivostok and the "yakuzas" of Japan.

External actors should adopt a strategy towards the DPRK of reinforcing the small openings to liberal social practice that are taking place (for instance, increased freedom of movement) by insisting on the incorporation of good labour practices in economic transfer agreements. Foreign governments could also provide training and funding to support the installation of liberal or Weberian-type state institutions in order to consolidate those changes. If a security deal were negotiated that removed the DPRK regime's fear of invasion, this would leave fewer excuses for domestic conservatives to oppose demobilization and would allow for the shifting of resources into civilian sectors, including economic development. The United States will have to take the lead in the security area, although a multilateral framework of negotiations will be necessary: a security agreement cannot be divorced from the economic assistance that will be needed for its own sake – to ensure human security for the majority – but also to help bring stability and freedom to the DPRK.

Given that financial assistance will come from the South Korean government and businesses (for national reasons) and, after political normalization, from Japan (as economic compensation for the colonial past), these governments should take the lead in devising acceptable principles and an appropriate format for DPRK financial transfers. External powers should agree to economic transfers, whether these be public or private, only if they are rigorously and publicly accounted for and if international standards of economic operations are demonstrably operationalized, including appropriate labour standards, health and safety guarantees, and accounting and audit procedures. This would mean project-based financial support for the DPRK as opposed to programmatic support of bilateral transfers to the DPRK government. Systematic training in conventional economic norms would have to accompany assistance. Public sector institution-building – in terms of a functioning central bank, the creation of an independent judiciary, and a competent bureaucracy in every area of state functions – would also have to be included in a package deal. Outside actors would and should not offer financial transfers to the DPRK unless they were reasonably confident that the direction of change would also bring an improved human rights regime to the DPRK. In other words, economic assistance must be accompanied by social and political change that is normatively acceptable to the global community – as signified by verifiable adherence to United Nations human rights regimes for instance.

A light multilateral framework, focused on technical tasks, could be organized on a similar basis to that of the Korean Peninsula Energy Development Organization (KEDO), which handled nuclear cooperation between the major stakeholders of the United States, South Korea, Japan and the DPRK from 1994 onwards. This would be a Korean Peninsula Economic Development Organization – based on the model inherited from KEDO and ostensibly operating primarily as a technical institution. Such a framework would allow all governments to save face. The DPRK would avoid difficult sovereignty challenges, because economic conditionality and assistance would not be directly channelled through South Korea and Japan. In much the same way that the European Coal and Steel Community acted for France vis-à-vis Germany in the early 1950s, a multilateral economic and technical institution could provide an "alibi" function for Japan and South Korea in the face of hostile public opinion, which might resent the transfer of public funds to the still distrusted neighbour, the DPRK.

Moving forward

As long as the state could reward most of its population, the Kim Il Sungist state system functioned reasonably effectively. Inherent flaws and fissures from its inception, however, meant that the chronic economic deterioration of the 1980s, combined with acute crisis in the mid-1990s, tore apart the always fragile system of state as "permanent campaigning political movement".

Since the socioeconomic transformation that began with the economic

crisis of the 1990s, the overriding rational objective of all individuals, social groups, and local and central government was physical survival. Individuals and communities were forced to fend for themselves and to
bypass the old forms of state. An unintended effect of the multitude of
disparate activities in pursuit of the objective of survival was the reconstitution of the state to allow, for the first time, the possibility of a transformation to a state model in which liberal democratic forms could become
possible. Economics was partially separated from politics, and the increasing autonomy of social groups, combined with a greater governmental willingness to permit sites of governance in non-state bodies, allowed
space for the growth of recognizably modern state-like institutions.

To a greater or lesser extent, local governments tolerated and cooper-
ated with new methods of socioeconomic interaction so as to ensure that
local populations could find the means to survive. Central party and governmental organizations at first vacillated, then condoned, then tried to
direct the new socioeconomic landscape created through self-help responses. At the same time, these organizations strengthened the role of
the military as a defence against regime instability.

External actors helped to shape the nature and direction of state reconstitution in the DPRK, often inadvertently. They possessed and continue to possess influence irrespective of their self-consciousness of the
ramifications of their activities. This reconstituted socioeconomic landscape provided opportunities for "intelligent intervention" by external
actors – to prevent the growth of the more negative aspects of social
change and to support the development of more positive change – such
as the creation of a state machinery and institutions that embody liberal
political values and help to safeguard citizens' rights rather than subordi-
nating them.

Increased freedom and economic prosperity have not arrived in the
DPRK as a result of socioeconomic reconstitution and changes to the
state form, but the unanticipated effect of crisis has provided the enabling
conditions for change to a liberal democratic state in the DPRK. The
process of state reconstitution is by no means complete and the possibilities for different outcomes are open-ended. The government and external actors could – consciously or otherwise – maintain policies that have
so far failed poor and hungry North Koreans. Alternatively, the government, whose prime responsibility it is to respond to the needs of citizens,
and external actors could choose policies that would reconstitute the
state to provide citizens with the foundations on which could be built economic development and political freedom. External actors also have responsibilities, and those that are not self-reflective about policy choices
run large risks of supporting the reconstitution of the state in the DPRK
in a direction that they might not anticipate or desire.

Making the DPRK work

The DPRK, unlike other states discussed in the present volume, is situated in a relatively stable region. It does not suffer to any significant degree from any of the frailties that the editors of this volume identify as characterizing potentially failing states – ethnic divisions, unequal distribution of resources, civil–military tensions, the proliferation of small arms. Neither does it suffer from the fragmented authority structure that Thomas G. Weiss and Peter J. Hoffman argue is characteristic of some problem states.[67] As the editors have noted in the Introduction, "states cannot be made to work from the outside". Given this premise, it is vital that international actors adopt strategies that are tailored to the realities of DPRK state and society. It is not enough to point to the failings of the DPRK – that is the easy part. The real challenge is to derive nuanced policies that have a chance of success.

In the end, the nature of state reconstitution matters only if the new state form can better address the needs, hopes and ambitions of the people who live within the state's territory. For children growing up in the DPRK today, who have known nothing but hunger as the most salient feature of their personal, social and economic landscape, such reconstitution could help to provide a framework for the provision of stable and reliable improvements to their conditions of life. Given the failure of old forms and the fragility of the new, there is an ethical imperative to make sure the new state "works" in the DPRK.

Notes

1. This chapter will use "DPRK" in preference to "North Korea" out of deference to the DPRK's own terminology. For discussion of the conventional interpretations, see Hazel Smith, "Bad, Mad, Sad or Rational Actor? Why the 'Securitization' Paradigm Makes for Poor Policy Analysis of North Korea", *International Affairs*, Vol. 76, No. 3, 2000.
2. See chapter 1 in the present volume.
3. Fred Halliday, "State and Society in International Relations", in Fred Halliday, ed., *Rethinking International Relations*, London: Macmillan, 1994, p. 79.
4. This chapter does not seek to offer a conceptual disquisition on Max Weber's understanding of modern political organization and how that framework might be used to interrogate the empirical data available on the DPRK. It does, however, employ Weberian insights to frame the argument and organize the available material. Weber provides a potentially rich source for excavating social and political change in the DPRK. See, particularly, Max Weber, *Economy and Society*, New York: Bedminster Press, 1968, Vols 1–3.
5. For a highly pro-Japanese view of the development of the port towns, see Bank of Chosen, *Economic History of Chosen*, Seoul: Bank of Chosen, 1920, pp. 98–112. A description of northern Korea, from the Daedong river (which runs through Pyongyang) up to the Yalu, which straddles the China/Korea border, and which constitutes a large part of

present-day DPRK, is of "a stretch of country in part uninhabited ... frequented by bands of Korean robbers and Chinese bandits". See, further, Angus Hamilton, *Korea*, London: Heinemann, 1904, p. 187.

6. For a North Korean analysis, see Sok Chang-sik, "Experiences of State-Building in the Democratic People's Republic of Korea", in Ken'ichiro Hirano, ed., *The State and Cultural Transformation: Perspectives from East Asia*, Tokyo: United Nations University Press, 1993, pp. 328–343.

7. Weber argues that what is distinctive about the modern state is its combination of a limitation of powers and a separation of powers as a method of "distribution of competence among its various organs". See Weber, *Economy and Society*, Vol. 2, p. 652.

8. The military in the Soviet Union normally stayed out of domestic politics and subordinated itself in policy terms to the party. The military and the party could be at odds with each other because they were organizationally and normatively separate institutions – as was most dramatically shown in the attempted military coup against President Gorbachev in August 1991. See Malcolm Mackintosh, "The New Russian Revolution: The Military Dimension", in Max Beloff, ed., *Beyond the Soviet Union: The Fragmentation of Power*, Aldershot: Ashgate, 1997, pp. 87–104.

9. For discussion of how the local government evolved also as local administration, see Sok Chang-sik, "Experiences of State-Building", pp. 334–335.

10. The DPRK blamed the collapse of communism in the former Soviet Union on the "non-politicization of the[ir] army". See "Ever Victorious Sword-High Priority Army Politics", *Korea Today*, 12 December 1999, *Juche* 88, p. 2.

11. For numbers, see the very useful annual *The Military Balance*, a publication of the International Institute of Strategic Studies (IISS). See, for example, IISS, *The Military Balance 2001–2002*, London: Oxford University Press, 2001, pp. 196–197.

12. For detail of military organization, see ibid., p. 196.

13. The information in this paragraph comes from direct observation through visiting the DPRK over 13 years but most specifically from working with North Koreans in the DPRK for 18 months between 1998 and 2001. It is also the product of indirect observation from hundreds of conversations with other international residents in the DPRK and with North Koreans throughout the country.

14. This was an explicit policy. See Sok Chang-sik, "Experiences of State-Building", p. 340.

15. Adrian Buzo's account of the development of the Kim Il Sung dynasty stresses the formative impact of the guerrilla heritage on methods of political operation. My argument is not that this is not correct – it is – but that what is important is how this process happened. This heritage, in other words, is constitutive of state and societal patterns of organization in very specific and historically constituted institutional ways. These specific institutional forms can be deconstructed, analytically and practically, that is, changed through political and social activity. See Adrian Buzo, *The Guerrilla Dynasty: Politics and Leadership in North Korea*, Boulder, CO: Westview Press, 1999.

16. For detail on the philosophy and practical implementation of a fusion of bureaucracy and party interest, see Sok Chang-sik, "Experiences of State-Building".

17. "Theses on Education", in Foreign Languages Publishing House, *Korea Guidebook*, Pyongyang: Foreign Languages Publishing House, 1989, pp. 80–81.

18. Weber, *Economy and Society*, Vol. 3, p. 956.

19. Sok Chang-sik, "Experiences of State-Building", p. 341.

20. A useful description of the work points allocation system for food distribution is found in Lola Nathanail, *Food and Nutrition Assessment of the DPRK*, Rome: World Food Programme, 1996.

21. The evidence suggests the converse, which is that, even in times of chronic food shortage and a policy move by the government to the market, as in 2002, the mechanisms

stayed in place such that a basic minimum of food reached the entire society. The nutrition survey of 2002, organized and audited by the international humanitarian community, demonstrates for instance that there was no statistically significant difference between the nutritional status of urban children and that of rural children, a strong indication of efforts to distribute basic rations to all social sectors. See Central Bureau of Statistics DPRK, "Report on the DPRK Nutrition Assessment, 2002", mimeo, Pyongyang, 20 November 2002, *Juche* 91.

22. Until 1996, when farmers' markets were given some latitude to buy and sell outside the state plan, private or farmers' markets existed but under such tight restraints that they could not provide a significant volume of extra commodities for consumption and distribution, and the rules governing selling and buying were not significantly different from state distribution in that prices, although higher than at public distribution outlets, were controlled. See Hy-Sang Lee, *North Korea: A Strange Socialist Fortress*, London: Praeger, 2001, pp. 208–211.

23. I develop the idea of the human security trade-off in the DPRK as the basis for state-building in the DPRK and the eventual disintegration of the trade-off after the economic and food crises of the 1990s in Hazel Smith, *Hungry for Peace: International Security, Humanitarian Assistance, and Social Change in North Korea*, Washington, DC: United States Institute of Peace Press, forthcoming.

24. The 27 rooms of the "Hall for the Period of the Anti-Japanese Revolutionary Struggle display relics and materials which are associated with President Kim Il Sung's revolutionary family, his early revolutionary activity and the brilliant history of the anti-Japanese armed struggle" (Editing Committee of the Album of the Korean Revolution Museum, *The Korean Revolution Museum*, Tokyo: Miraisha, 1975, Vol. 2, p. 4). The elaborate Revolutionary Martyrs' Cemetery on Mount Taesong in Pyongyang is dedicated to 100 leaders of the anti-Japanese struggle and is a national monument that Koreans from all over the DPRK visit to pay their respects. See *Pyongyang Review*, Pyongyang: Foreign Languages Publishing House, 1995, pp. 71–72. Few newspapers or magazines are without the obligatory reference to the past crimes of the Japanese. See, for example, "The Japanese Government Must Apologize for Their Past Crimes of Sexual Slavery and Make State Compensation", *Korea Today*, Vol. 12, December 1999, *Juche* 88, pp. 47–48; "President Kim Il Sung's Eternal Country", *Korea Today*, Vol. 9, September 2001, *Juche* 90, p. 10.

25. Weber, *Economy and Society*, Vol. 1, p. 31.

26. Even in 1999, after a limited opening to the West had taken place, a DPRK official representation to a United Nations Human Rights Committee could state: "The state does not tolerate the expression of ideas that severely infringe upon the honour and dignity of others or state security and public order" (*Second Periodic Report of the Democratic People's Republic of Korea on Its Implementation of the International Covenant on Civil and Political Rights*, 25 December 1999, reproduced in International Covenant on Civil and Political Rights, Human Rights Committee, CCPR/C/PRK/2000/2, mimeo, 4 May 2000, p. 31).

27. In a sense, all economic activity in a planned economy possesses ontological irrationality, because it is not determined by cost–benefit, market-driven imperatives. Economic irrationality does not, however, necessarily imply bureaucratic irrationality, which is the point I develop here. On planned economies, see Weber, *Economy and Society*, Vol. 1, pp. 110–111.

28. In the DPRK it is common to see men and women sleeping in the middle of the day (on tables, in vehicles) because they have been engaged all night in extracurricular physically intensive activities such as building roads, civil defence or party festivities. It is also not uncommon to see collective groups of workers engaged in work-based activ-

ities where the tasks are spread out over long periods of time because there are no economic imperatives encouraging workers to complete work efficiently or speedily.

29. For the DPRK account of economic growth, see Hong Song Un, *Economic Development in the Democratic People's Republic of Korea*, Pyongyang: Foreign Languages Publishing House, 1990. For a detailed account of growth but from a normatively and epistemologically critical perspective, see Hy-Sang Lee, *North Korea*.

30. Foreign Languages Publishing House, *Korea Guidebook*, p. 138.

31. For Chinese assistance, see Robert Scalapino, "China and Korean Reunification – A Neighbour's Concerns", in Nicholas Eberstadt and Richard J. Ellings, eds, *Korea's Future and the Great Powers*, Seattle: University of Washington Press, 2001, pp. 107–124. For Russian perspectives on Russian relations with the DPRK, see the excellent compilation by James Clay Moltz and Alexandre Y. Mansourov, eds, *The North Korean Nuclear Program: Security, Strategy, and New Perspectives from Russia*, New York: Routledge, 2000.

32. Evgeniy P. Bazhanov, "Russian Views of the Agreed Framework and the Four-Party Talks", in Moltz and Mansourov, *North Korean Nuclear Program*, p. 219.

33. "North Korea: External Trade" on the Links2 website, available at ⟨http://www.link2exports.co.uk/regions.asp?lsid=1968&pid=1281⟩.

34. For information on flood damage, see UN Development Programme and DPRK government, "Documents Prepared for the Thematic Roundtable Meeting on Agricultural Recovery and Environmental Protection", mimeo, Pyongyang, May 1998. On the destruction of grain reserves, see Ken Quinones, "The American NGO Experience in North Korea", mimeo sent to author, 12 March 2002. The Food and Agriculture Organization (FAO) and the World Food Programme (WFP) had reported, however, that grain stocks were already depleted by 1995 so that they were at a "negligible" level. See FAO/WFP, "Special Report: Crop and Food Supply Assessment Mission to the Democratic People's Republic of Korea", mimeo, 22 December 1995, p. 4.

35. World Food Programme, "Emergency Operation DPR Korea No. 5710.00: Emergency Food Assistance for Flood Victims", in WFP, *WFP Operations in DPR Korea as of 14 July 1999*, Rome: WFP, undated (but 1999).

36. There has been a great deal of spurious speculation about the death toll from the famine in the DPRK. An exception is the rigorous analysis by Suk Lee, "Food Shortages and Economic Institutions in the Democratic People's Republic of Korea", unpublished doctoral thesis, Department of Economics, University of Warwick, January 2003.

37. Trade with China as a coping mechanism is reported in FAO/WFP, "Crop and Food Supply Assessment, Special Alert, No. 267", mimeo, 16 May 1996. Coping mechanisms are discussed in detail in FAO/WFP, "Crop and Food Supply Assessment", mimeo, 6 December 1996, p. 10.

38. W. Courtland Robinson, Myung Ken Lee, Kenneth Hill and Gilbert M. Burnham, "Mortality in North Korean Migrant Households: A Retrospective Study", *The Lancet*, Vol. 354, No. 9175, 24 July 1999.

39. On the innovative coping strategies of households, see FAO/WFP, "Special Report: Crop and Food Supply Assessment", 12 November 1998, p. 16.

40. The discussion on dollarization in this paragraph is from Hazel Smith, "La Corée du Nord vers l'économie de marché: Faux et vrais dilemmas", *Critique Internationale*, No. 15, Paris, April 2002.

41. I interviewed dozens, maybe hundreds, of public service officials including doctors, teachers, nursery and orphanage care staff, food administrators, public health officials, and water engineers throughout the country between 1998 and 2001. Most of them were visibly undernourished and continued to work without real wages and with only intermittent access to basic food supplies. Without exception, discussion would focus on the difficulties facing the people they were serving, not their own difficulties.

42. For a comment on recovery in the farming sector, see FAO/WFP, "Crop and Food Supply Assessment", 25 June 1998, p. 7.
43. FAO/WFP, "Crop and Food Supply Assessment, Special Alert, No. 275", mimeo, 3 June 1997, p. 4.
44. FAO/WFP, "Special Report: Crop and Food Supply Assessment", 29 June 1999, p. 10.
45. FAO/WFP, "Crop and Food Supply Assessment", 6 December 1996, p. 10.
46. Hazel Smith, *WFP DPRK Programmes and Activities: A Gender Perspective*, Pyongyang: WFP, December 1999.
47. The DPRK government, in reporting on its progress on implementing its commitments under the International Convention on the Rights of the Child, which it ratified in 1991, noted that the economic crisis of the 1990s had, among other things, compromised the quality of education because of "irregularities in provision of textbooks and other educational and learning materials" (Democratic People's Republic of Korea, "National Report", written for the 5th Ministerial Consultation for the East Asia and Pacific Region, mimeo, May 2000). Damage to schools and educational institutions was outlined in National EFA 2000 Assessment Group Democratic People's Republic of Korea, "National Assessment Report: The Implementation of the 'World Declaration on Education for All' ", mimeo, September 1999, *Juche* 88, pp. 33–34.
48. For DPRK official comment on the "arduous march" and the "forced march", see "Editor's Note" in Kim Sung Un et al., *Panorama of Korea*, Pyongyang: Foreign Languages Publishing House, 1999.
49. Reports of the Onsong riot are in "Chinese Influence on the Rise in Pyongyang", 5 November 1999, *Stratfor.com Global Intelligence Update*, available at ⟨http://www2.gol.com/users/coynerhm/chinese_influence_on_pyongyang.htm⟩; *NAPSNet Daily Report*, 2 November 1999, available at ⟨http://www.nautilus.org/napsnet/dr/9911/NOV02.html#item7⟩; Bradley Martin, "The Koreas: Pyongyang Watch: The Riot Act?", 3 November 1999, available at ⟨http://www.atimes.com/koreas/AK03Dg01.html⟩.
50. A full discussion of the development of food production at county and provincial level and attempts at local food self-sufficiency is in Hy-Sang Lee, *North Korea*.
51. On methods of "socialist" construction, see Hy-Sang Lee, *North Korea*. On the grain deficit, see FAO/WFP, "Special Report", 22 December 1995.
52. I discuss early contact with international humanitarian agencies in Hazel Smith, " 'Opening up' by Default: North Korea, the Humanitarian Community and the Crisis", *Pacific Review*, Vol. 12, No. 3, 1999.
53. An official DPRK publication notes that "the mission of the chairman of the National Defence Commission is the highest official duty of the state ... [It] constitutes a sacred official duty symbolic and representative of the glory of the motherland and the nation's dignity" (Kim Sung Un et al., *Panorama of Korea*, p. 52).
54. FAO/WFP, "Special Report", 12 November 1998, p. 10.
55. See, for example, Hazel Smith, *CARITAS Five-Year Evaluation of Programmes and Projects in the DPRK*, Hong Kong: CARITAS-Hong Kong, 2001.
56. Central Bureau of Statistics, DPRK, "Report on the DPRK Nutrition Assessment, 2002", mimeo, Pyongyang, 20 November 2002, *Juche* 91.
57. *CNS DPRK Report No. 15*, November–December 1998, available at ⟨http://cns.miis.edu/pubs/dprkrprt/98novdec.htm⟩.
58. *NAPSNet Daily Report*, 23 July 2002, available at ⟨http://www.nautilus.org/napsnet/dr/0207/JUL23.html#item9⟩.
59. Hazel Smith, "North Korean Foreign Policy in the 1990s: The Realist Approach", in Hazel Smith et al., eds, *North Korea in the New World Order*, London and New York: Macmillan and St. Martin's Press, 1996.
60. Numbers of counties from "World Food Programme in DPR Korea as at 31 December 2002", map, mimeo, 2002.

61. The discussion in this paragraph is from Smith, "La Corée du Nord".
62. Weber argues that "the development of the *money economy* is a presupposition of a modern bureaucracy" (Weber, *Economy and Society*, Vol. 3, p. 963; emphasis in original).
63. FAO/WFP, "Crop and Food Supply Assessment", 25 June 1998, p. 2.
64. Kim Jong Il even spoke highly of the more extensive Russian reforms on a visit to the country in 2001. See *Online Pravda*, 4 August 2001, available at ⟨http://english.pravda.ru/diplomatic/2001/08/04/11769.html⟩.
65. The 2003 state budget reflected these priorities, with 14.9 per cent allocated to military spending. See "Report of Finance Minister on State Budget for 2003", *People's Korea*, available at ⟨http://www.korea-np.co.jp/pk/190th_issue/2002032907.htm⟩.
66. For detailed discussion on how external actors conceptualize the DPRK, see Smith, "Bad, Mad, Sad or Rational Actor?"
67. See chapter 14 in the present volume.

9

Afghanistan's weak state and strong society

Amin Saikal

Despite all the changes in and around Afghanistan since the country's foundation as an identifiable political unit over two and a half centuries ago, and since the late 1970s in particular, Afghanistan has persistently highlighted the difficulties confronting a weak state in dynamic relationship with a strong society. With the exception of two short periods when the Afghan state exercised a noticeable degree of regulatory and distributive capacity, power and politics in Afghanistan have by and large been personalized rather than institutionalized. The authority of successive central governments has remained weak in comparison with the strength of micro-societies, which have functioned more or less as autonomous enclaves shaped by ethnic, tribal, sectarian and linguistic allegiances and the role of dominant personalities. Although the upheavals of the past 24 years affected these micro-societies and rendered Afghanistan a severely disrupted state, they do not appear to have deformed the micro-societies to the extent that would permit a strong post-Taliban state to emerge easily.

The challenge ahead for post-Taliban governments, the United Nations and the international community is to influence the kind of state Afghanistan should be. Should it be a centralized unitary state or a relatively decentralized state, with strong national institutions and sufficient resources to regulate micro-societies' activities in relation to themselves and the central government and to prevent their cross-border ties from making Afghanistan vulnerable to outside interference and intervention?

193

This chapter explains the fundamental factors underlying the crisis of the Afghan state for most of its life. It also examines the attempts of the Karzai government and its international backers, the United Nations and the United States in particular, to map out a new state for Afghanistan. Finally it outlines some of the dynamic issues that could underpin the viability and stability of an Afghan state. The chapter contends that, unless Afghanistan is transformed into a multi-level state where dynamic interactive relationships are established between the central authority and micro-societies, and among the latter through appropriate, institutionalized processes of political, economic, social and security reconstruction, Afghanistan is likely to remain in the wilderness for years to come. There is even the risk of the country's reverting to the darkness of the pre-Karzai administration era.

The historical context

The Afghan state has been in a condition of crisis for most of its life, since the country's emergence as an identifiable political unit from 1747. It has gone through so many internal political and social upheavals, foreign interventions and invasions that it has largely existed as a seriously fractured or disrupted political entity.[1] For the bulk of the nineteenth century, it functioned as little more than a cluster of divided principalities, with Kabul, Kandahar and Herat serving at times as capitals of rival power groups. After the initial phase of its consolidation in the second half of the eighteenth century, the only other periods when Afghanistan enjoyed political and territorial coalescence and stability, with a central government in Kabul capable of exercising influence over other power centres in the country, were from the 1880s to the early 1920s and from 1930 to 1978. The first period was marked by the British-backed autocratic rule of Amir Abdul Rahman Khan (1881–1901) and his son Habibullah Khan (1901–1918). The former applied violence and "internal imperialism" as a policy means to build national unity and a functioning system of national governance and administration.[2] The latter, as a somewhat enlightened nationalist, autocratic ruler, relied on his father's power consolidation to introduce a number of liberal social and educational reforms and to open up Afghanistan for wider interactions with the outside world. This was followed by a phase of independence from Britain and of intense modernization under Habibullah's reformist nationalist son, Amir Amanullah Khan (1919–1929). Yet it was this phase that also generated a serious micro-society-based backlash, prompting many conservative ethnic, tribal and religious opponents of Amanullah's reform to revolt.[3] Amanullah's decision to flee to Italy opened the way, following less than a year of rule by a rebel leader, Habibullah Kalakani, for the longest period of political stability in modern Afghan history under the Musahiban dynasty (1930–1978).

The Musahiban dynasty was headed by General Mohammed Nadir – a brother-in-law and former defence minister under Amanullah. Ending a self-imposed exile in France, Nadir led a revolt and secured the throne for himself and his three brothers with help from south-eastern Pashtuns (the largest, though tribally divided, single ethnic group in Afghanistan) and British India. Nadir and his brothers formed the Musahiban family. Although Nadir Shah was assassinated in 1933, he was succeeded by his son Mohammed Zahir Shah, who ruled first at the behest of his uncles, Mohammed Hashim Khan and Shah Mahmoud Khan, and subsequently under the influence of his rival cousin, Mohammed Daoud, until 1963 when he was finally able to govern in his own right. In July 1973 he was overthrown while in Italy by Mohammed Daoud.

Daoud declared Afghanistan a republic, but was in turn overthrown and killed in a violent coup in April 1978 by a pro-Soviet communist clique, exposing Afghanistan to a period of bloody internal conflict, foreign invasion and ideological extremism. During this phase, lasting until late 2001, the communists failed to consolidate power, despite the Soviet occupation of Afghanistan in the 1980s. Similarly, the US-backed Islamic resistance groups (the mujahidin), who took over the reins of power in April 1992, could not unite and govern Afghanistan effectively. Afghanistan became vulnerable to a "creeping invasion" by neighbouring Pakistan and takeover of most of the country by the Pakistan-backed medievalist Islamic Taliban and their Arab allies, Osama bin Laden and his al Qaeda network.[4] Al Qaeda's terrorist attacks on New York and Washington, DC, on 11 September 2001 prompted the United States to launch a counter-terrorist military campaign, dismantling the Taliban–al Qaeda rule and replacing it with an internationally backed administration led by US-linked former mujahidin and anti-Taliban Pashtun figure Hamid Karzai. The Afghans are now once again challenged, though this time with an unprecedented amount of assistance from the international community, to achieve national unity and rebuild their country, with a new lasting political order.

Crisis factors

Numerous factors have contributed to the crisis of the Afghan state. Some have been internal and others external in nature, but the interaction between the two and the Afghans' approach in managing these dynamics have repeatedly held the Afghans back from building a viable, coherent and peaceful state.

The mosaic nature of Afghan society is one of these factors. Afghanistan has traditionally been composed of numerous micro-societies or associations of individual and group actors, within which key relations between actors are defined by certain shared norms and the behaviour of actors is to a degree patterned and predictable. Since different norms may be shared to different extents, a geographical unit may simultaneously embrace an emerging "common society" (marked by the increasing acceptance of certain key norms) and many "micro-societies" (defined by the persistence of norms particular to the "micro-society" under discussion). This reflects the fact that an individual lives in not one but *many* worlds, and survives most easily when circumstances do not cause the demands of these different worlds to conflict.[5]

The Afghan micro-societies have historically been delineated along tribal, ethnic, linguistic and sectarian lines, coalescing around influential leaders claiming religious powers or capable of dispensing material and security benefits, generally on a patrimonial basis. The whole process of state-building and state-functioning in Afghanistan has been heavily influenced by the ability of national leaders to create a coherent central core and to forge a coalition of these micro-societies with dynamic relationships among themselves and with the central core. This has been critical in determining the authority, power and legitimacy of central governments. The more relations between the core and the micro-societies and among the latter have been interactive and cooperative, the greater the chances of creating a stable political order in the country. This was the case during the leadership of Ahmed Shah Durani (1747–1773): although a coalition of Pashtun tribes formed the original core under Ahmed Shah's charismatic and militarist leadership, it was Ahmed Shah's ability in generating interaction between this core and micro-societies, together with military expeditions that kept many elements of the core preoccupied, that allowed the Afghan state to evolve. The process was consolidated during the 20-year rule of his son Timour Shah, but could not last much beyond that.

Chief among the reasons for its discontinuity was the fact that the process was inherently disintegrative. It depended too much on personalized politics and charismatic leadership, and lacked the necessary degree of legal-rational norms and practices, participatory mechanisms and inner elasticity to enable it to absorb external shocks, which were caused not only by irregularities in the behaviour of the micro-societies but also by the rising tide of Anglo-Russian imperial rivalry in the region. Another variable that was, and still is to some extent, pertinent to the politics of

Afghanistan and a number of other Muslim countries concerned the practice of royal polygamy and foreign intervention. Under Islamic law, Muslim males are allowed to take four wives (provided that they can provide equally for all four and that the first wife consents to the taking of the second wife, and so on), and Islam does not prohibit concubinage. As a result, until the rule of Amanullah Khan, virtually all Afghan rulers took more than one wife and many concubines – for reasons ranging from power relationships to self-satisfaction. However, the male children of the concubines had the same rights to the throne as the children of legal wives. A ruler's designation of someone other than the eldest son from the first wife as heir led many times to inter-dynastic power struggle and armed clashes, plunging Afghanistan into a perpetual state of warfare for most of the nineteenth century.[6]

This not only undermined the process of building the necessary domestic structures and mechanisms for national unity and a participatory political order, but also exposed Afghanistan to the rivalry of the major powers of the time, Britain and Russia. As various contenders for the throne allied themselves with the rival powers as a source of security, the two powers welcomed the opportunity to exploit this in support of their respective interests. The result was an intense interplay between domestic and exogenous factors determining the shape and functions of the Afghan state and its place in world affairs.

The only times when the Afghans achieved a breathing space (albeit in spasmodic fashion) were during the rule of Abdul Rahman Khan and his son Habibullah Khan, but that was largely because the British had achieved what they wanted: control of Afghanistan's foreign affairs and finances and the two Afghan rulers' pandering to British India. Yet this situation unravelled with Amanullah's brand of radical nationalism in pursuit of Afghanistan's full independence and speedy Western-style modernization. Amanullah's goal of independence antagonized the British, prompting him to look, though in many cases reluctantly, to the Soviets for support. Moreover, his process of modernization of a traditionally Islamic and socially divided society inevitably generated serious backlashes, which were partly fuelled by the British to contain the spillover effect of Amanullah's radical nationalism on British India.

The overthrow of Amanullah's monarchy and its replacement with Nadir Shah's dynastic rule coincided with a lull in the traditional Anglo-Russian rivalry. The Soviet Union became too preoccupied with Stalin's processes of consolidation of his dictatorship, and the British found themselves impaired by the Great Depression and rising nationalist movements in their Indian and Middle Eastern colonies. This, together with the ability of Nadir Shah and his successor to maintain good relations with the British while at the same time assuring the Russians that they would not give policy favours to British, helped the Afghans to restart a process of state-building. The rule of Nadir Shah, his son Mohammed Zahir Shah and his nephew Mohammed Daoud brought the longest and most sustained period of consolidation of the Afghan state, with functioning governmental structures. The stability of this period was underlined by an alliance between the monarchy, the religious establishment and powerful figures of various micro-societies. The process of change and development was by and large marked by authoritarianism, conservatism and gradualism.

It was accelerated only when Daoud became prime minister in 1953 and found the international climate of the Cold War conducive to achieving what Amanullah had failed to accomplish. Despite his aversion to Marxism–Leninism per se, but in light of Washington's lack of strategic interest in Afghanistan at the time, Daoud rapidly became dependent on the Soviet Union for military and economic aid – to modernize, on the one hand, and to overcome micro-society-based domestic challenges and a simmering border dispute with Pakistan, on the other.[7] By now, Pakistan, together with Afghanistan's western neighbour, Iran, had drifted into the US orbit.

This had two consequences. The first was that, although Washington was jolted to counter the Soviet influence by providing some economic assistance, Afghanistan became a *rentier* state. Another was that many in the Afghan ruling elite eventually felt that a degree of symmetry needed to be injected into Afghan–Soviet relations through certain domestic and foreign policy changes. After Daoud's resignation in 1963 over complications in relations with Pakistan, his successors under King Zahir Shah embarked on a process of "quasi-democratization". Yet the process soon proved to be not only ill defined and culturally provocative, but also unacceptable to Daoud, because it was aimed in part at denying him the opportunity to make a political comeback. With the help of pro-Soviet elements in the armed forces, he seized power in 1973 through a palace coup and declared Afghanistan a republic.

The central government under Zahir Shah and then Daoud certainly succeeded in expanding its writ beyond the major centres of population through traditional processes of coercion, co-optation, patronage building, foreign aid and the provision of basic services. But Daoud was not a democrat; he was essentially an autocratic nationalist modernizer, with a leaning towards a socialist mode of development. He failed to promote pluralist participation through either integrative or federative mechanisms, or to pursue foreign policy objectives and priorities that would reduce his vulnerability to the Soviets and their Afghan allies without antagonizing them. His overthrow by a pro-Soviet communist clique, followed by the Soviet invasion of Afghanistan, led to extensive political, economic and social fracturing of the Afghan state.[8]

The conflict that ensued was marked by a proxy war between the Soviet Union and the United States. The Soviets finally withdrew from Afghanistan in defeat in 1989, but the United States failed to play an effective role in the management of post-communist Afghanistan, making the country vulnerable to regional actors. Pakistan emerged as the main interventionist, given its extensive cross-border ethnic Pashtun ties, its alliance with the United States during the Soviet occupation and its regional ambitions. Pakistan's support of, at first, the destructive mujahidin leader Gulbuddin Hikmatyar, and then the Taliban and an alliance between this militia and the al Qaeda terrorist network, which brought the Taliban money and Arab fighters as a mechanism of control in Afghanistan, triggered unanticipated disasters. Washington's initial silence on these developments contributed to this.[9]

As Afghanistan was rapidly transformed into a hub for religious and political extremism and international terrorism, the anti-Taliban United Front resistance (the so-called Northern Alliance), composed of mainly non-Pashtun groups and led by Commander Ahmed Shah Massoud, found itself increasingly isolated. The United States treated the United Front as yet another Afghan faction, unworthy of American support. Only the al Qaeda attacks on New York and Washington finally drove the United States to act, by declaring war on terror and launching a military campaign, with widespread international support, in Afghanistan. The aim was to bomb the Taliban out of power, to dismantle the al Qaeda network and to punish its leaders and operatives; at the same time, the operation would end Pakistan's "creeping invasion" and replace the Taliban with an internationally acceptable Afghan government.[10] US President George W. Bush undertook this with a pledge to remain engaged in Afghanistan – doing "nation-building" – for as long as necessary to secure, stabilize, democratize and reconstruct Afghanistan.

The long years of conflict had two main consequences for Afghanistan. One was the unravelling of the power structure, the national framework, and the interactive relationships between central authority and micro-societies that the Nadiri regime had built since the early 1930s. Another was the fragmentation of power and the emergence of various local power holders and their disintegrative manipulation of micro-societies for their personal purposes. In the process, of course, the boundaries of the micro-societies and the inner dynamics of each micro-society in terms of patterns of leadership, power, authority and loyalty had changed. However, what did not seriously alter were the ethnic, tribal, linguistic and sectarian composition and traditional values and practices which underpinned people's affiliation within each micro-society and across micro-societies.

It was no longer the traditional tribal, religious and ethnic leaders around whom the micro-societies revolved, but rather a new breed of leaders, in the form of armed commanders or local hegemons – what have commonly become known as "warlords". Although wearing the mantle of the traditional leaders, the new breed acted as security providers, with distributive and patronage powers. The US military campaign enabled the United Front – despite Massoud's assassination by al Qaeda agents two days before 11 September 2001 – to liberate northern, central and western Afghan provinces and to confine the remnants of the Taliban and al Qaeda in the south. It also opened up the space for various leaders and micro-societies to become reassertive in post-Taliban Afghanistan. This development was further reinforced when, in the absence of a credible and powerful central authority, the United States found it expedient to support some of the old and new hegemons with money and arms in order to achieve its goals.

The reconstruction of the Afghan state

The immediate challenge confronting Afghanistan was to decide what kind of new state it should reconstruct out of the ashes of the old one and how to achieve this objective, with an eye to three important issues. One was to keep in mind that the Afghan traditions and practices of political legitimation, and therefore the processes by which it would be generated, needed to be culturally relevant. Another was to help realign the diverse micro-societies and their multiple leaders, with competing ethnic-tribal and sectarian interests and claims on power, into a new durable national framework. The third was to address the demands of the international community in terms of transforming Afghanistan from a theocratic state and a nest for international terrorism into a democratic state with a broad-based and internationally acceptable government. In this respect, two players emerged as critical. The first was the United Nations, which had been involved in Afghanistan in various conflict resolution and peace-making roles since the early 1980s and was now entrusted with the task of playing a "central role" in helping the Afghan people to establish a transitional administration for the formation of a new legitimate government. The UN role came to be personified by Lakhdar Brahimi, who was appointed as the Secretary-General's Special Representative for Afghanistan in October 2001 to supervise Afghanistan's transformation. The second was the United States, which was now the main security provider and without whose support the United Nations could do little, but which had its own geopolitical expectations focused on the vindication of its war on terror in Afghanistan and beyond.

To address and reconcile these conflicting imperatives, Brahimi found it appropriate to work for a transformation of Afghanistan that would aim at creating a lasting, stable political order, based on an interactive relationship between the political, economic and security dimensions of Afghanistan's reconstruction. Given the urgency to fill the power vacuum created by the fall of the Taliban and the need of the United States and its coalition partners to avoid being seen as occupying forces, Brahimi opted for a process that would commence with an elite settlement (which enjoys a historical tradition in Afghanistan) and end with a general election (an unfamiliar process in Afghanistan but necessary to satisfy the demands of the international community) within a three-year timeline.

The Bonn Conference that Brahimi convened in late November to early December 2001, with the support of the United States and other major powers, Afghanistan's neighbours and the European Union, was more of an exercise in ethnically and politically driven elite power-sharing than in popular legitimation. It brought together the representatives of only four groups: the militarily powerful United Front, the politically desirable "Rome group" of ex-King Zahir Shah, and two other smaller clusters with strong Pashtun representation – "the Cyprus group" and "the Peshawar group". With considerable arm-twisting on the part of the United Nations and the United States, the conference produced the Bonn Agreement of 5 December 2001 as a means to set in motion Afghanistan's process of transformation.[11] The Agreement basically prescribed a set of processes and mechanisms whereby a legitimate political order could be created in several stages. It prescribed the immediate establishment of an Interim Administration, one of whose main functions would be to convene within six months an emergency Loya Jirga (the traditional Afghan tribal Grand Council) to legitimize the creation of a Transitional Administration, which would in turn pave the way for a regularly elected, democratic government by mid-2004.

The Bonn participants endorsed a commitment to the principles of constitutionalism, institution-building, an independent judiciary, observation of human rights and democratization, as well as the right of the United Nations to have a "central role" and the presence of foreign forces to operate in support of Afghanistan's transition. They also agreed on Hamid Karzai – a Pashtun who was little known inside Afghanistan – as a compromise choice to head the Interim Administration and on a list of factional figures to fill cabinet positions. As such, the Bonn Agreement underlined the importance of both the Afghan traditional mechanisms of legitimation, for instance the Loya Jirga, as well as Western-type processes and tools of democratization.

As for the questions of what kind of state Afghanistan should be and what form of government it should have, the Bonn Agreement remained largely silent. It made no mention of the nature of a future central authority or how micro-societies should be brought back in relation to one another and to the central authority within a nationally acceptable framework. Such details were understandably left to be worked out in the course of transition, although the underlying contention on the part of most of the Afghan delegates seemed to be that Afghanistan needed a strong state with a unitary system of governance, which the Afghans had historically recognized as imperative even if they had not been very successful at achieving it.

The first two stages prescribed by the Bonn Agreements have been implemented, with less political turmoil than might have been expected. Despite some disquiet about the disproportionate weight given to the United Front, especially the native Panjshiri followers of the late Massoud, Karzai's Interim Administration took up office on 22 December 2001, with the full endorsement of the international community and with security provided by the forces of the United States and its coalition partners. Those local power holders who showed reluctance to attend the swearing-in ceremony were cajoled by the United States and United Nations to acquiesce. A 5,000 strong International Security Assistance Force (ISAF), including a substantial NATO component, was deployed in Kabul by late February 2002 to ensure security in the capital and to form, for all practical purposes, the backbone of the Interim Administration. The Bush administration announced a long-term partnership with Afghanistan and pledged to rebuild the country and not abandon it again. At the Tokyo International Conference of January 2002 on Reconstruction and Assistance to Afghanistan, 61 countries and the World Bank pledged US$4.5 billion, of which US$1.8 billion was earmarked for 2002.[12]

The Interim Administration established an Independent Commission to organize an emergency Loya Jirga, made up of elected and appointed delegates, which convened for 10 days in June 2002. Although the Loya Jirga was marred by many irregularities, with power holders within and outside the Interim Administration overrepresented, and by the United States' interventionist role in influencing the outcome according to its preferences, it still proved to be a success in the circumstances. It provided an important forum for women, who had especially been targeted by the Taliban's discriminatory behaviour, and for various ethnic voices to be heard. It also served as a significant traditional means to legitimize

Hamid Karzai, who won an overwhelming vote of support to head the Transitional Administration.

Since then, in collaboration with Brahimi's office, President Karzai has moved to implement the other provisions of the Bonn Agreement, including promulgation of a new constitution by a constitutional Loya Jirga in October 2003, and institution of the necessary steps to organize a new national army, to reform the judiciary and public service, and to prepare for elections. Many of the measures have, of course, faced the usual administrative, procedural and personnel problems associated with a transitional phase in a disrupted society, and some of them have failed to meet targets. On the whole, this has not been for lack of trying to achieve the objectives set by the Bonn Agreement. To this extent, both the Karzai government and its international backers can claim that they are to a considerable degree on course.

However, the daunting problems confronting the government have been not in the area of implementing the Bonn Agreement, but rather whether what has been implemented is likely to generate the appropriate foundations for a lasting, legitimate and democratic political order and a stable, secure and coherent Afghan state. It was clear from the start that, to ensure the survival of the government as an extension of the war on terror, Afghanistan needed a lot more than a change of regime and the provision of sufficient humanitarian, economic and military assistance to make Kabul secure. Political stability was always conditional upon the creation of a government with a widespread writ, the generation of nationwide security, and reconstruction. This would entail a capacity to change the Afghans' culture of the gun to a culture of peace and to keep Afghanistan's neighbours, especially Pakistan, at bay. Progress in all these areas has been very limited. The Karzai government has remained very weak, and many local power holders, who draw on various kinds of micro-societal support and legitimacy, have grown in power and are capable of acting independently or in defiance of the central government – to the extent that Afghanistan's journey on the path of viability and stability is seriously threatened.

Little has been achieved in relation to reintegrating many of the local hegemons into some kind of national frame of unity. Similarly, a big question hangs over what kind of governmental system would be most appropriate in piecing Afghanistan together effectively to ensure the country's long-term viability. The preference of the Karzai leadership and some of its international backers, especially the United States, seems all along to have been to create a presidential, unitary system of government, underpinned by a mixture of traditional and democratic processes and practices of legitimation. This is what in fact is enshrined in the new constitution, based on an assumption that only a strongly central state, backed by an effective national army and security and police forces, could ensure Afghanistan's reconstruction as a stable, secure and democratic state.

However, this assumption is challenged by those who are conscious that a move down this path of development could easily lead to a bloody power struggle between the central government and local or regional power holders. They argue that it could deprive Afghanistan of the degree of political elasticity that it needs in its present circumstances to incorporate the local hegemons into a national system. Meanwhile, a powerful centralized army in a state such as Afghanistan, which has experienced so much disruption, carries a serious risk of making politics vulnerable to military interventions, as has happened in the country twice before. Although recognizing the importance of initial centralization of power for policy innovation, a substantial body of expert opinion tends to favour the eventual development of a more decentralized state in Afghanistan. If this evolution into a functioning multi-level state is to be achieved, eight imperatives must be satisfied.

The first is to develop a central, popularly legitimated government with sufficient distributive, dispensary and defensive powers to act as the focus, promoter and protector of national unity and as the embodiment of national sovereignty.

The second is to allow the functioning micro-societies sufficient internal autonomy. This should enable influential powerbrokers and actors to remain content, with incentives not to mount serious challenges to the central authority either individually or in alliance with one another. Instead, the aim should be to create the necessary opportunities and incentives for them to cooperate with the central authority and become part of it. One way to achieve this is through a parliamentary federal structure.

The third imperative is to provide as strong a regional basis as possible for micro-societies. At present the micro-societies are enveloped within 33 provinces, constituting a large number of administrative divisions and making the task of governance burdensome in a medium-sized country such as Afghanistan. The regionalization of micro-societies should be based on combining several overlapping micro-societies into a north and north-eastern region, comprising mainly Tajiks, to cover the area right to the northern gates of Kabul; a north and north-western region, to include predominantly Turkmans and Uzbeks; a central region, made up of Hazaras; a western zone composed of Heratis and the surrounding people with mixed ethnic elements; a southern region, comprising Kandaharis and other southern Pashtuns; a south-eastern region, involving the Pashtuns of Paktia and Paktika and surrounding zones; and an eastern region, made up of Nangarhari and Kunara Pashtuns. Yet Kabul must remain a focus of the central government and therefore a focus of all regionalized micro-societies, and it must have the necessary constitutional and enforcing powers to protect the rights of minorities within each region.

The fourth imperative relates to a demand for a specific kind of economic reconstruction. Infrastructural and economic development have to be planned and implemented in such a way as to forge linkages between local and national projects and therefore between the micro-societies and between the micro-societies and central government. It is this goal towards which the responsible Afghan agencies, especially the ministries of finance, planning and national reconstruction, and foreign donors and international organizations, especially the United Nations, should work, with as much Afghan involvement as possible through the central government and regional authorities, depending on the division of functions as agreed upon within a constitutional framework.

The fifth imperative concerns capacity-building and the building of civil society. This cannot be realized by the Afghans on their own. Yet the foreign help that is needed must be brought into the country in such a way as not to make the Afghans feel inferior and culturally irrelevant, whether it is in the area of know-how and managerial skills or technical and industrial development. The role of outsiders should be to empower the Afghans themselves to build a capacity for long-term processes of change and development.[13] What Afghanistan needs most in the next decade is to build a vibrant and responsible civil society within an appropriate constitutional framework. This is something that must be achieved as a precursor to democratization – not as a result of it. International opinion must be patient if a Western-type democracy is not generated in the short run;[14] the Afghans will have to be helped to create the necessary conditions for a democratization that will bear their cultural marks but at the same time will be embedded in notions of transparency, accountability and responsibility, with an emphasis on the protection and provision of basic human rights.

The sixth imperative concerns foreign aid and reconstruction.[15] Originally, many analysts claimed that what Afghanistan needed was a kind of Marshall Plan, but Western policy makers, most importantly US Secretary of State Colin Powell, argued that, despite its total devastation, Afghanistan did not need reconstruction aid on a massive scale. Powell contended that a lot could be achieved with a small amount of money. The US$4.5 billion promised for reconstruction at the Tokyo conference of January 2002 was considered to be what Afghanistan could efficiently absorb over the next five years. This simply squashed the concern of many analysts, who argued at the time and subsequently that Afghanistan actually required some US$15–20 billion during that period. The problem was compounded when the donors could not fulfil their pledges in full.

Of the US$1.8 billion promised for 2002, only US$890 million was released.[16] Even then, much of this was spent on emergency humanitarian
needs and the costs of maintaining UN and NGO offices in Afghanistan.
In the end, all the Karzai administration actually received was US$90
million – a figure that could hardly enable it to pay the salaries of its employees, let alone boost public confidence in its distributive capacity.

When the national budget of Afghanistan for 2002 was set at US$560
million, which seemed very frugal for a war-torn country with a population of 22 million, the Afghan finance minister was justified in complain-
ing in early April 2003 that Afghanistan was receiving far less foreign
aid per head than Bosnia and Kosovo. As a consequence, despite all the
initial excitement, Afghanistan's reconstruction has made a very slow
start.[17] Only one substantial reconstruction project – the Kabul–Kandahar–Herat highway, at a cost of US$180 million – saw the light of day in
2003, and even this was running well behind schedule. The reconstruction
dimension of regenerating a viable Afghan state was in serious trouble.
Washington was finally prompted to reconsider the issue of funding and
reconstruction in mid-2003, promising to provide a further US$1 billion
in aid to expedite Afghanistan's process of rebuilding.[18] Another donor
conference was held in Berlin in March 2004, but its promise of a further
US$8 billion in aid to Afghanistan over the next three years is yet to be
realized.

The seventh imperative relates to security. At best the security situation in the country has remained fragile and unpredictable.[19] Although
ISAF has helped to make Kabul relatively secure, the security of the
remainder of the country rests with local hegemons and the umbrella operations of US forces against the remnants of the Taliban and al Qaeda.
Although the latter, backed from early 2003 also by Hikmatyar's supporters in a common anti-American cause, have been incapable of seriously
threatening the Karzai government as long as ISAF and the 11,000 US
and allied troops operate in Kabul and the country, respectively, they
have managed to make many areas, especially in the Pashtun-dominated
south and south-east, increasingly insecure. In the absence of a professional national army,[20] police force and border guards, which will take
years to build, the security situation in many parts of the country remains
fraught with danger. The opposition's targeting of not only foreign and
Afghan security forces but also aid workers and visitors has caused
much anxiety among the NGO communities. This state of insecurity has
had a profound impact on the ability of the Karzai government to consolidate and expand its writ and to accelerate the process of national reconstruction. Although initially resisting the expansion of ISAF to provide
security in other major cities beyond Kabul for reasons of both costs and
casualties, Washington has supported the creation of "provincial recon-

struction teams". These teams, with the involvement of Special Forces of the United States and its allies, are anticipated to perform a dual rebuilding and security role. However, unless they are extremely well resourced, with a capacity for decisive and extensive engagement, they are likely to face severe problems of civil–military cooperation and to fail to produce the desired results.

The eighth imperative concerns the position of the Afghan diaspora. Despite the initial enthusiasm on the part of many educated Afghans in the West to return to Afghanistan, few have found the overall situation conducive to doing so. With factionalism, family connections, nepotism and bribery becoming rampant inside and outside the Karzai administration, there is little incentive for skilled Afghans to trade the comfort of their existence in Western countries for elusive patriotic commitments. The Afghan diaspora is quite sizeable and Afghanistan needs many elements of it for reconstruction. But this cannot happen until a viable political order and a stable and secure environment are achieved. At the same time, this objective cannot be realized without the help of the diaspora. In this respect, Afghanistan is caught in a vicious circle that needs a circuit breaker sooner rather than later. What is required is for the central government to set up a powerful search committee to draw up a list of highly qualified Afghans abroad, who could be invited and enticed to fill a number of positions across the board in the government. The process has to be systematic and judicious, with full presidential weight behind it. The reason that this has not been done thus far is that ethnic politics, factionalism and nepotism have stood in the way. This is, however, a problem that needs to be overcome rapidly in order to meet the acute shortage of trained people until such time as a new generation of educated and specialized Afghans becomes available from within the country.

Conclusion

Afghanistan is in the throes of a very difficult historical situation. It faces many painful choices and uncertainties. Its reconstruction into a stable democratic polity, characterized by a strong centralized/decentralized state, is a serious challenge and a test not only for the Afghans but also for the international community. It requires the Afghan leadership and its international supporters, most significantly the United Nations and the United States, to be more bold and innovative in their approach to state-building than has been the case so far. It is crucial that they put Afghanistan on a path of change and development that could integrate its micro-societies into the frame of a centralized/decentralized state. The

United Nations, the United States and NATO, which took over the command of ISAF on 11 August 2003 for an indefinite period, will have to remain engaged in Afghanistan for at least 10 years to ensure stability and security on a large scale and to keep Afghanistan's predatory neighbours at bay on a long-term basis. Anything less than this could see Afghanistan drift backward, enabling the country's neighbours to reactivate their past interferences in Afghanistan in pursuit of conflicting regional interests. As the situation stands, Afghanistan is at risk of remaining a disrupted state. Given the lack of secessionist impulses, it could become, at least politically if not territorially, a failed state, at the cost of a loss in the war on terrorism.

Notes

1. For a discussion of what constitutes a disrupted state, see Amin Saikal, "Dimensions of State Disruption and International Responses", *Third World Quarterly*, Vol. 21, No. 1, February 2000, pp. 39–49.
2. See Hasan Kakar, *Government and Society in Afghanistan: The Reign of Amir Abd al-Rahman Khan*, Austin: University of Texas Press, 1979.
3. Leon B. Poullada, *Reform and Rebellion in Afghanistan: King Amanullah's Failure to Modernize a Tribal Society*, Ithaca, NY: Cornell University Press, 1973.
4. Ahmed Rashid, *Taliban, Militant Islam, Oil & Fundamentalism in Central Asia*, New Haven, CT: Yale University Press, 2000, Part 1.
5. For a detailed discussion, see Amin Saikal and William Maley, *Regime Change in Afghanistan: Foreign Intervention and the Politics of Legitimacy*, Boulder, CO: Westview Press, 1991, Ch. 2.
6. Amin Saikal, *Modern Afghanistan: A History of Struggle and Survival*, London: I. B. Tauris, 2004, Ch. 1.
7. See J. Bruce Amstutz, *Afghanistan: The First Five Years of Soviet Occupation*, Washington, DC: National Defense University Press, 1986, pp. 19–49.
8. See William Maley, *The Afghanistan Wars*, London: Palgrave Macmillan, 2002, Chs 1–2.
9. See Amin Saikal, *Islam and the West: Conflict or Cooperation?*, London: Palgrave Macmillan, 2003, pp. 95–110.
10. For a discussion of American objectives, successes and failures, see Richard Falk, *The Great Terror War*, New York: Olive Branch Press, 2003, Ch. 3.
11. For the full text of the Bonn Agreement, see *Agreement on Provisional Arrangements in Afghanistan Pending the Re-establishment of Permanent Government Institutions*, UN Doc. S/2001/1154, 5 December 2001.
12. For details, see Amin Saikal, "Afghanistan after the Loya Jirga", *Survival*, Vol. 44, No. 3, Autumn 2002, pp. 47–56.
13. See Simon Chesterman, "Walking Softly in Afghanistan: The Future of UN State-building", *Survival*, Vol. 44, No. 3, Autumn 2002, pp. 37–45.
14. For a discussion, see Andreas Wimmer and Conrad Schetter, *State-Formation First: Recommendations for Reconstruction and Peace-Making in Afghanistan*, Bonn: ZEF Discussion Papers on Development Policy, 2002, esp. Chs 8–8.2.
15. For a discussion, see Chris Johnson and Jolyon Leslie, "Afghans Have Their Memories:

A Reflection on the Recent Experience of Assistance in Afghanistan", *Third World Quarterly*, Vol. 23, No. 5, 2002, pp. 861–874.

16. Sohil Abdul Nasir, "Afghanistan: The More It Changes ...", *Bulletin of the Atomic Scientists*, March/April 2003, p. 48.

17. Ali A. Jalali, "Afghanistan in 2002: The Struggle to Win the Peace", *Asian Survey*, Vol. 43, No. 1, January/February 2003, pp. 181–182.

18. *New York Times*, 27 July 2003.

19. Russell Skelton, "War Is Over, But There's No Peace", *Sydney Morning Herald*, 26–27 April 2003.

20. For a discussion of the difficulties in building a new Afghan army, see Anja Mannuel and P. W. Singer, "A New Model Afghan Army", *Foreign Affairs*, Vol. 81, No. 4, July/August 2002, pp. 44–59.

Part IV
Successes

10

Success in Mozambique?

Michel Cahen

Is Mozambique a successful state? Is it a state that has, in fact, worked? As a country independent only since 1975, Mozambique is obviously a success story – above all a success of international mediation. A war (1977–1992) ended that had begun as a war of regional destabilization of the new "Marxist" republic by Southern Rhodesia and apartheid South Africa, but soon evolved into a civil war. Free and fair elections were held in 1994 and again, though not so fairly, in 1999. Pluralism, parliamentarianism, partial media freedom and economic liberalism have been embraced in Mozambique. Trials with political implications are allowed to run their course. Even the International Monetary Fund (IMF) often congratulates Mozambique, which remains a major recipient country, for being a "good pupil". Most foreign governments regard the situation as stable with Frelimo, the former Marxist and now liberal party, in power.

Mozambique has undoubtedly been one of the African countries that, along with Algeria and Tanzania, has attracted the most sympathy in politically committed intellectual circles. Frelimo's emancipatory project succeeded in appealing to "Marxist–Leninists" as well as to priests. Of the five lusophone (Portuguese-speaking) African countries, Mozambique seemed to be the most radical. It took the "transition to socialism" more seriously than did Cape Verde; it seemed to be less pro-Soviet than Agostinho Neto's Angola; it also seemed to set a different intellectual tone from Guinea-Bissau and the archipelago state São Tomé e Príncipe.

The moral rigour of the Frelimo regime, marked by leaders' privileges but no corruption; an avowed but non-aligned transition to socialism; a genuine rural policy; a project of "people's democracy" with sometimes spectacular features; and, finally, first President Samora Machel's undeniable personal charisma – these certainly explain much of the attention that Mozambique has received. Roughly twice as many articles have been written and theses defended about Mozambique as about the others.

Yet this country of such promise, this kind "analytical landscape", experienced a terrible internal war that caused over 1 million deaths from a population of 14–16 million. The South African policy of destabilization, which fomented war, nevertheless laid the foundations for the present political arrangement. In particular, South Africa's aggression overdetermined the analysis of the conflict as purely external in nature. On this basis, it was argued that Renamo, the rebel Mozambique National Resistance, had no social base in the country – anyone who argued otherwise was consciously or unconsciously playing apartheid South Africa's game. As a result, much more importance was placed on South African and United States covert operations than on the real, internal war.[1] The "secret war", paradoxically, was better known than the public war. This lag in research has yet to be overcome.[2]

There is, today, an "optical" problem of analysis comparable to that during the war, which was seen through the lens of South African destabilization. In particular, this chapter argues that Mozambique's present fame as a "good pupil" on a neo-liberal model hides deeply disturbing domestic problems of social and political stability. These tensions will be examined through Mozambique's history and by comparison with neighbouring Angola. The chapter then re-evaluates Mozambique's past decade of democracy. The central argument is that building up the institutions of the state has overshadowed the need for engagement at the level of society and the nation.

Mozambique up to democracy (1962 to 1992–1994)

It is customary to say that Frelimo, founded in June 1962 in Dar-es-Salaam, Tanzania, united previously existing ethno-nationalist or regional organizations. The merger thus supposedly made possible a transition to modernist nationalism for the whole country, so that sustaining ethnic expressions beyond that time was "divisive" and "reactionary". This reading of the political conflicts inside Mozambican nationalism has been upheld to the present day within Frelimo and among its sympathizers around the world.

Mozambican nationalism and "tribalism"

Frelimo was in reality a new organization that, under strong Tanzanian pressure, brought together only parts of the membership and leadership of the existing organizations. Most of the cadres of these organizations either rejected the merger or accepted it while maintaining their own organization, or left the "unified" movement. This does not change the fact that Frelimo managed to grow more than all the earlier organizations. The difference, however, had less to do with its more developed and "modern" anti colonial programme than with the social identities and trajectories of which it was the bearer.

In fact the "uniqueness process" of 1962–1965, which nonetheless made possible the emergence of a dominant organization, was not the expression of either the unification of Mozambican anti-colonialism or the large-scale emergence of nationalism. It is thus crucial to understand those questions of 1962–1965 in order to grasp the country's weaknesses today.

The failure of a real process of unification reflected the great asymmetry of the country's elite groups. The origin of this contemporary asymmetry may be found mainly in the Portuguese decision in 1907 to move the capital city from Moçambique Island to Lourenço Marques (now Maputo) in the far south. This was intended to plug the colony into booming Transvaal and Witwatersrand capitalism: the colony had to earn its living as a provider of railway and harbour services (Maputo is on Delagoa Bay). Since the beginning of contemporary colonization, Mozambique has been highly dependent, but not on its "home country" of Portugal. The whole of its development during the twentieth century marginalized the old elite of the Zambezi valley, Zambezia and the north-east – the "old Mozambique" of Portuguese merchant colonization through the ages. The switch from merchant to capitalist colonization was not just an economic process but a socio-spatial one. This marginalization was so effective that the members of the old elite were incapable of genuinely integrating themselves into Frelimo, which was dominated, at the level of its political cadres, by the urban, modern and socially bureaucratic new elite of the far south.[3] One could say that the members of the old elite felt like aliens there, and quickly formed dissident currents, which were termed "bourgeois", "tribalist" or "reactionary". Frelimo's history thus reproduced unchanged the phenomena of marginalization characteristic of contemporary colonization. It is not surprising that some of these "lumpen-elites" were later to be found involved in or close to Renamo.

Nevertheless, there was a qualitative turning point between the movements that emerged in 1958–1962 and Frelimo. The earlier movements expressed an "identity nationalism" that comprised, above all, a determination to free the land and expel the Portuguese so as to be masters in their own homeland and not a Mozambican state project. The limits of such a project seem obvious, but at least the movements expressed the strength of existing feelings. Frelimo arose not as the fusion of these feelings but as their negation – "a single people, a single nation, from the Rovuma to Maputo",[4] and therefore a single freedom front and, afterwards, a single party. The denial of ethnic and social identities was at work very early on in Frelimo's language and, through successive approximations in its military-political practice, parallel to the denial of traditional values and structures, such as chiefdoms. By the time the first Frelimo President, Eduardo Mondlane, was killed in 1969, the negation was complete. Anti-colonialism was made synonymous with nationalism – as if the will to see Portuguese people leave had itself created a new common identity throughout Mozambique, erasing the identity of former groupings. The "nation" was thus not just a project; it was a project directed against the existing earlier nations. Nationalism was *induced* in the anti-colonial social movement, not *produced* by it. With independence, state nationalism was completely identified with the nation-state, and authoritarian modernization with the nation-building process. The national project *was* the nation, proclaimed, imposed and identified with the party. Frelimo was in essence not a state party but a "nation party". However, its nationalism did not express something national; rather it was directed against it (the first nations). This nationalism was actually "nationism", the "pro-nation project", and not the project of liberating existing (first) nations.

James Mayall explains something close to this when he writes that anti-colonial nationalism was overwhelmingly a political rather than a cultural, ethnic or religious phenomenon.[5] The problem that occurred more radically in Mozambique than in other colonized lands was that its anti-colonial nationalism prevented the merging of the state nationalism produced by the urban micro-elite and the "identity nationalisms" produced by the first nations.[6] Mozambique was to be not the nation-state of the first nations, a nation of nations, but the nation-state *against* the nations. This political, cultural and social paradigm was to have the greatest weight in the dynamics of the new independent republic over subsequent decades.

Indeed, there was nothing original about this process in Africa: the imitation of a European, more or less homogeneous nation-state was relatively common. There are certain "Afghan" aspects in the Mozambican process, which reflected the experience and mode of existence of the very small, southern, urban, assimilated African elite, produced by and within the colonial state apparatus with its specific twentieth-century characteristics.

The fact that Portugal was the colonial state at the heart of this process was itself important. Europe's oldest nation-state, whose frontiers have barely changed since the thirteenth century, Portugal is particularly homogeneous linguistically and in its Catholicism. Although the "Soviet" political model was very visibly at work in Mozambique, the Portuguese social model was all-powerful among the elite in Lourenço-Marques, who imagined Mozambique's future to fit what they already knew. Interestingly, the two models were not necessarily inconsistent. Marxist discourse in its Stalinist version corresponded well to the southern elite's national project: a single party as the crucible of the nation, a homogeneous nation, a single national language, the state as main actor in the economy and site of elite reproduction, authoritarian paternalism, and so on. Stalinist Marxism in Mozambique was not an expression of friendship towards the East; rather it was primarily the way that was found to express the *Westernization* of this small elite.

One of the leitmotifs of the sympathy for Frelimo that emerged in the West was doubtless its self-proclaimed anti-racism and anti-tribalism. But Frelimo's anti-racism and anti-tribalism are incomprehensible if not situated in this framework. With Portuguese colonialism just behind it and Southern Rhodesia and apartheid South Africa next door, these virtues indeed had great appeal. They opened up the possibility of survival for white and mixed-race Mozambicans, and made it possible to think that there would be no ethnic or religious discrimination. The reality was very different, though not because these principles were betrayed; on the contrary, it was because they were applied.

In fact, it was not seen clearly enough from the beginning that this anti-tribalism and anti-racism consisted above all in hostility towards the original social structures among the peasantry, which were identified with "feudalism" and "obscurantism", and towards any cultural, regional or ethnic diversity. From the beginning, anti-racism and anti-tribalism had a dual nature: there was a classical, sympathetic dimension of hostility to racial and ethnic discrimination; but, at the same time, there was a fierce denial of the relevance, even of the existence, of all the different communities. This denial was very concrete. At the same time that Samora Machel claimed "There are no more whites or blacks, only Mozambicans", he banned European communal organizations as well as ethnically rooted African ones. He fought against the old settlers not only as a *class* (the Luso-colonial and Luso-Mozambican petty bourgeoisie) but as a *community*. The early imposition of a single party – although Frelimo would not have run much risk by organizing elections in 1975 – had the function of hindering any expression of different identities or different regional social trajectories, under the pretext of denouncing "neo-colonial" and even "police" groups.

Anti-racism and anti-tribalism were thus inextricably linked to hostility towards Mozambican society itself. The objective was the rapid production of a European-style nation through a process of authoritarian modernization. Naturally this process particularly benefited the social groups who had been able to take control of the state, primarily those located in Maputo. Since they expressed themselves only through a "national" discourse, without ever publicly revealing their own identity, the denial of ethnicity classically served to disguise the strong ethnicity of southern groups, particularly those of the Shangaan.

Can one then say that the Frelimo state was a tribal state? This was the argument made systematically by Renamo. Mirroring the charges that Frelimo made against it, Renamo consistently criticized Frelimo's "tribalism".[7] It is one thing, however, to say that "pan-Mozambican" *nationalism* served as a cover for Shangaan, Ronga or Tsua ethnicity, and quite another to say that the Mozambican state itself had a particular ethnic character. Even if the country's elites were not represented in a balanced way in the Frelimo leadership, Frelimo was never exclusively southernist. Cadres of every ethnic origin, everywhere, were formed by it, during the armed struggle as well as after independence. Although a social power group that came together under southernist ethnic hegemony crystallized around Frelimo, Frelimo cannot be reduced to that group. That would in any event have been completely ineffective for the management of the state: Frelimo needed to build genuine local relay networks. Frelimo is certainly rooted in a strong "family feeling", but it is not an ethnically rooted party group as such.

Renamo was even more specific in its charges: it argued that Frelimo was the heir of the "Gaza empire" of King Ngungunhana.[8] The memory of this head of state's exactions was still vivid among the non-Nguni peoples whom he dominated, particularly among the Ndaus, the people of the former guerrilla commander Afonso Dhlakama. But Renamo's accusation called for meticulous historical research. It is far from obvious that the lineages born of the Gaza epic were the genesis of nationalism in Mozambique's south and of Frelimo's support. This polemic about the "Gaza empire" actually hid the social history of Frelimo, which had cadres of southern origin who were not descended from Ngungunhana lineages, but on the contrary were very often already assimilated (products of the colonial state).

Renamo propaganda thus oversimplified the situation to the point that it ultimately obscured it, including even aspects that could have served its own ends. In fact, although the Frelimo state cannot be classified on conceptual and historical levels as a tribal state, this does not change the reality that its day-to-day functioning reproduced the process of marginalization begun by twentieth-century colonialism. There was not a break with the past, there was a continuation: the location of state institutions in the country's far south, in a capital plugged in to the South African economy and seen as the prototype of the nation; literacy campaigns entirely in Portuguese and adapted to the most urbanized groups; the authoritarian policy of building the state apparatus in the bush; a pricing policy that favoured the cities – these and other factors continued the marginalization of the religious, social, regional and ethnic groups that had been marginalized under earlier regimes.

In this way there was a reproduction of a constellation of marginalized groups, whose interests and imaginations were different or even contradictory. This centrifugal cycle, set in motion or kept in motion by the Frelimo political and social model, was obviously exacerbated by the collapse of the administration and services caused from the moment of independence by the departure of the overwhelming majority of managers and by Rhodesian and South African aggression.

The war and the vote

The civil character of the Mozambican war has been the subject of intense, sometimes very disagreeable, polemics. In fact, the debate had to do not so much with the nature of the war as with the nature of Renamo. Was it a simple, apolitical, warrior apparatus whose strings were held by the apartheid regime? If so, the war was an outside aggression. Or was Renamo a military movement following a trajectory from a "warrior social body" to a political party, equipped with a minimal social base? If the latter, the war was a civil war. The 1994 elections partially settled the question. Since Renamo won more than one-third of the vote, winning in areas that had been continuously under Frelimo administration, it clearly had some sort of local support base.

But acknowledging the reality of the "civil war" quickly leads to another question: was this war a peasant revolt? This is the thesis that has always been defended by the pro-Renamo lobby in London. In fact, these are two very different questions. One can note only that Renamo sometimes received a warm welcome, managing to organize this welcome, to become part of the grave crisis of Mozambican society and to be a particular expression of it, and succeeded in recruiting thousands of soldiers, some of whom were volunteers. A section of Mozambican society identified with the war that Renamo was already carrying on from the outside. In addition, in a peasant revolt or even in a classic politico-military movement, guerrillas are not tightly sealed off from the population, whereas Renamo maintained an impermeable barrier between its military apparatus and the populations turned over to the *regulos* (officially recognized local chiefs). This was therefore not a peasant war that arose locally from societies under attack. There is no contradiction in asserting that the war was a civil war and, at the same time, saying that it was not a peasant revolt. One could parenthetically make an analogy with Yugoslavia, which recently experienced a war that no one denies was a civil war, without there ever having been any genuine popular uprisings. Peasant dissension would never have been militarized without the introduction of an outside guerrilla force; only the classic phenomenon of passive resistance would have developed. Without any response from Mozambican society, Renamo would have remained the small warrior group envisaged by its sponsors.

This leads directly to the point at issue: the ethnicization of the conflict and of the country. Apart from the fact that a map of the conflict provides evidence against it, the fact that processes of marginalization gave rise to resentments of an ethnic type among many Mozambicans does not mean that certain ethnic groups as such took to guerrilla warfare, as the Karen did in Malaysia or the Mau-Mau in British Kenya. Peasant societies may rebel but they tend to be splinter groups from larger ethnic groups or clans, always deeply rooted in previous history. Besides, the stronghold of Zambezia and Nampula had a regional dimension that went beyond any particular ethnic group. This suggests that, although ethnic considerations were undoubtedly a factor, the war cannot be defined as an inter-ethnic conflict. In this respect, the Mozambican situation was quite different from that in, say, Yugoslavia.

It may also explain why the UN Operation in Mozambique – known by its Portuguese acronym ONUMOZ – was a success. The war had deeply divided the whole country, affecting every region and a variety of ethnic groups, even if Frelimo and Renamo had remained more powerful in certain regions. Each county, sometimes each village, had been split. Within the country, there were no well-established areas controlled by each side, as there were in Angola. Each side was thus more or less present throughout the country, and society as a whole wanted peace. ONUMOZ was welcomed by the inhabitants and was able to control both military groups from the points where it was established.

The 1994 elections opened up a new period in Mozambican political life. Both the main parties used ethnic-based arguments. Renamo attacked southern domination and promised better power-sharing among ethnic groups, which it mentioned by name. Specifically, Dhlakama never talked about "Mozambicans" in his speeches but always referred to people in the bush by their ethnic designation. Frelimo attacked Renamo's ethnic language, but it resorted on at least one occasion to an openly tribalist stratagem in order to instil fear of northern revenge in the south. This was not characteristic of the campaign as a whole, however.[9]

These 1994 elections ended in victory for both parties. Frelimo won the presidential and legislative elections (with a majority of deputies but a minority of votes) in a process accepted by the international community. Renamo, although "defeated", won a stunning victory in legitimizing itself: the "bandits" proved that they represented almost 40 per cent of Mozambicans and the majority in the most populous provinces.

Freed from the war, did citizens vote along ethnic lines? There were reasons to fear that they would. Many African political parties are in effect bound to a fixed set of policies by the IMF and the World Bank, which prevents them from putting forward any real alternative policies and thus leaves them to distinguish themselves through regionalism and ethnic appeals. How did this play out in Mozambique in 1994?

The first point to note is Frelimo's crushing victory in the four southern provinces. With the exception of Govuro, Renamo did not win a plurality in a single district in the four southern provinces. In the capital it was able to win a modest share of the vote among migrants from the north and a minority of the Indian community. The situation was particularly striking in Gaza, and was further accentuated in this province's cities. An even closer, district by district, analysis in particular localities would show that entire communities rejected Renamo in the southern region. Such a massive vote means that there are not really any political currents; it is the community as such that has reacted. As a result, despite the fact that the southern provinces – except the capital – have only modest demographic weight, Frelimo won about 45 per cent of its total national vote in this region.

A second point has to do with Renamo's landslide victory in Sofala province, its absolute majority in Manica and Zambezia provinces, and its plurality in Tete and Nampula provinces. Renamo secured victories in the most populous provinces and those that contribute most to GDP. Nonetheless, only Sofala province showed an (upside-down) equivalent of the southern political landscape, with overwhelming percentages at the district level. In the two demographically decisive provinces that ensured Renamo's national political weight – Zambezia and Nampula – the party most often won only relative majorities at the district level, or absolute majorities that rarely rose as high as 75 per cent of the electorate. This meant that everywhere, not only at the district level but also generally at the local level, communities were divided. Even in those central and northern districts where it won, Renamo did not, on average, attain results comparable to Frelimo's in the southern districts.

A third point concerns the three provinces where the anti-colonial armed struggle was particularly intense. In Tete, Renamo won, coming just short of an absolute majority. In the far northern provinces of Cabo Delgado and Niassa, by contrast, Frelimo booked a clear but not overwhelming victory. Frelimo's victory in the far north resembles Renamo's victory in the centre: the communities were divided, with the sole exception of the Macondes (Mueda and Muidumbe). It therefore does not seem as if the war of liberation is still an electoral factor, at least at the provincial level. The Macondes on their own were not enough to make Frelimo win in Cabo Delgado.

Generally one can detect a very important pattern: Renamo was much weaker where it lost than Frelimo was where it lost. Renamo was virtually excluded from some areas, whereas Frelimo was present almost everywhere.

On the ethnic level, the conclusion may seem surprising: Frelimo benefited much more from the ethnic vote than Renamo did. The Shangaan, Ronga and Tsua ethnic groups voted for Frelimo as communities, Frelimo's scores in the areas where it predominated varying from 78 to 82 per cent. At the other end of the country, the Maconde ethnic group also remained loyal to Frelimo en masse in its rivalry with other ethnic groups for hegemony within Cabo Delgado province.

Renamo, even in the districts where it won, rarely attained such results, generally remaining below 75 per cent. Although the numerically modest Ndau group seems to have voted en masse for Renamo, the Makhuwas did not vote as a bloc for Renamo, and this is the country's largest ethnic group. By contrast, the Senas, supposedly anti-Vandau and "therefore" pro-Frelimo, in reality voted by a majority for the ex-rebels. It was the regional factor, not the ethnic factor, that worked in Renamo's favour, because of the resentment felt throughout the centre towards the east and south. Intra-ethnic and clan divisions played a role, as did social differentiations and different relationships with the state dating back to colonial times. The phenomenon of coastal societies had an impact as well. So the answer to the question posed at the beginning can be only a nuanced one. Overall, the ethnic question had a major impact on the election results. The Makhuwas certainly voted as Makhuwas (not just as Mozambicans). But as Makhuwas they were divided between two different parties. Thus the elections did not, on the scale of the whole country, follow full-fledged ethnic lines. Nonetheless, they were a red alert for Frelimo: once the "party of the whole people" under single-party rule, it has largely become the party of the south. The elections expressed what existed before but could never be expressed politically. From its bases in the south, Frelimo has to leap over the immense, populous centre and north before finding majority support again in the far north. This is a huge blow to the myth of national homogeneity and, in fact, a potential danger to territorial integrity.

Happily for Frelimo, Renamo decided to boycott the 1998 municipal elections (*autárquicas*). Beyond the material difficulty of organizing them, the real danger for Frelimo was the social division of power in the provinces. If major city halls came under Renamo control, the diffusion of southern cadres throughout the whole state apparatus would be slowed. Despite its national majority, Frelimo would no longer be able to exercise its political and social hegemony everywhere. This problem recurred in subsequent municipal elections in late 2003, when Renamo participated and won four cities (including the second largest, Beira), all in central and northern districts. In such a context there is a very real danger of an escalation in ethnic or even openly tribalist tensions.

Nevertheless, things have not gone that far yet. The war and then the elections definitely turned ethnicity into a political issue; that is, there has undoubtedly been a process of politicization of ethnicity. But the politicization of ethnicity is not synonymous with the politicization of ethnic groups. It has not yet produced a "political ethnic group" in which the community would become totalitarian and exclude the autonomy of the individual citizen. Although there have been such tendencies, particularly in the south, in Frelimo's favour, no ethnic group even in these regions voted 100 per cent or even 95 per cent for one party. This means that tendencies towards tribalism (political ethnic groups) do indeed exist, but are far from having the inevitability of a lit fuse – 15 years of civil war and sharply polarized general elections have not yet brought them to the point of exploding. Everything will depend now on socioeconomic developments.[10]

However, before studying the new democratic period in Mozambique (since 1994), it is useful to present a brief comparative analysis between the Angolan and Mozambican wars. Why did war come to an end in Mozambique but continue for another 10 years in Angola?

Disturbing Angola, reassuring Mozambique?

In studying different relationships to a national project, there seems to be a striking contrast between Angola and Mozambique, though both were colonized by the same power and have many other points in common. In Angola, colonial history had produced at least three elites whose status was not equal but was comparable enough to fuel rivalry. The Creole elites of largely Mbundu origin were socialized in the capital according to the modes of the colonial state apparatus, which offered them various bureaucratic and service jobs, mostly under the influence of the Catholic Church. The elite of the Bakongo north, socialized by using the Congolese and Zairian frontier as a resource and by the urban crafts of Kinshasa, was a sort of trading petty bourgeoisie, for the most part Protestant (Baptist). There was also the elite of the Ovimbundu plateaus of the mid-south, heirs of small grain-growing kingdoms, who, if Protestant, had often been converted by Congregationalists. These three elites hardly knew each other and hardly ever came across each other in their economic, social and spiritual trajectories, but they were sufficiently self-confident to fight over the Angolan nation, beginning by forming different nationalist movements: Movimento Popular de Libertação de Angola (MPLA), Frente Nacional de Libertação de Angola (FNLA) and União Nacional para a Independência Total de Angola (UNITA).

The psychological landscape was and remains quite different in Mozambique. The old elites of the country's centre and north had been so marginalized by twentieth-century colonial history that they had to emigrate southwards in order to survive (from the north to Beira, then from Beira to Maputo). Except for a few brief moments of glory, they did not manage to achieve autonomous political expression. I have already noted that the formation of Frelimo in 1962, far from expressing the unification of Mozambican nationalism, reflected the extraordinary political weakness of the non-southern elite groups, who never really managed to integrate themselves into Frelimo, either leaving the movement or being violently repressed. Frelimo's history thus reproduced colonial marginalization, but the resulting rancour was very different from that in Angola.

When Jonas Savimbi led rallies of UNITA for the 1992 elections in Angola, its banners always said "*É a nossa vez*" ("It's our turn"). The subtext was that "the northerners" – also described as "settlers' sons" – had governed for 17 years, and now the time had come for the authentically African southerners to take over. Given that the Bakongo no longer had any means of political expression after the disintegration of the FNLA, two elites were fighting openly over who owned the nation.

In Mozambique, the psychology of the conflict was totally different. Although Renamo always denounced the "tribalism" of a state dominated by certain ethnic groups, there was nevertheless only ever one nation-party. The Frelimo enemy remained the model for Renamo. Neither Renamo nor the central and northern elite groups that supported it ever had – or have now – the means to put themselves forward as an alternative. Their demand was not to "take over the nation" but to join it.

This explains in large part why UNITA was completely different from Renamo. At the heart of UNITA was a small political group building up to war against the Portuguese and the MPLA. It was later backed by South Africa on such a scale that it became a real, fully equipped army, lacking only an air force and a state, led by an officer corps who lived well off the war. This massive support then combined with diamond mining to turn UNITA into a very specific kind of guerrilla force, which did not need the population in order to live but in fact fed the population.[11] This incomplete journey from political group to warrior social body – some political dimension of its activities always remained – largely explains UNITA's 1992 electoral defeat, which revealed its inability to "re-civilize" itself. On the other side, the MPLA state was 95 per cent dependent on oil revenues and was no more than an "offshore state". In the Angolan civil war, the belligerents did not need the population, whose existence was in fact an inconvenience to them. No one wanted peace and it would arrive only by way of a military defeat of one of the sides. This is what eventually happened to UNITA's military wing in 2002, leading to a significant revival of its weak political apparatus.

Renamo was originally a warrior group, although the support it received from Rhodesia and South Africa was very modest. Renamo was a beggars' barefoot army; it had no stable officer corps; it lived with and off the population. Because of this, in order to survive it had to get through to a Mozambican society in crisis. Its leadership understood early on that it could survive only politically: its goal was to win political recognition from Frelimo, which it obtained with the opening of the Rome negotiations in 1992. True, the United Nations had learned from the Angolan disaster, but it was also dealing with two belligerents who, for different reasons, wanted peace. The trajectory thus led from a warrior social body to a political group. Renamo succeeded in "civilizing" itself.

Even the international context was only partially comparable (for Angola the Cold War, and for Mozambique a regional conflict between apartheid and the so-called "frontline states"): whereas South Africa wanted to overthrow MPLA power completely, it wanted only to force Frelimo to change. The internal contexts of the Angolan and Mozambican wars also showed considerable differences, explaining why the United Nations was able to play a positive role on the shores of the Indian Ocean.[12] In order to be effective in Angola, the United Nations would have had to intervene against the ongoing conflict, against *both* armed forces, and mobilize the population along those lines. This was not at all part of its remit or practice.[13] In Mozambique, with far greater resources, the United Nations was able to intervene in the resolution of the conflict, but only after the end of the war. Furthermore, ONUMOZ (the UN Operation in Mozambique) took place after long negotiations involving Zimbabwean and Kenyan mediation and, above all, the Community of Sant'Egidio. Sant'Egidio brought Frelimo and Renamo leaders face to face with no other country being present. This "indigenization" of the process produced a genuinely Mozambican decision to stop the war. The United Nations did not participate in the negotiations and had only to manage their results. ONUMOZ succeeded in becoming an autonomous internal political force, respected (and sometimes hated) by both sides.[14]

This "bit of luck in its troubles" that Mozambique has enjoyed nonetheless remains more precarious than it seems, and not because Renamo

might go back to the bush. Wiu triumphant neo-liberalism ethnicize social and regional tensions – something that 15 years of civil war did not
achieve?

Democratic Mozambique?

I have already mentioned the reproduction in Mozambique of a constellation of marginalized groups whose interests and visions were different
or even contradictory. This constellation was able to become a coalition,
but only thanks to the dynamics of war: the young man excluded from
the academic system; the unemployed person compulsorily deported
from Maputo to the far north in 1983; the humiliated traditional chief;
the ethnic cultures despised by local state authorities; the peasant refusing to enter the communal village – all these experiences were producing
hostility towards Frelimo and the state, but only military dynamics allowed them to unite and express themselves. The common enemy was
"communism" and "Marxism–Leninism".

It might have been expected that the second general election in 1999
would show a decrease in support for Renamo. After all, Frelimo was
now capitalist, sympathetic towards traditional chiefs, very concerned
with religious issues, and open to African mother tongues. Renamo,
meanwhile, no longer had UN money to conduct its electoral campaign.
Nevertheless, it was the "behaviour" described earlier (not respecting
the peasant societies, not diversifying the ethnic component of state
power, not developing the northern regions as well as the southern ones,
etc.) that was to prove the most influential factor.

The first "red alert" had been the local elections of 1998 in 33 towns
and cities (including Maputo). Renamo had boycotted the elections, but
its call for a boycott clearly could not explain the fact that 85 per cent
of voters stayed at home.[15] Indeed, Frelimo's reaction to its election in
all the towns by huge majorities of the 15 per cent who did vote was significant: complete indifference. "In the United States too, abstention
rates are high," they said. More than ever, it appeared that, since the
elections had kept the party in power in the cities and towns, nothing
else mattered. Is democracy the continuation of hegemonic power by
other means?

It was therefore with a high degree of self-confidence that Frelimo entered the race for the presidential and legislative elections of 3–5 December 1999. Nevertheless, the results were not good for the party. First, in
comparison with the 1994 race, voter turnout was down: only 70 per cent
(presidential election) and 67 per cent (legislative election) of 7 million
registered adults. Second, whereas in 1994 the former rebel leader Dhla-

kama had received fewer votes than his party did, this time he obtained far more. The "polarization" between only two candidates (against 14 in 1994) certainly contributed to this increase: Renamo and Frelimo obtained 39 per cent and 49 per cent of the vote, respectively, but Dhlakama achieved 48 per cent against 52 per cent for Joaquim Chissano, the incumbent president. This represented a slight increase for Renamo (+1.03 per cent) and a huge increase for Dhlakama (+14.81 per cent). The image of the former warrior chief had decisively changed: he was now a credible alternative choice. Furthermore, the electoral geography revealed an intriguing phenomenon. The Renamo party had improved its results in places where it was already more powerful, making a striking divide between the regions north and south of the Sabi River.[16] It was as if, in spite of the profound political weakness of Renamo, large parts of the population were using Renamo and its leader to express their exasperation with the Maputo regime. The "rightist" Renamo was supported by a social movement extending far beyond it that could be described as "left wing", whereas the formerly Marxist Frelimo, as we have seen, was the elite party.

Because of the closeness of the vote for the two candidates and because there were some serious suspicions of fraud,[17] Renamo asked for a recount and refused to recognize the legitimacy of the new president and new government. From that moment on there was persistent instability, which grew towards the end of 2000 when, on 9 November, mass demonstrations by Renamo were violently repressed.

It was not the Renamo leadership that had mobilized people against the government in such a coherent way. On the contrary, its political attitude remained hesitant and uncoordinated in the area of propaganda. However, the social base of Renamo was far more mobilized against the results and the government in the central and northern regions of the country, and the Renamo leadership was obliged to organize the 9 November mass demonstrations in order to maintain its influence over its base. On 22 November, the prominent journalist Carlos Cardoso was killed, an assassination linked with his accusations in his weekly magazine a few days before of high-level corruption. This was the second such case, the economist António Siba Siba Macuacua having been killed in Maputo in August.

The years 2001 and 2002 were more peaceful, with the political scene being dominated by preparations for the local elections in late 2003 and the third general election in December 2004. But this tranquillity should not be presumed to be the norm. In spite of taking advantage of pluralism and neo-liberalism to broaden the social group in power slightly, Frelimo has maintained its monopoly of power at every level of the state,[18] thus expressing the deep crisis of an impoverished authoritarian paternalism that does not allow any sharing. Such behaviour is not just economic but also an ethnic, political and regional process. This explains why "communism" may still be a unifying enemy: "communists" are still in power. Feelings that the state is unrepresentative remain very strong. Deep-rooted and long-standing ethnicities, historical colonial asymmetries and the current social and political relationship with the state are combining to produce dangerous tensions.

Towards instability and violence?

On 13 June 2002, at its eighth National Congress, Frelimo chose Armando Guebuza as its presidential candidate. This choice was far from insignificant. Guebuza was one of the main organizers of the 1983 "Operation Production", which involved expelling all "unproductive" persons from the cities and sending them into the bush where they were obliged to "produce". Thousands of people were deported and many of them died of starvation; others joined Renamo. Before that, Guebuza had been the organizer of the compulsory "villagization" of the Limpopo Valley in 1977 and 1978. During the presidency of Joaquim Chissano, he became minister for transport, a key portfolio. He is said to have become very rich.

Why choose such a candidate? His ethnic mix may be good (Sena, a central ethnic group, and Ronga, a southern one) but it was not the main reason. Furthermore, Guebuza is not popular in the south, where people have not forgotten who he is and what he did. This would not lead southern people to vote for Renamo, but it could provoke mass abstentions and therefore victory for the former rebels. However, the leadership of Frelimo took the 1999 results very seriously, and realized that it was now necessary to face the possibility of a legal Renamo victory. In this context, local, regional and national executives looked for a "strong" candidate, in contrast to the excessively "soft" President Joaquim Chissano. The decision was not an "open" political one but primarily an internal decision by the party apparatus. This indicates that it was inconceivable that Frelimo could lose power – for economic reasons, obviously, but also for "ideal-type" reasons. As we have seen, Frelimo was built as a nation-party: Frelimo is the nation; Frelimo is the "organized people", the Mozambican family. It is supported by the international community as a competent party, the guarantor of the much-desired "stability", in contrast with the politically weak and disorganized barefoot Renamo.

In order to organize the elections, the National Elections Commission (on which Frelimo has a majority) elected its new president on 23 January 2003. He is from the (Protestant) Christian Council of Mozambique, which has historically close links with Frelimo.

Another issue is that, although Sant'Egidio and ONUMOZ succeeded in "indigenizing" the peace process, making it a domestic one and not just an externally imposed settlement, this has not produced an emergent civil society and a feeling of community as a nation. It has been much more a peace process than a democratization process. For historical reasons that have already been mentioned, any "third force" aside from Frelimo and Renamo has a very narrow social space (except in the capital city), and urban civil society has remained very weak.[19]

One sign of this is the complete absence of calls for any kind of "Truth and Reconciliation Commission" or other transitional justice. This may seem surprising given that the civil war involved a lot of war crimes on both sides. But this is the point: the crimes were on both sides, and neither the leaders nor the population have much interest in such a catharsis. Nonetheless, a popular kind of "transitional justice" was practised at local levels. For example, when a child soldier who, at the time of his forced recruitment by Renamo, had been obliged to kill some people from his village (sometimes even his own parents) returned home, the local religious leaders conducted rituals to pacify the vengeful spirits of the murdered persons and to allow the child to be readmitted to the community.[20]

This local-level transitional justice may explain why there has not been any massive demand for a "modern" transitional justice. The rituals' aim was not to judge or even to forgive, but to accept back soldiers from both sides. Some societies have been so deeply wounded that they need amnesia more than amnesty. This is perfectly understandable, perhaps even healthy. But the fact that this issue has been faced only locally has obviously weakened the national process of building both civil and political societies. Following a successful peace process, both Frelimo and Renamo have remained distinct "worlds" within the same country, without any political, social, economic or, increasingly, ethnic communication and dialogue – two populations, two Mozambiques.

The fear now is of two possible dangerous trends: the "Zimbabwean" or the "Malagasy" scenarios. In the former case, Frelimo, led by Armando Guebuza, would be prepared to do anything in order to stay in power. Even if it is not possible in Mozambique to conduct a campaign like that of Robert Mugabe against white farmers, this could involve appeals to ethnic groups, intimidation and fraud. In the "Malagasy" scenario, Renamo would have enough force actually to challenge results it considered fraudulent, with quasi-revolts in a number of cities and towns and the proclamation of Dhlakama as president. But this could not be a genuine parallel to Malagasy, because the main protest would not be in the capital city, which is ethnically close to Frelimo. There would, instead, be a geographical split, perhaps more reminiscent of the fragmentation of Somalia, with the northerners paralleling the experience of those in Somaliland. Such pessimistic scenarios for Mozambique may not materialize, but it would be irresponsible not to contemplate them.

Conclusion

Mozambique is not a failed state, but it is a weak and authoritarian state in danger of further disruption. Neither decentralization nor domestic federalism would be a panacea, because they raise the question of what would be decentralized or federalized. Which spaces? Which power relationships? The problem lies within the nature of the state: making the state work is primarily a question of finding ways for heterogeneous African populations grouped together by colonial caprice to achieve appropriate expression. Is it a question of coming back to classical good governance in order to improve state-building? Perhaps, but improving state-building must rely not upon enlightened despotism – no despotism is able to remain enlightened for long – but on first developing society's capacities to demand, impose and obtain accountability. There can be no political society without civil society.

During the Frelimo "Marxist–Leninist" period (1975–1989) Mozambique was one of Africa's most Weberian states – minimally corrupt, ideal-type, with a functioning bureaucracy – but this Weberian state was unable to help people achieve a better life or actual social progress. One of the main reasons was the denial of the original social relationships within the population and the authoritarian modernization process to which it has been submitted. Now "Marxism" has gone but, rather than a "socialist transition", it was more a local and contextualized way for an urban micro-elite to express its desire for nationalist Westernization. What has survived best from the "Marxist" period is indeed state nationalism. Neo-liberalism has weakened the capacity to impose it, but it is very much alive. Mozambican people are still to be "modernized", "organized", "integrated", and so on. High technology in foreign private companies may have replaced heavy tractors from Bulgaria on state farms – for the marginalized peasant, is this model of social development so different?

More generally speaking, when the nation does not pre-exist and when a state, for political or economic reasons, does not have the means to be a welfare state or even a socially promoting state, its capacity to build a nation is weakened. When, furthermore, nation-building is based on the negation of social identities – when "for the nation to live the tribe must die"[21] – not only does it not produce a nation, but it provokes anti-state reactions that find expression along existing fault lines, notably ethnic ones. Such centrifugal forces may be stronger than the centripetal ones.

That means that, at the extreme periphery of the world economy, nation-building must be conceived as the formation of nations of nations, and not of "nations against identities", with deep respect for the original social relationships within the society. Mozambique should not, therefore, be seen as having moved from civil war to civil strife, and from there to civil society. It has successfully handled the transition from war to peace, but there it has, for the time being, halted.

Notes

1. For examples of such an "externalist thesis" by Western scholars explaining the war in Mozambique, see Joseph Hanlon, *Mozambique. Who Calls the Shots?*, Bloomington, IN: James Currey/Indiana University Press, 1991; John S. Saul, *Recolonization and Resistance in Southern Africa in the 1990s*, Toronto: Between the Lines, 1993; William Minter, *Apartheid's Contras: An Inquiry into the Roots of War in Angola and Mozambique*, London: Zed Books, 1994; and, more open to nuances, Merle L. Bowen, *The State against the Peasantry: Rural Struggles in Colonial and Postcolonial Mozambique*, Charlottesville, VA: University Press of Virginia, 2000.
2. See, for example, João Paulo Borges Coelho and Sérgio Nathú Cabá, *Elementos para a história social da guerra em Moçambique, 1978–1992*, Maputo/Dakar: Codesria, forthcoming. For an "internalist" explanation of the civil war, see Christian Geffray's classic *La Cause des armes au Mozambique: Anthropologie d'une guerre civile*, Paris/Nairobi: Karthala/CREDU; Michel Cahen, *Les Bandits: Un historien au Mozambique, 1994*, Paris: Publications du Centre Culturel Calouste Gulbenkian, 2002.
3. For a detailed discussion of this historical trajectory, see René Pélissier, *Naissance du Mozambique: Résistance et révoltes anticoloniales (1854–1918)*, Orgeval, France: Pélissier, 1984; Malyn Newitt, *A History of Mozambique*, Bloomington, IN: Indiana University Press, 1994; Michel Cahen, "Mozambique: Histoire géopolitique d'un pays sans nation", *Lusotopie* (Paris: L'Harmattan), 1994.
4. Rovuma and Maputo are two border rivers in the far north and far south of the country.
5. See chapter 2 in this volume.
6. On identity nationalism, see Michel Cahen, "L'Anticolonialisme identitaire: Conscience ethnique et mobilisation anti-portugaise au Mozambique (1930–1965)", in Colette Dubois, Marc Michel and Pierre Soumille, eds, *Frontières plurielles, Frontières conflictuelles en Afrique subsaharienne*, Paris: L'Harmattan, 2000, pp. 319–333.
7. On Renamo's mimicry of Frelimo, see Michel Cahen, "'Entrons dans la nation!': Notes pour une étude du discours politique de la marginalité. Le cas de la Renamo du Mozambique", *Politique Africaine* (Paris: Karthala), No. 67, October 1997, pp. 70–88.
8. The Gaza empire was the Nguni state in southern Mozambique during the nineteenth century. The last king was Ngungunhana, defeated by Portuguese troops in 1895.
9. See Michel Cahen, "*Dhlakama é maningue nice!*' An Atypical Former Guerrilla in the

Mozambican Electoral Campaign", *Transformation: Critical Perspectives on Southern Africa*, No. 35, 1998, pp. 1–48. For electoral mapping, see Luis Cerqueira de Brito, *Cartografia Eleitoral de Moçambique – 1994*, Maputo: Livraria Universitária, 2000.

10. See Michel Cahen, "Nationalism and Ethnicities: Lessons from Mozambique", in Einar Braathen, Morten Bøås and Gjermund Sæther, *Ethnicity Kills? The Politics of War, Peace and Ethnicity in Sub-Saharan Africa*, London: Macmillan, 2000, pp. 163–187.

11. A comparison with certain Latin American narco-guerrillas is thus not wholly justified, since the latter exploit the coca-growing population.

12. For a discussion of the role of ONUMOZ, see Alex Vines, *"No Democracy without Money": The Road to Peace in Mozambique (1982–1992)*, CIIR Briefing Paper, London: Catholic Institute for International Relations, 1994; United Nations, *The United Nations and Mozambique, 1992–1995*, New York: UN Department of Public Information, 1995; João Bernardo Honwana, *A Sustainable Peace? The United Nations and Mozambique*, Lisbon: Instituto de Estudos Estratégicos e Internacionais, 1996. See also note 14, below.

13. See Christine Messiant, "Angola, les voies de l'ethnisation et de la décomposition", *Lusotopie* (Paris: L'Harmattan), 1994, pp. 155–212, and *Lusotopie* (Paris: Karthala), 1995, pp. 181–212; "Angola: Le retour à la guerre ou l'inavouable faïllité d'une intervention internationale", *L'Afrique politique* (Paris: Karthala; Bordeaux: Centre d'étude d'Afrique noire), 1994, pp. 199–229; "MPLA et UNITA: Processus de paix et logique de guerre", *Politique africaine*, No. 57, March 1995, pp. 40–57; "Fin de la guerre, enfin, en Angola. Vers quelle paix?", *Politique Africaine* (Paris: Karthala), No. 86, June 2002, pp. 183–195.

14. On Sant'Egidio, international mediation and the peace process in Mozambique, see generally Beth Strachan, *Mozambique: The Quest for Peace – The Political, Social and Economic Context 1980–1994 – A Select and Annotated Bibliography*, Johannesburg: South African Institute of International Affairs, 1996; Stephen Chan and Vivienne Jabri, eds, *Mediation in Southern Africa*, London: Macmillan, 1993; Cameron Hume, *Ending Mozambique's War: The Role of Mediation and Good Offices*, Washington, DC: United States Institute of Peace Press, 1994; Roberto Morozzo della Rocca, *Mozambico: Dalla guerra alla pace: Storia di una mediazione insolita*, Milan: San Paolo, 1994; Chris Alden, *Mozambique and the Construction of the New African State. From Negotiations to Nation Building*, Houndsmill: Palgrave, 2001; Éric Morier-Genoud, "Sant' Egidio et la Paix: Interview de Don Matteo Zuppi et Riccardo Cannelli", *Le Fait Missionnaire* (Basel), No. 13, October 2003, pp. 119–145.

15. On local powers, local elections and mass abstention in Mozambique, see Brigitte Lachartre, "Élections municipales et démocratisation au Mozambique", *Politique Africaine* (Paris: Karthala), No. 75, October 1999, pp. 161–169; Carlos Serra, ed., *Eleitorado incapturável. Eleições municipais de 1998 em Manica, Chimoio, Beira, Dondo, Nampula e Angoche*, Maputo: Universidade Eduardo Mondlane, Livraria Universitária, 1999.

16. For a more detailed analysis of the results, see Michel Cahen, "Mozambique: L'Instabilité comme gouvernance?", *Politique Africaine* (Paris: Karthala), No. 80, December 2000, pp. 111–135.

17. See, for instance, *Carter Center Commends Mozambicans on Elections, but Calls for Greater Transparency in Resolving Complaints*, 23 December 1999; *Carter Center Final Report on 1999 Elections in Mozambique*, 24 August 2000; both available at: ⟨http://www.cartercenter.org⟩. The official results may be found in A. Carrasco et al., *General Elections 1999*, Maputo: Technical Secretariat for Electoral Administration, 2001.

18. On the "statist privatization" process by Frelimo in Mozambique, see M. Anne Pitcher, *Transforming Mozambique: The Business of Politics, 1975–2000*, Cambridge: Cambridge University Press, 2002.

19. Brigitte Lachartre, *Enjeux urbains au Mozambique. De Lourenço Marques à Maputo*, Paris: Karthala, 2000.
20. See Alcinda Honwana, "Children of War: Understanding War and War Cleansing in Mozambique and Angola", in Simon Chesterman, ed., *Civilians in War*, Boulder, CO: Lynne Rienner, 2001, pp. 123–142; Alcinda Honwana, *Espíritos vivos, tradições modernas, possessão de espíritos e reintegração social pós-guerra no sul de Moçambique*, Maputo: Promédia, 2002.
21. This slogan had long been one of the South African ANC (before Nelson Mandela's invention of the "rainbow nation" concept).

11

State-building, national leadership and "relative success" in Costa Rica

Abelardo Morales-Gamboa and Stephen Baranyi

Costa Rica is a small, middle-income country with 4 million inhabitants which has distinguished itself as an example of a "successful" democratic state since the mid-twentieth century. During the Cold War the country managed to avoid the most profound problems faced by its neighbours – dictatorships, civil wars and foreign interventions. Its institutions have subsequently faced new challenges, including economic liberalization through free trade agreements and privatization, and pressures to transform an activist welfare state. The regional crisis of the late Cold War era and the new wave of market-oriented reforms have tested the legitimacy of the state and the capacity of its institutions to respond to unprecedented challenges.

This chapter analyses the ways in which the state and other national actors have behaved within the institutional framework that emerged during the colonial period and was decisively consolidated from the late 1940s onwards. The chapter is divided into four sections. First we explain the historical bases and institutional pillars of the "Costa Rican model". Then we examine the strategies through which national actors confronted the regional crisis during the 1980s. After examining current national debates on economic liberalization and the related crisis of political representation, we conclude with reflections on the relevance of the Costa Rican experience for global debates on state-building.

This account of Costa Rican history connects with several threads that run through this volume. It explores the notion introduced by Sebastian von Einsiedel in chapter 1 that state failure and success are properly regarded as lying on a continuum, by showing how Costa Rica consolidated itself at the successful end of this continuum in the second half of the twentieth century. The Costa Rican example also helps to unpack the familiar dichotomies of strong/weak states/societies by examining the institutional arrangements – liberal democracy, demilitarization, a mixed economy and a welfare state – and the sense of nationhood that have been central to Costa Rica's success. The chapter highlights the importance of enlightened leadership, the judicious management of power and an enabling international environment for the process of state-building. It also demonstrates how a successful state can maintain its status even when one of these variables changes dramatically – as happened when Central America became a quintessential "bad neighbourhood" in the 1980s. Finally, like the regional studies and the chapter on Mozambique, this study illustrates the ambiguous impact of economic globalization, reminding us that success is fragile and depends on appropriate national responses to major challenges. By focusing the spotlight on national leadership, institutions and policy options, this chapter and the study of Singapore that follows offer an interesting counterpoint to the emphasis by other authors on the role of the international community in preventing state failure.

Historical bases and institutional pillars

Costa Rica is an unusual case in the Latin American context. It is one of the oldest and most stable democracies in the region. Its model of equitable economic and social development stands in stark contrast to those of its immediate neighbours, Nicaragua and Panama, and even to those of larger, more distant neighbours such as Colombia and Guatemala. The historical explanation for this achievement is a social model that, particularly since the post-colonial period, has been based on the development of stable political institutions, give-and-take (as opposed to winner takes all) relations among political elites and the progressive integration of subordinate groups' interests through socioeconomic redistribution and political participation.

The roots of this model go back to the colonial era, when Costa Rica played a marginal role in the Spanish empire. The colonial occupation began in 1560, four decades later than in the rest of Central America.[1] A small indigenous population and limited natural resources offered few incentives for large-scale slave trading, mining or plantation agriculture, with the result that the territory did not attract large armed forces. The distance from the Captaincy General of Guatemala allowed the province to remain at the margin of colonial power struggles and to develop local conflict management mechanisms.

After independence in 1821 – and particularly in the late nineteenth century – Costa Rica prospered owing to the fortunate convergence of national and international trends. Expanding international coffee markets generated dynamic economic growth and an isolationist policy shielded Cost Rica from the foreign interventions that plagued its neighbours. The country was led by fairly enlightened elites who developed stable political parties, fair electoral mechanisms, public education, relatively benign security forces and a culture of tolerance. As noted by Edelberto Torres, although the discourse of a homogeneous, egalitarian smallholder society has been somewhat exaggerated, this "founding myth" had the virtuous effect of contributing to social integration and stability over the generations.[2]

The historical contrasts between Costa Rica and its Central American neighbours were accentuated in the twentieth century as those societies suffered from military coups, armed conflicts and military interventions led or supported by the United States. Meanwhile the Costa Rican model showed signs of increased consolidation, particularly during the 1948–1980 period of equitable economic growth and political stability. It is worth looking at the five pillars of that model in some detail.[3]

Liberal democracy

The consolidation of liberal democratic institutions and the corresponding culture of "give-and-take politics" have enabled political elites to maintain overall control of society while managing intra-elite competition. Indeed, relatively free and fair elections have been the norm, with two exceptions (in 1917 and 1948), and the mantle of government has passed from one set of elected civilian leaders to another for over a century. Though women became full citizens in electoral terms only after 1948 and indigenous minorities have suffered historically, civil and political rights were not violated to the extent that they were in neighbouring societies.

Social conflict has certainly been a part of the country's history, for example between workers and management on banana plantations. The basic difference from the rest of Central America is that political crises resulted not in the dissolution of liberal democratic institutions but rather in their restoration and consolidation. Dissent has generally been channelled through the parliamentary opposition and free media, which have provided alternatives to the corrosive influence of political rumour mills in neighbouring societies. The political legitimacy of this system has rested on the popular belief that liberal democracy is the best way of balancing social order and progress.

In 1948, this order was interrupted by the "Costa Rican Civil War". The 38-day war was triggered by a series of electoral irregularities and accusations of fraud against the ruling National Republican Party–Civil Vanguard Party coalition. This coalition included a modernizing faction of the landed oligarchy, the Communist Party and elements in the Catholic Church. Its political practices were contested by a coalition of small farmers, urban professionals and social democrats that coalesced around the National Liberation Army, led by José Figueres Ferrer.[4] This crisis did not amount to state collapse, but it clearly represented state failure – in the Weberian sense of losing the monopoly of force and in the wider sense of a breakdown in the social contract.

The war was ended through peace negotiations, which resulted in the formation of a new Junta de Gobierno (Governing Council), a new constitution and elections, the proscription of the Communist Party (for two decades), the dissolution of the army, and the maintenance of the social reforms initiated by the previous government. Ironically, the institutions and norms of liberal democracy were consolidated by the conflict and its negotiated settlement, since elections were confirmed as the mechanism for facilitating the future transfer of power. Social reforms initiated under Communist leadership, such as the adoption of a Labour Code, were also deepened – instead of being reversed as they were in neighbouring countries such as Guatemala in the 1950s.

José Figueres was elected as president with 65 per cent popular support in 1953. After a period out of politics he was re-elected in 1970. The norm of give-and-take politics that he helped to institutionalize prevented him from aspiring to the presidency more often, but his National Liberation Party (PLN) dominated the political scene well into the 1980s. The legitimacy of these new political leaders rested on strong support, particularly by small farmers and the urban middle classes, for an activist public sector and liberal democratic institutions.

Demilitarization

The army was disbanded in 1949. The institution did not play a major role in the civil war since the conflict pitted the forces led by Figueres against brigades led by the Communist Party. The victors could have institutionalized their own military forces, but they calculated that they did not require an army to consolidate the regime.

A key factor underpinning this calculus was the considerable popular support enjoyed by the social democratic coalition, as indicated by the

PLN's impressive string of electoral victories. The support of the United States, not least because of the anti-communist credentials of Figueres and his followers, was another crucial enabling factor.

None of this would have been possible if the army had been more powerful militarily and politically. Historically, the military had been weak. In some campaigns during the nineteenth century, the government had recruited reserves but the army remained small and the military budget remained inferior to education expenditures. With few exceptions, military officers were minor players in politics. The absence of major security threats such as well-organized insurgencies or serious border conflicts also provided few opportunities for military intervention in political life.

Demilitarization meant that Costa Rica had to rely on the Inter-American Treaty of Reciprocal Assistance, and particularly on the development of a special security relationship with the United States. During the Cold War this relationship essentially traded support for US positions in international affairs for the maintenance of an arm's length relationship from Washington on matters of domestic policy. This approach was unique from a regional standpoint: Panama and Nicaragua also supported US Cold War strategies, but their foreign policies were linked to deep US political and military involvement in their domestic affairs. In addition, until the late 1970s Costa Rica maintained a policy of studied isolationism, or non-involvement in its neighbours' conflicts and political crises.

A mixed economy

During this period the Costa Rican economy experienced spectacular growth – an average annual rate of 6.5 per cent from 1950 to 1980. Other Central American economies also grew at impressive rates during this period, but what distinguished Costa Rica was that the benefits of growth were shared widely through public sector activism.[5]

The economic boom was based partly on the steady increase in the prices of traditional exports such as coffee and bananas. Yet growth included the significant diversification of production through import substitution industrialization linked to emerging national and regional markets. It also saw the creation of semi-autonomous public sector entities to regulate market relations or provide services in key areas such as banking, electricity, telecommunications, housing, transportation and infrastructure. A key innovation was the establishment of state institutions to regulate price relations between producers and commercial intermediaries in the countryside. Another was the state-fostered growth of a vibrant rural cooperative movement. The fiscal basis for these innovations was the common tax imposed on coffee production in 1949, under the Junta de Gobierno led by Figueres. This tax, which set a historical precedent and boosted government revenues, was supported by rural smallholders and by the emerging urban middle classes.

The welfare state

The civil war also spurred the consolidation of a welfare state that is still the envy of many developing countries. Important innovations included the extension of guaranteed universal access to adequate public education and health services, the provision of subsidized housing, and minimum wage laws enforced in urban centres as well as in the countryside.

Some of these reforms – especially the Labour Code and the Costa Rican Social Security Fund (CCSS) – had been initiated by the Communist Party during its coalition rule in the mid-1940s. By including them in its programme, the social democratic National Liberation Party managed to co-opt parts of the Communist Party's social base and use this support to pressure the landed oligarchy to accept fair taxes, fair wages and other "costs" of social peace.

A sense of nationhood

The last pillar of Costa Rican exceptionalism is the strong sense of collective nationhood that was entrenched after 1948. Costa Ricans had a long-standing image of themselves as a democratic, smallholder society quite distinct from the rest of Central America. This self-conception was rooted in the fact that this was primarily a European settler society with modest ethno-cultural differences and socioeconomic disparities – certainly compared with diverse and polarized societies such as Panama or Guatemala. The emergence of strong civil society organizations, such as the craft and trade unions that flowered in the 1920s, reinforced this sense of uniqueness.

This mythical sense of identity was enhanced by the outcome of the civil war, by the consolidation of new state–civil society relations and the resultant accentuation of differences from neighbouring countries. After 1948, the self-image of Costa Ricans as "the Swiss of Central America" became a cornerstone of national consciousness.

However, by the late 1970s the Costa Rican model could no longer be sheltered from the deepening regional crisis. In the 1980s the government also came under increasing pressure, from domestic and international sources, to implement market-oriented reforms. How has Costa Rican society managed these enormous challenges on the basis of the model consolidated during the post-1948 era?

The regional crisis and Costa Rican foreign policy

During the crisis from the late 1970s to the mid-1990s Central America experienced profound transformations. Repression and low-level conflict escalated into full-blown civil wars in Nicaragua and El Salvador, and to a lesser extent in Guatemala. Conflict had dramatic human and economic consequences, causing several hundred thousand deaths and disappearances, several million refugees and internally displaced persons, and a severe economic recession. Thinly veiled dictatorships were gradually transformed into more liberal democratic political systems with participation by political parties associated with insurgent forces, civil society and increasingly free mass media. In three cases, these changes were facilitated by negotiated peace settlements. US hegemony in the region was challenged and re-engineered, but not dismantled. The historical bookends of this regional crisis were the fall of the Somoza dynasty and the beginning of the Sandinista revolution in Nicaragua (July 1979) and the signing of comprehensive peace accords in El Salvador (December 1992) and then in Guatemala (December 1996).[6]

Although Costa Rica did not directly experience war or revolution, its proximity to the countries in conflict, especially Nicaragua, compelled it to adopt a more active foreign policy. The essence of this approach was an attempt to distance San José from Washington – particularly from the Reagan administration – and to contain the influence of foreign insurgencies and communist parties. During the period from 1978 to 1990, the resources invested in this foreign policy caused considerable tensions with the United States. The policy was also controversial with domestic constituencies that espoused divergent views on the Sandinista regime, the extent to which it threatened Costa Rican stability and the best way of dealing with the revolution to the north.

These divergences explain the shifts and inconsistencies of Costa Rican foreign policy over time. During the early years, the social Christian government of Rodrigo Carazo turned a blind eye to, and in some instances supported, insurgent groups fighting against the Somoza dictatorship in 1978–1979; the social democratic government of Luis Alberto Monge did the same with those fighting against the Sandinista regime from 1982 to 1986. The authorities publicly denied this rearguard support in both instances, used diplomatic channels to maintain the international image of a democratic and pacifist state and continued to explore negotiated solutions to the wars. Nonetheless, Costa Rica moved from a position of tension with the United States in the late 1970s to a posture of diplomatic support for the Reagan administration's Nicaragua policy by 1982.

The absence of an army and the decay of the Inter-American Treaty of Reciprocal Assistance as the basis for collective security placed Costa

Rica in a difficult position: it had to use diplomacy to keep the war off its territory, secure the confidence of its neighbours and regional middle powers, and ensure cooperation by the United States. In 1983 Washington intensified its pressure to obtain direct Costa Rican support for the Nicaraguan counter-revolution. US military assistance increased, as did the size of Costa Rica's security forces and their clandestine support for anti-Sandinista insurgents.

Owing to these contradictions in its foreign policy, Costa Rica was not invited to join the Contadora Group formed in May 1983 to forge a diplomatic solution to the region's conflicts. Indeed, its increasing belligerence towards the Sandinista government and its de facto support for the Reagan administration's policies compelled the four Contadora member states to define Costa Rica as a party to the conflicts.[7] This rebuff by important Latin American middle powers was a blow to the national myth and to the actors who believed that the country's interests would be best served by a more neutral approach.

The Monge government's attempt to forge a new balance among these domestic and external pressures started with the "Proclamation of Neutrality" issued at the end of 1983. This document stated that Costa Rica was an ally of the United States and reiterated the country's commitment to democracy and liberty, while declaring a position of neutrality vis-à-vis armed conflicts involving third parties in the region. The statement was nevertheless the subject of intense debates between pro-United States and anti-Sandinista forces, which included certain right-wing politicians, large business and media groups, opposed to a self-defined "pacifist movement" that included intellectuals, moderate politicians, students, professionals and pro-Sandinista groups. These societal differences were reflected within the state, especially between the main political parties and even between different government agencies.[8]

In the mid-1980s the Contadora initiative began to run out of steam. Ironically this coincided with increased questioning of the Reagan administration's policies in the region, in Washington and beyond – not least because of the so-called "Iran–Contra" arms sales scandal. In this context the new social democratic government of Oscar Arias began moving towards a more active and coherent peace-making policy in the region. In August 1987 Costa Rican diplomats managed to get the five Central American presidents to sign up to the "Esquipulas II Plan". This home-grown framework – premised on a simultaneous movement towards internal dialogue and democratization, a cessation of external support to all insurgencies in the region, and multilateral cooperation to verify the agreements and rebuild the region – marked a new phase of regional peace-making.[9]

The Arias government's foreign policy initially stoked the fires of internal and international tensions. On the domestic front, opponents of the 1983 Proclamation of Neutrality also came out against the Esquipulas process. Yet the Arias administration had been elected on a clear pro-peace platform in 1986, and it used its diplomatic success with Esquipulas II to consolidate popular support for an activist foreign policy. Large marches and public opinion polls indicated broad public support for this approach. The magic of the Arias discourse was that it reconnected with the popular myth of Costa Rica as a peaceful democratic country while dramatically moving beyond its isolationist subtext. As such, it captured the people's imagination and ensured the domestic backing required to end all support to Nicaraguan counter-revolutionaries and their US masters.

Internationally, the Reagan administration felt betrayed by San José since it viewed Esquipulas II as a process that would legitimize Sandinista rule, weaken the Contras and ultimately undermine US military strategy. Tensions with Washington increased dramatically in 1988–1989. Despite these pressures, the Arias government intensified its foreign policy activism, kept all the Central American governments on board despite their ideological differences, and gradually brought the Contadora Group, the United Nations, the Organization of American States, Canada and the European Community on side. The support of these countries and multilateral organizations was crucial to the verification and implementation of the Esquipulas II accords. This broad support also proved crucial to counterbalancing the pressures of the Reagan administration, and it opened the door to a pragmatic reorientation of policy by the Bush team from 1989 onward. The collapse of the socialist bloc and the end of the Cold War were also enormously important enabling factors for these developments.

In Nicaragua these trends converged with the elections of February 1990, which were won by the United Nicaraguan Opposition headed by Violeta Barrios de Chamorro. The decision by the Sandinistas to accept these results and allow the incorporation of Contra combatants into social life, in return for leaving important elements of Sandinismo in place – all within the framework of the Esquipulas II accords – paved the way for the gradual de-escalation of the war in that country.

The end of the war in Nicaragua also put an end to the old polemics over Costa Rican foreign policy. New debates came to the fore, particularly regarding the country's social and economic policies. Costa Rica remained involved in the regional summit process, which concentrated more and more on regional cooperation in the economic, social and environmental spheres. During the 1990s the focus of foreign policy shifted from Central America to the hemisphere and to emerging opportunities in global markets.

This shift began at a time when the persistent recession and political instability in Nicaragua continued to affect the Costa Rican economy negatively, particularly through the arrival of 300,000 new economic migrants in search of employment opportunities. Nicaragua remained a foreign policy concern and bilateral relations stayed strained, despite political changes in Managua. This was reflected in ongoing tensions associated with the disputed border along the San Juan River and the improvised character of responses to the challenge of increased north–south migration.

Nonetheless, the priority accorded to Nicaragua and the rest of the region gradually declined, as debates on strategies for optimal insertion into wider markets increased in salience. Three developments raised the profile of the latter set of issues: the negotiation of free trade agreements with extra-regional states; market-oriented reforms and the privatization of certain public sector entities; and the application of other structural adjustment measures.

Economic liberalization and the crisis of consensus

In fact the first wave of market-oriented reforms began in the mid-1980s, during the regional conflict. The first Structural Adjustment Program (SAP/PAE I) was applied by the Monge government beginning in 1985; SAP/PAE II and III were negotiated and implemented under the Arias and Calderon administrations. These programmes were negotiated with the international financial institutions but could not ignore pressure from domestic actors whose interests were affected by the measures.

The overarching goal of these policies was to ensure the competitive insertion of the Costa Rican economy into emerging export and foreign investment markets. Within this framework, the functions of the state, the scope of the mixed economy and the coverage of welfare programmes began to be questioned by critics of the established model. Several concrete measures were adopted from the mid-1980s onward to modify the system: the state's monopoly in financial markets was ended and a mixed banking system was established; state enterprises, such as distribution outlets of the agricultural production board (Consejo Nacional de Producción), were privatized; public infrastructure markets were opened to private participation. Finally, a debate on the privatization of public telecommunications, electricity and insurance service providers was initiated.[10]

These economic reforms enabled the development of new lines of revenue-generating activities, which counterbalanced the decline in coffee prices and the imposition of tariff barriers to banana exports to the

European Union. As the regional security climate improved, the market for tourism expanded, and by the early 1990s tourism had become the principal source of foreign revenues. The most dramatic change in this regard, however, was the establishment of a large production complex by the US electronics firm Intel in the mid-1990s. This development was the result of personal lobbying by President José Maria Figueres (son of José Figueres Ferrer) during his administration from 1994 to 1998. The foreign sales of this firm alone have constituted an average of 30 per cent of the total annual exports of Costa Rica since 1997. The establishment of the Intel complex is often seen as the tipping point in Costa Rica's shift from an agro-industrial to a post-industrial economy based on international commerce, tourism and services.

The Achilles heel of this new model, however, is a persistent gap between macroeconomic growth and the distribution of its benefits. The country's GDP grew by an average of 4 per cent annually during the 1990s. By 1999 the annual GDP growth rate had hit an impressive 8 per cent, of which 5 per cent was due to the Intel production complex. Unemployment remained at 6 per cent throughout the decade, which is quite low by regional standards – although some analysts suggest that this reflected an increase in women's labour market participation to compensate for decreased family incomes. As indicated in table 11.1, poverty and extreme poverty also increased in the early 1990s, before levelling off at around 21 per cent and 6 per cent, respectively, in 2000. Most worrisome, however, were significant increases in income inequality, as re-

Table 11.1 Household poverty in Costa Rica, 1990–2000 (per cent)

Poverty level	1990	1991	1992	1993	1994	1995	1996	1997	1998	1999	2000
Poor	27.1	31.9	29.4	23.2	20.0	20.4	21.6	20.7	19.7	20.6	21.1
Extremely poor	9.2	11.7	9.3	6.9	5.8	6.2	6.9	5.7	5.3	6.7	6.4
Unable to meet basic needs	17.9	20.2	20.1	16.3	14.2	14.2	14.7	15.0	14.4	13.9	14.8
Other households	72.9	68.1	70.6	76.8	80.0	79.6	78.4	79.3	80.3	79.4	78.9
Total	100.0	100.0	100.0	100.0	100.0	100.0	100.0	100.0	100.0	100.0	100.0

Source: Synthesized from the annual *Proyecto Estado de la Nación* reports, 1996–2002. Original data gathered by the Dirección General de Estadísticas y Censos, with measurement adjustments in 1996.

flected by changes in the Gini coefficient: from 0.419 in 1990 to 0.429 in 1994 and 0.454 in 1999.[11]

The drive to privatize public services has yet to affect core social services. Still, the fiscal crisis and the high level of internal indebtedness have imposed severe restrictions on public expenditures in the areas of education, health and housing. These cutbacks have eroded the universal coverage of social services and increased the attractiveness of private alternatives to those who can afford them. The same factors brought the public pensions system to the verge of bankruptcy, prompting institutional reforms and the opening of the pensions market to private funds.

Not surprisingly, these measures have been associated with conflicts between the so-called "globalizers" and the beneficiaries of the activist welfare state. The globalizers include actors associated with agro-exports, international commerce, tourism and private banking. These groups control the new sources of wealth generation and have begun to wield corresponding influence on politics and international trade policies in particular. The political leaders and technocrats who have run the state since the early 1990s emerged from or are closely associated with these strata; their interests are linked to production for extra-regional rather than national or regional markets. The new political elites are framing their project within the discourse of "political environmentalism". This vision posits that the key to Costa Rica's successful insertion into globalization is the exploitation of the country's biodiversity within a socioeconomic model based on equity, sustainability and respect for the environment.

The debate over this vision, as well as its policies and practices, is proving to be more socially contested than the debate over foreign policy strategies in the 1980s. On the other side of the social equation we find a heterogeneous array of national agricultural and industrial producers, commercial intermediaries, public employees and other workers, students, the poor and other historical beneficiaries of the activist welfare state. Many of these constituencies experienced a diminution of benefits from the mixed economy and public welfare programmes. Many began to lose confidence in the state and particularly in the main political parties. Despite their internal differences, these actors became defenders of the activist welfare state, protesting against the privatization of telecommunications and electricity services and against the opening of insurance markets to private funds.

Large public protests and intense debates in the media have not been reflected in major differences between the two main political parties because both parties now represent elites who see their interests bound up with market-oriented reforms. However, these political elites have had to moderate some of their measures in response to popular opposition. Reforms to the pensions system were imposed in the late 1990s despite massive public protests, yet this spawned a deep conflict between the political elites and the teachers' unions, which had been allies of successive governments but broke ranks when it became clear that their members would bear the brunt of the reforms. There was no room for negotiation, the reforms were rushed through Congress with a presidential decree that was approved by parliamentarians without public debate, and a procedural pillar of the historical consensus collapsed overnight.[12]

The new political elites and the globalizers were unable to impose a similar outcome in the debates on the liberalization of telecommunications and electricity. During the first round of debate in Congress in 2000, the two main political parties approved a bill that would have significantly reduced the role of the public sector in the provision of energy and telecommunications services. This debate was also seen as the first step in a process to privatize insurance and banking services fully.

The reform proposal rested on the argument that there was an urgent need to improve the quality of services, reduce state debts and ensure private investment in areas where the state had limited fiscal capacity. Nevertheless, the content of the bill and the process through which it was approved generated the country's largest social protest movement in living memory. The Rodriguez administration (1998–2002) had tried to negotiate the reform package with its opponents, but the first round of congressional debate indicated that it had misjudged the degree of consensus during the discussions. The opposition National Liberation Party also misjudged this consensus when it supported the bill in the first debate; when the degree of popular opposition to the package became clear, the PLN formally withdrew its support for the measures.

The legacy of this social movement goes far beyond the withdrawal of the liberalization package. First, the movement explicitly reaffirmed the identification by a large part of the population with institutions that since 1948 had been the bastions of the activist welfare state and whose management by transnational enterprises was seen to jeopardize hard-won universal access to basic public services. Second, the movement revealed a worrying degree of public disenchantment with the process of policy-making, and particularly with the primary institution of representative democracy: Congress. Strong concerns were voiced about the domination of Congress by the Office of the President through clientelistic practices. Third, the prominent participation of students in the social movement highlighted widespread sentiments of rebellion among youth directed at the institutions of public authority. The stand-off led to the historically unprecedented establishment of a Mixed Commission, with the participation of parliamentarians and representatives of social organizations, to negotiate reforms to the electricity and telecommunications sectors. Yet by this time irreparable damage had been done to the Costa Rican model and to its democratic credentials.

It is important to distinguish between this situation and the crisis of governance that occurred in 1948 or the ones that periodically make neighbouring countries almost ungovernable. Costa Rica is not on the verge of a breakdown in its constitutional order. Yet the "crisis of 2000" certainly revealed a deep divide between political elites who appear to have abandoned the ideals of the 1948 model and large sections of the population for whom that model remains a key part of their collective identity.

This divide has led not to a popular rejection of the Costa Rican model, but rather to disaffection with the political parties and other elites who seem to be abandoning its social democratic content and procedures. One indication of this tendency is the increase in electoral abstention rates from a historical average of 20 per cent to over 30 per cent in the February 2002 elections. In that election the two main political parties also suffered unprecedented losses and new parties gained seats; as a result, Congress has had to learn to deal with the vagaries of a multi-party legislature.

On the positive side, this has opened the political system up to new actors and issues. Civil society organizations, the judiciary and public ombudspersons have become more influential in the process. Demands are emerging for the expansion of these new participatory spaces, not just through Congress but also through a re-democratization of local politics and greater public input into the management of state entities. Whether Costa Rica will be able to find a way of continuing to insert itself competitively into the global economy, address growing socioeconomic inequities and renew its democratic institutions will be a major test over the coming years.

Reflections on the legacy of a successful state

This chapter has told the story of a small, less developed society and how it has confronted three major challenges over the past half-century. The 1948 civil war is the only one of these crises that could reasonably be classified as an instance of "state failure". We have seen how social democratic elites pulled the country out of that crisis by consolidating a model based on five pillars: an inclusive liberal democracy, demilitarization, a mixed economy, a welfare state and a strong sense of nationhood. That model, which positioned Costa Rica at the successful end of the state failure–success continuum, could be described as "a capable state resting on the judicious management of power in a strong society". It was rooted in earlier historical developments, including a relatively benign presence of colonial institutions, and enabled by US policy in the aftermath of the Second World War.

The Costa Rican model allowed the country to prevent the descent into civil war and foreign intervention experienced by its neighbours in the 1980s. It provided the backbone that enabled successive governments to craft an independent, activist foreign policy in favour of negotiated peace in the region, at a time when US policy was still pulling in the opposite direction. That model was also one of the factors that helped Costa Rica position itself to reap the benefits of economic liberalization from the 1980s onwards. However, some of the market-oriented reforms adopted to facilitate the competitive insertion into the global economy, combined with insufficient attention to established democratic procedures in recent years, have generated new social conflicts that call into question the longevity of the model itself. Fortunately these conflicts have also generated new spaces for public participation and debate on national priorities, thus opening the door to a renewal of the Costa Rican model within the framework of liberal globalization.

The account of Costa Rica as a relatively successful state – particularly compared with its Central American neighbours but also with many other developing countries – suggests a number of modest insights for the current debate on state failure. First, like the story of Singapore, this case reminds us that "fixing failed states", protecting citizens and preventing violent conflict are not just missions for the international community or resurgent empires. They are, first and foremost, missions for domestic actors, and in many instances national actors manage to find their own solutions to major crises. Sometimes the best approach for the international community might be to back off, support actors building indigenous or regional solutions, and not support poor leaders or entrenched elites even when their discourses echo great power or big business interests. Sadly, this insight in the 2001 report by the International Commission on Intervention and State Sovereignty is sometimes lost in debates on the responsibility to protect.[13]

Second, it reminds us that lasting solutions are made up of more than a series of conjunctural decisions and sectoral policies. The key to Costa Rican exceptionalism is the set of institutional arrangements and cultural understandings consolidated after the 1948 civil war. In the Costa Rican case, the factors explaining why this worked include: the vision of certain elites and of leaders such as José Figueres; a promising but historically rooted national correlation of forces and political culture (including the absence of strong autonomous security forces); an integrated strategy, namely the adoption of an integrated approach to democratic governance and economic and social policy as well as to foreign policy; and an enabling international environment, at least until the late 1970s. Although certain Costa Rican institutions differ from those in Singapore, notably in the degree of political liberalism and the type of security forces, others are remarkably similar, and both models share three central ingredients: enlightened leaders, a coherent institutional response and international space to consolidate a national system with modest foreign involvement.

Third, the Costa Rican case suggests that even when one of these ingredients shifts remarkably – as occurred when the region collapsed into war and US policy came to privilege military intervention in the region's affairs during the 1980s – coherent governance arrangements can enable visionary leaders to forge creative solutions, prevent state failure and even help neighbouring countries.

Finally, this case also reminds us that nothing should be taken for granted, especially not success. As noted in other chapters, the current round of economic globalization has created immense opportunities and challenges for state-building. Costa Rica is having difficulties managing this tension, despite its glowing record in comparison with its neighbours and with countries such as Colombia, Mozambique and Pakistan. Indeed, recent developments in the "Switzerland of Central America" have shown that successful governance is fragile, and that it must be renewed to preserve its core values while adapting to changing international conditions.

The strategic challenge for Costa Ricans is how to combine institutional approaches that were successful in earlier eras with the innovations required to benefit from the new global political economy. Many other countries undoubtedly envy Costa Rica for being able to focus on managing success. Some might also draw lessons from this country's remarkable achievements, as well as from its ongoing attempts to grapple with the tensions inherent in managing democratic governance and equitable development in the current world order.

Acknowledgements

We acknowledge the research and creative input of Ana Marcela Rodriguez, as well as the valuable comments of the editors and peer reviewers. We are also grateful for the support of our respective institutions, FLACSO Costa Rica and the North–South Institute.

Notes

1. In the 1540s the colonial administration passed laws to protect indigenous peoples and prohibit their enslavement. This norm and the absence of high-value natural resources acted as disincentives to Spanish settlement. See Wendy Kramer, W. George Lowell and Christopher H. Lutz, "La Conquista Española de Centroamérica", in Julio Pinto

Soria, ed., *Historia general de Centroamérica: El régimen colonial*, San José, Costa Rica: FLACSO, 1994. See also Juan Carlos Solórzano, *La búsqueda del oro y la resistencia indígena: campañas de explotación y conquista de Costa Rica (1502–1610)*, San José, Costa Rica: Universidad de Costa Rica, 1987.

2. Edelberto Torres Rivas, "Contrapunto entre reforma y revolución: La democracia en Costa Rica y Guatemala", in Jorge Rovira, *La democracia en Costa Rica en el Siglo XXI*, San José, Costa Rica: Editorial de la Universidad de Costa Rica, Fundación Ebert and Instituto de Investigaciones Sociales, 2001.

3. For an excellent analysis comparing the consolidation of liberal democratic and authoritarian political institutions in Costa Rica and Guatemala, see Deborah J. Yashar, *Demanding Democracy: Reform and Reaction in Costa Rica and Guatemala, 1870s–1950*, Stanford, CA: Stanford University Press, 1997.

4. Víctor Hugo Acuña, *Conflicto y reforma en Costa Rica: 1940–1949*, San José, Costa Rica: Editorial Universidad Estatal a Distancia, 1992; John Patrick Bell, *Guerra civil en Costa Rica: Los sucesos políticos de 1948*, San José, Costa Rica: Editorial Universitaria Centroamericana, 1981; Juan Diego López, *Los cuarenta días de 1948: La guerra civil en Costa Rica*, San José, Costa Rica: Editorial Costa Rica, 1998; Manuel Rojas, *Lucha social y guerra civil en Costa Rica: 1940–1948*, San José, Costa Rica: Editorial Porvenir, 1979; Jacobo Schifter, *La fase oculta de la guerra civil en Costa Rica*, San José, Costa Rica: Editorial Universitaria Centroamericana, 1981.

5. The economies in Central America grew by an average of 5 per cent annually in real GDP terms from the 1950s to the end of the 1970s, significantly exceeding the 3.2 per cent average annual population growth. Yet the Costa Rican economy grew fastest, at an average of 6.5 per cent during this period, possibly owing to the redistributive policies that were put in place at the outset. See Victor Bulmer-Thomas, *La economía política de Centroamerica desde 1920*, San José, Costa Rica: BCIE-EDUCA, 1989.

6. The crisis in Panama, leading to the US invasion against the Noriega regime in December 1989, was related to the Central American crisis but had a distinct dynamic. As such, its impact on Costa Rican foreign policy will not be analysed here.

7. The Contadora Group was composed of Colombia, Mexico, Panama and Venezuela. Its intense diplomatic process generated three major regional peace treaties. Though these were never signed, they laid indispensable foundations for the Esquipulas II accord and subsequent national peace agreements.

8. For example, between 1982 and 1986 certain chiefs of the Rural Assistance Guard (GAR) openly supported the operations of anti-Sandinista insurgents, whereas another sector of government, particularly in the foreign ministry, tried to maintain channels of communication with the government in Managua.

9. This section is based on Carlos Sojo, "La política del aliado inteligente: Costa Rica y Estados Unidos 1988–1989", in Gabriel Aguilera, Abelardo Morales and Carlos Sojo, *Centroamérica de Reagan a Bush*, San José, Costa Rica: FLACSO, 1991; Carlos Sojo, *Costa Rica: Política exterior y sandinismo*, San José, Costa Rica: FLACSO, 1991; Luis Guillermo Solís, "Costa Rica: La política exterior y los cambios en el sistema internacional en los ochenta", in Manuel Villasuso, ed., *El nuevo rostro de Costa Rica*, San José, Costa Rica: CEDAL, 1992; Fransisco Rojas, *Costa Rica y el sistema internacional*, San José, Costa Rica: Fundación Friedrich Ebert, 1990.

10. This section draws heavily on Mary Clark, *Gradual Economic Reform in Latin America: The Costa Rican Experience*, New York: New York University, 2001; Juan Rial and Daniel Zovatto, *Urnas y desencanto político: Elecciones y democracia en América Latina 1992–1996*, San José, Costa Rica: IIDH/CAPEL, 1998; Marcela Rodríguez, "El financiamiento de los partidos políticos en México, Costa Rica y Colombia: Un análisis comparativo de sus reformas", thesis for Licenciatura degree, Universidad de Costa Rica,

San José, Costa Rica, 1999; Mitchell Seligson, "Problemas en el Paraíso? La erosión en el apoyo al sistema político y la centroamericanización de Costa Rica, 1978–1999", in Jorge Rovira, ed., *La democracia en Costa Rica en el Siglo XXI*, San José, Costa Rica: Editorial de la Universidad de Costa Rica, Fundación Ebert and Instituto de Investigaciones Sociales, 2001; Manuel Solís, "Entre el cambio y la tradición: El fracaso de la privatización de la energía y las telecomunicaciones en Costa Rica", *Revista de ciencias sociales*, No. 95, Universidad de Costa Rica, 2002.

11. Data synthesized from the annual *Proyecto Estado de la Nación* reports, 1996–2002; original data gathered by the Instituto Nacional de Estadisticas y Censos. For an excellent analysis of these trends for Costa Rica and the region, see Juan Pablo Pérez-Sáenz, Katherine Andrade-Eekhoff, Santiago Bastos and Michael Herradora, *La Estructura social ante la globalización. Procesos de reordenamiento de social en Centroamérica durante la década de los noventa*, San José, Costa Rica: FLACSO and CEPAL, 2004. The Gini coefficient is an aggregate measure of income inequality. Measures range from 0 for perfect equality to 1 for perfect inequality: countries with measures between 0.2 and 0.35 are considered to have fairly equal income distributions, whereas countries with measures from 0.5 to 0.7 are seen to have highly unequal income distributions. By sliding from 0.419 to 0.454 between 1990 and 1999, Costa Rica moved closer to the high income inequality patterns of its neighbours. See Michael P. Todaro, *Economic Development in the Third World*, 3rd edn, New York: Longman, 1985, pp. 145–147, for details on how Gini coefficients are calculated.

12. According to Costa Rican law, three legislative assembly debates are required before a bill can be approved as law, and parliamentarians should hold a vote at the end of each debate.

13. International Commission on Intervention and State Sovereignty, *The Responsibility to Protect*, Ottawa, Canada: International Development Research Centre, 2001. The focus at the Progressive Governance Summit in July 2003 on the *Responsibility to Protect* report's recommendations regarding international intervention is symptomatic of this tendency to forget the report's other insights – including its position on the primary responsibility of national governments to protect their own citizens. See, for example, the coverage in CBC News Online, 14 July 2003. For a welcome exception to this tendency, see Ramesh Thakur, "Chrétien Was Right: It's Time to Redefine 'Just War'", *Globe and Mail*, 22 July 2003. This being said, it is certain that international military intervention is the only viable option in certain extreme circumstances. That is why the adoption by international institutions of criteria for intervention akin to those set out in the *Responsibility to Protect* report remains an important objective.

12

From vulnerability to success: The British withdrawal from Singapore

Patricia Shu Ming Tan and Simon S. C. Tay

Best known for its economic success, Singapore's singular experience in state-building may seem an unusual choice for inclusion in this book. But the strength and reach of today's city-state belie its fragile beginnings and ongoing concerns for its future. In fact, any study that hails Singapore's success must give equal or greater attention to its sense of vulnerability; many of the reasons for state failure outlined by Sebastian von Einsiedel in this volume – geographical disadvantages, the lack of a political culture or common social heritage, and ethnic divisions – applied to Singapore at its independence.[1] Against this background, the present chapter focuses on an important juncture in history for the success or failure of the Singapore state: the withdrawal of British troops in 1971.

This historical analysis of Singapore's experience reinforces the suggestion already made in the previous chapters: that self-sustaining stability and growth can be fostered only in an environment of self-directed evolution. Although long-term success can never be guaranteed, a state is more likely to survive and thrive in an environment of decisive internal implementation. This example also demonstrates how canny cooperation with external actors, driven by keen foresight of both local goals and international interests, is as crucial a parameter of effective local leadership as is credibility with the population.

This chapter therefore refrains from discussing solely when and how the international community intervened to support the state in this historically fragile moment. Instead, it examines how the cessation of an external actor's involvement may be re-cast as an important state-building exercise. Although Singapore's experience, in its specific historical context, is not likely to be repeated in the future, the recent examples of East Timor and Afghanistan demonstrate the importance of managing the disengagement of external actors, whose withdrawal can disrupt not only internal and external security but also the fabric of everyday life. Singapore's experience demonstrates how an integrated response by the government can create opportunities for foreign policy, domestic social policy and economic development from this transition.

Externally, Singapore's experience was that of an emerging state actively courting engagement with selected international actors, counterbalancing the diminished presence of one with increased involvement by others. By shifting the configuration of international involvement, the leadership tailored international cooperation to the new state's needs and long-term goals. The role of Israeli advisers and the assistance afforded by the United Nations Development Programme (UNDP), for example, were integral to the development of Singapore's defence and economy, respectively. Furthermore, by clearly defining the parameters of engagement, Singapore ensured its relationship with external actors could not be construed as dependence. This is a crucial distinction, because immediate solutions to vulnerability in the form of external assistance may diminish the legitimacy of the state in the longer term, in the eyes of both its citizenry and the international community.

The experience of Singapore suggests that answers may be present not only in the form of external assistance, but also within the country and the very crisis at hand. The international community can assist internal state-building, but can never substitute for the development of local capacity. This chapter also proposes that institutions such as civil society, although important, are insufficient in themselves in the absence of a stable functioning state. Given the necessity of a state that is internally conceived and driven, there is every need to hope for leaders who are committed to the collective good in their strategic planning.

Defining success for the state

In the decolonization that followed the end of the Second World War, some colonies, such as Singapore, enjoyed a number of advantages over their fellow emerging states. The British had appreciated the island's strategic importance, defined by its unique location, for over a century.[2] Its position and natural harbour had established the island as a centre for entrepôt trade. By the 1970s, Singapore was already the world's fourth-largest port.[3] Singapore also benefited from the economic and political foundations that were part of its colonial legacy. An intact civil service and a respect for the rule of law facilitated institution-building after independence. Singapore's success, however, must be compared with countries that were in analogous situations at that time. These post-colonial small and micro-states have since adjusted to independence with varying degrees of success.

In fact, Singapore's advantages were counterbalanced by instability, internally and in the region. Singapore would very likely have failed any test of viability in the 1960s. Even Lee Kuan Yew, architect of Singapore's eventual rapid development, believed at that time that the island of Singapore was an unviable entity as an independent state, calling an independent Singapore "a political, economic, and geographical absurdity".[4]

South East Asia could have been considered a classic "bad neighbourhood" 40 years ago, replete with conditions perfect for creating unstable states:

In the 1960s, the outlook for regional security and stability in Southeast Asia was particularly grim, the region was portrayed variously as a "region of revolt," the "Balkans of the East," or a "region of dominoes." The weak socio-political cohesion of the region's new nation-states, the legitimacy problems of several of the region's postcolonial governments, interstate territorial disputes, intra-regional ideological polarization and intervention by external powers were marked features of the geopolitical landscape of Southeast Asia.[5]

The boundaries of Singapore and nearby states reflected colonial legacies and political rationales rather than the ethnic or social realities of the region. Ethnic conflict, for example, was rooted in loyalties and identities that reached far beyond the state borders. The island was sandwiched between larger neighbours that had previously disdained the small state's sovereignty. As Lee Kuan Yew observed in 1966, "Your neighbours are not your best friends."[6] Singapore also had been the target of communist-led disturbances, which in turn triggered inter-state and domestic violence. The resultant danger to life and property did not help in attracting the foreign investment that Singapore needed badly.

In the case of Singapore, peace could be realized only by circumscribing local unrest as internal issues. Thus "domesticized" from the scope and source of regional conflict, the state could address these problems with new pan-ethnic goals of social cohesion. Such goals, however, were not self-evident and had to be articulated in the aftermath of Singapore's unanticipated separation from Malaysia in 1965.

In the light of these troubled beginnings, the example of Singapore shows how "success" is contextually defined. The world often seems short of success stories about the making and management of states. Although many states have emerged since the Second World War and the Cold War, few have achieved economic development, state legitimacy and freedoms for their peoples. Against this stark and somewhat bleak background, some champion Singapore as an example of success that can and should be emulated by others. Others qualify or denigrate Singapore's achievements by classifying Singapore as a "soft authoritarian" system. Such comments tend to focus on perceived shortcomings in freedoms of speech, the media and the development of a political opposition, as compared with the models of liberal democracy practised in the developed Western societies. Such criticism of Singapore grew stronger in the wake of the end of the Cold War, when theorists such as Samuel Huntington and Francis Fukuyama argued for a "third wave" of democracy and the "end of history". Criticism has ebbed somewhat as the Singapore state continued to show effective responses to new challenges, such as the Asian financial crisis and the security concerns of international terrorism after 11 September 2001.

This chapter cannot resolve that entire and often ideologically driven debate. The characteristics of what constitutes a successful state – indeed, the very elements of "success" – may change over time and shift in perspective, according to changes at both international and national levels. The present chapter hopes, more modestly, to examine a historical incident to consider how a moment of vulnerability was turned to stability and even advantage in preparing for future and still unresolved challenges for the state. With the caveat that the response of the People's Action Party (PAP) government in the 1970s cannot be replicated wholesale, either in Singapore today or in any other part of the world, this case-study presents a useful perspective on what forms of intervention, by international partners and by the national government, facilitated Singapore's successful emergence from this particular historical crisis.

Background to Singapore's experience

Singapore had long been strategically important for British military interests in South East Asia. After the Second World War, the headquarters of the British Far East Land Forces, the Far East Station of the Royal Navy and the Far East Air Forces of the Royal Air Force were all stationed in Singapore. Singapore's strategic significance, however, would wane as the UK Labour government, elected in October 1964, reconsidered the costs and merits of its overseas defence commitments, especially the expensive military deployment East of Suez.[7] The July 1966 sterling crisis further forced deflationary measures upon the United Kingdom. By the end of that year, a resolution calling for withdrawal was passed with a sizeable majority. British forces were to be reduced by half during 1970–1971 and completely withdrawn by the middle of the decade. However, the devaluation of sterling in November 1967 accelerated intentions to wind down the United Kingdom's military capability in the region completely by 1970–1971.[8]

Singapore thus had some warning of the anticipated withdrawal, a luxury that may not exist in other situations. Nevertheless, the withdrawal presented the young nation with a set of pressing problems that complicated its first years as an independent republic.

Unlike the post-colonial societies addressed by James Mayall earlier in this book,[9] Singapore did not emerge through anti-colonial nationalism. Singapore's post-colonial independence had been achieved through merger with Malaya to form Malaysia in 1963. Differences over the political and economic roles of Singapore within a federal Malaysia, however, proved increasingly irreconcilable. In August 1965, Singapore and Malaysia separated.[10] Singapore's sudden independence was fraught with insecurity. Malaysia's threat of force accompanying the acrimonious proposal for separation immediately caused Singapore to view its closest neighbour with much trepidation.[11] Singapore's dependence on the Malaysian state of Johor for water exacerbated its perception of its own vulnerability. The price and supply of water continue to be a point of dispute between Malaysia and Singapore. To this day, bilateral relations between the two states are marked as much by the realities of physical, functional, communal and historical closeness as by competitiveness and differences in outlook.

Singapore faced other internal and external threats to its security and stability at independence. The spectre of the recent communist insurgency (known as the Emergency) continued to loom large. Indonesia's policy of *konfrontasi* (Confrontation), initially Sukarno's statement of opposition to the formation of Malaysia, demonstrated the proximity of powerful destabilizing factors. Its resolution, under Indonesia's new leadership of Suharto, lent cold comfort to Singapore because Malaysia and Indonesia had proceeded to cement post-*konfrontasi* cooperation in "an appeal to a common Malay blood brotherhood".[12]

Such messages were particularly troubling to multi-ethnic Singapore. In terms of race and ethnicity, Singapore may be considered a Chinese enclave within South East Asia. Three-quarters of the population were Chinese, approximately 14 per cent Malay and about 8 per cent of South Asian origin. Not only was the population of Singapore at that time ethnically diverse, it was also sharply segregated across the island. As discussed in several other chapters of this book, the volatility that stems from ethnic divide is an important structural cause of conflict. Ethnic and religious antagonisms were raw and tensions between these groups had already erupted in serious race riots in July 1964.[13] Domestically, independence was perhaps most problematic for the Malay population, who suddenly found themselves in a minority position, in contrast to their counterparts across the Straits in Malaysia. Moreover, the close geographical and historical relationship between Malaysia and Singapore meant that any inter-ethnic strains were more than a domestic issue; communal violence in Kuala Lumpur in 1969, for example, spilled over to Singapore.

Finally, the retention of British bases was important to Singapore in economic terms. British bases provided for some 16 per cent of employment,[14] and the proportion of wealth attributable to the military presence was estimated to account for 14 per cent of the country's GDP. If handled badly, the withdrawal could have had devastating effects on the domestic economy and local population, which was already struggling under an unemployment rate of 14 per cent.[15] Faced with population growth at a rate of 4 per cent, the state needed quickly to develop a core of industries that would provide gainful employment and sustained growth to the nation-state.

External responses: Managing and engaging international partners

Although Singapore's legal status as an independent country has never been substantively challenged, asserting this independence and re-casting relationships with countries such as the United Kingdom and Malaysia required much effort. In the case of the United Kingdom, Singapore needed to engage its former colonial power, while shifting from its role of defence client to that of a defence partner. In the case of Malaysia and Indonesia, Singapore had to exert its sovereignty while maintaining the social and economic ties that reflected the geopolitical realities of the region.

For small and developing states, managing the actions of significant international actors sometimes appears impossible. After unsuccessfully trying to persuade the Australian, New Zealand and Malaysian leaders to lobby collectively with him against withdrawal, Lee travelled to London alone. He secured a postponement of the final withdrawal from Singapore by nine months. Crucially, this delay straddled the 1970 elections, which, as Lee had calculated, Labour lost.[16]

Lee's last-minute effort to manage the withdrawal process on less unilateral terms suggests that size may be less important than the ability to match goals with the interests of the greater power. Following the Conservative victory, Lee drew upon the Tory reluctance completely to relinquish the United Kingdom's role as a world leader to persuade Edward Heath, the Conservative leader, of the symbolic importance of a physical presence of troops.[17] Under this suggestion, the United Kingdom, and by extension Australia and New Zealand, would continue to be engaged in the region under economically manageable terms.[18] In early January 1970, Heath agreed to stem the withdrawal, committing the British forces still remaining in Singapore to a balanced five-power force that also included Australia, New Zealand and Malaysia.[19] As a result, 4,500 British troops remained in Singapore until March 1976.[20]

This five-power concept was in line with Singapore's emerging foreign policy, which reflected a new political equality among the five Commonwealth partners.[21] This required careful balance. On the one hand, Singapore needed to keep old actors (the United Kingdom) engaged. On the other, it sought to counterpoint the waning influence of the original relationship with other parties. Reconfiguring the bilateral colonial relationship into a multilateral defence arrangement suited all parties without loss of face. The United Kingdom remained engaged with reduced commitment and Australia's alliance with the United States indirectly introduced another significant actor in regional security. Singapore would continue to cultivate its defence and trade relationships with the United States, whose interest Singapore regarded as essential for the preservation of stability in the region.

The Singapore government sought the attention and presence of external stabilizing powers such as the United Kingdom and the United States to temper the turbulent geopolitics of the region. At the same time, however, the realities of geographical destiny could not be shirked. Regional cooperation had to be built, and Singapore sought to engage its larger neighbours in cooperative security and economic development through bodies such as the Association of South East Asian Nations (ASEAN), which was established in 1967.

This brief overview of Singapore's foreign and defence policy in the crucial 1960s and 1970s provides an insight into how the new Singapore government managed the inevitability of British troop withdrawal. When the withdrawal seemed more rapid than originally planned, Lee Kuan Yew appealed to the balance of interests within the British Parliament to secure a delay of the withdrawal and to propose a modified British presence in the region. Moreover, the government understood the drivers of political power in its neighbours. Although Singapore's leaders prized rationality in their own ranks, they realized that this was not a basis upon which policy could be communicated. Taking a realistic view of political will as the driver for all major decisions, including intervention, sustaining a presence and aid, they relied less on calculations of the limits of defence capability or damage to self-interest to preserve regional security, and more on pursuing the formation of a cooperative framework within which each member could play an active role.

Throughout this period, the government also invoked Singapore's difficult circumstances in the name of effecting wide-ranging change, including developing the armed forces and overhauling the economy. The vulnerability of Singapore was real as well as perceived, externally bolstered by Singapore's position between Malaysia and Indonesia and internally generated by its fragility of identity and diversity of citizenry.[22] In some contrast to Michel Cahen's analysis of the dangers of state- and nation-building, the Singapore experience was one of active downplaying of existing social relationships and vigorous promotion of new shared experience and challenges that the entire population would have to face together.[23]

Domestic responses: Earning legitimacy and building state institutions

The period coinciding with the withdrawal of British troops was one of nation-building. The internal challenge of giving shape to the nascent state exacerbated the uncertain economic and security conditions. These faltering beginnings were employed as a rallying cry for the nation, instilling a sense of urgency for development at both the individual and state levels. Policies to address domestic issues were couched in terms of nation-building based on a rhetoric of survival that facilitated both "pragmatic acculturation" and the establishment of new national symbols and institutions. National Service, housing programmes and a new national education programme were created as pan-ethnic institutions so that Singaporeans could identify Singapore as state, nation and home.

Such nation-building was necessary to address the prevalent ethnic tension. Under British rule, the different immigrant communities nurtured different national loyalties, and did not identify as a group. Social and support structures for the Chinese population, for example, were based on clan associations, which maintained close links to China. The Chinese built their own schools through collected donations, using textbooks published in China. "Culturally," as Lee Kuan Yew recalls in his memoirs, "they lived in a world apart."[24] The South Asian populations also tended to identify with the subcontinent rather than with their new abode. As indicated earlier, the Malay population had cause to feel disenfranchised over Singapore's separation from Malaysia. In fact, at independence, only two members of the first People's Action Party (PAP) cabinet had been born in Singapore.[25] Not only did the deep rifts between these societies threaten the internal stability of the new country, but the immigrant nature of these communities collectively resulted in a population that had little stake in the future of the state. There was no existing nation preceding the formation of the state; instead, the borders of the newly independent state had to define the nation within it.[26]

Sweeping reforms of this scale and nature required the active participation of the citizens, both in abandoning entrenched habits and in embracing new norms and behaviours. For example, the National Service Ordinance, passed by the British Colonial Government in 1952 to train troops in the light of the deteriorating relationship with Indonesia, had to be curtailed as a result of its unpopularity.[27] Although the National Service (Amendment) Act was passed in Parliament in March 1967, opposition to conscription, especially amongst the majority ethnic Chinese community, was strong.[28] The acquiescence of the citizenry in government policy, a quality by which Singapore is sometimes characterized today, was non-existent in the 1960s and 1970s.

In response to protests about National Service, the government employed the impending British troop withdrawal to raise awareness of Singapore's defence needs. It launched the Singapore Defence Fund in January 1968 as "a useful propaganda exercise"; contributions to the Fund were celebrated as patriotic acts supporting the sovereignty of the new republic. "Contributions from individuals, companies and institutions received publicity in the daily newspapers ... By July 1969, the Fund had collected $8.5 million."[29] Extensive public education campaigns were launched and festive send-offs were organized for the families of young men embarking on their service.

To test people's appetite for change, the government also advanced elections by seven months. This was particularly important because the PAP had shifted its platform considerably since its initial rise to power. At that time, Lee Kuan Yew had campaigned for merger with Malaysia, which had failed in 1965. The PAP now had to garner popular support for its policies for an independent Singapore. A victory would give the PAP a fresh mandate to meet the economic and military challenges of the withdrawal. The government, moreover, realized that it had to address industrial and labour relations if it was to deliver the economic development on which it was staking its legitimacy. In addition to its new agenda, therefore, the PAP needed to distance itself from its traditional supporters – trade unions and militant Chinese leftists – who had previously been the cause of low productivity, worker unrest and high wage demands.

The PAP's victory in March 1968 was crucial in allowing the government to move ahead with its policies, especially in the fields of security and economic development. Having visibly earned authority from the populace to address the major challenges ahead, the new government proceeded to cooperate with international actors to plan and implement the necessary structural changes. The salient lesson from Singapore's experience of engagement with international actors is that rapid and sustainable development can be possible only when local ownership of projects clearly defines the consultative process.

In the case of defence, Singapore needed to build its capability rapidly. After initially seeking, and not receiving, assistance from non-aligned Asian and African countries, the Singapore government embarked upon a comparative study of different models of national defence. It selected the Israeli system over the Swiss and Finnish models, "as Israel was considered to possess one of the most impressive citizen armies in the world and her system of training was fast and compressed".[30] Exploratory missions travelled to Israel to see the Israeli model at first hand, to observe training and to negotiate terms of cooperation. An Israeli military mission was stationed in Singapore between the end of 1965 and May 1974.[31] Crucially, the advisory role of the Israeli trainers was clearly defined. They had no command functions; instead, British-trained regular and volunteer Singaporean officers were trained by the Israelis and given direct responsibility for building up Singapore's new forces.[32]

Singapore's state-building efforts reinforce the importance of viewing problems and plans in context, so that all policies work in concert to achieve broad, tangible goals. In this respect, the goal of social cohesion was not pursued in a vacuum, but influenced almost every aspect of domestic policy. National Service, for example, did not merely facilitate the rapid build-up of the Singapore Armed Forces to operational capacity and competence. Just as importantly, it provided a common experience for citizens across all ethnic groups. The choice of Israel as a defence partner provided useful nation-building analogies of embattled sovereignty and a dogged pursuit of survival, reinforcing the state's mantra of self-reliance in the wake of the British withdrawal. National Service has since become a cornerstone of a new national consciousness, rising in social status as a training ground for future leaders, especially among the National Service officer ranks and the professional soldiers.

In the case of economic development, the government sought international expert assistance immediately after gaining self-rule in 1959. In its request for an industrial survey mission from the United Nations Bureau of Technical Assistance Operations (the predecessor of the United Nations Development Programme), Singapore was careful to ensure the relevance of the project to its needs. The state made clear its own diagnosis of the Singapore economy, and specified that the assistance should focus on how Singapore could supplement its commerce with a manufacturing sector that met international standards. The separation from Malaysia severed Singapore's access to its key market for its manufactured goods, and spurred the government to orient its manufacturing to the export market.[33]

To this end, the state asked for experts with experience in industrialization in their home countries, specifically small, industrialized countries such as the Netherlands, Sweden, Belgium and Israel. Albert Winsemius, who had been successful in attracting foreign investment in the Netherlands, led the team's efforts in 1960 and 1961.[34] In response to the mission's report, many of its recommendations were promptly implemented. Far-reaching changes in tax structure, industrial relations, worker training and economic promotion were put in place to develop key industrial sectors and to create jobs rapidly. An Economic Development Board (EDB), a non-political, multi-faceted body that focused on investment promotion and attracting foreign companies to Singapore, was also established.[35] By 1970, the 10-year industrialization programme had yielded the desired reduction in unemployment and significant growth in the manufacturing sector.[36] Equally importantly, several members of the original team were to maintain long-standing advisory relationships with Singapore, reflecting the degree of trust and cooperation between the consultant and client state.

The improvement in the Singapore economy was not, however, any guarantee of Singapore's success in the long term. By the end of the first 10 years of industrialization, Singapore had enjoyed only two strike-free years. The British decision to close its military facilities in Singapore came as a blow, because the withdrawal was estimated to result in 30,000 direct job losses (about 16 per cent of all employment) and 40,000 more indirect ones.[37]

The British naval bases in Singapore, designated the Far East Station of the Royal Navy, were extensive, and some of the busiest between Japan and Sydney. The British withdrawal meant that the bases would dwarf Singapore's skeletal navy. They would lie redundant unless converted to civilian use. Drawing personnel from the Economic Development Board, the government assembled industry heads, economists and advisers to set up a Bases Economic Conversion Unit under the Prime Minister's Office, "to manage and convert the military facilities to productive use and to find alternative employment for the workers".[38] The team was immediately dispatched to Malta, from which the British military had withdrawn the year before. The team investigated how Malta had transformed the British naval base to civilian economic use, and built upon this knowledge to commercialize the military naval bases with the assistance of Swan and Hunter dockyards, the same firm that had managed the conversion of Malta's shipyards.[39]

Through taking stock of the material and human resources available and a clear assessment of the strategic development necessary for economic growth, the withdrawal of the British navy spurred the development of Singapore's modern shipping industry. This goal, however, included more than physical and technical technology transfer; it depended on upgrading the skills of workers.

With the mandate from the recent elections to transform Singapore's economy, the government initiated a crash programme to retrain the workers, most of whom were clerical and naval workers. This project, a collaboration between the Economic Development Board and the Ministry of Education, converted the workers' skills to civilian industrial purposes through evening and weekend classes.[40] Ship-building and repairing were supported as an industrial complement to Singapore's port activities and contributed significantly to Singapore's development in the decades ahead. The concurrent development of the armed forces provided yet another platform for learning and international technology transfer.

The implications of "success"

The general issues raised by the analysis in this chapter are not unique to post-colonial transitional states. States that currently rely heavily on the international community for the provision of law and order, security and even basic goods need to prepare for the day when these resources are withdrawn. Singapore's development of its defence capabilities and implementation of its economic reform policies under the protective British umbrella may be perceived as luxuriously deliberate today, but were considered rushed in the 1960s. Historical examples of successful state-building, from postwar Europe to Singapore, should be a salutary reminder to international actors and client states that successful disengagement cannot happen overnight. In the case of the Philippines, for example, domestic turmoil prioritized nationalism over economic, diplomatic and security sense during the withdrawal of the American troops. Reneging on significant "base-related compensation" and rejecting the three-year phased withdrawal offered by the United States, President Corazon Aquino ordered American forces to withdraw from Subic Bay in just one year. "The time had come", she said, "to close the books on a colonial vestige."[41] Her decision was politically popular on the domestic front, but left the country with a significant equipment, skill and revenue gap.[42]

Was Singapore a "success" in its emergence from the potential crisis posed by the withdrawal of British troops soon after its independence?

Full recognition of the likely impact of the withdrawal revealed opportunities for furthering other vital state objectives. The economic disaster that threatened to follow the British withdrawal was averted through a redeployment of military (especially naval) facilities and skilled labour. This enabled the development of the modern port of Singapore, in line with the government's push for industrializing the economy away from a reliance on entrepôt trade. The need to build its armed forces from scratch also justified universal National Service. Conscription of Singaporean males addressed the defence requirements of the state, but also served as an important institution unifying the ethnically and socio-economically divided citizenry.

Several key aspects of this historical analysis, however, stand in stark contrast to present-day practices and preferences. The form and delivery of the international assistance given to Singapore contrast with the practice of almost all of today's efforts in transitional authority and state-building. First, Singapore did not adopt any externally dictated template for development. Instead, Singapore consciously selected practices from a range of other countries to emulate and adapt. These development strategies did not conform to the prevailing international consensus on state-building.

Second, Singapore received the most useful international assistance from teams that brought depth of experience from successful implementation of similar programmes in their own countries. In seeking to implement these plans, Singapore combined its own administrative elite with specially selected foreign experts, who, in many cases, remained to assist Singapore for extended periods. These experts brought more than crucial lessons from their own work in their countries. In a number of cases, they assisted Singapore by providing a network of key global contacts, such as foreign investors.

A third and related difference is that the state sought coherence in inter-nation assistance, so that changes in the security, domestic and economic arenas complemented one another. Many critics argue that Singapore's success has been primarily economic. This particular example demonstrates how defence, regional stability, economic success and domestic harmony were regarded as interlinked goals of statehood and self-determination, a philosophy that has underpinned much of Singapore's development policies. The Singapore example therefore reasserts the importance of leaders who can effectively and legitimately undertake this project for the public good with a long-term perspective.

Critics also posit that, in the pursuit of development, the state has evolved to cement the dominance of the ruling party, the PAP. Indeed, the vulnerability and potential crisis caused by the withdrawal of British troops created a situation in which key institutions of the state were challenged. Quite consciously, the PAP government responded by galvanizing a public consciousness that spanned ethnic differences, creating the conditions in which key institutions of the state could be established in order to bridge the historical and potential divides among a people who had almost no common language, ethnicity, religion or other characteristics to undergird the formal notion of citizenship. Singapore may be considered an "uncommon democracy", as coined by T. J. Pempel, in which the political actors who led the people through the crisis enjoy a special historical relationship with the electorate.[43] Amin Saikal's chapter on Afghanistan in this volume cautions that personalized politics and charismatic leadership, though sometimes effective, are seldom sustainable. It may be argued, however, that the dominance of the PAP has been a result rather than a goal of Singapore's state-building policies. As Lee Kuan Yew posits:

a country needed more than a few dignified and able men at the top to get it moving. The people as a whole must have self-respect and the will to strive to make a nation of themselves. The task of the leaders must be to provide or create for them a strong framework within which they can learn, work hard, be productive and be rewarded accordingly.[44]

In this regard, Singapore may not be the liberal democracy that critics hold up as the standard for today's new states, but the cluster of disparate immigrant communities that formed its population has evolved into a stakeholder society. Such a society is rooted in the recognition that strong states may be able to enforce policy, but success can occur only if the policy goals resonate with the population at the individual level. As demonstrated in this chapter, such legitimacy is a crucial precondition of the successful implementation of radical changes in the fabric of everyday life.

With respect to the crisis examined in this chapter, as well as to other subsequent challenges, the PAP government pursued policies that built a functional and psychological framework within which each citizen could actively contribute toward the development of the fledgling state. Each challenge, be it fighting corruption, eliminating secret societies and gangs, responding to communist insurgency, "social engineering" language, combating litter or espousing "meritocracy", was therefore an opportunity to create a shared symbol for a new nation. A prime example of these symbols is the institution of National Service, created in response to the crisis examined in this chapter.

Conclusion: The evolution of the state

The very conditions that threaten the viability of the state may present opportunities for the state to demonstrate its relevance to the population.

The danger of examining "successful states" for lessons, however, lies in the seduction of deterministic thinking – just because challenges have been met with relative success in the past, it is tempting to believe that future and quite different challenges can be similarly met and resolved.

Singapore's past progress, for instance its management of the British military withdrawal discussed in this chapter, showcases the paradox of success and change. Success tends to perpetuate habits and institutionalize practice, streamlining thinking and response along well-tested lines. Yet these same habits and institutionalized practices can inhibit the changes necessary for success at the next stage. In fact, the city-state's emergence from the potential crisis of the 1970s may be characterized by the government's willingness to adopt policies contrary to conventional habit or wisdom. Many of the new policies were precisely directed at rectifying the existing economic and security arrangements based on colonial policies, such as dependence on entrepôt trade, reliance on external actors (the United Kingdom and Australia, in particular), a marked disparity in income levels and standards of living[45] and racial segregation. In handling this multifaceted crisis, the state sought to reform Singapore's economy, society and defence relations in response to the changing regional and global circumstances, while persuading the populace to subscribe to a new version of citizenship – one demanding participation in institutions that initially appeared onerous and foreign.

To date, Singapore may be judged to have succeeded in meeting not only the particular challenge of the British troop withdrawal, the focus of this chapter, but also other economic and sociopolitical challenges. Looking forward, however, there is no guarantee that the state will successfully face the challenges presently confronting it, or those that will arise in the future. Studies of Singaporean policy responses often employ the phrases "management of success" or "re-engineering success". These imply moderated efforts to build on or fine-tune the formulas that have brought Singapore this far. Not only may this perspective prevent nimble, creative and context-appropriate responses, it may prove inadequate in the light of the increasingly complex challenges facing states today.

Although Singapore has in many ways moved "from Third World to First",[46] new threats continually confront it. Since 2001, Singapore has experienced economic weakness, with no or (by its high standards) low growth. The 11 September 2001 attacks in New York and Washington, DC, the US-led war on terrorism, and the Bali bombing of 12 October 2002 have also brought new insecurities to Singapore, including the detention of Singaporeans on suspicion of plotting terrorism. The capacity and capability of the state agencies have also come into sharper focus for examination as other problems arise: joblessness, an accident involving a naval patrol ship and a commercial vessel, and public health scares.

These challenges continue unabated as the state and society prepare for a transition in leadership of the PAP from the "second generation", led by Prime Minister Goh Chok Tong, to a "third generation", led by Deputy Prime Minister Lee Hsien Loong, son of the founding prime minister, Lee Kuan Yew. This "third generation" leadership is consciously exposed and evaluated by its responses during these crises. Such questions of both effectiveness and legitimacy inevitably affect the nature of the state and its relationship with its citizens, given the paramount and currently irreplaceable position of the PAP.[47]

In each of these cases, the state has had to respond domestically and in cooperation with international partners. As always, a realistic evaluation of capability and ambitions must be paired with a willingness to implement structural change. Hence, any functional policy reform should catalyse changes to the process – the nature of politics, public consultation and the citizen's relationship to the state. In order for the state to evolve in tandem with new global and domestic challenges, it is equally important continually to redefine both the tools for achieving success and the very definitions and attributes of state success.

Notes

1. See chapter 1 in this volume.
2. In April 1946, the United Kingdom had separated Singapore from the other Straits Settlements and established it as a separate Crown Colony. No state's strategic significance, however, is permanent. The capriciousness of world attention is even more relevant today. See chapter 16 by Simon Chesterman in this volume.
3. Stanley S. Bedlington, *Malaysia and Singapore: The Building of New States*, Ithaca, NY: Cornell, 1978, p. 212.
4. Quoted in Obaid Ul Haq, "Singapore's Search for Security", in Stephen Chee, ed., *Leadership and Security in Southeast Asia*, Singapore: Institute of Southeast Asian Studies, 1991, p. 118.
5. Amitav Acharya, *Constructing a Security Community in Southeast Asia: ASEAN and the Problem of Regional Order*, London: Routledge, 2001, p. 24.
6. Lee Kuan Yew, "Prime Minister's Speeches, Press Conferences, Interviews, Statements", mimeo, National University of Singapore, 1966, quoted in Ul Haq, "Singapore's Search for Security", p. 121.
7. Kin Wah Chin, *The Defence of Malaysia and Singapore: The Transformation of a Security System 1957–1971*, Cambridge: Cambridge University Press, 1983, pp. 127, 133.
8. Ibid., pp. 133–137.
9. See chapter 2 by James Mayall in this volume.
10. Michael Leifer, *Singapore's Foreign Policy: Coping with Vulnerability*, London: Routledge, 2000, p. 31. Leifer suggests that separation was not "foisted" on Singapore and that there had previously been some negotiation between Singapore and Malaysia. However, the lack of advance planning for coping with independence in Singapore indicates that separation still came as a shock.
11. Kuala Lumpur had amassed and alerted troops in Johor, just across the Causeway from

Singapore. "If Singapore had become the unstable factor within Malaysia, it now began, having gained its independence, to view Malaysia as a source of its own insecurity" (Chin, *Defence of Malaysia and Singapore*, p. 104).

12. Leifer, *Singapore's Foreign Policy*, p. 37.

13. Bedlington, *Malaysia and Singapore*, p. 209.

14. Chin, *Defence of Malaysia and Singapore*, p. 40. One-sixth of Singaporean labour was employed by the armed forces.

15. I. F. Tang, "A Lemon or a Rolls-Royce", in Chan Chin Bock, ed., *Heart Work*, Singapore: Singapore Economic Development Board, 2002, p. 19.

16. Chin, *Defence of Malaysia and Singapore*, pp. 141–142.

17. Ibid., p. 170.

18. Australia and New Zealand had based their commitment on the condition of the United Kingdom's presence in the region.

19. Leifer, *Singapore's Foreign Policy*, p. 160.

20. Ul Haq, "Singapore's Search for Security", p. 130.

21. Chin, *Defence of Malaysia and Singapore*, p. 172.

22. In this respect, a sense of vulnerability may be distinguished from real insecurity. Leifer writes of the Singapore government's conviction that "size and location should not add up to destiny". This belief has driven its efforts "to keep the futures of the Republic out of the play of solely regional forces that cannot be fully trusted" (Leifer, *Singapore's Foreign Policy*, p. 161).

23. See chapter 10 by Michel Cahen on Mozambique in this volume.

24. Lee Kuan Yew, *The Singapore Story: Memoirs of Lee Kuan Yew*, Singapore/New York: Prentice Hall, 1998, p. 167.

25. Bedlington, *Malaysia and Singapore*, p. 58.

26. Cho-Oon Khong, "Singapore: Political Legitimacy through Managing Conformity", in Muthiah Alagappa, ed., *Political Legitimacy in South East Asia*, Stanford, CA: Stanford University Press, 1995, p. 116.

27. Heng Chee Chan, "Singapore", in Z. H. Ahmad and H. Crouch, eds, *Military–Civilian Relations in South East Asia*, Singapore/New York: Oxford University Press, 1985, p. 140. The National Service Ordinance of 18 November 1952 required all male Federal citizens between the ages of 21 and 28 to register for national service.

28. The government was aware of the low social status accorded by the Chinese to the military; as the popular Chinese proverb goes: "good sons do not make soldiers, just as good iron is not made into nails."

29. Chan, "Singapore", p. 142.

30. Ibid., pp. 140–141. Singapore's initial appeal reflected its determination to remain nonaligned.

31. Benjamin Beit-Hallahmi, *The Israeli Connection: Whom Israel Arms and Why*, London: Tauris, 1988, p. 26.

32. Martin Choo, ed., *Singapore Armed Forces*, Singapore: Public Affairs Department, Ministry of Defence, 1981, p. 20.

33. Export orientation demanded that Singaporean manufacturing meet international standards. The shift from import substitution to export orientation in the mid-1960s forced Singapore to address the problem of industry standards and quality control.

34. Ian Patrick Austin, *Pragmatism and Public Policy in East Asia*, Singapore: Fairmont International, 2001, p. 112. In fact, Winsemius was reportedly to be initially reluctant to work on Singapore as he thought it would be a "losing proposition" in the light of the communist threat facing Singapore. Tang, "A Lemon or a Rolls-Royce", p. 19. Winsemius was quoted as reflecting how Singapore was initially "bewildering. There were always strikes, violent strikes, all communist inspired. And inside the Government there

were also communists" (K. B. Chow, M. L. Chew and Elizabeth Su, *One Partnership in Development: UNDP and Singapore*, Singapore: United Nations Association of Singapore, 1989, p. 19).

35. Linda Low, M. H. Toh, T. W. Soon, K. Y. Tan and Helen Hughes, eds, *Challenge and Response: Thirty Years of the Economic Development Board*, Singapore: Times Academic Press, p. 34. The EDB is one of the main statutory boards that displays the sort of technocratic management and close relationship with the government for which modern Singapore is often criticized.

36. Chow et al., *One Partnership in Development*, p. 23.

37. S. Dhanabalan, untitled chapter in Chan, ed., *Heart Work*, p. 29.

38. Ibid.

39. K. H. Ang, untitled chapter in Chan, ed., *Heart Work*, pp. 232–233.

40. Low et al., eds, *Challenge and Response*, p. 239.

41. Christopher Sandars, *America's Overseas Garrisons: The Leasehold Empire*, Oxford: Oxford University Press, 2000, p. 125. See also J. Woodcliffe, *The Peacetime Use of Foreign Military Bases*, Dordrecht: Martinus Nijhoff, 1992; R. Pringle, *American Interests in the Islands of South East Asia*, New York: Columbia University Press, 1980.

42. Acharya, *Constructing a Security Community*, p. 140. The Philippines had been almost totally dependent on the United States for protection against external threats, and the crumbling of goodwill between the United States and the Philippines led to the Americans removing practically all military equipment. This stands in contrast to the British withdrawal from Singapore, where all military equipment, including buildings and bases, was left intact for Singaporean military or civilian use.

43. T. J. Pempel, ed., *Uncommon Democracies: The One-Party Dominant Regimes*, Ithaca, NY: Cornell University Press, 1990.

44. Lee, *The Singapore Story*, p. 132.

45. Austin, *Pragmatism and Public Policy*, p. 84. Lee Kuan Yew and Goh Keng Swee rejected colonial economic policies because they failed "to deliver broad economic development".

46. This phrase is borrowed from the title of the second volume of Lee Kuan Yew's memoirs. Lee Kuan Yew, *From Third World to First*, New York: HarperCollins, 2000.

47. Simon S. C. Tay, "The Coming Crisis, Domestic Politics in Singapore in and from 2001", in *Perspectives 2002*, Singapore: Institute of Policy Studies, pp. 12–24.

Part V
Choices

13

Early and "early late" prevention

I. William Zartman

State collapse and failure are extremely difficult to prevent, not because they represent insoluble challenges but because they are the work of human error, either deliberately or as externalities. Compared with the deliberate efforts of Mobutu Sese Seko and then Joseph Kabila in Zaire, Samuel Doe and then Charles Taylor in Liberia, Mohammed Siad Barre in Somalia, François Duvalier, Raoul Cedras and then Jean-Bertrand Aristide in Haiti, Burhanuddin Rabbani and then Mohammed Omar in Afghanistan, structural problems and political and economic market failures are relatively easy to overcome. This is to suggest not that the work of state failure and collapse is only that of egregious rulers, just that they are easier to identify than collective forces of government and opposition; the work of the Algerian junta or of the Revolutionary Armed Forces of Colombia (FARC) and their colleagues has been just as fatal to good governance and state survival as has a single ruler bent on self-serving self-destruction. The challenge is how to prevent governments and oppositions from collaborating to commit politicide.

To do this, one must begin with a diagnosis of the illness and of the right of the doctors to intervene when the patient does not admit its condition. This involves cultivating an early awareness of the problems among potential interveners, and then an examination of the possible measures of early prevention of a generic sort and of later intervention of a more specific nature. These are the five topics of this chapter: the nature of state collapse, the mandate to intervene, the guidelines for intervention, and the means of early and "early late" prevention (policy standards and direct measures). Yet, despite a focus on the difficulties posed by the determined agents of collapse and failure, it must be recognized that the challenge of good governance and the strengthening of state institutions encompass the whole subject of comparative politics, which has been under consideration but not settled since it was introduced by Aristotle[1] and Kautilya,[2] among others, two and a half millennia ago. The current treatment may hope to contribute to the discussion but will assuredly not provide any final solutions.

Collapse and failure: The nature of the process

States, as the authoritative political institutions that are sovereign over a recognized territory, perform four functions: rule-making, rule enforcement, security and representation. They can fail to perform one or more of these functions without fully collapsing. As these failures accumulate, however, the state weakens its ability to perform its functions in other areas until, in the end, "structure, authority (legitimate power), law and political order have fallen apart and must be reconstituted".[3] Interventions to prevent failure and collapse can therefore address specific shortcomings or respond to their cumulative effects. The first type is particularly difficult because it means interfering in the operations of an otherwise ongoing concern, although it could also be the case that the otherwise unthreatened institution might welcome sectoral assistance. The second is particularly difficult because it faces more or less total crumbling of state functions that might otherwise give support to reconstruction, and because any remaining claimant to authority is likely to feel all the more threatened by interventions.

Failure evokes the image of a car falling off a cliff in a movie or an object falling down a flight of stairs – landing or teetering on each step, struggling to recover balance, and then tumbling down to the next step, where it grapples uncertainly with balance, and so on. At any step, the object may recover its equilibrium; at any stage, the state may regain its coherence, overcome its sectoral failure and start to climb back up the steps to full functionality. In the falling, failing process, interventions can help a state resolve specific challenges, strengthening both the policy response to the problem and the machinery to provide it. But when the state hits bottom and collapses, it needs full reconstitution or reinstatement of its machinery – institutions, rules, personnel – before it can take on policy-making. Unfortunately, such sequencing is impossible, since the business needs to start operating before the new management is yet in place. The magnitude of the task underscores the need for preventive measures.

There are two types of state that pose different types of problem in such prevention: weak/soft and hard/brittle states.[4] Weak/soft states are flabby constructions, incapable of decision and execution, incompetent in providing internal and external security, prone to repeated failures. Egypt in the early 1950s, Somalia in the mid-1960s, Ghana in the late 1970s, Ecuador in the early 1990s, even France at the end of the Fourth Republic, are examples, as is Afghanistan (as discussed in this volume).[5] They need help in dealing with pressing problems, in strengthening component institutions, in training and setting up replacements for weak or absent mechanisms, and in countering threats that prey on weaknesses. This is the state-building function – mistakenly called "nation-building" in the current loose formulation – which currently constitutes an important need. In all the cases mentioned above, it was a military coup that restored fibre to the state, although such a drastic turn of politics need not be necessary. Less dramatic instances of foreign assistance helping domestic efforts to prevent a weak state from collapse were French assistance to Côte d'Ivoire in 2003 and US help to Colombia in the early 2000s and to Mexico in the early 1980s.

Hard/brittle states are oppressive, rapacious constructions, unrepresentative, kleptocratic, centred on their pivotal figure, vulnerable to collapse with a crash but creating vacuums about themselves beyond the ruler's castle walls that prevent easy reconstruction. They need to be reminded of acceptable standards of behaviour, constrained to reform and to open up, made accountable, and assisted with transitions or, if incorrigible, simply replaced. This is the regime change function, involving much more than just military operations. It is perpetually torn between the drastic option of removing the unreformable egregious ruler by direct intervention and the tenuous possibility of gradually transforming the repressive regime by pressure. The latter eventually may be realized only at the time of succession, remembering that hard rulers tend neither to choose soft successors – as Kim Il Sung, Siaka Stevens, François Duvalier and Hafez el-Assad, among many others, have shown – nor to lose power to soft replacements – as Mobutu Sese Seko, Samuel Doe and Hassan al-Bakr, among others, have experienced. North Korea, as discussed in this volume, is a telling example of a hard/brittle state.

Both types of state however pose the question of the permissible degree of intervention, a term used to designate any sort of action that "comes into" the sovereign domain of a state, whether indirect pressure or direct interference.

The mandate to intervene

The pulse of politics is wild and erratic. The decades of the Cold War usually saw "intervention" coupled with "Soviet", or in some cases with

"American", but in each case loaded with opprobrium. Only in the 1980s did the United States become involved in openly supporting other countries' political parties, an activity it had done covertly in earlier years but one that Soviet internationalism had carried out throughout the century. The expansion of "The Children of NED" (National Endowment for Democracy) – the International Republican Institute (IRI) and the National Democratic Institute (NDI) – into partisan activity and party support abroad marked a new turn in US policy, as did open support for "our Freedom Fighters", anti-communist guerrillas in Soviet-supported countries. From another angle in the same period, the international financial institutions (IFIs) – the World Bank and the International Monetary Fund – began to include political criteria such as governance and institutionalization in their financial relations with developing countries and even approached a veiled political conditionality in their lending.[6]

In the last decade of the twentieth century, after the end of the Cold War, the United States shied away from any muscled intervention until it was too late (as in Liberia), apologized for its inaction (as in Rwanda), and then entered late with overwhelming diplomacy (as in Bosnia) and destruction (as in Kosovo). The excuses involved the Viet Nam and Somali syndromes, despite the fact that polls showed that American public opinion would support international action and even body bags if appropriately explained and justified. Once in the new century, while much of the rest of the world clung to the same spirit, the United States massively invaded a country that posed no immediate threat to its security in the name of preventing a long-term danger, of removing a long-time despot and of introducing democracy, then saved the skin of a rapacious, elected dictator and hundreds of his citizens in an attempt to install order and responsible government. All of the above actions over the half-century were condemned from various quarters, just as stoutly as they were defended as appropriate and necessary. What gives the right to intervene?

Clearly it is the subject or object of the intervention – the shortcoming to be prevented – that confers a mandate or legitimacy on the intervener, but there is no agreed threshold of seriousness that compels intervention. Yet there is a growing feeling – evidenced by this very discussion – that, in circumstances still to be consensually defined, the failure and collapse of the responsible agency justify intrusive foreign action. The rise of attention to conflict prevention at the end of the Cold War was marked by a search to define appropriate measures and legitimate occasions. Such definitions are necessary, lest the protection against intervention that the Peace of Westphalia in 1648 afforded to smaller states be completely overturned in favour of the larger ones. The decade since the early 1990s has seen a number of official diplomatic and academic nongovernmental efforts to address the problem.

On the side of official diplomacy, efforts took place, as might be expected, within the settings of international institutions. An initial attempt of importance was the first-ever meeting of heads of state and government of the UN Security Council in January 1992, which concluded with a call for "analysis and recommendations on ways of strengthening ... the capacity of the United Nations for preventive diplomacy".[7] This produced UN Secretary-General Boutros Boutros-Ghali's pioneering *Agenda for Peace*, which was endorsed by the UN General Assembly at the end of the year. Measures noted included confidence-building measures, fact-finding, early warning, preventive deployment and demilitarized zones; the contribution of peace-building to further conflict prevention was also noted. In a statement remarkable for a report to sovereign states (and one whose spirit doubtless eventually cost him his job), Boutros-Ghali noted the fundamental position of state sovereignty and integrity, but also that "the time of absolute and exclusive sovereignty ... has passed; its theory was never matched by reality. It is the task of leaders of States today to understand this and to find a balance between the needs of good internal governance and the requirements of an ever more interdependent world."[8]

On the regional level, a notable attempt to address the questions of measures and mandates was the Swedish initiative in connection with the Swedish presidency of the European Union in the first half of 2001. The occasion provided the basis of a 1999 report, *Preventing Violent Conflict*, designed to focus and energize Swedish and eventually EU policy.[9] The focus was on developing a culture of prevention, for which the rationale and justification appeared in the initiative to be almost self-evident. Although diplomatic measures were emphasized, military measures were included, and there was little concern about the dangers of intervention or sovereign interference.[10]

The 2000 meeting of the G-8 foreign ministers in Miyakazi, Japan, produced a document, the *Miyakazi Initiative for Conflict Prevention*, focusing on strategies for reducing conflict.[11] Its strategy of "chronological comprehensiveness" covered structural prevention, early and late prevention, and post-conflict peace-building. Again, the focus was more on strategies than on justifications for intervention.

The subject was also addressed by academic analysis carried out within non-governmental research organizations. Three academic works aimed at an audience of practitioners as well as analysts appeared in the mid-1990s to pursue the argument about conflict prevention. The Council on Foreign Relations undertook a group study on *Enforcing Restraint: Collective Intervention in Internal Conflicts*, focusing on legitimacy and effectiveness in six cases.[12] Legitimacy was linked to a collective decision but also to the effectiveness of international organizations facing new challenges. The US Institute of Peace also published a strategic toolkit and analysis for conflict prevention, *Preventing Violent Conflicts: A Strategy for Preventive Diplomacy*.[13] The need to overcome debilitating conflicts and crises was implicitly viewed as reason enough for the necessary interventions, of which a whole range was provided. The Brookings Africa project sponsored a collective work, *Sovereignty as Responsibility: Conflict Management in Africa*, that looked little at prevention but focused on intervention, primarily conceived as mediation.[14] Rather than sovereignty being viewed as a protection of the state, it was seen as a responsibility, which was to be exercised by the state and shared by other states if the primary state did not exercise its own responsibility for the welfare of its people. Intervention was justified by failed or repressive states' loss of legitimacy and by the existence of the "higher authority ... of [the] international system ... to ensure that states conform to accepted norms or face the consequences".[15] The work was inspired by the 1991 Kampala Document promoted by President Olusegun Obasanjo, which contained the declaration that "domestic conditions constituting a threat to personal and collective security and gross violations of human rights lie beyond the protection of sovereignty".[16]

The two paths of attention came together in the Canadian-sponsored International Commission on Intervention and State Sovereignty (ICISS), whose 2001 report *The Responsibility to Protect*, takes up the same theme to state that "the primary responsibility for the protection of its people lies with the state itself", but "where a population is suffering serious harm, as a result of internal war, insurgency, repression or state failure, and the state in question is unwilling or unable to halt or avert it, the principle of non-intervention yields to the international responsibility to protect".[17] It also declares, in bold type, that "prevention is the single most important dimension of the responsibility to protect". It seeks to shift the debate from the "right to intervene" to the "responsibility to protect", citing the rise in humanitarian concerns, the weakness of new states and the shift in attention from state security to human security. Prevention is highlighted as of particular importance, as the most direct translation of protection before the damage occurs; it is divided into structural or root-cause prevention and direct or conflict prevention, and military intervention is circumscribed by a just cause threshold, precautionary and operational principles, and right authority.[18]

These various verbal affirmations suddenly collided with reality during the military operation against Iraq in March 2003.[19] Although the US Operation Iraqi Freedom was clearly provided for in the previous discussions, referring to repressive regimes and gross violations of human rights, and ambiguously provided for in its many resolutions calling on Iraq to disarm or face "serious consequences", the Operation was criticized by a large body of opinion, in the United States and abroad. Misnamed a pre-emptive operation – it did not respond to any imminent attack – this was a preventive war variously justified in official statements as an implementation of repeated UN resolutions calling for the removal of Iraq's nuclear, biological and chemical weapons of mass destruction, a phase in the war against al Qaeda terrorism, and an action to remove a repressive regime in order to permit democratization. As in the case of Boutros-Ghali's affirmations a decade earlier, the UN Security Council found that articulation of the criteria for intervention was one thing and their operationalization was another.

In sum, the debate on the justification of preventive intervention in sovereign states usually centres on the conditions themselves, where state failure and collapse, as well as repression and human rights violations, stand as conditions to be prevented. The mandate covers physical as well as functional intervention – that is, military as well as civilian interference in internal affairs and also external pressures and inducements affecting state policies and policy-making. The mandate is not unambiguous, however.[20] Its main limitation is proportionality or "no net harm", taken from the laws of war; in other words, the cure should not be more costly or damaging than the illness.[21]

Even such limitations leave some important contradictions and tensions unresolved. One is between the inherent egalitarianism among sovereign states and the paternalism exercised by those who claim the right to intervene, even for others' sake: who are the preventers and who the prevented? Another is the mechanism for change in a hierarchical society of nations: how are newcomers to elite status to be treated and included? A third is the degree or threshold of imperfection required to justify prevention: how bad does it have to be? And a fourth is: how far to go? Conditions clearly leading to state collapse can certainly justify friendly warnings and predictions from fellow sovereign states and strident broadcasts from non-governmental organizations (NGOs). But, if they are not heeded, does this justify threats and promises, invasions and subversions? And, even if such measures are legitimized by events and conditions, do they justify the intervening agency's expenditure of public or private treasure and attention, and even lives? The answer is doubtless found in the soft and subjective terrain of cost–benefit calculations. But if the answer to these last two questions is likely to be negative, should the initial effort be made at all?

For the record, two arguments coming from different directions stand firm against preventive intervention for state-building and should be briefly noted. One is the classical position based on indivisible sovereignty, which gives the state the licence to do what it wants within its boundaries, protected against intervention from abroad. The doctrine, coming from the Peace of Westphalia in 1648, was designed and works as a protection of weak states against strong states, and that spirit still poses the most significant challenge to the counter-doctrine of sovereignty as responsibility.

The other argument is solidly based on the spirit of democracy and states that a people has the government it deserves. The argument emerges from the notion of popular sovereignty and the nation-state that grew out of the French Revolution. It considers government to reflect the political culture of the nation, not just the mechanics of a selection process (except in that the selection process itself reflects the national political culture). Thus, it considers Mobutu, Barre, Hussein and Stalin to be products of popular sovereignty in Zaire, Somalia, Iraq and Russia, as much as Bill Clinton and George W. Bush, François Mitterrand and Jacques Chirac, and Luiz Inácio Lula da Silva and Zelia Cardoso de Mello are in the United States, France and Brazil. Any attempt to intervene preventively is pointless in this view, because it runs foul of the national ways of doing things, including failing and collapsing – or maintaining – states.

Although these two views, as a whole, need to be rejected for the present discussion to continue, they contain crucial elements that should nevertheless be considered. The mandate to intervene, or the legitimacy or justification of intervention, still begs a clear definition, which it needs whether it is delivered by the UN Security Council or claimed by a state or group of states acting alone.

The guidelines for intervention

Beyond the mandate, preventive intervention requires a number of other norms and guidelines for practice. These include early warnings, standards for "non-collapsing behaviour" for states, rules of the game for preventers, and institutions and policies for prevention.

It cannot be restated too often that early warnings abound; the problem is early awareness: the ability to listen to, to hear and to act on the early warnings. Academic analyses and government files are filled with indications of state failure and impending collapse, even if the exact dates of the crash are not predictable. Yet, curiously, discussions of prevention repeatedly return to the need for early warning systems, when the real need is to overcome such problems as signal unreliability, bureaucratic inertia, the overshadowing of future dangers by current crises or a preoccupation with fire over smoke, the depletion of credibility by false warnings or the "cry wolf" problem, and other obstacles to policy makers' hearing and responding to the abundant multiple signs of impending failure.[22] Surprises in this business are rare, but deafness is widespread.

Many of these problems require a conscious decision to give attention to and credit for proactive efforts at prevention, instead of simply reactive policy-making. The US Agency for International Development (USAID) has its conflict assessment, the UN Development Programme (UNDP) its early warning assessment, the Central Intelligence Agency (CIA) its State Failure Task Force, the Fund for Peace its analytical model.[23] As noted, the effort of the Swedish government to thrust prevention on the European Union and its standard practices is laudable and revealing of the difficulties, as was the earlier attempt by Boutros-Ghali to draw the attention of UN Security Council members to the problem. However, a real problem remains: the analytical inability to distinguish storm warnings that precede hurricanes from those that do not.[24]

A similar challenge on the other side of the problem is the absence of standards of healthy behaviour for "successful" (non-failing or non-collapsing) states. Once again, literature abounds on such matters as good governance, indices of freedom, structural adjustment policies and comparative politics in general, but clear consensual standards are not available, nor are they likely to be, given the nature of the subject and the differences in individual cases. The relation between structural or root causes and state failure and collapse is still under discussion and certainly not direct. Not all poverty, demographic pressure, class stratification, ethnic division or even repression produces conflict (and vice versa), and not all conflict is preventable or even dysfunctional. Not only are the minimum conditions of sociopolitical health under constant debate, but they are dynamic and responsive by nature. Democratization can produce erratic results and short-term setbacks; economic fundamentals and policies are in constant interaction; social expectations unsettle apparently stable conditions. Often middle-range state health requires short-term shocks, with a potential for destabilization in themselves.

The rules of the game for preventers and interveners are still unclear, given the absence of standards for successful preventers' behaviour. Even if standards of state health were available and the threshold of unhealthiness were clearly discernible, the limits of remedy remain uncertain. As the debate over the Iraq intervention clearly shows, it is easier to be eloquent about what needs to be prevented than about how to prevent it. Since collapse and failure are cumulative processes, there are innumerable cases of states that have begun the slippery slide and caught themselves in time, early or late, by their own efforts or with the help of external friends. It is the ones that fall through the net of advisable and acceptable practices that pose the problem. For those that are resolved to fail and collapse, a fundamental question remains how much intervention is permissible, of what kind, and at what stage.

Finally, a subset of the previous question concerns the agency of prevention. There is general consensus that collective action, with collective responsibility, is preferable to individual action. A relevant principle is subsidiarity, which requires that responsibility be borne at the lowest level; if it is not exercised by the state itself, it should be assumed by the neighbours in the region. In part, but only in part, this is a matter of capability, which is another element involved in the mandate; often, multiple interveners are needed to amass the required capability to prevent the expected damage. The problem arises, however, when one or a small number of interveners have the capability and do not feel they need to share responsibility and its associated restraints with a larger collectivity (when sharing might actually lower interveners' capabilities as well). The other side of the problem occurs when the members of the collectivity refuse to assume responsibility, leaving it to one or a smaller number, and only in the last resort to the international community organized in the United Nations. Mediating problems include questions of interest, of free-riding and of uncertainty.[25] These problems too have no clear answer but it is necessary to consider them. With such considerations in mind, it is possible to turn directly to questions of early and late prevention.

Early prevention: Building regimes for generic prevention

The best way of accomplishing early prevention would be to remove the structural or root causes. Not only is such a goal utopian, but, as noted, the relation between structural weakness and state failure and collapse is not direct. In addition, to be able to deal with root causes, standards would be required to guide appropriate action. Once accepted standards of behaviour are in place, they can be used as guidelines for states to respond to their own challenges and problems and also for third parties to assist them in achieving appropriate responses. It is here that early prevention can begin, with the construction of international regimes – "principles, norms, rules, procedures and programs that govern the interactions of actors in specific issue areas"[26] – for dealing with situations likely to lead to state failure and collapse. Regimes are not enforceable; they do not prevent state problems per se. But they foster prevention in three ways: they guide and justify actions by states to achieve and maintain their own good functioning, suggesting actions to take and legitimizing them against opposition; they constitute normative standards and practices by which states can be held accountable, offered assistance and subjected to pressure; and they provide both a rationale for more direct intervention and a charter for its goals and programmes.

A number of areas lend themselves to this type of regime-building, and some have already been the subject of such efforts. These include democracy, ethnic relations, displacement, corruption, human rights and fiscal responsibility, as discussed below; others could be suggested.[27] It is significant that together these regimes cover the essential area of the prevention of state failure and collapse. It is hard to imagine new areas for regime-building.[28] This does not mean that the regimes are complete or perfect; regimes are continually under construction, as problems, power and interests, and approaches change.[29] On the contrary, it means that existing regimes need reinforcement, completion and acceptance, rather than being extended to new subjects.

Democratization

Democratization is a process of accountability. Current analysis – perhaps mixed with a bit of faith – holds that states are best strengthened by the establishment of a healthy and functioning relationship between governors and governed. This should provide regular occasions for the current governors to account for their stewardship and for the governed to choose and to repent of their previous choice, under conditions of free choice of candidates, free discussion of issues and protection of the law. Publication of such standards and reference to them by governments and NGOs in their operations reinforce the norms, and specific activities serve to put them into effect. Although such activities can stand on their own rights and norms, they are strengthened by reference to a common set of standards, functioning as part of the overall regime. Thus, election monitoring makes most sense as part of a regime of democratization rather than as a discrete activity, as do programmes in the training of the judiciary and the rule of law or programmes in responsible journalism and the role of the media.

A democratization regime is not only a set of standards for target states; it is also a policy guideline for interveners, either from a distance through pressures and incentives or directly. Democratic standards provided the basis for pressure from the United States and the IFIs on Kenya in 1997, Cameroon in the mid-1990s and Peru in 2000 to conduct free and fair multi-party elections. They justified the US intervention in the Philippines in early 1986 and would have served just as well to justify a decertification of the Liberian elections of the previous year, or active support of a freer election process in Serbia in 1996. Where taken, the actions went far to prevent a hard, brittle state from moving closer to collapse; where not taken, the inaction preceded preventable failures and collapse.

Ethnic relations

Ethnic relations are a subject of increasing importance as the ages of nationalism and then of social consciousness give way to an age of sub-nationalisms. Recent research findings indicate that highly multi-ethnic and essentially single-ethnic nations tend toward stability, but pluri-ethnic situations with a dominant ethnic group are the most conflict prone.[30] Further study indicates that, within this situation, relations among groups tend towards conflict if one group is heavily favoured in the distribution of benefits or if another group is subject to discrimination and repression. There are statistics but no indices for ethnic relations as yet, although they have been called for, and the publication of an index of ethnic concentration in government positions, along with ethnic mentions in various human rights reports, would be useful.

Ethnic relations pose their own difficulties for preventive action. Standards for healthy ethnic relations can be useful for evaluating stability and for conditioning development when used by distant funding sources, for example. World Bank programmes were criticized for not heeding expert advice about the dangers of skewing benefits toward the majority Hutu ruling group in Rwanda in the early 1980s; experts foresaw the Tutsi reaction that finally overthrew the government, but not before the genocide took place.[31] However, as relations between Rwanda and its neighbours show, tribal overhang can serve as a too convenient justification for interference in a neighbouring state. Many conflicts, from Sudetenland to Kivu, have been pursued rather than prevented in the name of protecting oppressed (and, incidentally, ethnically related) minorities. Like any tools, standards must be used carefully and put into the right hands.

Population displacement

Population displacement, either between states as refugees or within states as internally displaced persons (IDPs), is governed by two complementary regimes. Refugee regimes cover the rights to asylum, resettlement, return and remain, and IDPs are covered in a set of Guiding Principles.[32] Although broadly accepted, these norms and standards are not universally applied; they nevertheless form the basis of dealing, however imperfectly, with situations of state failure and collapse. Displaced populations result from state functions of welfare, security and order, and the regime serves to guide efforts to deal with these symptoms, if not with their causes.

Corruption

Corruption is already the subject of a robust regime, in the hands of the NGO Transparency International. Its most important preventive function is to shine the light of publicity on deserving states, which in turn serves to empower domestic opposition and, more broadly, world public opinion. Such attention then finds its way into the practice of other states, such as through the provisions in US law against side-payments in business dealings at home and abroad. No direct foreign interventions have taken place in the name of anti-corruption, but indirect interventions, such as USAID training programmes against corruption, find their justification under the umbrella of the regime. Further enforcement of the regime's principles depends on domestic legislation and effective court systems, items contained in the standards of the regime itself.

Human rights

Human rights constitute a large area for regime-building. This was tackled directly in the monumental statement contained in the Universal Declaration on Human Rights, adopted by the United Nations in 1948; more specifically, it is monitored vigorously by Human Rights Watch and the Ligues des Droits de l'Homme, among others. The regime is also strengthened by sectoral statements and activities related to its many components. An example is the Convention against Torture, which worked its way through the United Nations until its adoption in December 1984; it is monitored by the Committee against Torture and other bodies, was advanced by a strong campaign led by Amnesty International, and has been strengthened by additional instruments, including an Optional Protocol in December 2002.[33] Building respect for human rights is a slow process, but despoiling them is sometimes a deadly process within the offending state, even if judgement day may be long in coming. Yet humanitarian causes have justified direct intervention – in Iraqi Kurdistan, Somalia, Kosovo and finally Iraq itself – and have provided the legal basis for international tribunals, from Nazi Germany to Rwanda and Yugoslavia. None of these actions has been without debate, despite a well-codified regime, and none has prevented state collapse. Yet the aspiration is that the demonstration and deterrent effect of retribution after the fact in these cases will dissuade leaders from similar atrocities in other cases.

Fiscal responsibility

Fiscal responsibility has been the subject of a regime created under the auspices of the IFIs, expressed in such statements as the Washington Consensus.[34] Although a regime has not been devised that would eliminate poverty, the structural adjustment guidelines are designed to avoid the economic irresponsibility that can lead directly to state collapse. These guidelines form the basis of enforcement measures contained in relations with the IFIs. It should be noted, however, that this issue area is an instance where the regime has not simply grown but has changed course dramatically over the years, as different standards have evolved for appropriate policies to prevent poverty.

Uncertainty is not the only problem inhibiting the use of international regimes as standards of state conduct to prevent state collapse. In addition to positive consequences, most regimes also have negative side-effects or externalities, and costs are incurred in producing their benefits. The fiscal responsibility required by the IFIs may entail cutting social programmes in health, education and welfare or requiring payments for them. Human rights, refugee and IDP norms, as well as standards for handling ethnic minorities (and majorities), can be destabilizing, at least in the short run, and can impose additional operating costs on the government. Democratization can lead to instability in its initial stages, and even to bad government on occasion. Were such standards of behaviour unambiguously beneficial, it would be easier to have them adopted. The point is less that there is no perfection in this world than that even accepted standards for prevention require fine-tuning, policy choices and costs that make prevention debatable and resistance natural.

It might seem that the regimes are lofty and anodyne compared with the brutal and dirty processes of state failure and collapse. Enumerating the highest standards of state health might appear to be a matter for angels when what is needed is dealing with devils. Without such standards, however, action for curing sick states becomes ad hoc and contradictory, lacking justification and coordination. As consensual methods of problem-solving, regimes coordinate and facilitate the generic prevention of state failure and collapse. Although universal in their standards and coverage, they are applicable individually to specific states in need of diagnosis and prescriptions.

"Early late" prevention: Intervening before it is too late

Regimes, and the pressures and encouragements they legitimize, have been helpful in the innumerable cases of state failure and state collapse that have been averted. But they have not been sufficient in all cases. On occasion, more direct measures in the early part of the final phase of collapse are necessary to make states work and to avoid the extreme measures of state reconstruction. Salient among these are mediation, convocation and deposition. Examples of their use are necessarily more specific than those of generic measures.

Mediation

Mediation is useful in preventing collapse when the state fails to deal effectively with an internal segment of the population to the point where dissatisfaction takes the form of insurgency, rebellion or other armed conflict.[35] The segment may be an ethnic or other identity group suffering from perceived discrimination or a social category or class suffering from poverty and neglect. Mediation is appropriate when the state response is inadequate to the situation, when government, as a party to the conflict, loses its position as conflict manager, and when the interests of all the sides need to be incorporated in order to end the violence and restore a functioning political system. When the state is not fully in charge, it is no longer able to preside over a hierarchical hearing between government and aggrieved parties. Mediation, like any negotiation, carries with it the implication that the parties are equal in standing (even if not in power), that they have legitimate interests to be protected, and that none of them is seeking suicide.

For the mediation to work, valid spokespeople for the various parties are required. If there are many parties or the spokespeople are not clearly authorized, the mediator may first have to form coalitions and to designate spokespeople for mediation purposes, necessitating deeper involvement in internal politics and seriously complicating the task. For example, at Dayton, the United States arranged for Serb President Slobodan Milosevic to speak for the Bosnian Serbs and Croatian President Franjo Tudjman to speak for the Bosnian Croats, although this was not without complications for the process and the subsequent implementation of the Dayton Accords.

Mediation in an internal conflict is generally resisted by governments, since it implies that a government cannot handle its own problems, that the rebellion deserves recognition and equal standing before the mediator, and in the end that the only resolution will be a new political system that accords the rebellion a place in legitimate politics.[36] It was under these assumptions that the Community of Sant'Egidio (backed by the United States, Russia, Portugal, Italy, Zimbabwe, Kenya and Zambia) mediated between Renamo and Frelimo in Rome in 1990–1992, and that Portugal, the United States and the United Nations mediated between UNITA and the MPLA in Estoril in 1992, in Lusaka in 1994 and in Luanda in 2001–2002 to overcome state failure and prevent state collapse in Mozambique and Angola, respectively. Since mediation inevitably works both to strengthen the weaker party – the rebellion – and to save the state while reforming it, it is to be undertaken only when conditions suggest that the current state failure is serious and is likely to continue to be so to the point of impending collapse.

Mediation is exceptionally difficult in some types of state collapse – where cultural clashes are paramount, where the rebellion takes on a terrorist form and where the rebels have an independent source of funding that allows them to enjoy their Sherwood Forest existence. For example, it has been hard to find an appropriate mediator in the Algerian, Colombian or Sierra Leonean conflicts. Some French and Algerian officials have called for mediation in Algeria in the war that is pitting state terrorism against Islamist terrorism, but there is little to mediate between these two extremes and there are few mediators (and certainly not France or the United States) that would be acceptable to both sides. The diligent efforts of Sant'Egidio in 1995 brought together disparate opposition parties to form a political middle where none had previously existed, but they were unable to overcome Algerian nationalist resistance to bringing these parties (which included the Islamic Salvation Front) together with the government. Similarly, in Colombia, ideology and the drug trade have made the Revolutionary Armed Forces uninterested in seeking a solution from talks with the government, despite the state's valiant attempts to find a basis for discussion, and various would-be mediators have found no purchase on the situation. In Sierra Leone, the Revolutionary United Front proved unworthy of mediation and broke the Abidjan (1996), Conakry (1997) and Lomé (1999) agreements brokered by West African mediators. In such cases, it is only when the terrorists are exhausted and completely isolated from a population alienated by their tactics that they become amenable to a return to civil politics; then the conflict becomes susceptible to mediation. Otherwise they must be defeated. Mediation as a means of preventing failure and collapse is not merely a matter of making peace; it must be a means of reforming and restoring the political fabric of the state in order to make it functional again.

Convocation

The convocation of a conference of the remaining political forces in the country – an extended form of mediation – is necessary to restore the state to working order when that order has broken down and many parties are in contention in the resulting power vacuum. At this point, efforts to reassemble a legitimate state structure need to come from the outside, since little state authority remains, even though a political organization bearing the name of the collapsing state may still be one of the contending parties. Such convocations usually take place outside the collapsing state: Arab states convened national conferences on Lebanon in Damascus in 1976, Geneva in 1983, Lausanne in 1984, Damascus in 1985 and Taif in 1989; West African states convened conferences of Liberian warring parties at Yamoussoukro several times in 1991, Cotonou in 1993, Geneva in 1994, Akosumbo in 1995 and Abuja in 1995 and 1996; states in the Horn of Africa hosted conferences on Somalia in Djibouti in 1991 and Addis Ababa in 1992; the president of Gabon and the special representative of the secretary-general of the Organization of African Unity called conferences of the warring parties to the Congolese elections in Libreville in 1993 and 1997; the United States convened a conference of the Haitian parties in New York in 1993 and of the Bosnian parties in Dayton, Ohio; southern African states convened the Congolese parties in Sun City in 2002. Many of these instances could have occurred earlier; for example, conferences were proposed to bring together the Yugoslav parties in 1990 and 1991, the Somalis in 1988 and earlier in 1991, and the Zaireans/Congolese in 1997 and 1999.[37]

Because convocation is required in conditions where state authority has been severely weakened, it needs an unusually steady hand. Commitment, perseverance and skill are required, along with a number of more specific elements. Rather than limiting participation to the convenors' own friends or the moderates, the parties to the conflict need to be involved as parties to the solution. They need to be kept at work until their subject is fully covered and not allowed to leave with merely a cease-fire or when deadlock, superficial agreement or conference fatigue sets in. The resulting agreements need to cover the allocation of power, the structuring of institutions and the implementation of details, and to create confidence-building measures during and after the intervention in order to allow the parties to check on their progress as they move from conflict to reconstruction. The convenors need to mediate as communicators, formulators and even manipulators, and not leave outcomes to the devices of the conflicting parties.[38] These elements have made the difference between convocations that successfully prevent further state collapse and those that fail.

Deposition

The deposition[39] of egregious rulers needs to be considered in the extreme case (which unfortunately is not rare) where repression and state collapse can be unambiguously traced to the long rule of a debilitating dictator operating on a shrinking power base in a hard/brittle state. By alienating ever larger numbers of citizens but destroying the organized opposition, such dictators create a vacuum around themselves. Saving the state depends on removing the ruler: hopes of reform are vain; mere power-sharing only prolongs the pain. The assumptions of prevention through deposition are antithetical to the ideas behind mediation and convocation: mediation restores the relationship between a failing government and a rebellious opposition in a new state system, and convocation brings together the parties to fill the vacuum left by a departed egregious ruler. Left to itself, the final stage of state collapse will remove the ruler in its own, costly way and complete the vacuum. Deposition of the ruler seeks to effectuate that result earlier and in such a way as to fill the vacuum, so that total collapse can be prevented and legitimate authority reinstated.

Deposition is an extreme but not unthinkable form of intervention. Jacobo Arbenz, Jean Bédel Bokassa, Idi Amin Dada, Bernard Coard, Ferdinand Marcos, Manuel Noriega, Jean-Claude Duvalier, Raoul Cedras (eventually), and Saddam Hussein were deposed, respectively, in Guatemala in 1954, Central African Republic in 1979, Uganda in 1979, Grenada in 1983, the Philippines in 1986, Panama in 1989, Haiti in 1986, 1994 and 2004, and Iraq in 2003. For the most part, the agent was the United States, although it operated with the United Kingdom in Iraq; France was the agent in the Central African Republic and was involved in Haiti; and Tanzania was the agent in Uganda. Some of these interventions were condemned by international opinion, sometimes more for the principle than for the particular instance. The African interventions were roundly criticized by the Organization of African Unity, but the results were greeted with relief and member states were content to allow France and Tanzania to effect them.

There are three non-military ways of removing egregious rulers: vote them out, talk them out or buy them out (or a combination of all three). The alternative is to force them out. Marcos and Noriega were voted out of office but it took American intervention to bring them to recognize the vote; a similar policy of decertifying the falsified elections in Liberia in 1985 could have brought Doe to retire and saved the lives of thousands and the state itself. In Zaire, the Sovereign National Conference had elected a prime minister, Etienne Tshisekedi, which would have allowed Mobutu to retire in dignity; diplomatic intervention with a little military backing by the "troika" (United States, France and Belgium) in 1991, 1993 or 1994 could have enforced that retirement, obviating the deaths and crisis of the rest of the decade. Forceful American interventions on a number of occasions after 1991 might have restored Bertrand Aristide to power in Haiti, as former President Carter was finally able to accomplish in 1994 with the threat of a US military intervention behind him. Ten years later, having alienated much of his population by corruption and repression, Aristide was talked out and given exile before the armed gangs got him.

Removal by election has the strong advantage of providing a successor and thereby limiting the dangers of a political vacuum, but it often needs active intervention by external patrons to take effect. If elections are regarded as a valued tool for stability and succession, there should be no hesitation about intervening to enforce them when necessary. Indeed, a few crucial enforcements work to reduce the need for similar actions on subsequent occasions.

Even if voting provides the means, talking (and sometimes buying) is usually required as well, as the above cases show. Like hostage negotiations, early retirement negotiations become possible when they shift from the original demands to conditions for asylum. The difference between failure and success in evacuating Doe between 1985 and 1990, Mobutu between 1990 and 1997, Siad Barre between 1988 and 1991, and Cedras and company between 1991 and 1994 was diplomatic intervention to offer security in exchange for status; here the attractiveness of the trade-off depends on the interveners' ability to portray the insecurity inherent in the current course. Cornered, Doe in 1990, Siad Barre in 1991, Cedras in 1993, Mobutu in 1991 and 1993, and Hussein in 2003 turned down offers of early and secure retirement, doubtless feeling that the chances of holding on were still favourable. Reportedly, the personal decision was based on Doe's mysticism, Siad Barre's desperation, Mobutu's pride, and the belief of both Hussein and the Haitian junta that the United States would not put up even if it did not shut up. Interveners need to convey the idea that "the game is up" and missed opportunities offer plenty of evidence of the value of seizing the occasion early rather than waiting until it is too late. The fate of Doe, Barre, Noriega, Mobutu and Hussein is no prettier than that of their own citizens, suffering because of their leader's delayed deposition.

Some extreme cases require extreme means – military intervention – in addition to diplomacy, negotiation, persuasion and negative and positive inducements. Military force was the means of preventive deposition in the case of Panama, the Central African Republic, Uganda, Grenada and Haiti, in a sense in Somalia, and in the greatest sense in Iraq. Although these are serious means to be evaluated carefully against the costs of the current state of affairs and its likely prolongation, the larger danger comes from the aftermath. If removal by military means is designed to prevent egregious state failure and collapse and to make the state work again, it must actually produce a restored and functioning state. When force is used against a state, even or especially a collapsed one, the forces of order – the military or powerful police – are needed as much to fill the ensuing vacuum and provide law and order during the transition as to remove the ruler.

Conclusion

Early prevention through international regimes has provided a growing set of regulations, rules, norms, principles and expectations that have played an important, if indeterminate, role in preventing state failures and collapse and restoring the effective functioning of the existing state. These standards serve as guidelines both for state governments and for external agencies – states, intergovernmental organizations and NGOs – that work to keep them healthy. As safety nets, however, they have holes, and states sometimes fall through on specific policies and onto a more general slide to collapse. "Early late" prevention through diplomatic and even military intervention provides specific means of forestalling that slide before it actually reaches its end. These means have not been used with as much success or as early as they could, and have been invoked more often after the fact – as "late late" methods – than before. This is eloquent expression of the need for more awareness and sustained action in the face of state failures and impending state collapse.

Between these two types of response lies a large and diffuse band of opportunities to help states overcome debilitating policy failures before they accumulate to open the path toward collapse. Preventive measures in these areas are addressed to particular social or economic issues or to institutional problems of policy-making, as discussed in some of the previous chapters, and have found some use. This larger gap needs to be filled if state collapse is not to become a more frequent feature of the world scene.[40] It is a gap occupied by negligent policies and obstinate strategies that provoke failure and lead to collapse, but that are far enough from peace-disturbing situations and gross human rights violations to elude justifications for decisive external intervention. It is a gap populated by Côte d'Ivoire under Henri Konan Bedie, by Iraq during the first decades of Saddam Hussein, by Zimbabwe under Robert Mugabe, by Sierra Leone under Joseph Momoh and before him under Siaka Stevens, by Zaire under Mobutu Sese Seko, by the Republic of Congo under Denis Sassou Nguesso, by Algeria under Chadli Benjedid, by Turkmenistan under Saparmurad Niyazov, and by Cameroon under Paul Biya, among the many leaders bent on failing policies and obdurate resistance to external counsel.

These leaders have made inappropriate choices in socioeconomic policies, led corrupt regimes, and alienated and repressed significant parts of their populations. Somewhere down the road their states have fallen apart as a result (or in the last two cases are close to doing so). Yet interested external states either have not been moved enough to help them make the state work or have met deaf ears from the leaders in question. Unlike the two categories of preventive action analysed above – early and "early late" prevention – which are conceptually clear even though they present some conjunctural gaps and have by no means always been effected, this larger range of preventive needs is not even conceptually well understood and is very little seized upon in practice. Once the operational gaps in the structural and proximate prevention measures have been filled, it is to this larger, amorphous area that attention next needs to be turned and the conceptual dimensions worked out. But it is precisely this area in which the mandate and the measures are most difficult to determine, returning this discussion to its beginnings.

Notes

1. See, e.g., Aristotle, *Politics*, trans. Ernest Baker, London: Cambridge University Press, 1948.
2. *Kautilya Arthasastra* [440], trans. R. Shamasastry, Mysore: Mysore Publishing House, 1960.
3. I. William Zartman, ed., *Collapsed States: The Disintegration and Reinstitution of Legitimate Authority*, Boulder, CO: Lynne Rienner, 1995, p. 1.
4. Gunnar Myrdal, *Asian Drama*, New York: Vintage, 1971; Joel Migdal, *Strong States and Weak Societies: State–Society Relations in the Third World*, Princeton, NJ: Princeton University Press, 1988.
5. Jean Lacouture and Simone Lacouture, *Egypt in Transition*, New York: Criterion, 1958; David Laitin, *Politics, Language and Thought: The Somali Experience*, Chicago: University of Chicago Press, 1977; Naomi Chazan, *An Anatomy of Ghanaian Politics*, Boulder, CO: Westview Press, 1983; Juan Linz and Arturo Valenzuela, eds, *The Failure of Presidential Democracy: The Case of Latin America*, Baltimore, MD: Johns Hopkins University Press, 1994; Herbert Lüthy, *France against Herself*, New York: Praeger, 1955.
6. UN Development Programme, *Governance for Sustainable Growth and Equity*, New York: UNDP, 1997; International Bank for Reconstruction and Development, *World Bank Development Report: The State in a Changing World*, Washington: IBRD, 1997; Robert Picciotto and Eduardo Wiesner, eds, *Evaluation and Development: The Institutional Dimension*, New Brunswick, NJ: Transaction, 1998.
7. UN Doc. S/23500, 31 January 1992, in Boutros Boutros-Ghali, *An Agenda for Peace*, New York: United Nations, 1995, pp. 117–118.
8. Boutros-Ghali, *Agenda for Peace*, p. 44. See the statements made by Kofi Annan after the Kosovo intervention in 1999.
9. Foreign Ministry of Sweden, *Strategi för konfliktförebyggande og konflikthantering*, Stockholm: Foreign Ministry, Ds 1997:18; Foreign Ministry of Sweden, *Preventing Violent Conflict – A Swedish Action Plan*, Stockholm: Foreign Ministry of Sweden, Ds 1999:24.
10. Peter Wallensteen, ed., *International Intervention: New Norms in the post-Cold War Era?*, Uppsala: Uppsala University Department of Peace and Conflict Research, Report 45, 1997; International Security and Information Service, *Restructuring for Conflict Prevention and Management: EU Restructuring Conference Report and Comments*, Brussels: ISIS Europe, 1999; Saferworld, *Preventing Violent Conflict: Opportunities for the Swedish and Belgian Presidencies*, London: Saferworld and International Alert, 2000; Anita Björkdahl, "Developing a Toolbox for Conflict Prevention", in *Preventing Violent Conflict – The Search for Political Will Strategies, and Effective Tools*, Stockholm: Swedish International Peace Research Institute, 2000, appendix I.
11. G-8, *Miyakazi Initiative for Conflict Prevention*, Miyakazi, Japan: G-8, 2000.
12. Lori Fisler Damrosch, ed., *Enforcing Restraint: Collective Intervention in Internal Conflicts*, New York: Council on Foreign Relations, 1993.

13. Michael Lund, *Preventing Violent Conflicts*, Washington, DC: US Institute of Peace Press, 1996.
14. Francis Deng et al., *Sovereignty as Responsibility*, Washington, DC: Brookings, 1996.
15. Ibid., pp. 32–33.
16. Olusegun Obasanjo, *The Kampala Document*, New York: Africa Leadership Forum, 1991; Francis Deng and I. William Zartman, *A Strategic Vision for Africa*, Washington, DC: Brookings, 2002, p. 165.
17. International Commission on Intervention and State Sovereignty, *The Responsibility to Protect*, Ottawa: International Development Research Centre, December 2001, available at ⟨http://www.iciss.gc.ca⟩, p. xi.
18. ICISS, *The Responsibility to Protect*, pp. xii–xiii, 22–27, 47–69.
19. For a good review of the ends and means, see International Crisis Group, "Iraq Policy Briefing: Is There an Alternative to War?" Amman/Brussels: ICG, Middle East Policy Report No. 9, 24 February 2003.
20. ICISS, *The Responsibility to Protect*, p. xii.
21. This is different from the false-Hippocratic judgement absolute, "first, do no harm". As *Responsibility to Protect* recognizes, there is a cost to prevention. See I. William Zartman, *Preventive Diplomacy and Conflict Resolution*, Ditchley Conference Report D98/15, Ditchley Park, 1998; Christine Ruggere, "Quoting the Hippocratic Oath", *Science*, 29 October 1999, p. 901.
22. I. William Zartman and Guy Olivier Faure, eds, *The Dynamics of Escalation and Negotiation*, Ann Arbor: University of Michigan Press, 2004.
23. Suzanne Verstegen, *Conflict Prognostication*, The Hague: Clingendael, 1999.
24. I. William Zartman, *Cowardly Lions: Missed Opportunities to Prevent Deadly Conflict and State Collapse*, forthcoming.
25. Mancur Olson, *The Logic of Collective Action*, New York: Schocken, 1965; Zartman, *Cowardly Lions*; Rudolf Avenhaus and Gunnar Sjöstedt, eds, *Negotiating Risk*, Laxenburg: International Institute of Applied Systems Analysis, 2003.
26. The term is used here in its international sense, as referenced, and not in its domestic sense of an administration or type of government (as in "regime change", discussed below). See Marc Levy, Oran Young and Michael Zürn, "The Study of International Regimes", *European Journal of International Relations*, Vol. 1, No. 3, 1995, p. 272; Stephen Krasner, ed., *International Regimes*, Ithaca, NY: Cornell University Press, 1983; Andreas Hasenclever, Peter Mayer and Volker Rittberger, *Theories of International Regimes*, New York: Cambridge University Press, 1997.
27. Note that mandate is in itself a regime, where principles, norms, rules, procedures and programmes govern acceptable behaviour, as shown by debates in regard to Rwanda, Cambodia, Solomon Islands (discussed in a previous chapter) and Iraq, among others.
28. There is one more subject that needs consensual rule, unfortunately beyond the reach of regimes, and that is a two-term limitation on presidencies. Many of the most egregious rulers did well during their first decade and ran out of ideas thereafter, turning to repression to maintain their power habit. Military rule was then adopted as the means of succession, rather than elections, and the slippery slope of failure to collapse had begun.
29. Bertram I. Spector and I. William Zartman, eds, *Getting It Done: International Regimes as Negotiation*, Washington, DC: United States Institute of Peace, 2003.
30. Paul Collier and Anke Hoeffler, "Greed and Grievance in Civil War", Washington, DC: World Bank, Policy Research Paper 2355, 2000; Ibrahim Elbadawi and Nicholas Sambanis, "Why Are There So Many Civil Wars in Africa", *Journal of African Economies*, Vol. 9, No. 3, 2000, pp. 244–269; Nicholas Sambanis, "A Review of Recent Advances and Future Directions in the Literature on Civil War", *Defense and Peace Economics*, Vol. 14, No. 3, 2002, pp. 215–243.

31. Rene Lemarchand, *The World Bank in Rwanda*, Bloomington: University of Indiana African Studies Program, 1982; Peter Uwin, *Aiding Violence: The Development Enterprise in Rwanda*, West Hartford, CT: Kumarian, 1998.
32. Francis Deng and Roberta Cohen, *Guiding Principles on Internally Displaced People*, New York: United Nations, 1998.
33. Anna Korula, "The Regime against Torture", in Spector and Zartman, *Getting It Done*.
34. World Bank, *The Washington Consensus*, Washington, DC: IBRD, 1999.
35. See Saadia Touval and I. William Zartman, eds, *International Mediation in Theory and Practice*, Boulder, CO: Westview Press, 1985; Jeffrey Z. Rubin, ed., *The Dynamics of Third Party Intervention*, New York: Praeger, 1981; C. R. Mitchell and Keith Webb, eds, *New Approaches to International Mediation*, New York: Greenwood, 1988; Jacob Bercovitch and Jeffrey Z. Rubin, eds, *Mediation in International Relations*, New York: St Martin's Press, 1992; Jacob Bercovitch, ed., *Resolving International Conflicts*, Boulder, CO: Lynne Rienner, 1996; Jacob Bercovitch, ed., *Studies in International Mediation*, New York: Palgrave, 2002; Marieke Kleiboer, *International Mediation*, Boulder, CO: Lynne Rienner, 1997.
36. I. William Zartman, ed., *Elusive Peace: Negotiating to End Civil Wars*, Washington, DC: Brookings, 1995, esp. chap. 13.
37. Zartman, *Cowardly Lions*.
38. Saadia Touval and I. William Zartman, "International Mediation after the Cold War", in Chester A. Crocker, Fen Osler Hampson and Pamela Aall, eds, *Turbulent Peace: The Challenges of Managing International Conflict*, Washington, DC: United States Institute of Peace Press, 2001.
39. As can be seen, the term is used here in its primary dictionary sense of deposing a leader and not in its narrow legal sense of a testimony.
40. David Cortright, ed., *The Price of Peace*, Lanham, MD: Rowman & Littlefield, 1997.

14

Making humanitarianism work

Thomas G. Weiss and Peter J. Hoffman

The spread of state failure and the crisis of governance are accompanied by burgeoning vulnerable populations amid shifting political and institutional sands. A collapsing state, let alone a failed one, is unable to provide food, shelter, sanitation, health care and physical protection. Those who would come to their aid face not only the usual challenges of emergency relief (mustering the political will and resources to respond and complementing other recovery efforts beyond the emergency stage) and the protection of human rights, but the additional hazards inherent in "stateless" complex emergencies – violence and the politicization of aid. The modern international humanitarian system, inadequately funded and designed specifically to address the horrors of inter-state conflict, is now plagued by additional shortcomings resulting from humanitarian crises associated with state failure.

Whereas earlier chapters have depicted the drivers and cases of state failure, this chapter examines "stateless" complex emergencies from the perspective of on-the-ground humanitarian agencies and suggests improvements and strategies for achieving outcomes better in line with intentions. For humanitarians, the crumbling capacities of fragile states in the 1990s, coupled with the emergence of a variety of powerful non-state actors, necessitate at least a rethinking of practical responses, if not the wholesale overhaul of the international humanitarian system. Making humanitarianism work in the face of state failure – that is, saving lives without fuelling further conflict or raising the spectre of the "well-fed dead" –

requires agencies to assess actors in operational environments and then formulate appropriate forms of engagement that stress the political health of afflicted societies.

Humanitarians are "first responders" and thus are often thrust into uncertain political territory populated by a wide array of actors. Although they focus on populations at risk, other actors are just as important. Efforts to recognize this reality tend to paint other actors with far too broad brushstrokes and often miss the essence of the problem; popular narratives of "good guys" and "bad guys" obfuscate the reality that only rarely are such binary distinctions clear-cut.

Unpacking the politics of war-torn societies reveals a three-fold problem for humanitarians. The first is identifying and promoting those actors that facilitate humanitarian operations, contribute to reconstruction efforts and support peace-building; in short, they need to nurture civil society or peace-oriented non-state actors. The second is limiting relations with and curtailing the influence of those rogues that profit politically or economically from war; this involves marginalizing and navigating "uncivil" society or spoiler non-state actors. The third is distinguishing those that have the potential to contribute to humanitarian action but may not, and then finding strategies and tactics for transforming their interest structures toward fostering peace; this means assessing and cultivating ambiguous partners or unreliable non-state actors.

The only first-order principle for humanitarians should be the sanctity of life. Operational "principles", including neutrality and impartiality, are means not ends; they are not moral absolutes. They necessarily take a back seat to more consequentialist calculations about the likely results from helping particular non-state actors. There is little room for humanitarians who refuse tough judgements and provide succour without discrimination. The age of innocence, if there ever was one, is over.[1] Instead of responding hastily, there is an urgent need to slow down and to reflect before acting. In order to mitigate the perils of a "grey humanitarianism", agencies should recognize the implications of entanglements and incorporate strategies for addressing ambiguous situations.

This chapter begins by examining how humanitarian operations are shaped by state failure and the mushrooming numbers of non-state actors. Next, it discusses the traditional shortcomings of the humanitarian system with particular emphasis on its inability adequately to address the implications of state failure. Finally, the chapter searches for solutions. In order to remain true to their own values, humanitarians should critically reflect on new dynamics to develop tools and strategies better suited to today's crises. This realization has been too slow in coming; as Larry Minear notes, "adaptation to the new realities has been for the most part lethargic and phlegmatic".[2]

State failure, non-state actors and humanitarian challenges

In most humanitarian disasters, aid agencies engage directly with state authorities. But in situations where central authority is failing or has failed, agencies must make other arrangements. This section fleshes out the gamut of relevant non-state actors – from peace-oriented to spoiler and everything in between – and pinpoints resulting humanitarian challenges.

State failure and non-state actors

The weakening and disappearance of central authority have been a boon to non-state actors of all stripes and sizes. Only rarely do failing states entail complete anarchy; usually beneath the veneer of formal institutions there remain rudiments of order. Such "orders" – or "durable disorders" – are still grounded in arrangements among actors representing political, military and economic power.[3] The absence of centralized political power allows non-state actors to operate unfettered by law and to assume a larger and often pernicious role. Where vacuums of authority exist, humanitarian agencies are obliged to work with non-state actors instead of governments. Table 14.1 reviews such actors. Understanding interests and their durability in a particular society is essential if humanitarian agencies are to forge and manage productive relationships in war zones.

Everyone is affected by state failure, but its impacts are distributed unevenly. First and foremost for humanitarians are vulnerable populations, those who rely on the state for essential services, who clearly suffer from a crisis of governance. Others have different points of contact with humanitarian agencies; for example, a temporarily displaced farmer may receive food but also seeds. Agencies have automatically and viscerally provided relief to victims, but they must increasingly evaluate their operational environments. Reflection must precede reaction.

Civil society

Frustrations with or a lack of state authorities and ideological preferences have led humanitarians to engage civil society (or "peace-oriented"

Table 14.1 Types and examples of non-state actors

Spoilers	Unreliable non-state actors	Civil society
Warlords	Leaders of political movements	NGOs
Mafia	Legitimate business	
	Employment seekers	
	Private military companies	

non-state actors), whose primary mission is assistance, development and stability. Many non-governmental organizations (NGOs) are or could be assets for humanitarian agencies in distributing aid, promoting reconciliation and supporting reconstruction and development. As part of "civil society", groups such as human rights organizations and trade unions are an easy case: they are viable partners for aid agencies even if their capacities are often feeble.

"Spoilers"

Also an easy case – to be eschewed rather than embraced – is "spoilers", whose destructive behaviour and hostility dispel the "romance" of any idealistic notions of the private sector.[4] "Spoilers" hardly share liberal values; they operate without reference to or even knowledge of international conventions and are intrinsically destabilizing. Protracted wars and state collapse "give a comparative advantage to sociopaths",[5] but the crises they engender are not exclusively populated by misanthropic gunfighters whose behaviour and interests can be written off as maniacal or beyond calculation. War and aid play rational economic roles.[6] Many spoilers pursue interests that may appear "irrational" to outsiders or on measures of the aggregate welfare of afflicted societies, but are quite "rational" on narrower calculations.

While states are failing or rebuilding, unusual predatory economic opportunities abound: a market for protection services, illicit and destabilizing commerce, and aid manipulation. New political economies that thrive with the prospect of state failure, or ongoing state failure, drive actors to concentrate their energies on controlling commerce. As a result, spoilers pursue profits, with "taxation" for protection a prime tactic for enrichment.

Commercial activity in the context of state failure may be premised on maintaining disorder and violence. Profiteers benefit from high prices: staples such as grain or gasoline are "priced" to reflect costs plus margins to enrich speculators and intermediaries. A second form of criminally distorting commerce is the exploitation of natural resources by private interests. Greed and the opportunity to finance political projects and military campaigns lead many non-state actors to focus on securing access to natural resources. Examples of natural resources that fall into this schema include minerals (diamonds, cobalt, coltan, bauxite, gold and oil) and high-value agricultural commodities (tropical hardwoods and certain fruits and vegetables).[7]

Finally, observers have pointed out that aid has inadvertently fuelled war. Assistance given without reflection may not only become the object of struggle but also actually create the potential for violence. Outside assistance in the response to the Rwandan genocide ignored and then reinforced the structural violence within a society, which made possible the murder of some 800,000 individuals.[8]

As stakeholders in complex emergencies, spoilers' interest in humanitarian assistance derives from its potential to perpetuate rather than mitigate conflict. Moreover, international aid and security jobs with aid agencies are a prized source of income. Perennial spoilers risk being marginalized after a negotiated peace, the onset of reconciliation, the establishment of the rule of law, and the prospect of a peacetime economy. After the crisis, resources brought by aid agencies – goods, jobs, rent and contracts – can no longer be manipulated to help sustain their patronage relations with supporters, and soldiers and racketeers who committed serious crimes cannot return to their communities.

Warlords, militias and armed groups have a political base that rests firmly on persistent insecurity, fear and division. Their aim is not to establish legitimate political order but to provide protection for security, political and economic payoffs. "My gun is my job" is the economic rationale behind warmongering. Every continent has its well-known examples of young, unskilled and unemployed members of militias – some kidnapped or forcibly recruited as children[9] – being rewarded with access to war booty.

Although fundamentally grounded in economic interests, illegitimate business organizations and mafioso present comparable challenges. Complex emergencies produce a class of war merchants and profiteers whose activities include killing competitors, drug trafficking, smuggling, toxic waste dumping and piracy, in addition to their usual predatory economic practices such as driving up food prices. Aid agencies often encounter problems tendering bids for transportation and money exchange with borderline criminals who are well positioned to reap the fruits of aid brought to mitigate the suffering of others. In some instances, the very presence of aid agencies constitutes a security threat to groups involved in illegal commerce, especially when expatriate staff are well informed.

The "grey" area: Unreliable non-state actors

Beyond the extreme categories understood by the conventional frameworks currently utilized by humanitarian agencies there exists an enormous expanse of grey. There are a wide variety and number of non-state actors who might best be characterized as "unreliable", because their interests are such that they may or may not be viable partners for humanitarians. The distinction is fuzzy between spoilers, on the one hand, who are adamant about their opposition and thus have crossed the "point of no return", and unreliable non-state actors, on the other hand, who could be enticed into legitimate commerce, politics and employment. Many fluctuate in orientation over time, and others appear two-faced in seeking assistance for themselves and their allies but fighting to prevent access to opponents.

For example, from 1994 to 1998 in eastern Zaire, aid recipients were also combatants – a phenomenon called "refugee-warriors".[10] Given the experiences of the 1990s, it is more exact to speak of "victim-belligerents" – those who spur, and suffer from, conflict. Humanitarians attuned to existing programming categories regarding combatants and non-combatants and the indelibility of such designations may inadvertently marginalize potential allies and buttress potential enemies. Four illustrations of such unreliable actors suggest potential trade-offs in the "grey" area.

First, the leaders of political movements, factions, self-declared regional authorities and secessionist groups present a mixed bag for humanitarians. One of their chief objectives is to win recognition and demonstrate authority over defined territories and peoples. A truly effective scheme has been to act as an intermediary between local populations and external aid agencies. To be the "sole legitimate authority" in an area of operations tends to legitimize a claim. This chronic problem for aid agencies was exemplified by Hutu *génocidaires*, who manipulated camp residents and also aid agencies in eastern Zaire. In some zones of state collapse, traditional clan or communal leaders reassert their roles. Although an asset in some emergency responses, their legitimacy may reflect an ability to protect and promote a group's interest rather than the community's. This can lead to aid operations being disrupted or halted because of a deadlock among elders. Research in Somalia indicates the extent to which traditional authority structures were helpful to delivery but hurtful to state-building.

Second, legitimate business constitutes another blend of promise and peril. Local commercial interests can be pivotal in shaping the operating environment. Merchants and traders are major stakeholders in the price of basic commodities, which can be undermined by the availability of relief goods in local markets. Private sector providers of key services in veterinary medicine, health care and even potable water see profits dwindle when aid agencies provide goods for free. Well-intentioned relief can make enemies of legitimate local businesspeople, prompting them to sabotage wells, drive food convoys away or even incite violence against aid agencies. One of the more astute measures used in Somalia in 1993 was to make foodstuffs commercially available, rather than free, which forced hoarders to dump their commodities and enticed legitimate traders back into business.[11] Sometimes powerful external commercial interests – such as oil, mining and timber companies – can become obstacles to relief efforts or even spark conflicts that trigger humanitarian crises. Notable current examples are the foreign oil companies operating in the "scorched earth" area of southern Sudan or in mineral-rich parts of the eastern Congo.

Third, the case of employment seekers reveals more trouble. When unemployment approaches 100 per cent and people are desperate for work to feed themselves and their families, external aid agencies may constitute virtually the entire formal monetized sector. Stories of drivers working for external agencies who earn 10 times the salary of a senior government official are accurate. The negative impact on the local economy includes skyrocketing rents and inflation, prostitution and parallel markets. When hiring procedures are perceived to have been unfair, aid agencies can be confronted with spurned applicants. In other cases, fired local staff can become a security problem.

Fourth, "private military companies" (PMCs) are contracted primarily by governments (and occasionally by large corporations) to provide security services – to protect key economic assets, train the military and support combat operations. Executive Outcomes, hired in Sierra Leone by the government to defeat the insurgency and secure diamond mines, is an often-cited illustration because its additional military punch prevented imminent state failure.[12] Over the past decade, the use of private security forces has grown, and there is no longer a visceral rejection of such mercenaries, even by humanitarians.[13] Significant logistical capabilities and firepower are obliging agencies to entertain partnerships once viewed as anathema.[14]

Humanitarian challenges of non-state actors

Aside from problems in mobilizing resources and logistics, insecurity in failing or failed states challenges humanitarians to reconsider how aid and protection are provided. To develop better strategies for addressing state failure, they need to consider both direct and indirect obstacles to their work.

Direct impediments: Violence and access

Two primary and interrelated hurdles directly impede the work of humanitarians – violence and access. Violence begets insecurity, which frequently blocks aid efforts and threatens personnel. High-profile examples include the executions in Chechnya of Fred Cuny and six Red Cross nurses. A review of aid workers killed in recent years attests to this disconcerting trend.[15] Kidnapping, threatening and assassinating local staff present a conundrum for agencies attempting to emphasize indigenous capacity-building, because local staff are even more vulnerable than expatriates.

Access to those in need is essential, but outbreaks of violence and insecurity jeopardize efforts. Creating safe areas or corridors of tranquillity is often a first step, if not the first sticking point, for humanitarians, but getting the green light from elements that control territory often proves tortuous and uncertain.

"Indirect obstacles": The unintended consequences of aid

Two strains of malfeasance, economic and political, can be considered "indirect" insofar as they do not necessarily hinder humanitarian efforts but they do skew impacts. Money and aid are often extorted or stolen from relief agencies upon passing through checkpoints (this is euphemistically dubbed "taxation"). Looking the other way is often justified as the cost of doing business. Although non-state actors may not provide any of the basic services of a competent government, they often enrich themselves by serving as gatekeepers for those in need. Demands for contracts, including the provision of security (for example by the "technicals" in Somalia), may also be part of the package.

A related economic perversion is market manipulation. Even in crises, markets remain channels for relief, so it is essential that external aid not corrupt or destroy them. Efforts to control currency rates or the prices of key commodities are obvious levers. Hoarding and parallel markets are another way to distort relief efforts by undermining local producers. In Afghanistan, for instance, the economic power of Pashtuns is based on their connections to markets in Pakistan, which tilt the benefits of assistance and reconstruction in their favour.[16] A milder form of manipulation consists of ignoring or eroding local capacities.[17]

The politicization of aid is another significant indirect obstacle. Some observers believe that all forms of aid are innately political, and therefore classifying a particular instance as "politicized" has little meaning. The task is to isolate those rationales and challenges that are utilized to dramatically alter the course of political outcomes. Disputes arise over the allocation of aid, jobs and contracts, and the distribution of relief often occurs according to political, economic or ethnic cleavages. Camps of refugees or internally displaced persons (IDPs) can be manipulated by militias as "bait" to attract international relief. Misuse of camps for recruitment and regrouping is commonplace.

Humanitarians now work with people who have been forcibly moved to refugee or IDP camps, but many victims may also be loyal supporters of those responsible for a crisis. Although charity always seems worthwhile, food, clothing and shelter are fungible and free up other resources for the war effort. Moreover, control of access to international assistance is a means of rewarding supporters and punishing opponents. Fake charities that present themselves as the local counterparts of international non-profits are little more than fronts for rogues and are also widespread.

They often are attempts to "capture" agencies, monopolize jobs and aid, prevent assistance from being distributed to adversaries, and control information. In the worst cases, external agencies inadvertently become a virtual logistical support unit for militias; their local armed guards are basically encamped members of militias on the payroll.

By working with spoilers, humanitarian organizations may grant legitimacy to otherwise illegitimate actors. Formal relations with spoilers implicitly acknowledge their authority, and a relief role bolsters their claims of legitimacy.[18] This problem was less acute, or perhaps more awkward and less common for UN agencies, before civil wars and non-state actors became routine parts of their mandates. For instance, in the 1980s UNICEF was chosen to lead Operation Lifeline Sudan because women and children were deemed exceptional; UNICEF's dealing with the Sudanese Liberation Army did not necessarily imply international recognition.[19] At present, few barriers to entry exist for humanitarians in war zones, and virtually all UN agencies and a gaggle of NGOs vie for a share of the aid market. Helping affected populations usually takes precedence over possible downstream problems of unpalatable partners.

Shortcomings of the humanitarian system and state failure

Compounding efforts to differentiate among non-state actors are three problematic dynamics within the international humanitarian system. First, current mechanisms were designed to respond to international wars and often are ill suited to "stateless" complex emergencies. Second, the survival instinct of organizations leaves them vulnerable to the whims of donors, which in turn foster turf wars. Third, the international humanitarian system is under-capacitated and overworked, which fosters a triage mentality as agencies attempt to match principles, resources and programming to a swelling stream of crises. These flaws impede the questioning of assumptions and standard operating procedures. They lead to ad hoc approaches, piecemeal policies and incoherent outputs. To the extent that any lessons learned remain relegated to file-drawers, coffee tables or book jackets, the concept of learning is absurd. Indeed, it is more accurate to speak of "lessons spurned". Alex de Waal rues an international humanitarian system with an "extraordinary capacity to absorb criticism, not reform itself, and yet emerge strengthened".[20]

The first long-standing structural problem exacerbated by state failure is that the existing system is largely geared to earlier crises. Experiences in the First and Second World Wars led to an emphasis on persons forcibly displaced across international boundaries. Furthermore, the nature of these humanitarian crises did not threaten the viability of governance, and relief was delivered with the consent of the warring parties. The principles of neutrality and impartiality that emerged from responding to international conflicts and natural disasters became shibboleths. However, refugees have been diminishing over the past decade while those internally displaced – that is, who physically remain within their own countries – by civil wars have been increasing dramatically. The number of refugees at the beginning of the twenty-first century was generally agreed to have shrunk to below 15 million, but the number of IDPs is at least twice that – depending on who is counting, 20–30 million displaced by wars and a similar number displaced by natural disasters. When IDP data were first gathered in 1982, there were only 1 million, at which time there were about 10.5 million refugees. Ironically, the fastest-growing category of war victims still has no institutional sponsor or agreed international legal framework, whereas refugees, whose numbers are diminishing, benefit from well-developed institutional and legal efforts through the UN High Commissioner for Refugees (UNHCR). Various stop-gaps have been instituted to fill this void, but the humanitarian machinery is engineered to respond to inter-state conflicts. The prevalence of non-state actors is treated as an aberration rather than the norm.[21]

The second major complication is perverse funding patterns.[22] Donors – be they public (bilateral or multilateral) or private (foundations and individuals but also operational NGOs that are conduits for public funds) – contribute resources when disaster strikes but only for a particular crisis and for a limited duration. Thus, short-sighted or incomplete plans and incoherent implementation are widespread. "Most donor behaviour is really rational from a donor point of view," notes Deputy Emergency Relief Coordinator Carolyn McAskie. "However, the sum total of all donor behaviour doesn't produce a rational whole."[23] Donor imperatives structure how operational agencies cast their efforts. Since donors' interests fluctuate, agencies often dedicate their energies more to appeasing donors than to designing appropriate programming. Donor agendas invariably seek out "glamorous" high-profile actions, leaving a lack of resources for other nagging but neglected humanitarian issues.

In addition to such donor snarls, turf wars bedevil overall performance. Several case-studies of NGOs illustrate that organizational interests can trump those of the victims.[24] Agencies design programmes with an eye more towards assuring their relevance and role than effective relief and protection. One UN practitioner has noted that coordination occurs not by command but rather, if at all, by consensus or default.[25]

Resources and capacity are already scarce, and state failure is an additional strain. Asking humanitarians to devote more of their funds to analysis is problematic. High stress and burn-out rates for officials assigned to complex emergencies are widespread. Recent efforts to upgrade administration and train personnel are an important start, but the magnitude of the problems suggests the need for more radical efforts to enhance flexibility, increase professionalism and retain talented personnel.

The collective impact of these shortcomings is hard to quantify, but the performance of the international humanitarian system is undoubtedly being eroding. The image of a "global fire department" – endlessly scurrying from crisis to crisis, lost in a desperate rush to bring immediate relief with no time to develop appropriate methods – aptly captures reality. As one military observer commented: "The need for a concerted approach ... contradicts the current independence of each responding agency and organization in an international response."[26] The creation by the United Nations of the Office for the Coordination of Humanitarian Affairs (previously the Department for Humanitarian Affairs), the Inter-Agency Standing Committee (IASC) and the Executive Committee for Humanitarian Affairs disguises the reality that there is no central decision-making. The existence of NGO consortiums also does not imply meaningful coordination among private agencies. The consolidation of humanitarian machinery that was rejected in the so-called UN reform of 1997 should be reviewed.[27]

Improvisation continues to be the hallmark of the status quo. General Romeo Dallaire, who commanded the paltry UN peacekeeping force that was powerless to halt the Rwandan genocide in 1994, looked back over the 1990s as "a decade of adhocracy".[28] Actually, improvisation connotes more order, certainty and responsiveness than the present underfunded patchwork truly delivers. Ad hocery is bad enough in a natural disaster, but in the ebb and flow of authority and security in "stateless" complex emergencies it is tragically wasteful. A jumbled response can produce resentment in areas of operations, stir conflict and undercut support for humanitarians.

The search for solutions: Improving intelligence and strategies

Making humanitarianism work involves greater understanding of the humanitarian fog of war: who is to be helped and how? Two necessary steps are gathering better information in the field and refining context-specific tactics within alternative strategies.

Humanitarian intelligence

At the most basic level, humanitarianism means bringing aid to the suffering, which in an ideal world would consist of accountable transactions from aid providers to needy recipients. However, the complex political overlay of state failure and humanitarian action has altered the equation. The humanitarian impulse must be tempered with data about who benefits most – the victims or the spoilers who see crises as political or economic opportunities. Currently, when agencies wonder whether a particular non-state actor merits trust or suspicion, humanitarians have neither the inclination to analyse them nor readily available information about their interest structures or the likely result of cooperation. The growing realization that aid has complicated if not fuelled wars requires field staff and policy makers to make better assessments of the agendas, authority and abilities of non-state actors. An independent review of field experience suggests that the operational tool most in demand but in shortest supply is humanitarian intelligence,[29] a view shared by the IASC: "Knowledge of how belligerents and others perceive the situation may provide 'early warning' to humanitarians. A key to effective protection and planning is anticipating and responding to next moves."[30]

Assessments are essential to framing agencies' options for engagement. Determining whether an unreliable non-state actor can become a partner for agencies and how to promote such a transformation is a central collective challenge for international humanitarian responses in failing or failed states. A case can be made that, in certain circumstances, even the behaviour of some spoilers is subject to modification. Members of militias who fight and loot because that is their only source of earnings have in Central America availed themselves of the opportunity to learn new skills in demobilization programmes. Business interests can shift from illegitimate to legitimate, as in the case of Somali hoarders who became merchants after the war. And even some warlords have played the political field as candidates for elected office in the Loya Jirga in Afghanistan.[31] The main obstacle to understanding is the dearth of solid data or even accurate descriptions of the politics and interests of non-state actors. Instead of relying on state-centric frameworks, humanitarians need to grasp the "transnational and networked characteristics" of war economies.[32]

Humanitarians require intelligence – substantial information-gathering and comparative analyses on the range of incentives and disincentives that are attractive to non-state actors[33] – and agencies should dedicate more resources to strengthening their assessment capacities. Background materials produced by scholars are an overlooked asset, and field personnel often underestimate the value of regular exchanges with academic specialists.[34] Furthermore, scholarly work would benefit from exposure to field personnel and agency perspectives. More important still is the timely information to be gathered from informal sources in the field: traders and truck drivers can advise on logistics; displaced persons can offer new information on military movements, roadblocks and landmines; journalists and business groups can help analyse power hierarchies and economic networks. In highly polarized environments, biases are an occupational hazard and the best insurance is to have broad samples.

Pooling information among agencies has its own problems, but greater sharing is essential. If waste and overlap are to be avoided and experiments attempted, donors should overcome their antipathy to increased overheads. Although investing in analytical functions may have less quantifiable impact than food delivery, it pays dividends in the medium term. If donors are concerned with overall efficiency and effectiveness – and, most of all, a humanitarian exit strategy – greater flexibility and resources are required to understand local contexts and to allow experimentation.

Strategies

In the build-up to or aftermath of state failure, humanitarians equipped with improved assessments should make tactical decisions with respect to non-state actors within four strategic options: neutrality and impartiality, confrontation, pragmatic adaptation, and co-optation. The current humanitarian protocols may be adequate for engaging civil society, but spoilers and the "grey" area are much more problematic. The key to engaging these sorts of non-state actor effectively is to change incentive structures.[35] The choices may not be as stark as the categorization in table 14.2 implies, but classifying strategies helps to clarify the options.

Neutrality and impartiality

Although the International Committee of the Red Cross (ICRC) is the "prophet" of the classic neutrality and impartiality approach, there are many other "priests".[36] Separating itself from politics and calling for a division of labour with other agencies (human rights advocates as well as aid purveyors) and military forces, the ICRC seeks to protect its classic stance. Other organizations pursue what might be labelled "non-partisanship", stopping short of advocacy but nonetheless engaging with belligerents on essential political issues.

Table 14.2 Strategies for engaging non-state actors

Spoilers	Unreliable non-state actors	Civil society
Confrontation	Occasional confrontation Co-optation Pragmatic adaptation	Neutrality and impartiality

In spite of protestations by traditionalists, "business as usual" is not a viable strategic option for many of today's humanitarian disasters. Although apt in earlier periods and still practical in many inter-state wars (and natural disasters), neutrality and impartiality are of limited applicability in "stateless" complex emergencies. Staying clear of politics is impossible and may make matters worse. Consent has little meaning when outside military forces intervene. One summary of a discussion by prominent agencies stated: "Many within the NGO community who initially believed that their organizations could play neutral roles in complex emergencies have begun to revise their views."[37] Even a proponent of neutrality has recognized that the experiences of the 1990s "have placed on the defensive people who have sought to preserve the consensual and civilian character of humanitarian action".[38]

Humanitarian action is innately and intensely political.[39] Even when actions are not intended as such, they are perceived as political. The evidence of conflicts and responses from the past 15 years suggests that maintaining artificial barriers between the humanitarian and the political thwarts programming.[40] Indeed, Mark Duffield and others have called for a more avowedly political posture. The "new or political humanitarianism" is an integral part of a set of relief, development and reconstruction activities required by the new wars.[41] Neutrality and impartiality remain useful in dealing with civil society but may be ineffective or even counter-productive with others.

Confrontation

Opposing or defying non-state actors can work against aid agencies and risk the lives of expatriate and local personnel. An agency's bargaining relationship is weak, whether measured by gun-power or will-power. Ratcheting up measures implies the willingness to withdraw, but non-state actors calculate that aid agencies' need to be present in a crisis will outweigh the costs of being entangled with spoilers.

Still, the threat to withdraw is a common tactic, often born of frustration and fatigue. A temporary suspension of operations can be useful if an agency can convince recipients to blame spoilers and not the agency itself. Moreover, intergovernmental organizations operate under orders from political masters and, unless a governing body of states approves confrontation (for example, the UN Security Council invoking its Chapter VII powers), there is little room for field personnel or even heads of agencies to confront belligerents. When High Commissioner for Refugees Sadako Ogata tried to suspend operations in Sarajevo after particularly egregious behaviour by Bosnian Serbs, Secretary-General Boutros Boutros-Ghali overruled her, presumably because the United Nations had no choice. Headquarters can press staff to remain on the ground to foster fund-raising and media objectives even if the actual field mission is dysfunctional in the eyes of those on the ground.

Suspension or withdrawal of aid activity is more effective under a united front. When a sole agency departs, this may be viewed as resulting from its misunderstanding and mishandling of local dynamics. If collective bargaining were undertaken by major agencies, the message would be unmistakable. However, unity is difficult, in that humanitarian agencies in the field often have mixed feelings for one another as well as diverging agendas, governing boards and donors. Selective suspension or withdrawal has symbolic rather than practical implications because other agencies can almost certainly make up the loss. Lonely defectors may occupy the high moral ground, but they increase the demand for other agencies whose boards and staff are conscious of "market share".[42] This, in turn, may lower the media profile of those who leave, which can affect fund-raising and programming for other activities as well.

Another argument against withdrawal is that relieving suffering is the reason humanitarian organizations exist. However, some agencies – for example, CARE Canada and Médecins Sans Frontières (MSF) International in eastern Zaire in 1995 – have reasoned that in certain situations they were doing more harm than good and left the scene. There is little point in wasting resources that deal with symptoms and lead to subsequent violence against those aided. As there is no shortage of crises and demands for help, resources should be channelled to contexts where aid is not frittered away or used to fuel conflicts. Confrontation is most likely to work as a strategy for humanitarians with the groups that are the least problematic, namely civil society and some malleable non-state actors.

Pragmatic adaptation

Faced with extortion from spoilers and obstructionists, many aid agencies opt to sup with the devil in order to aid at least some needy populations. The most common tactical concessions include agreeing to diversion at the point of entry as well as employment and contracts for individuals specified by warlords.

Utilitarian logic always operates on a slippery slope; at some point the good an aid agency is doing may be offset or overwhelmed by the damage wrought by Faustian tactical bargains. That harm can be measured: the weapons procured by warlords with the relief aid handed over as a "tax"; the precedents set for future transactions; and the empowerment of warlords. As the most expedient and least risky way to manage the short-term problem of spoilers and unreliable non-state actors, pragmatism remains a popular option.

To ensure that pragmatism is not sheer opportunism, some NGOs have experimented with subcontracting to merchants and paying only for what was delivered – that is, making recipient communities themselves responsible for distribution. To limit extortion, others have tried to negotiate as a group. The monetization of foodstuffs, rather than free deliveries, is yet another method.

Co-optation

Some non-state actors may be more obstructionist than spoiler. In some instances, their behaviour is driven by short-term economic calculations and survival. To the extent that external actors possess carrots and sticks, they can reshape interests and modify behaviour. Hence, effective policies focusing on co-opting non-state actors become an important strategic option that requires input from the field and headquarters.

At the same time, the transformation of warlords into elected officials, of bandits into police officers, and of mafioso merchants into legitimate businesspeople is usually well beyond the capacity of aid agencies. Shifts in the structure of interests are not amenable to quick fixes. Perhaps among the exceptions to this rule are demobilization programmes, which can provide skills training and financial incentives to soldiers to put down their weapons. Nonetheless, success is likely only during genuine economic recovery; otherwise, efforts to co-opt soldiers may lead to disgruntled, unemployed people who return to banditry. Contracting the delivery of food aid to businesspeople is another instance of successful co-optation.[43] The essence is to create stakeholders in law and order.

Behaviour towards aid agencies hinges on weighing short- versus longer-term benefits. With a short time horizon, decision-making tends to be myopic and non-state actors ask themselves, "Why work with an agency controlling substantial wealth and goods if they are likely to depart shortly?" The short-term nature of emergency responses – many disbursements must occur within three to six weeks – invites local actors to behave expediently, which translates into confiscating as many resources as quickly as possible.

Some humanitarian organizations have long-standing experience in war-torn communities. In these instances, long-term interests in maintaining an agency's presence can neutralize obstructionists. However, an ongoing presence in communities is impossible unless donors make financial commitments for the future. To facilitate the elaborate calculations and subtle manoeuvres discussed here, donor criteria will have to change. This seemingly obvious reality has yet to penetrate donor capitals or the Development Assistance Committee of the Organisation for Economic Co-operation and Development.

Conclusion

Contemporary humanitarian disasters induced by crises of governance have led to much soul-searching but no radical rethinking of responses, let alone a restructuring of the international humanitarian system. The groping and coping of the past decade are an indication of good faith though disappointing performance. Indeed, the growing willingness to be self-critical is an encouraging sign among humanitarian organizations, albeit more visible in NGO than in UN circles.

The bottom line is that effective delivery and protection demand a better understanding of non-state actors and tailored operating strategies. Some practitioners may be sceptical about the benefits of information-gathering and empirical research. But this is not an argument for paralysis by analysis. Recent experiences demonstrate that good intentions and charitable impulses afford openings to parasitic elements. Therefore, humanitarian intelligence is not an ornamental luxury but a necessary building-block in crafting effective programming.

The aftermath of the 2003 war in Iraq and the ever-widening war against terrorism in such places as Afghanistan, Chechnya and Indonesia made clear that the challenges of fragmentation and humanitarian action are hardly relics of the twentieth century. The conflict in Iraq and the contested occupation demonstrate that some facets of inter-state war are still relevant for humanitarians: functioning government bureaucracies to distribute aid and cooperative civil and military forces to ensure access and security.[44]

At the same time, however, for the coming decade as for the last, non-state actors will represent an increasing share of the challenges in every war zone and thereby undermine traditional arrangements and methods. In Iraq, as in Afghanistan, the defeat of the previous regime's military caused the collapse of the central political authority, leaving other centres of authority to proliferate. Although many previously repressed groups may emerge as part of a vibrant civil society and eventually become assets, humanitarians should be prepared to encounter far more problematic actors.

In Iraq, agencies will contend with various spoiler and obstructionist elements who see no role for themselves in a US-dominated Iraq – some with ties to the Saddam Hussein regime (defeated soldiers from the Republican Guard, senior government officials, Baath party leadership, fedayeen paramilitary factions, tribal leaders from Tikrit, and corrupt economic interests), others with links to extremist or terrorist groups. Beyond Iraq and the challenges that it presents, al Qaeda poses a different sort of hurdle, that of the transnational spoiler, whose presence in a wide range of conflicts suggests that humanitarians should develop strategies for operating in common areas of activity. Such future emergencies will likely feature a dearth of order and a multitude of diverse actors with equally divergent interests in a fluid and insecure environment. Responses geared mainly to the challenges presented by state actors or even by unambiguous non-state actors will not suffice.

Finally, it is worth recognizing how making humanitarianism work helps to make states work. Although humanitarianism is designed to address the suffering associated with weak or failed states, its implications go far beyond an emergency phase. The dangers of interacting with uncertain actors have both strategic and tactical consequences for humanitarians. As the above analysis spells out, there are resulting operational problems. Furthermore, when humanitarians grant legitimacy to unsavoury parties through working relationships, the underlying humanitarian strategy is also harmed because support for those who violate human rights sows the seeds of future repression and emergencies. Therefore, a crucial dimension to making humanitarianism work is establishing reliable relationships with legitimate partners.

Those whose primary agenda is to create effective states often share the concerns of humanitarians, but their overriding priority tends to be stability and order. A subset of this group, aptly dubbed "human rights hawks", seeks not merely effective states but just states that work, even if it means a resort to force. Humanitarian efforts usually go hand in hand with this muscular human rights agenda, but it is essential to appreciate that they are not one and the same. Making humanitarianism work saves lives; making states work saves (or establishes) the institutions that protect and nurture societies. Until we get the former right, the latter will be forever wronged.

To return to the main focus of this chapter, the word "dilemma" is often used to describe the challenges faced by humanitarians in "stateless" complex emergencies, but "tough choices" would be more appropriate.[45] Doing nothing is morally acceptable in confronting a true dilemma – two alternative courses of action, each bearing the potential for unintended and direct (but nonetheless unavoidable and equally undesirable) consequences. Better understanding and clearer engagement strategies will not make difficult decisions easy, but they will make them possible and palatable. Ways and means can be found to mitigate the worst aspects of spoiler activities and perhaps to co-opt other non-state actors whose interests are subject to influence and change.[46]

Albert Einstein once said, "The problems that exist in the world today can not be solved by the level of thinking that created them." This chapter has chronicled two such failures, one of states torn by strife and the other of the international humanitarian system. The humanitarian impulse remains vital, but the performance of humanitarians themselves has come under fire. Aid agencies more aware of and astute about their practices, environs, impacts and options will help to make humanitarianism work.

Notes

1. This argument was originally made in Thomas G. Weiss, "Principles, Politics, and Humanitarian Action", *Ethics & International Affairs*, Vol. 13, 1999, pp. 1–22. Rethinking the enterprise is a theme of Hugo Slim, *A Call to Alms: Humanitarian Action and the Art of War*, Geneva: Centre for Humanitarian Dialogue, 2004; Fiona Terry, *Condemned to Repeat? The Paradox of Humanitarian Action*, Ithaca, NY: Cornell University Press, 2002, pp. 241–243; and Adrian Wood, Raymond Apthorpe and John Borton, eds, *Evaluating International Humanitarian Action: Reflections from Practitioners*, London: Zed Books, 2001.
2. Larry Minear, *The Humanitarian Enterprise: Dilemmas and Discoveries*, Bloomfield, CT: Kumarian, 2002, p. 7.
3. Mark Duffield, "Globalization, Transborder Trade, and War Economies", in Mats Berdal and David M. Malone, eds, *Greed and Grievance: Economic Agendas in Civil Wars*, Boulder, CO: Lynne Rienner, 2000, pp. 70–74; also see William Reno, "Shadow States and the Political Economy of Civil War", in ibid., p. 44.
4. Fred Halliday, "The Romance of Non-State Actors", in Daphné Josselin and William Wallace, eds, *Non-State Actors in World Politics*, New York: Palgrave, 2000, p. 23.
5. William J. Reno, *Warlord Politics and African States*, Boulder, CO: Lynn Rienner, 1998, p. 71.
6. David Keen, *The Economic Functions of Violence in Civil Wars*, Oxford: Oxford University Press, Adelphi Paper 320, 1997; and Mark Duffield, *Global Governance and the New Wars: The Merging of Development and Security*, London: Zed Books, 2001.
7. Several studies have examined the role of natural resources in fuelling contemporary conflicts in Angola, Cambodia, the Democratic Republic of Congo, Indonesia, Liberia and Sierra Leone. See Duffield, *Global Governance*, pp. 161–201. Also, several UN reports document the widespread plunder of mineral wealth in contemporary conflicts: *The Causes of Conflict and the Promotion of Durable Peace and Sustainable Development in Africa*, Report of the UN Secretary-General to the Security Council, UN Doc. A/RES/57/296, April 1998; more recently, the link to the war in the Democratic Republic of Congo is covered in *Final Report of the Panel of Experts on the Illegal Exploitation of Natural Resources and Other Forms of Wealth of the Democratic Republic of Congo*, UN Doc. S/2002/1146, 16 October 2002.
8. Peter Uvin, *Aiding Violence: The Development Enterprise in Rwanda*, West Hartford, CT: Kumarian, 1998; Terry, *Condemned to Repeat?*, pp. 186–192.
9. See, for example, Ilene Cohn and Guy S. Goodwin-Gill, *Child Soldiers: The Role of Children in Armed Conflict*, Oxford: Clarendon Press, 1994; and Graça Machel, *The Impact of War on Children*, New York: Palgrave, 2001. Useful data can be found in UNICEF, *Progress since the World Summit for Children: A Statistical Review*, New York: UNICEF, 2001.
10. Terry, *Condemned to Repeat?*, pp. 155–170, also pp. 5–9, 34. For a discussion of "refugee-warriors", see Aristide R. Zolberg, Astri Suhrke and Sergio Aguayo, eds, *Escape from Violence: Conflict and the Refugee Crisis in the Developing World*, New York: Oxford University Press, 1989.

11. Andrew S. Natsios, "Humanitarian Relief Intervention in Somalia: The Economics in Chaos", *International Peacekeeping*, Vol. 3, No. 1, Spring 1996, pp. 68–91. Also see Thomas G. Weiss, *Military–Civilian Interactions: Intervening in Humanitarian Crises*, 2nd edn, Lanham, MD: Rowman & Littlefield, 2004, chap. 4.

12. Jeremy Harding, "The Mercenary Business: 'Executive Outcomes'", *Review of African Political Economy*, Vol. 24, No. 71, March 1997, pp. 87–97; Herbert Howe, "Private Security Forces and African Stability: The Case of Executive Outcomes", *Journal of Modern African Studies*, Vol. 36, No. 2, 1998, pp. 307–331.

13. Doug Brooks, "Messiahs or Mercenaries? The Future of International Private Military Services", *International Peacekeeping*, Vol. 7, No. 4, Winter 2000, pp. 129–144; Christopher Spearin, "Private Security Companies and Humanitarians: A Corporate Solution to Securing Humanitarian Spaces?", *International Peacekeeping*, Vol. 8, No. 1, Spring 2001, pp. 20–43; and Steven Brayton, "Outsourcing War: Mercenaries and the Privatization of Peacekeeping", *Journal of International Affairs*, Vol. 55, No. 2, Spring 2002, pp. 303–329.

14. This trend began in the 1990s and is increasing. Michael Bryans, Bruce D. Jones and Janice Gross Stein, *Mean Times: Humanitarian Action in Complex Political Emergencies – Stark Choices, Cruel Dilemmas*, Toronto: University of Toronto, 1999; International Alert study in collaboration with the Feinstein International Famine Centre at Tufts University, Workshop on *The Politicization of Humanitarian Action and Staff Security: The Use of Private Security Companies by Humanitarian Agencies*, April 2001, available at ⟨http://www.international-alert.org/pdf/pubsec/Tuftrep.pdf⟩; Tony Vaux, Chris Seiple, Greg Nakano and Koenraad van Brabant, *Humanitarian Action and Private Security Companies*, London: International Alert, March 2002. Secretary-General Kofi Annan has also indicated that the United Nations has considered contracting PMCs; see *Thirty-Fifth Annual Ditchley Foundation Lecture*, UN Doc. SG/SM/6613, 26 June 1998, available at ⟨http://www0.un.org/News/Press/docs/1998/19980626.sgsm6613.html⟩.

15. See Denis King, "Paying the Ultimate Price: Analysis of the Deaths of Humanitarian Aid Workers (1997–2001)", 15 January 2001, available at ⟨http://www.reliefweb.int/symposium/PayingUltimatePrice97-01.html⟩.

16. Sarah Collinson, ed., *Power, Livelihoods, and Conflict: Case Studies in Political Economy Analysis*, London: Overseas Development Institute, HPG Report 13, 2003, p. 18. For a more general discussion of market manipulation, see Duffield, "Globalization", pp. 74–79, and "The Political Economy of Internal War: Asset Transfer, Complex Emergencies and International Aid", in Joanna Macrae and Anthony Zwi, *War & Hunger: Rethinking International Responses to Complex Emergencies*, London: Zed Books, 1994, pp. 56–57; and David Keen and Ken Wilson, "Engaging with Violence: A Reassessment of Relief in Wartime", in Macrae and Zwi, *War & Hunger*, p. 217.

17. See Mary B. Anderson and Peter J. Woodrow, *Rising from the Ashes: Development Strategies in Times of Disaster*, Boulder, CO: Westview Press, 1987; and Mary B. Anderson, *Do No Harm: How Aid Can Support Peace – Or War*, Boulder, CO: Lynne Rienner, 1999.

18. Terry, *Condemned to Repeat?*, p. 44.

19. See Larry Minear et al., *Humanitarianism under Siege: A Critical Review of Operation Lifeline Sudan*, Trenton: Red Sea Press, 1991; Francis M. Deng and Larry Minear, *The Challenge of Famine Relief: Emergency Operations in the Sudan*, Washington, DC: Brookings, 1992.

20. Alex de Waal, *Famine Crimes: Politics and the Disaster Relief Industry in Africa*, Oxford: James Currey, 1997, p. vi.

21. See Thomas G. Weiss, "Internal Exiles: What Next for Internally Displaced Persons?", *Third World Quarterly*, Vol. 24, No. 3, June 2003, pp. 429–477.

22. De Waal, *Famine Crimes*, and Michael Maren, *The Road to Hell: The Ravaging Effects of Foreign Aid and International Charity*, New York: Free Press, 1997, criticize humanitarian agencies that benefit from local populations on the dole.

23. Quoted by Larry Minear and Ian Smillie, *The Quality of Money: Donor Behaviour in Humanitarian Financing*, Somerville, MA: Humanitarianism and War Project, April 2003, p. 5. See also Joanna Macrae et al., *Uneven Power: The Changing Role of Official Donors in Humanitarian Action*, London: Overseas Development Institute, HPG Report 12, 2002.

24. Alexander Cooley and James Ron, "The NGO Scramble: Organizational Insecurity and the Political Economy of Transnational Action", *International Security*, Vol. 27, No. 1, Summer 2002, pp. 5–39, especially p. 34; Dorothea Hilhorst, "Being Good at Doing Good? Quality and Accountability of Humanitarian NGOs", *Disasters*, Vol. 26, No. 3, 2002, pp. 193–212, especially p. 196; and Terry, *Condemned to Repeat?*, p. 233.

25. Antonio Donini, *The Policies of Mercy: UN Coordination in Afghanistan, Mozambique, and Rwanda*, Providence, RI: Watson Institute, Occasional Paper No. 22, 1996, pp. 26–41.

26. John Mackinlay, *Globalisation and Insurgency*, Oxford: Oxford University Press, Adelphi Paper 352, 2002, p. 100.

27. Thomas G. Weiss, "Humanitarian Shell Games: Whither UN Reform?" *Security Dialogue*, Vol. 29, No.1, March 1998, pp. 9–23.

28. Romeo Dallaire, "Keynote Address", 24 April 2001, conference organized by CARE Canada and the Humanitarianism and War Project.

29. Stanley Foundation, *Humanitarian Action and the United Nations on the Ground*, Muscatine, IA: Stanley Foundation, 2003.

30. Inter-Agency Standing Committee, *Growing the Sheltering Tree: Protecting Rights through Humanitarian Action*, Geneva: IASC, 2002, p. 5; see also pp. 49–55.

31. For example, see "Evaluating Implementation Tasks" and "Case Studies", the second and third parts of Stephen John Stedman, Donald Rothchild and Elizabeth Cousens, eds, *Ending Civil Wars: The Implementation of Peace Agreements*, Boulder, CO: Lynne Rienner, 2002, pp. 139–659.

32. Duffield, "Globalization", pp. 69–90.

33. Mats Berdal and David M. Malone, "Introduction", in Berdal and Malone, eds., *Greed and Grievance*, p. 13.

34. The Social Science Research Council's Conflict Prevention Program is attempting to systematize outside information for the United Nations, available at ⟨http://www.ssrc.org/programs/conflictprev/⟩.

35. David Keen, "Incentives and Disincentives for Violence", in Berdal and Malone, eds, *Greed and Grievance*, p. 37.

36. Hugo Slim, "Sharing a Universal Ethic: The Principle of Humanity in War", *International Journal of Human Rights*, Vol. 4, No. 2, Winter 1998, pp. 28–48. See also Michael Ignatieff, *The Warrior's Honor: Ethnic War and the Modern Conscience*, New York: Henry Holt, 1997. David Rieff has come full circle and argues for a return to traditional approaches in *A Bed for the Night: Humanitarianism in Crisis*, New York: Simon & Schuster, 2002.

37. Marc Lindenberg and Coralie Bryant, *Going Global: Transforming Relief and Development NGOs*, Bloomfield, CT: Kumarian, 2001, p. 81.

38. Minear, *The Humanitarian Enterprise*, p. 116.

39. David Forsythe's classic book is entitled *Humanitarian Politics: The International Committee of the Red Cross*, Baltimore, MD: Johns Hopkins University Press, 1977, and argues that the ICRC was engaged politically. Forsythe continues and updates this theme in *The Humanitarians: The International Committee of the Red Cross*, Cambridge: Cambridge University Press, forthcoming 2005.

40. S. Neil MacFarlane and Thomas G. Weiss, "Political Interest and Humanitarian Action", *Security Studies*, Vol. 10, No. 1, Autumn 2000, p. 142.
41. Duffield, *Global Governance*, especially chap. 4.
42. See Cooley and Ron, "The NGO Scramble", and Rieff, *A Bed for the Night*.
43. In addition, the IASC notes that "Private Contractors Can Sometimes Venture Where UN Vehicles Cannot", *Growing the Sheltering Tree*, p. 40.
44. Owing to the effects of sanctions and how food is distributed in Iraq, a large portion of the population subsisted on what the Baghdad regime provided: "Sixty per cent of the population, 16 million people, depends completely on the food ration for their survival, which provides 2,200 calories a day, well below the average Iraqi intake of 3,159 calories before the Gulf War. An estimated 2.03 million children under-five and one million pregnant women will face moderate to severe malnutrition" (*Likely Humanitarian Scenarios*, released by Campaign Against Sanctions in Iraq, 10 December 2002, paras. 23–28, available at ⟨http://www.casi.org.uk/info/undocs/war021210.html⟩).
45. An edited volume commissioned by the ICRC mixed both notions in the title; see Jonathan Moore, ed., *Hard Choices: Moral Dilemmas in Humanitarian Intervention*, Lanham, MD: Rowman & Littlefield, 1998.
46. This line of argument was first developed in Thomas G. Weiss and Cindy Collins, *Humanitarian Challenges and Intervention*, Boulder, CO: Westview Press, 2000, chap. 4.

15

Transitional justice

Alex Boraine

Although the nature of failed states and the reasons for their dis-integration vary widely, such states are almost always characterized by weak and dysfunctional criminal justice institutions. All of the weak or failing states in this volume, from Pakistan to the Democratic Republic of Congo, from the Solomon Islands to Colombia, demonstrate how the absence of the rule of law is tied to broader questions of state legitimacy and, ultimately, state weakness. Furthermore, massive and systematic human rights abuse is often both a cause and a symptom of state failure. In order to make states work, it is imperative to return to the rule of law, which is fundamental to the maintenance of a free society. This in turn necessitates accountability for transgressions against the law. But what does accountability really mean? In his provocative and thoughtful book, *Radical Evil on Trial*, Carlos Nino poses several key questions: "How shall we live with evil? How shall we respond to massive human rights violations committed either by State actors or by others with the consent and tolerance of their governments?"[1] Following Kant, Nino argues that gross human rights violations are so abnormal and inexplicable that they can only be termed "radical evil". The killing of more than 6 million people and the unimaginable sufferings of countless more cannot be treated as a "normal" crime; to describe it in any terms less than "radical evil" insults the victims and contributes to the obscenity.

In trying to come to terms with genocide, crimes against humanity and other massive atrocities, not only does our moral discourse appear to reach its limit, but it also emphasizes the inadequacy of ordinary measures that usually apply in the field of criminal justice. Abnormal atrocities, it can be argued, demand abnormal measures.

There is, however, no unanimity amongst politicians, lawyers and philosophers about what these measures ought to be. Nino leaves no doubt as to where he stands: "I believe ... that some measure of retroactive justice for massive human rights violations helps protect democratic values."[2] But this only begs the question: what is meant by "some measures of retroactive justice"? Clearly, the issue of retroactive or transitional justice remains uncharted and there are far-reaching moral, political and legal problems, which deserve detailed study and vigorous debate. Despite these widely divergent views and the fact that impunity has been the norm rather than the exception, many countries and international agencies have sought accountability from those responsible for gross violations of human rights. The major response, in terms of accountability, is, invariably, the imposition of criminal sanctions on those who violate the law. In this way, the rule of law is vindicated, not only by punishing the perpetrator but also by emphasizing to society in general that such behaviour is intolerable. However, the search for justice is much more complicated than simply following the usual approach of trials and prosecutions.

In considering transitional justice and making states work, the approach ought to be holistic. By that I mean we should never approach any failed state on the way to recovery with a fixed dogmatic programme, even if the intention is good and accountability is the goal. The approach should be based on a careful analysis of the overall needs of the society and, in particular, the need for peaceful coexistence and development. Therefore, transitional justice ought to be considered as embracing accountability, truth-seeking and truth-telling, reconciliation, institutional reform and reparations.

This chapter begins by exploring the transitional context in which questions of accountability arise and how the mode of transition affects the kind of justice pursued. Within this context, I then examine judicial mechanisms of accountability, specifically the use of international courts and tribunals, and non-judicial mechanisms, including truth and reconciliation commissions and the vetting of public officials. Each of these mechanisms is analysed in terms of its potential contribution to accountability, reconciliation and state-building. The chapter concludes by emphasizing the importance of local consultation and holistic approaches to accountability in rebuilding states.

The transitional context

Balancing the past and the future

Pursuing justice in a normal situation involves enormous difficulties; when one attempts to do this in countries undergoing transition, the problems are intensified. There is a need to balance two imperatives. On the one hand, there is the need to return to the rule of law and the prosecution of offenders. On the other hand, there is a need to rebuild societies and embark on the process of reconciliation. In helping to make states work, it is important, therefore, to balance accountability with the shoring-up of fragile emerging democracies. The overall aim should be to ensure a sustainable peace, which will encourage and make possible social and economic development.

To put it in another way, should we attempt to deal with the past or should societies focus on the future? Timothy Garton Ash reminds us that "there is the old wisdom of the Jewish tradition: to remember is the secret of redemption".[3] Along similar lines, Lev Tolstoy asks:

People say why recall the past? What is the good of remembering what has been swept away? What is the good of irritating the nation? How can one ask such questions? If I suffered from a serious and dangerous disease and recovered or was cured from it, I would recollect the fact with joy. I would be disturbed by it only if I was still ill or if I'd taken a turn for the worse and wanted to deceive myself.[4]

On the other hand, there are powerful voices urging that the best way to deal with the past is to forget and move on. To be fair, for many it is not so much a question of ignoring the atrocities that have been committed as a concern to consolidate and protect a newly emerging democracy. Of course, there are some who simply wish to ignore the past because of their own involvement in it. But there is a defensible position, which calls for moving towards the future and not allowing the past to destroy or inhibit the new democracy.

Certainly, the experience of Mozambique is illustrative of this tension. As Michel Cahen notes in chapter 10 in this volume, the civil war split communities and pitted neighbour against neighbour. Many leaders in Mozambique argued against a national truth and reconciliation process, in part because they feared it would divide, rather than unite, the new state. Yet the controversial nomination as Frelimo's 2002 presidential candidate of Armando Guebuza, who played a key role in the relocation of "unproductive" people from the cities to the villages, demonstrates that Mozambique's past has been neither addressed nor forgotten.

Professor Bruce Ackerman has strongly criticized those who "squander moral capital in an ineffective effort to right past wrongs – creating martyrs and fostering political alienation, rather than contributing to a genuine sense of vindication". Indeed, he says, "moral capital" is better spent educating the population about the limits of the law rather than engaging in a "quixotic quest after the mirage of corrective justice". He cautions that any attempts to engage in corrective justice will generate "the perpetuation of moral arbitrariness and the creation of a new generation of victims".[5]

Uri Savir, an Israeli negotiator, makes this point very powerfully when he refers to the day when he and Palestinian negotiator Abu Ala arrived at their first understanding – never to argue about the past:

I ... told him: "You are a threat, because you want to live in my home. In my house."

"Where are you from?" he asked.

"Jerusalem," I replied.

"So am I," he continued, somberly. "Where is your father from?"

"He was born in Germany."

"Mine was born in Jerusalem and still lives there."

"Why don't you ask about my grandfathers and their forebears? We could go back to King David," I said, making no effort to hide my anger. "I'm sure we can debate the past for years and never agree. Let's see if we can agree about the future."

"Fine," he said, barely above a mumble.

We had arrived at our first understanding. Never again would we argue about the past. This was an important step, for it moved us beyond an endless wrangle over right and wrong. Discussing the future would mean reconciling two rights, not readdressing ancient wrongs.[6]

But the answer is surely not either/or. Once it is agreed that there must be the balancing of imperatives, then it is surely both/and. In other words, we should deal with the past and not dwell in it, but what measures are taken have to be informed by the nature of each transition and the political space for accountability. For example, when the bombing stopped in Afghanistan, some advocated the immediate introduction of trials and prosecutions. However, it was clear that the major problem confronting Afghanistan was not, in the first instance, accountability but security – the return of the refugees, food for those who were in danger of starving, and a measure of good governance so that law and order could be introduced and maintained. The same is true of Iraq. Although it is desirable to prosecute those who committed human rights violations during Saddam Hussein's dictatorship, the first imperative is to stop the looting, to return to some measure of law and order, and to enable Iraqi leaders and people to begin taking part in future decision-making, which will restore some semblance of stability and peaceful coexistence.

Modes of transition

A country's particular mode of transition and level of political restriction define the parameters of the choice between competing theories of retro-active justice.[7] Despite the heavy emphasis on the duty to punish, the fact of the matter is that in the majority of transitions the deciding factor has not been international law. It can be argued that, in practice, decisions made by transitional governments around issues of retroactive justice are not choices at all and are little affected by moral or legal considerations. Instead, such decisions on the form that justice can take – be it trials, truth commissions, ad hoc international tribunals or amnesties – are dictated in most instances by the mode and politics of the particular transition.

Modes of transition can be defined in terms of four categories: (1) full defeat in an armed war (for example, the treatment of Germany after the Second World War); (2) transition through a dictator's loss in an election (for example, Chile); (3) transition through compromise and negotiations (for example, South Africa); and (4) transition from a long-standing communist regime (for example, East European countries).

Each mode presents its own set of institutional and political constraints, which, in turn, delineate the form of justice, from the most retributive model (prosecutions and trials) to more restorative models of justice (truth commissions and disqualification from public office) to no justice at all (impunity). In the context of a military victory (category 1), the only restriction is the victor's own sense of justice and long-term strategic considerations. For instance, Germany's military defeat in the Second World War was absolute in that the Nazi regime lost both political and military power. The Allied forces, because of their total victory, were able to opt for the most retributive model, the Nuremberg Trials.

Where transitions from totalitarianism occur after elections (category 2), greater political restrictions arise. Very often the former dictator maintains a strong power base (whether in the military or in civil society) and, prior to his or her departure, passes laws to grant amnesty for past human rights abuses. The new democracy, faced with an unstable political and social situation and no clear legal remedy, often seeks an amalgam of retributive and restorative models of justice, via truth commissions, reparations and limited prosecutions.

Where transitions occur through a process of peaceful negotiation between the democratizing force and the previous totalitarian regime (category 3), the political constraints become even more heightened. Negotiation politics require compromise, first and foremost. Thus, in a country that is attempting to accommodate all factions in a new democracy, justice by necessity becomes a restorative project of establishing moral, if not legal, truth. In such contexts, justice takes the form of truth commissions and limited amnesty. South Africa is a noteworthy example of this approach.

In the case of transitions from totalitarian communist regimes to democracy (category 4), political constraints all but preclude more retributive forms of justice. The nature of communism's teaching and practice has arguably had two discernible consequences: first, to rob even dissidents of the initiative and will, for a very long period, to act against those in authority, resulting in a weakness or absence of civil society; and, second, to create a technocratic government of such pervasiveness in society that large numbers of individuals in communist countries achieved a level of complicity with the regime unparalleled by other non-communist totalitarian regimes. Post-totalitarian transitions to democracy in former communist countries are thus characterized by little retribution in the form of trials and little truth-seeking in the form of truth commissions. Instead, these nations have taken refuge in general laws of lustration, which only implicitly admit a history of misdeed by barring the accused from future participation in government.

The case of Afghanistan blurs the lines between these categories. Although many liken the US defeat of the Taliban to the defeat of the Nazi regime, Afghanistan is unlikely to initiate prosecutions in the near future. One factor preventing immediate prosecutions – and hampering Afghanistan's recovery, according to Amin Saikal in chapter 9 in this volume – is the continued military strength of local power holders, which is similar to the regimes in category 2, where former dictators continue to hold power. The current ruling authority was cobbled together as a result of negotiations, whereby negotiating parties – themselves complicit in human rights abuse in the past – divided up the spoils of the Afghan state, which in some ways is analogous to category 3 transitions. And, similar to the fate of communist regimes, 25 years of continual conflict destroyed Afghan civil society, which only now is beginning to assert itself.

All of this illustrates that such categories can amount to only a broad framework for understanding the relationship between transitions and transitional justice, rather than a predictive model. Within this framework, two general trends are evident. First, the more that peaceful coexistence is a stated goal of the transition, the greater the political restrictions faced by the transitional government. Second, history bears out that, as the level of restriction increases, transitional societies turn away from strictly retributive models and towards more restorative models of justice.

Prosecutions

The Nuremberg Trials

The Nuremberg Trials constitute a watershed moment in international justice. The trials, which lasted from 1945 to 1949, were conducted by the victorious Allies following the crimes committed by Nazi Germany directly preceding and during the Second World War; 19 Nazi leaders were convicted of crimes against humanity, among other charges, of whom 10 were executed by hanging. More than 50 years later, discussion still rages over the merits of the Nuremberg Trials. When it is borne in mind that as late as 1944 the British Foreign Office and Winston Churchill, together with Stalin, proposed lining the Nazi leaders up against a wall and shooting them without trial, it is to the credit of Justice Jackson and others that trials were actually held. The trials were often referred to as "victors' justice", in part because of the controversial prosecution of "aggression" but also because many critics, and some legal experts, believe due process was not observed. Obviously, many Germans viewed the trials simply as revenge by the Allies for the Holocaust and other war crimes committed by Hitler and his Nazi Party. The Tokyo Trials were equally contentious and they were followed by trials held by many of the European countries that had been overrun and occupied by the Nazis during the Second World War.

Despite these reservations, there can be no denial that the Nuremberg Trials represented the first concerted action by the international community to deal in a systematic manner with what Nino describes as "radical evil". When one bears in mind the thousands of people who must have been involved in the atrocities in light of the 19 Nazi leaders convicted in Nuremberg, it illustrates the limitations of law and the built-in, ad hoc amnesty for those who were never brought before the court. This points to the serious problem of selectivity, which is the only way to assign individual responsibility for mass atrocities, but it also means that many of those responsible will escape prosecution. This process of selectivity diminishes the sense that all perpetrators have been called to account for their actions and it tarnishes the hallmark of fairness that should characterize prosecutions and the upholding of the rule of law.

The International Criminal Tribunals for the former Yugoslavia and Rwanda

In 1992, the Security Council of the United Nations adopted Resolution 780, which established the appointment of a Commission of Experts to investigate violations of international humanitarian law in the former Yugoslavia. This very important step led, ultimately, to the appointment of the International Criminal Tribunal for the Former Yugoslavia (ICTY) in The Hague. This was 40 years after Nuremberg, but quite clearly influenced by the Nuremberg Trials. Following the 1994 genocide in Rwanda, which, in a brief period of three months, saw approximately 800,000 people slaughtered, the Security Council established the International Criminal Tribunal for Rwanda (ICTR).

Despite severe challenges and delays in both tribunals, the Hague Tribunal in particular has succeeded in bringing several leading culprits to trial. The indictment against Slobodan Milosevic was the first ever to be brought against a sitting head of state. As of August 2002, 25 investigations still needed to be brought to the indictment stage, but could potentially result in an additional 100 accused by the end of 2004.[8] In many ways, the Tribunal has failed to reach its original goals. As of July 2003, 91 indictees had appeared before the ICTY, but only 37 had been tried.[9] There are currently 18 fugitives with public arrest warrants against them, including Ratko Mladic and Radovan Karadzic, respectively the military and political leaders of the Serb Republic, in addition to an unknown number of fugitives under sealed indictments. One of the most serious drawbacks of ad hoc tribunals, certainly in the cases of The Hague and Rwanda, is the length of time a trial takes. Dusko Tadic was the subject of the ICTY's first trial. The case lasted only 75 days, but the period between his being taken into the custody of the Tribunal (24 April 1995) and the final appellate decision on 26 January 2000 was almost five years in length. Furthermore, the Tribunal, with its major focus on prosecution, has not been able to achieve any meaningful reconciliation in the former Yugoslavia. Perhaps it was asking too much of the Court to attempt this, but it certainly was part of its mandate.

The International Criminal Tribunal for Rwanda suffered even more reversals and difficulties. The ICTR is based in Arusha, Tanzania, although its investigative base is in Kigali, Rwanda. Nine years after its creation and more than five years since the first trial in 1997, the ICTR has handed down 11 judgments, including one acquittal, as of June 2003.[10] The ICTR has detained at least 60 indictees, yet some of the masterminds of the genocide, whether indicted by the ICTR or not, are said to be walking free. The International Crisis Group described the performance of the ICTR as "lamentable", noting that between July 1999 and October 2000 the ICTR heard only one "substantial case", that of Ignace Bagilishema, the former mayor of the village of Mabanza.[11] Reports of mismanagement, corruption and alleged irregularities in ICTR's operations led to reform efforts that have gradually increased ICTR's capacity and effectiveness. Nevertheless, bearing in mind that the annual budget is approximately US$90 million, the limited nature of the ICTR's achievements is extraordinary.

The point is that, although the idea of an international tribunal is a noble one, its mandate is almost impossible to fulfil and one has to question whether the money and resources that have been made available to these two tribunals were warranted, considering the contribution they have made to accountability in the broadest sense of that term. The ICTR's mandate to contribute to reconciliation in Rwanda was made even more difficult by the government's arrest and detention of over 120,000 people, most of whom languished in jail for many years without trial. It is not surprising the government has finally decided to release a large number of these detainees. It is also not surprising that the government has decided to move away from the formal courts and established an indigenous system of justice known as "Gacaca" (this word derives from the Kinyarwanda word meaning a patch of grass, usually under a tree, where people used to meet to discuss or settle disputes within communities). Achieving justice through prosecutions is not as easy as it might seem.

The International Criminal Court

These ad hoc tribunals will be phased out and their place will be taken by the newly established International Criminal Court. The International Criminal Court (ICC) is a treaty-created body whose powers are derived from the consent of the state parties. This means that, although it is a court, its findings are binding only on those who have ratified the treaty. The fact that the United States, China and Russia have not ratified the treaty is a significant and serious handicap to the work of the Court. Moreover, the Court's jurisdiction applies only to criminal conduct that has occurred since the statute's entry into effect on 1 July 2002. It is hoped that, because this is not an ad hoc body but a permanent body, it will be able to conduct its affairs and make its decisions not selectively but on a clearly defined programme. It is hoped also that the Court, with its 18 judges, will not make the mistake of spending an inordinate amount of time on a single case or incur vast expenditure. The Court can act only when a state is either unwilling or unable to deal with human rights violations in that state; the first task of the Court is to encourage and enable those countries to conduct their own programmes of justice. The Security Council has the right to refer certain matters to the Court but, because several powerful permanent members have yet to ratify the treaty, it may use this right sparingly.

Thus, even though we have advanced to the setting of a permanent international court, there are still shortcomings and it is impossible to deal with the true intent of justice by court procedures alone. The aim of transitional justice is surely wider than punishing the guilty. It is the establishment of a just society, which means establishing and consolidating democratic institutions. National courts will continue to play a major role in dealing with excesses in their own countries, but many of these countries do not have adequate legal systems in which to deal fairly, impartially and efficiently with matters that deserve to be brought to trial. It would make far more sense, therefore, for additional revenue and human resources to be placed at the disposal of these legal systems, thus enabling national courts to prosecute their own crimes rather than leave it to an international court.

Hybrid courts

In light of the shortcomings of the International Criminal Tribunals, the United Nations shifted its focus in the late 1990s to negotiating the establishment of hybrid courts in East Timor, Sierra Leone and Cambodia. These courts, which rely on both international and national staff, procedures and laws, are established through negotiations with government parties and, security permitting, conduct proceedings in the countries concerned. In comparison, the ICTY and the ICTR, which were established under Chapter VII of the UN Charter by the Security Council, take place in The Hague and Tanzania respectively, which limits the involvement of local populations. Despite these improvements, these hybrid courts, like the ICTY and ICTR, will be able to prosecute only a limited number of people because of limited resources combined with the need to ensure due process and accountability for individuals.

Non-judicial mechanisms

Truth and reconciliation commissions

One of the non-judicial mechanisms that has gained great prominence over the past 10 years is the truth and reconciliation commission. It was first used in Latin America but has since spread to many other parts of the world. There have been approximately 30 such commissions, with varying degrees of success. Currently, at least four commissions are under way: Morocco, Sierra Leone, East Timor and Ghana. Several others are in the offing, including the Democratic Republic of Congo (DRC).

The truth commission, as indicated by its title, is concerned first and foremost with the recovery of truth. Through truth-telling, the commission attempts to document and analyse the structures and methods used in carrying out illegal repression, taking into account the political, economic and social context in which these violations occurred. In some ways, it is unfortunate that the word "truth" is used. Beyond its Orwellian overtones, many critics rightly feel that it is impossible for all the truth ever to be known. Antjie Krog, a South African poet and writer, tells of her own difficulty with the word "truth":

The word truth makes me uncomfortable. The word truth still trips the tongue. I hesitate at the word ... I'm not used to using it. Even when I type it, it ends up as either "turth" or "trth". I've never bedded that word in a poem. I prefer the word "lie." The moment the lie raises its head, I smell blood because it is there ... Where the truth is closest.[12]

Despite these necessary cautions, truth commissions have, in some instances, uncovered truth that has been quite deliberately suppressed by the state, and they have broken the silence by documenting, acknowledging and publicizing the truth based on the victims' stories of human rights violations. This focus on victims rather than perpetrators is one of the hallmarks of most truth commissions. Therefore, it does not substitute for courts or prosecutions, but rather complements the retributive aspect of justice with a greater emphasis on the restorative nature of justice.

In the South Africa Truth and Reconciliation Commission, we sought to distinguish four aspects of truth. The first is objective, factual or forensic truth. The Commission was mandated to "prepare a comprehensive report which sets out its activities and findings based on factual and objective information and evidence collected or received by it or placed at its disposal".[13] This meant that the Commission was required to make findings public on particular incidents with regard to specific people concerning what happened to whom, where and when, how and who was involved. The Commission was also responsible for findings on the context, causes and patterns of violations. Although I think Michael Ignatieff underestimates the influence and impact of some truth commissions, nevertheless his comments are salutary: "All that a truth commission can achieve is to reduce the number of lies that can be circulated unchallenged in public discourse."[14]

It follows that, in the South African context, it is no longer possible for so many people to claim that they "did not know". It became impossible for the political leaders who governed the apartheid state to deny that the practice of torture by the state security forces was systematic and widespread. It is also impossible to claim any longer that the accounts of gross human rights violations in ANC camps were merely the consequence of state disinformation.

The second aspect of truth we described as personal or narrative truth. Through the telling of their own stories, both victims and perpetrators have given meaning to their multi-layered experiences of the South African story. Through the media, these personal truths were shared with the broader public. In other words, an old tradition was at the centre of the Commission's work. One of the objectives of the South African Commission was to "restore the human and civil dignity of victims by granting them an opportunity to relate their own accounts of the violence of which they were the victims".[15] It is this part of truth commissions that, in a major way, complements the work of the courts, which focus almost entirely on the perpetrator and simply are not suited to give serious consideration to the stories of the victims.

The third aspect of truth is "dialogical truth". Dialogical truth is social truth, truth of experience that is established by interaction, discussion and debate. What is noteworthy here is that the process of acquiring the truth is almost as important as the process of establishing it. The process of dialogue involved transparency, democracy and participation as the basis of affirming human dignity and integrity.

Finally, the fourth aspect of truth is healing and restorative truth. The truth that the Commission was required to establish had to contribute to repairing the damage inflicted in the past and preventing its reoccurrence. But, for healing to be a possibility, knowledge in itself is not enough. Knowledge must be accompanied by acknowledgement and acceptance of accountability. To acknowledge publicly that thousands of South Africans, in this instance, paid a very high price for the attainment of democracy affirms the human dignity of the victims and survivors and is an integral part of the healing of society. Thus, there is a dual opportunity and responsibility on the one hand for victims to tell their story in their own words, using their own language, and on the other for those who were responsible for the suffering to tell their truth by acknowledging and accepting that responsibility.

A number of commissions have talked not only about truth, but also about reconciliation. If the word "truth" conjures up problems for many people, so does the word "reconciliation". It has religious connotations, especially in the Christian faith, and there are many who would prefer the word and the concept of reconciliation not to be used in commissions, which are seeking to recover the truth and focus on victims. At its best, reconciliation involves commitment and sacrifice; at its worst, it is an excuse for passivity, for siding with the powerful against the weak and dispossessed. Religion, in many instances, has given a bad name to reconciliation because it has often joined with those who exploit and impoverish entire populations rather than support the oppressed. When reconciliation calls for mere forgetting or for concealing, then it is spurious. In Argentina, the concept of reconciliation is regarded with deep scepticism. In that country, the Roman Catholic Church in large measure supported the military junta, and the perpetrators of human rights violations were always the first to call for reconciliation. The same is true of Rwanda, where religious groups and priests and nuns participated in the massacre of the Tutsis and, therefore, to talk about reconciliation is highly suspect and in this context is viewed as a call for amnesia. Unless the call for reconciliation is accompanied by acknowledgement of the past and acceptance of responsibility, it will be dismissed as cheap rhetoric. Perhaps one of the ways to achieve at least a measure of reconciliation in a deeply divided society is to create a common memory that can be acknowledged by those who created and implemented the unjust system, those who fought against it, and the many more who were in the middle and claimed not to know what was happening in their country. H. Richard Niebuhr put it succinctly:

Where common memory is lacking, where men and women do not share the same past, there can be no real community and where community is to be formed, common memory must be created. The measure of our distance from each other in our nations and our groups can be taken by noting the divergence, the separateness and the lack of sympathy in our social memories. Conversely, the measure of our unity is the extent of our common memory.[16]

The process of reconciliation can begin at different points in the transition of a country from a totalitarian state to a new form of democracy. For some, it begins at the negotiating table; for others, it begins when perpetrators are indicted and prosecuted. The release of political prisoners or the acceptance of a new constitution that guarantees fundamental freedoms may facilitate the beginning of reconciliation. For others, it is when free and open elections are held in which all citizens can participate. There are many starting points, but it is never a one-step process. The process is ongoing, especially in countries where oppression has been deep and lasting. And, if it is to succeed, reconciliation must affect the life chances of ordinary people.

In my view, reconciliation, both as a process and as a means of seeking an often elusive peace, must be understood through the lens of transitional justice. Reconciliation stands a better chance and is better understood if victims believe that their grievances are being addressed and that their cry is being heard, that the silence is being broken. For ethnically divided societies, such as in the South Pacific or the Great Lakes region of Africa, establishing individual guilt can make an important contribution to reconciliation by negating perceptions of collective guilt. When individual perpetrators arc held to account, when truth is sought openly and fearlessly, when institutional reform begins and the need for reparation(s) is acknowledged and acted upon, then reconciliation can begin. The response by former victims to these initiatives can increase the potential for greater stability and increase the chances for sustainable peace.

The process of reconciliation has often been hindered by the silence or the denial of political leaders concerning their own responsibility and the failure of the state. On the other hand, however, when leaders are prepared to speak honestly and generously about their own involvement or, at least, the involvement of their government or the previous government, then the door is open for the possibility of some reconciliation amongst citizens to happen. President Patricio Aylwin of Chile highlights what I believe is the irreducible minimum for reconciliation to have a chance – a commitment to truth. When he received the report of the Chilean Truth and Reconciliation Commission, he emphasized this point:

This leaves the excruciating problem of human rights violations and other violent crime(s), which have caused so many victims and so much suffering in the past. They are an open wound in our national soul that cannot be ignored; nor can it heal through mere forgetfulness. To close our eyes and pretend none of this ever happened would be to maintain at the core of our society a source of pain, division, hatred and violence. Only the disclosure of the truth and the search for justice can create the moral climate in which reconciliation and peace will flourish.[17]

For truth and reconciliation to flourish, serious and focused attention must be given, not only to individuals, but also to institutions. Institutional reform should be at the very heart of a transformation. The truth commission is an ideal model for holding together both retrospective truth and prospective needs. Unfortunately, most truth commissions have chosen to focus almost entirely on individual hearings. This is important and critical, but if commissions were to hold institutional hearings they would be able to call to account those institutions that were directly responsible for the breakdown of the state and the repressive measures imposed on citizens of that state. In at least one commission, an opportunity was created for spokespersons from the military, the police, the security forces, politicians, faith communities, legal representatives, the media and labour to give an account of their role in the past and, which is extremely important, how they saw their role in the future. In other words, it is not enough to be concerned merely about the past. We must deal with the past but we must not dwell on it, and we deal with it for the sake of the future.

On a recent visit to Serbia, it was quite clear that one of the major problems preventing that country from moving out from its very dark and ominous past into a brighter democracy was that the institutions remained almost exactly the same. The same police officers were controlling the police forces; the same generals were controlling the army. And this was true of all the major institutions. As I moved from one group of leaders to another, it was clear that, unless and until institutions are radically restructured, there will be little opportunity for growth, for development and for peace in Serbia. This is true not only of Serbia but of the former Yugoslavia as a whole. It also applies to Colombia, where Serrano and Kenny note in chapter 5 that the judicial system has virtually collapsed, and to the Solomon Islands, where according to Reilly and Wainwright in chapter 6 the current police force poses a threat to the state. It is true of all states that have failed and are in transition. In deeply divided societies where mistrust and fear are characteristic of that society, there must be bridge-building and a commitment, not only to criminal justice, but also to economic justice. For that to be a reality, institutions, as well as individuals, have to change.

Vetting

In common discourse, the term "vetting" generally refers to the examination of individual employment and other records for the purposes of hiring or firing persons in the workplace, although this chapter will deal only with vetting for the purpose of firing. As the chapters on Colombia, Pakistan and North Korea in this volume illustrate, abandoning the rule of law is not just the prerogative of leaders but can often permeate entire institutions. Vetting therefore becomes a central component of the justice reforms adopted by new governments attempting to respond to a legacy of human rights abuse and widespread corruption by assessing the culpability of rank-and-file government employees.

In its most familiar guise, vetting is the practice of removing individuals responsible for serious misconduct from public sector posts, including the police and prison services, the army, the intelligence services and even the judiciary. The vetting process typically comprises a thorough background check including a review of multiple sources of information and evidence to determine whether or not a particular official has been involved in past abuses. In addition, vetting tends to prescribe procedures that ensure that the accused is made aware of the allegations against him or her and given an opportunity to reply to those allegations in person or in writing before the body administering the vetting process.[18]

As a tool of transitional justice, vetting can contribute to making states work by reducing the likelihood of new abuses, increasing public trust in state institutions, and removing past abusers who, by their corrosive attitudes and actions, might otherwise present a direct threat to broader efforts to reform the public service. Vetting sends a clear message about the importance of accountability for the new government and can remove some obstacles to the prosecution of human rights abusers. Indeed, there is little point insisting on trials for human rights crimes and corruption if the very officials responsible for the trials are themselves directly implicated in past crimes. A further motivation for vetting is to restore the good name of those officials whose reputations have been unfairly tainted by association with the "bad apples" within their institution. In this sense, vetting can help increase employee morale, improve the external image of the institution and help attract new and better recruits.

A less obvious, but still important, motivation for vetting is that it can allow a government to achieve indirectly what it cannot achieve directly. As already noted, subjecting everyone implicated in past abuses to criminal trial is simply not possible. Criminal justice systems in transitional contexts tend to be weak, corrupt or both, and the number of perpetrators is usually too great for any judiciary to handle in a cost-effective, fair or expeditious manner. Indeed, attempting to prosecute all those implicated would be not only logistically impossible but also politically and economically destabilizing. Because vetting procedures are not burdened by the same standards of due process as criminal trials, they can process large numbers of cases more quickly and more discreetly. Vetting procedures can also be designed to include a wider range of significant non-criminal sanctions, including job termination, temporary bans on public employment, loss of employment benefits, and forms of restitution or community service. In this sense, vetting can serve as an important complement to criminal justice efforts, especially with respect to lower-ranking officials who would otherwise in most cases remain untouched by the arm of the law.

Before establishing a vetting mechanism, it is important to recognize that there may be various alternative ways to achieve vetting indirectly, such as using existing oversight mechanisms, privately informing individuals of the evidence against them, or eliminating and then re-establishing the organization in question. Once the decision has been made to establish an individualized vetting process, a host of other political, legal and practical matters must be taken into account.

Unlike a criminal trial, a vetting body is not a court and cannot order punishment by imprisonment. Consequently, the standards of due process applicable to a criminal trial are naturally and properly higher than those applicable to a non-judicial or quasi-judicial vetting mechanism. At the same time, any vetting body must apply a baseline standard of procedural fairness in order to be considered legitimate and fair. At a minimum, vetting procedures must provide an opportunity for an implicated person to refute adverse allegations as well as some form of appeal to an impartial body. More generally, a vetting body must be independent from political control and impartial, competent and prompt in carrying out its duties.

At the same time, the need for procedural fairness must be balanced against competing goals such as efficiency, accuracy, transparency and comprehensiveness. Important as it may be to remove abusers from positions of public trust, advocates of vetting must bear in mind the available supply of human capital; there may not be enough trained and competent personnel on hand to replace the vetted persons. In some instances, overly aggressive vetting could end up hurting not helping the public interest, at least in the short term. Vetting mechanisms must also consider the risk that vetted persons, particularly former army, police and intelligence officials, will simply turn to private crime after their dismissal. Countries such as Colombia, the DRC and the Solomon Islands, where vetting of the security sector appears to be both necessary and likely, must forcefully anticipate this challenge. To the degree possible, the body responsible for vetting ought to be authorized to consider ways in which the government might help to prepare vetted officials for a new life. Particularly in societies with high levels of unemployment and crime, consideration could be given to job retraining, civilian apprenticeship programmes and other forms of sustainable economic reintegration. Such measures, however, would have to be carefully formulated so as not to appear as or amount to rewards for past abuse.

All of these objectives need to be balanced against the constraints of time, limited human and financial resources, the size of the caseload and the availability of evidence, and possible legal constraints such as amnesty laws and statutes of limitation. The point is that, although the design of any vetting procedure needs to include certain core due process protections, it also needs to structure the procedure in a way that makes viable the very objectives it was established to achieve.

Conclusion

The rule of law and the fair, even administration of justice deserve our greatest respect. No society can claim to be free or democratic without strict adherence to the rule of law. Dictators and authoritarian regimes abandon the rule of law at the first opportunity and resort to naked power politics, leading to all manner of excesses. It is of central importance, therefore, that those who violate the law are punished. But, as we have seen, there are limits to law and we need to embrace a notion of justice that is wider, deeper and richer than retributive justice. Not only is it impossible to prosecute all offenders, but an over-zealous focus on punishment can make securing sustainable peace and stability more difficult. Further, to achieve a just society, more than punishment is required. Documenting the truth about the past, restoring dignity to victims and embarking on the process of reconciliation are vital elements of a just society. Equally important is the need to begin transforming institutions; institutional structures must not impede the commitment to consolidating democracy and establishing a culture of human rights. It follows that approaches to societies in transition will be multifaceted and will incorporate the need for consultation to realize the goal of a just society.

In seeking a peaceful transfer of power following conflict and bitter enmity, some countries have opted for a form of amnesty. This varies from country to country. Sometimes it takes the form of a general or blanket amnesty, such as the Evian Agreement ending the war between France and Algeria, for war criminals on both sides, and the amnesty by India and Bangladesh for Pakistani soldiers at the close of the Bangladesh War in 1971. Others have opted for a limited or conditional form of amnesty, such as East Timor, where immunity from prosecution can be granted for "lesser crimes" once the terms of the Community Reconciliation Agreement have been met, and South Africa, where amnesty was conditional upon full disclosure.

Many human rights groups and international organizations have condemned any form of amnesty as encouraging impunity and contradicting international law. It is important to view amnesties with grave suspicion, particularly when they are granted by the offending state or the armed forces. But the reality is that almost every state has used amnesties to bring about a cease-fire. It makes more sense, therefore, to consider amnesties on their merit rather than *prima facie* to reject all amnesties.

Some countries are facing very difficult transitions at the present time. The Sri Lanka government is locked in negotiation talks with the Tamil Tigers. Neither party has clean hands. Is it reasonable to assume that either of the parties will agree to prosecution? In Angola, there is an uneasy peace. Rebel soldiers have returned from the bush, but if large-scale prosecutions are demanded the likelihood is that they will return to the bush, the fighting will recommence and many more people will die.

Justice Sandra Day O'Connor, although mindful of the dangers of im-

punity, believes that amnesty does not necessarily undermine accountability. Referring to the South African model of conditional amnesty,
she writes:

This process has several advantages. First, because the amnesties granted under
this process are not designed to exculpate the state's own agents, but to expose
and acknowledge the crimes of a previous regime, the process promotes truth
and accountability. Secondly, the focus on reconciliation and healing ensures
that the process looks forward to strengthening the new democratic regime,
rather than looking backward toward retribution.[19]

Arguing against blanket amnesties and in favour of conditional amnesties, she concludes: "Despite the difficulties, the South African approach
appears to effectively balance these two goals, encouraging public accountability with the destabilizing effect of a fully fledged trial."[20]

This emphasizes the wisdom of looking at every country as unique in
its history, culture and political circumstances and in the nature of the
transition. External actors seeking to contribute meaningfully to a state's
rebirth must partner local organizations and leaders. Where civil society
is weak or non-existent, measures that strengthen their ability to conduct
open debates and discussions and their comparative knowledge of other
transitions will often be more effective in promoting the aims of transitional justice than simply imposing model transitional justice strategies.
One-size-fits-all approaches simply do not work and, although external
actors may question the independence and motives of their partners, any
solution that does not reflect their unique situation is likely to fail. As the
cases of Singapore, Mozambique and Costa Rica in this volume emphasize, any state-building effort must be locally owned to be sustainable.
International actors must not supplant, or substitute for, domestic actors.
This should not minimize the often influential role played by external
governments and non-governmental organizations. Through sharing
technical expertise, promoting access to individuals engaged in similar
exercises around the globe and contributing financial resources, external
actors can make a real difference – if their assistance is tailored to actual
needs on the ground as articulated by local actors. Sensitivity to, and ap-
preciation of, the local political, economic and social context could lead
to a more nuanced, practical and ultimately effective transformation of
the state.

Acknowledgements

This chapter draws on my previously published work *A Country Unmasked*, as well as my experiences as the Deputy Chair of the South

Africa Truth and Reconciliation Commission and, currently, as the President of the International Center for Transitional Justice (ICTJ). In particular I would like to thank Andrea Armstrong, a colleague at ICTJ, for her valuable comments. I would also like to thank Mark Freeman, whose work on vetting for ICTJ is also reflected in this chapter.

Notes

1. Carlos Nino, *Radical Evil on Trial*, New Haven, CT: Yale University Press, 1995, p. vii.
2. Ibid., p. vii.
3. Timothy Garton Ash, *The File: A Personal History*, New York: Vintage Press, 1997, p. 225.
4. Cathleen E. Smith, *Remembering Stalin's Victims*, Ithaca, NY: Cornell University Press, 1996, epigraph.
5. Bruce Ackerman, *The Future of the Liberal Revolution*, New Haven, CT: Yale University Press, 1992, pp. 72–73.
6. Uri Savir, *The Process: 1100 Days That Changed the Middle East*, New York: Random House, 1998, pp. 14–15.
7. This argument is more fully explored in my book *A Country Unmasked*, Cape Town: Oxford University Press Southern Africa, 2000, pp. 382–385.
8. *Ninth Annual Report of the International Tribunal for the Prosecution of Persons Responsible for Serious Violations of International Humanitarian Law Committed in the Territory of the Former Yugoslavia since 1991*, UN Doc. A/57/379, September 2002.
9. International Criminal Tribunal for the Former Yugoslavia, "Fact Sheet on ICTY Proceedings", available at ⟨http://www.un.org/icty/glance/index.htm⟩, accessed 10 July 2003.
10. International Criminal Tribunal for Rwanda, "ICTR Detainees – Status 26 May 2003", available at ⟨http://www.ictr.org/ENGLISH/factsheets/detainee.htm⟩.
11. International Crisis Group, *International Criminal Tribunal for Rwanda: Justice Delayed*, Brussels: International Crisis Group, 7 June 2001, available at ⟨http://www.crisisweb.org⟩.
12. Antjie Krog, *Country of My Skull*, Johannesburg: Random House, 1998, p. 36.
13. Republic of South Africa, *Promotion of National Unity and Reconciliation Act, No. 34 of 1995*, Section (4)e.
14. Michael Ignatieff, "Articles of Faith", *Index on Censorship*, Vol. 5, 1996, p. 113.
15. Republic of South Africa, *Promotion of National Unity and Reconciliation Act, No. 34 of 1995*, Section (3)(1)c.
16. H. Richard Niebuhr, *The Meaning of Revelation*, New York: Macmillan, 1941, p. 9.
17. President Patricio Aylwin, in a speech to the nation announcing the creation of the National Commission on Truth and Reconciliation, broadcast on Chilean TV on 24 April 1990.
18. Vetting is different from "lustration", a term that is commonly used in Eastern and Central Europe to refer to laws and policies of wide-scale dismissal and disqualification based not on individual records but on party affiliation, political opinion or association with a hitherto oppressive secret service. Many lustration laws were criticized internationally for violating fundamental standards of procedural fairness by inter alia punishing on the basis of collective not individual guilt, violating the presumption of innocence and the principle of non-retroactivity, imposing bans on elected or appointed positions (in violation of the prohibition against discrimination on the basis of political opinion),

unfairly limiting rights of appeal before judicial bodies, and relying too heavily on spurious communist-era records to prove unlawful or wrongful behaviour. For these and other reasons, vetting generally offers a preferable model for removing public officials guilty of serious professional misconduct.

19. Sandra Day O'Connor, "Foreword", in Richard J. Goldstone, *For Humanity: Reflections of a War Crimes Investigator*, New Haven, CT: Yale University Press, 2000, p. xiv.
20. Ibid., p. xv.

16

Transitional administration, state-building and the United Nations

Simon Chesterman

Is it possible to establish the conditions for legitimate and sustainable national governance – to make a state "work" – through a period of benevolent foreign autocracy under UN auspices? This contradiction between ends and means has plagued recent efforts to govern post-conflict territories in the Balkans, East Timor, Afghanistan and Iraq. Such state-building operations combine an unusual mix of idealism and realism: the idealist project that a people can be saved from themselves through education, economic incentives and the space to develop mature political institutions; the realist basis for that project in what is ultimately military occupation.

Such an approach is antithetical to many lessons presented in other chapters in this book: Singapore and Costa Rica were successes in large part despite foreign actions; Colombia and Pakistan are testimony to the dangers of allowing foreign governments a role in shaping a fragile state. As with much of the history of the United Nations, these concerns have been acknowledged in theory and then routinely challenged in practice.

In early 1995, chastened by the failed operation in Somalia, the failing operation in Bosnia and Herzegovina, and inaction in the face of genocide in Rwanda, UN Secretary-General Boutros Boutros-Ghali issued a conservative supplement to his more optimistic 1992 *Agenda for Peace*. The *Supplement* noted that a new breed of intra-state conflicts presented the United Nations with challenges not encountered since the Congo operation of the early 1960s. A feature of these conflicts was the collapse of state institutions, especially the police and judiciary, meaning that international intervention had to extend beyond military and humanitarian tasks to include the "promotion of national reconciliation and the re-establishment of effective government". Nevertheless, he expressed caution against the United Nations assuming responsibility for law and order or attempting to impose state institutions on unwilling combatants.[1] General Sir Michael Rose, then commander of the UN Protection Force in Bosnia (UNPROFOR), termed this form of mission creep crossing "the Mogadishu line".[2]

Despite such cautious words, by the end of 1995 the United Nations had assumed responsibility for policing in Bosnia under the Dayton Peace Agreement. The following January, a mission was established with temporary civil governance functions over the last Serb-held region of Croatia in Eastern Slavonia. In June 1999, the Security Council authorized an "interim" administration in Kosovo to govern part of what remained technically Serbian territory for an indefinite period. Four months later, a transitional administration was created with effective sovereignty over East Timor until independence. These expanding mandates continued a trend that began with the operations in Namibia in 1989 and Cambodia in 1993, where the United Nations exercised varying degrees of civilian authority in addition to supervising elections.

As the foregoing chapters have demonstrated, efforts to construct or reconstruct institutions of the state are hardly new: nation-building coincided with the dismantling of colonial structures, and efforts to support weak governance have long been a feature of UN post-conflict reconstruction. What was novel about the missions undertaken in Kosovo and East Timor was the degree of executive authority assumed by the United Nations itself, placing it in the position of an occupying power. Though this power was, presumably, understood to be exercised in a benevolent fashion, problems associated with foreign rule repeated themselves with some predictable results in the cases examined here.

The first section of this chapter surveys the brief history of UN transitional administration, before elaborating on three contradictions that have emerged in the conduct of such operations. The emphasis is on operations in which the United Nations has exercised some form of executive control – most prominently in East Timor, where it exercised effectively sovereign powers for over two years. More recent operations in Afghanistan and Iraq have shifted the terms of this debate: the state-building agenda in such operations has been determined less by the needs of the post-conflict society than by the strategic interests of the United States.[3] The second section therefore turns to the relationship between state-building and the war on terror.

The contradictions of transitional administration

Though colonialism is now condemned as an international crime, international humanitarian law – specifically the 1907 Hague Regulations and the Fourth Geneva Convention of 1949 – provides the legal basis for an occupying power to exercise temporary authority over territory that comes under its control. The occupying power is entitled to ensure the security of its forces, but it is also required to "take all the measures in his power to restore, and ensure, as far as possible, public order and safety, while respecting, unless absolutely prevented, the laws in force in the country". In addition to other positive obligations, such as ensuring public health and sanitation, as well as the provision of food and medical supplies, the occupying power is prohibited from changing local laws except as necessary for its own security and is limited in its capacity to change state institutions. As the purpose of transitional administration is precisely to change the laws and institutions, further legal authority is therefore required. In most of the cases examined here, that authority has tended to come from the UN Security Council. Here, as with much of the Council's work, practice has led theory, with some members of the Council and the wider UN community apparently antipathetic to the development of doctrine.

These UN missions, sometimes referred to as complex peace operations, bear a curious heritage. In the heady days of the early 1990s, traditional or "first-generation" peacekeeping, which was non-threatening and impartial and governed by the principles of consent and minimum force, was swiftly succeeded by two further generations. Second-generation or "multidimensional" peacekeeping was used to describe post–Cold War operations in Cambodia, El Salvador, Mozambique and Angola, but, retrospectively, might also have included the Congo operation in 1960–1964. Third-generation peacekeeping, sometimes called "peace enforcement", operating with a Chapter VII mandate from the Security Council, began with the Somalia operation. The genealogy was curious – the third generation appearing a mere six months after the second – but the terminology also misleadingly suggested a linear development in peacekeeping doctrine. Evolution is a more appropriate metaphor than selective breeding, with essentially unpredictable events demanding new forms of missions.[4]

If military doctrine developed through natural selection, civil administration was a random mutation. The fact that such operations continue to be managed by the UN Department of Peacekeeping Operations is suggestive of the ad hoc approach that has characterized transitional administration – a historical accident perpetuated by the reluctance to embrace temporary governance of post-conflict territory as an appropriate and necessary task for the United Nations. This was evident in the Brahimi Report on UN Peace Operations, which noted the likely demand for such operations as well as the "evident ambivalence" within governments and the UN Secretariat itself concerning the development of an institutional capacity to undertake them. Because of this ambivalence it was impossible to achieve any consensus on recommendations, so the Department of Peacekeeping Operations continues to play the dominant supporting role.[5]

These doctrinal and operational concerns are valid, but have frequently overshadowed the more basic political problems confronting transitional administration. I shall now discuss three sets of contradictions in the very idea of creating a legitimate and sustainable state through a period of benevolent autocracy: the means are inconsistent with the ends; they are frequently inadequate for those ends; and in many situations the means are inappropriate for the ends.

The means are inconsistent with the ends

The UN Mission in Kosovo (UNMIK) and the High Representative in Bosnia and Herzegovina govern through military occupation. In East Timor, the United Nations completed the task of decolonization. The fact that these powers have been exercised benevolently does not deprive them of their imposed character. More important than the benevolence of intention is the acceptance of the subject population that power is being exercised for ends that are both clear and achievable. The postwar experiences of Germany and Japan suggest that it is not impossible to create democracies through military occupation, but those operations were very different from more recent instances of transitional administration, with the possible exception of Iraq. Decolonization may be a more fitting model, but there are valid concerns about embracing such language only half a century after one-third of the world's population lived under colonial rule. Whatever euphemism is used, however, it is both inaccurate and counter-productive to assert that transitional administration depends upon the consent or "ownership" of local populations. It is inaccurate because, if genuine local control were possible, then a transitional administration would not be necessary. It is counter-productive because insincere claims of local ownership lead to frustration and suspicion on the part of local actors.

Clarity is central to the effective management of post-conflict reconstruction. Instead of institutional transformations, such as rejuvenating the Trusteeship Council or creating a new body to administer territories under the auspices of the United Nations, a modest but important area of reform would be to require clarity in three key areas: the strategic objectives; the relationship between international and local actors and how this will change over time; and the commitment required of international actors in order to achieve objectives that warrant the temporary assumption of autocratic powers under a benevolent international administration. Structured discussion within the UN Security Council would be one way to achieve this, and could take the form of transitional administration committees, modelled on the sanctions committees that now routinely monitor the implementation, effects and humanitarian impact of economic sanctions.

In a case such as East Timor, the strategic objective – independence – was both clear and uncontroversial. Frustration with the slow pace of reconstruction or the inefficiencies of the UN presence could generally be tempered by reference to the uncontested aim of independence and a timetable within which this was to be achieved. In Kosovo, failure to articulate a position on its final status inhibits the development of a mature political elite and deters foreign investment. The present ambiguity derives from a compromise that was brokered between the United States and Russia at the end of the NATO campaign against the Federal Republic of Yugoslavia in 1999, formalized in Security Council Resolution 1244 (1999). Nevertheless, it is the United Nations itself that is now blamed for frustrating the aspirations of Kosovars for self-determination.

Obfuscation of the political objective leads to ambiguity in the mandate. In a speech at the tenth anniversary of the Department of Peacekeeping Operations in 2002, Jacques Paul Klein, former Special Representative of the Secretary-General for the UN Transitional Administration in Eastern Slavonia (UNTAES), contrasted his own mandate with that governing international efforts to bring peace to Bosnia. The UN Protection Force in Bosnia was governed by no fewer than 70 Security Council resolutions and dozens of presidential statements. Political negotiating authority was divided between the United Nations, the European Union and the Contact Group. The Dayton Peace Agreement had 150 pages, 11 annexes, 40 pages of Peace Implementation Council declarations, 92 post-accession criteria for membership of the Council of Europe, and a host of further agreements – most of which were never fulfilled.

In contrast, the mandate of UNTAES contained just thirteen sentences that could be distilled into six quantifiable objectives.... My point here is twofold: if you start out and don't know where you want to go, you will probably end up somewhere else. And secondly, the mandate is the floor (but not the ceiling) for everything the Mission does. If the mandate is vague for whatever reason – including the inability of Security Council members to agree on a political end state – dysfunction will plague the lifespan of the Mission.[6]

This echoed sentiments in the Brahimi Report applicable to peace operations generally.[7]

Niche mandate implementation by a proliferation of post-conflict actors further complicates the transition. More than five years after the Dayton Peace Agreement, a "recalibration" exercise required the various international agencies present in Bosnia to perform an institutional audit to determine what, exactly, each of them did.[8] Subsidiary bodies and specialized agencies of the United Nations should in principle place their material and human resources at the direct disposal of the transitional administration: all activities should be oriented towards an agreed political goal, which should normally be legitimate and sustainable government. Ideally, the unity of civilian authority should embrace command of the military as well. In reality, the reluctance of the United States and other industrialized countries to put their troops under UN command makes this highly improbable. Coordination thus becomes more important, to avoid some of the difficulties encountered in civil–military relations in Afghanistan.

Clarity in the relationship between international and local actors raises the question of ownership. This term is often used disingenuously – either to mask the assertion of potentially dictatorial powers by international actors or to carry a psychological rather than a political meaning in the area of reconstruction. Ownership in this context is usually not intended to mean control and often does not even imply a direct input into political questions. This is not to suggest that local control is a substitute for international administration. As the operation in Afghanistan demonstrates, a light footprint makes the success of an operation more than usually dependent on the political dynamic of local actors. Since the malevolence or collapse of that political dynamic is precisely the reason that power is arrogated to an international presence, the light footprint is unsustainable as a model for general application. How much power should be transferred and for how long depends upon the political transition that is required; this in turn is a function of the root causes of the conflict, the local capacity for change and the degree of international commitment available to assist in bringing about that change.[9]

Local ownership, then, must be the end of a transitional administration, but it is not the means. Openness about the trustee-like relationship between international and local actors would help locals by ensuring transparency about the powers that they will exercise at various stages of the transition. But openness would also help the states that mandate and fund such operations by forcing acknowledgement of their true nature and the level of commitment that is necessary to effect the required transition.

Clarifying the commitment necessary to bring about fundamental change in a conflict-prone territory is, however, a double-edged sword. It would ensure that political will exists prior to authorizing a transitional administration, but perhaps at the expense of other operations that would not be authorized at all. The mission in Bosnia was always expected to last beyond its nominal 12-month deadline, but it might not have been established if it had been envisaged that troops would remain on the ground for a full decade or more. Donors contemplating Afghanistan in November 2001 baulked at early estimates that called for a 10-year, US$25 billion commitment to the country. In the lead-up to the war with Iraq, the Chief of Staff of the US Army was similarly ridiculed by the leadership of the Defense Department when he testified to the Senate that 200,000 soldiers would be required for postwar duties. Political considerations already limit the choice of missions, of course: not for lack of opportunity, no major transitional administration has been established in Africa, where the demands are probably greatest.

Resolving the inconsistency between the means and the ends of transitional administration requires a clear-eyed recognition of the role of power. The collapse of formal state structures does not necessarily create a power vacuum; political life does not simply cease. Rather, power comes to be exercised through informal political and legal structures, complicating efforts to construct political institutions and to instantiate the rule of law. Constructive engagement with power on this local level requires both an understanding of the culture and history as well as respect for the political aspirations of the population. Clarity will help here too: either the international presence exercises quasi-sovereign powers on a temporary basis or it does not. This clarity must exist at the formal level, but leaves much room for nuance in implementation. Most obviously, assertion of executive authority should be on a diminishing basis, with power devolved as appropriate to local institutions. This is not, therefore, an argument for unilateralism in the administration of post-conflict territories, but an argument for the transfer of power to be of more than symbolic value: once power is transferred to local hands, whether at the municipal or national level, local actors should be able to exercise that power meaningfully, constrained only by the rule of law. Unless and until genuine transfer is possible, consultation is appropriate but without the pretence that this is the same as control. In such situations, additional efforts should be made to cultivate civil society organizations such as local non-governmental organizations (NGOs), which can provide a legitimate focus for the political activities of the local population and lobby international actors. Where international actors do not exercise sovereign power – because of the size of the territory, the complexity of the conflict or a simple lack of political will – this is not the same as exercising no power at all. Certain functions may be delegated to the international presence, as they were in Cambodia and Afghanistan, and international actors will continue to exercise considerable behind-the-scenes influence either because of ongoing responsibilities in a peace process or as gatekeepers to international development assistance. In either case, the abiding need is for clarity as to who is in charge and, equally important, who is *going* to be in charge.

The means are inadequate for the ends

Speaking in Cincinnati, Ohio, on 7 October 2002, US President George W. Bush made one of his strongest early statements concerning the threat that Iraq posed to the United States. In the course of his speech, he also alluded to the aftermath of war, stating that the lives of Iraqi citizens would "improve dramatically if Saddam Hussein were no longer in power, just as the lives of Afghanistan's citizens improved after the Taliban".[10] Yet, 10 months after the Bonn Agreement, Afghanistan was hardly a success story – Bush's remarks could equally have been intended as an optimistic assessment of that troubled mission or a pessimistic downplaying of expectations for what might follow the impending war with Iraq.

Iraq is, of course, distinct from the UN transitional administrations considered here, but the ephemeral nature of international interest in post-conflict operations is, unfortunately, a cliché. When the United States overthrew the Taliban regime in Afghanistan, Bush likened the commitment to rebuild the devastated country to the Marshall Plan. Just over 12 months later, in February 2003, the White House apparently forgot to include *any* money for reconstruction in the 2004 budget that it submitted to Congress. Legislators reallocated US$300 million in aid to cover the oversight.[11] Such oversights are disturbingly common: much of the aid that is pledged either arrives late or not at all. This demands a measure of artificiality in drafting budgets for reconstruction, which in turn leads to suspicion on the part of donors – sometimes further delaying the disbursement of funds. For example, US$880 million was pledged at the Conference on Rehabilitation and Reconstruction of Cambodia in June 1992. By the time the new government was formed in September 1993, only US$200 million had been disbursed; this rose to only US$460 million by the end of 1995. The problem is not simply one of volume: Bosnia has received more per capita assistance than Europe did under the Marshall Plan, but the incoherence of funding programmes, the lack of a regional approach and the inadequacy of state and entity institutions have contributed to Bosnia remaining in financial crisis.[12]

Many of these problems would be reduced if donors replaced the system of voluntary funding for relief and reconstruction for transitional administrations with assessed contributions, such as presently fund peacekeeping operations. The distinction between funds supporting a peacekeeping operation and those providing assistance to a government makes sense when there is some form of indigenous government, but is arbitrary in situations where the peacekeeping operation *is* the government. Given existing strains on the peacekeeping budget, however, such a change is unlikely. A more realistic proposal would be to pool voluntary contributions through a trust fund, ideally coordinated by local actors or a mixed body of local and international personnel, perhaps also drawing upon private sector expertise. Even more modest proposals along these lines have faced stiff resistance from the larger donors – in part owing to concerns about accountability and additional red tape, in part owing to fears that this would remove the discretion to direct funds to projects that are more popular at home than they are necessary abroad. At the very least, a monitoring mechanism to track aid flows would help to ensure that money that is promised at the high point of international attention to a crisis is in fact delivered and spent.

Parsimony of treasure is surpassed by the reluctance to expend blood in policing post-conflict territories. In the absence of security, however, meaningful political change in a post-conflict territory is next to impossible. Unless and until the United Nations develops a rapidly deployable civilian police capacity, either basic law and order functions will be included as part of the military task in a post-conflict environment, or these functions will not be performed at all. The military – especially the US military – is understandably reluctant to embrace duties that are outside its field of expertise, but this is symptomatic of an anachronistic view of UN peace operations. The dichotomy between peacekeeping and enforcement actions was always artificial, but in the context of internal armed conflict where large numbers of civilians are at risk it becomes untenable. Moreover, as most transitional administrations have followed interventions initiated under the auspices or in the name of the United Nations, inaction is not the same as non-interference – once military operations commence, external actors have already begun a process of political transformation on the ground. And, as the Independent Inquiry on Rwanda concluded, whether or not a peace operation has a mandate or the will to protect civilians, its very presence creates an expectation that it will do so.

A key argument in the Brahimi Report was that missions with uncertain mandates or inadequate resources should not be created at all:

Although presenting and justifying planning estimates according to high operational standards might reduce the likelihood of an operation going forward, Member States must not be led to believe that they are doing something useful for countries in trouble when – by under-resourcing missions – they are more likely agreeing to a waste of human resources, time and money.[13]

Applied to transitional administration, this view finds some support in the report of the International Commission on Intervention and State Sovereignty, *The Responsibility to Protect*, which calls for the "responsibility to rebuild" to be seen as an integral part of any intervention. When an intervention is contemplated, a post-intervention strategy is both an operational necessity and an ethical imperative.[14] There is some evidence of this principle now achieving at least rhetorical acceptance: despite his aversion to "nation-building", Bush stressed before and during operations in Afghanistan and Iraq that the United States would help in reconstructing the territories in which it had intervened.

More than rhetoric is required. Success in state-building requires time and money, in addition to clarity of purpose. A lengthy international presence will not ensure success, but an early departure guarantees failure. Similarly, an abundance of resources will not make up for the lack of a coherent strategy; however, the fact that Kosovo has been the recipient of 25 times more money and 50 times more troops, on a per capita basis, compared with Afghanistan goes some way towards explaining the modest achievements in developing democratic institutions and the economy in Kosovo.[15]

The means are inappropriate for the ends

The inappropriateness of available means for the desired ends presents the opposite problem to that of the inadequacy of resources. Although the question of limited resources – money, personnel and international attention – depresses the standards against which a post-conflict operation can be judged, artificially high international expectations may nevertheless be imposed in certain areas of governance. Particularly when the United Nations itself assumes a governing role, there is a temptation to demand the highest standards of democracy, human rights, rule of law and provision of services.

Balancing these against the need for locally sustainable goals presents difficult problems. A computerized electoral registration system may be manifestly ill suited to a country with a low level of literacy and intermittent electricity, but should an international NGO refrain from opening a world-class clinic if such levels of care are unsustainable? An abrupt drop from high levels of care once the crisis and international interest pass would be disruptive, but lowering standards early implies acceptance that people who might otherwise have been treated will suffer. This was the dilemma faced by the International Committee of the Red Cross, which transferred control of the Dili National Hospital to national authorities in East Timor almost a year before independence.

Although most acute in areas such as health, the issue arises in many aspects of transitional administration. In the best tradition of autocracies, the international missions in Bosnia and Kosovo subscribed to the vast majority of human rights treaties and then discovered *raisons d'Etat* that required these to be abrogated. Efforts to promote the rule of law tend to focus more on the prosecution of the highest-profile crimes of the recent past than on developing institutions to manage criminal law in the near future. Humanitarian and development assistance is notorious for being driven more by supply than by demand, with the result that the projects that are funded tend to represent the interests – and, frequently, the products and personnel – of donors rather than those of recipients. Finally, staging elections in conflict zones has become something of an art form, though more than half a dozen elections in Bosnia have yet to produce a workable government.

Different issues arise in the area of human resources. Staffing such operations always takes place in an atmosphere of crisis, but personnel tend to be selected from a limited pool of applicants (most of them internal) whose skills may be irrelevant to the tasks at hand. In East Timor, for example, it would have made sense to approach Portuguese-speaking governments to request that staff with experience in public administration be seconded to the UN mission. Instead, it was not even possible to require Portuguese (or Tetum or Bahasa Indonesia) as a language. Positions are often awarded for political reasons or simply to ensure that staff lists are full – once in place, there is no effective mechanism to assess individuals' suitability or to remove them quickly if they prove unsuitable. A separate problem is the assumption that international staff who do possess relevant skills are also able to train others in the same field. Training is an entirely different skill, however, and simply pairing international and local staff tends to provide less on-the-job training than extended opportunities to stand around and watch – a problem exacerbated by the fact that English tends to be used as the working language. One element of the "light footprint" approach adopted in Afghanistan that is certainly of general application is the need to justify every post occupied by international staff rather than a local person. Cultivating relations with diaspora communities may help address this problem, serving the dual function of recruiting culturally aware staff and encouraging the return of skilled expatriates more generally.

The "can-do" attitude of many people within the UN system is one of the most positive qualities that staff bring to a mission. If the problem is getting 100 tonnes of rice to 10,000 starving refugees, niceties of procedure are less important than getting the job done. When the problem is governing a territory, however, procedure is more important. In such circumstances, the "can-do" attitude may become a cavalier disregard for local sensibilities. Moreover, many staff in such situations are not used to criticism from the population that they are "helping", with some regarding it as a form of ingratitude. Where the United Nations assumes the role of government, it should expect and welcome criticism appropriate to the sort of political environment it hopes to foster. Security issues may require limits on this, but a central element in the development of local political capacity is encouraging discussion among local actors about what sort of country theirs is going to be. International staff sometimes bemoan the prospect of endless consultation getting in the way of their work, but in many ways that conversation is precisely the point of their presence in the territory.

State-building and the war on terror

The primary barrier to establishing transitional administration-type operations in areas such as Somalia, Western Sahara and the Democratic Republic of Congo has to do less with the difficulty of such operations and more with the absence of political will to commit resources to undertake them. The "war on terror" has transformed this agenda, though triage is performed more according to the strategic priorities of the dominant actors, most prominently the United States, than to need. The operations in Afghanistan and Iraq are not transitional administrations as understood in this chapter, but they are suggestive of how the state-building agenda has changed.

In the course of the US-led intervention in Afghanistan in late 2001 – in particular, as the likelihood diminished of capturing Osama bin Laden "dead or alive" – a rhetorical shift became evident in the Bush administration's war aims. "Nation-building",[16] something that Bush had previously derided as inappropriate for the US military, came back onto the US agenda. And, with increasing frequency, the Taliban regime and its mistreatment of the Afghan civilian population were presented as the real evil, rather than being ancillary to the man and the organization that attacked the United States on 11 September 2001. These developments highlighted the changing strategic and political environment within which state-building takes place. The proximate cause was the adoption of state-building as a tool in the "war on terror", but underlying this was an emerging view that the United States should be more ready to use its power in the world.

Nation-building and the national interest

During the 2000 US presidential campaign, candidate Bush was openly critical of the use of US military resources for nation-building purposes. He affirmed this position once in office, including statements in July 2001 stressing that the United States military "should be used to fight and win war".[17] Bush made similar comments in the weeks after the 11 September 2001 attacks, when he stated that "we're not into nation-building, we're focused on justice".[18] Days before the United States commenced military operations in Afghanistan, however, the President's spokesperson marked a slight shift in position as it became apparent that international support for the impending conflict might depend on the broader consequences for the Afghan people: the United States had no intention of engaging in nation-building, but it would "help those who seek a peaceful, economically-developing Afghanistan that's free from terrorism".[19] This was elaborated by the President himself in a news conference after the military action had begun, including a more substantial role for the United Nations in rebuilding Afghanistan:

I believe that the *United Nations* would – could provide the framework necessary to help meet those conditions. It would be a useful function for the United Nations to take over the so-called "nation-building" – I would call it the stabilization of a future government – after our military mission is complete. We'll participate; other countries will participate ... I've talked to many countries that are interested in making sure that the post-operations Afghanistan is one that is stable, and one that doesn't become yet again a haven for terrorist criminals.[20]

US war aims thus evolved from a retributive strike, to a defensive response, and finally to embrace the broader goals of ensuring the stability of post-conflict Afghanistan. As the war aims changed, so, with the benefit of hindsight, did the asserted motivation for US military operations in the first place. This appeared to be a carefully scripted shift, as shown in two important speeches by President Bush. Speaking to the United Nations in November 2001, he equated the Taliban regime with the terrorists who had attacked the United States: the regime and the terrorists were "virtually indistinguishable. Together they promote terror abroad and impose a reign of terror on the Afghan people. Women are executed in Kabal's [*sic*] soccer stadium. They can be beaten for wearing socks that are too thin. Men are jailed for missing prayer meetings. The United

States, supported by many nations, is bringing justice to the terrorists in Afghanistan."[21] Then, in his 2002 State of the Union Address, Bush sought to expand this into a more general doctrine intimating that the US action stemmed from goals loftier than self-defence:

We have no intention of imposing our culture. But America will always stand firm for the non-negotiable demands of human dignity: the rule of law; limits on the power of the state; respect for women; private property; free speech; equal justice; and religious tolerance. America will take the side of brave men and women who advocate these values around the world, including the Islamic world, because we have a greater objective than eliminating threats and containing resentment. We seek a just and peaceful world beyond the war on terror.[22]

One year after the 11 September 2001 attacks, nation-building was implicitly included in the *National Security Strategy* issued by the White House. Much of the document elaborated and justified the concept of pre-emptive intervention; together with the stated policy of dissuading potential adversaries from hoping to equal the power of the United States, it implicitly asserted a unique status for the United States as existing outside of international law as it applies to other states.[23] At the same time, however, the *National Security Strategy* noted that threats to the United States now came not from fleets and armies but from "catastrophic technologies in the hands of the embittered few". In such a world, failing states pose a greater menace to US interests than do conquering ones.[24]

The transformed strategic environment presents both opportunities and dangers for state-building. Recognition that weak states can create threats that reach beyond their borders may increase the level of international interest in supporting those states, indirectly providing benefits to the populations. This argument has been made, for example, to encourage intervention for human protection purposes in Liberia by the United States and in the South Pacific by Australia, although in both cases the link with terrorism was tenuous.[25] The connection was also made in the *National Security Strategy*, which stressed that, when violence erupts and states falter, the United States will "work with friends and partners to alleviate suffering and restore stability".[26] When interventions are justified by the national interest, however, this may lower the standards to which post-conflict reconstruction is held. The level of physical and economic security required in Afghanistan to prevent it becoming a terrorist haven, for example, is not the same as that required for the basic peace and prosperity of the general population. This was reflected in the methods used by the United States to pursue its objectives in Afghanistan: by minimizing the use of its own troops in favour of using Afghan proxies, more weapons were introduced into a country that was already heavily armed, empowering groups that fought on the side of the United States – whether or not they supported the embryonic regime of Hamid Karzai. Many Afghans saw these power relations as reinforced by the Emergency Loya Jirga in June 2002, which appeared to show that the position of warlords and other local commanders would not be challenged by international actors.[27]

None of this, of course, is new. Coercive diplomacy, the use of force and military occupation have long been used by powerful states to further their interests; claims that occupation serves noble motives have an equally long pedigree. What is relatively new is the rejection of colonization as an element of foreign policy from around the middle of the twentieth century. Modern sensibilities therefore prevent explicit reference to occupation or colonization as a model for transitional administration, a constraint that at times prevents the learning of valuable lessons from decolonization in particular. There is a danger, however, that strategic interests may now begin to erode this prohibition in favour of a greater preparedness not merely to intervene, but to occupy and transform other states along the models of Afghanistan and Iraq. Such a development would be undesirable in principle, because it forms part of a broader attack on international law that proposes to order the world not around norms and institutions but around the benevolent goodwill of the United States.[28] And it would also be undesirable in practice, because it is far from clear that the United States is either willing or able to fulfil such a role.

The indispensable nation

In debates within the United Nations and elsewhere, much attention has been focused on the unwillingness of the United States to engage in state-building. But there is also some evidence that the United States is not well suited to such activities. The importance of domestic politics in the exercise of US power means that it has an exceptionally short attention span – far shorter than is needed to complete the long and complicated task of rebuilding countries that have seen years or decades of war, economic ostracism and oppression under brutal leaders. More importantly, when the United States has assumed state-building responsibilities, as in Afghanistan and Iraq, this was justified at home as an element of the war on terror. This was reflected in the strategies adopted in each case, with military priorities ranking well above political goals for either country.

The United States is not alone in suffering from foreign policy "attention deficit disorder", but its hegemonic position and global footprint increase the significance of this condition. The United States spends more on its defence budget than the next 15 countries combined, it is the only country with five military commands spanning the entire planet, and it is unrivalled in its capacity to move troops and hardware. Reference to US imperialism, which increased exponentially with the invasions of Afghanistan and Iraq, was common during the years of the Viet Nam War. What is different in its contemporary manifestation is that the discussion is often neither hostile nor apologetic – indeed, a common criticism of the perceived US empire is that it does not exercise its power sufficiently. Michael Ignatieff has termed this phenomenon "Empire Lite", though it bears similarities to the British policies of indirect rule.[29] Whereas indirect rule was developed in part out of weakness, however (notably the practical impossibility of administering Nigeria), US imperial ambivalence derives in equal part from its democratic traditions, its isolationist tendencies and its adherence to anti-colonial norms that it helped to establish. The potential for a US imperium is also constrained by the changed nature of how power is exercised: US military power may be unrivalled, but its economic strength is not. Both economically and culturally, the United States has greater influence than any other state, but that influence depends upon a free flow of capital and ideas that would be undermined by extensive reliance upon military might.[30]

This may change. How the United States manages its de facto empire and the choices that it makes between unilateral and multilateral responses to problems that are increasingly global will determine much of twenty-first-century history. Machiavelli advised his Prince that it was better to be feared than to be loved, but this was only because it was difficult to unite both qualities in one person.[31] It is perhaps a uniquely American notion that countries inferior in power to the United States should not resent their subordinate status – that, if it is nice enough, Washington might construct a benevolent empire in which all love it.[32] Afghanistan and Iraq may serve as proving grounds for this vision.

Conclusion

Above all we must remember that the ways of Orientals are not our ways, nor their thoughts our thoughts. Often when we think them backward and stupid, they think us meddlesome and absurd. The loom of time moves slowly with them, and they care not for high pressure and the roaring of the wheels. Our system may be good for us; but it is neither equally, nor altogether good for them. Satan found it better to reign in hell than to serve in heaven; and the normal Asiatic would sooner be misgoverned by Asiatics than well governed by Europeans.

(George Nathaniel Curzon[33])

A measure of the speed with which the UN Interim Administration Mission in Kosovo was established is the name itself. UN operations typically operate under an acronym, but "UNIAMIK" was dismissed as too much of a mouthful. "UNIAK" sounded like a cross between "eunuch" and "maniac" – associations judged unlikely to help the mission. "UNMIK" was the final choice, having the benefits of being short, punchy and clear. Only in English, however. Once the operation was on the ground, it was discovered that *anmik*, in the dialect of Albanian spoken in Kosovo, means "enemy". No one within the United Nations was aware of the confusion until it was too late, at which point instructions went out to pronounce the acronym "oon-mik".

Just as generals are sometimes accused of planning to re-fight their last war, so the United Nations' experiments in transitional administration have reflected only gradual learning. Senior UN officials now acknowledge that, to varying degrees, Kosovo got the operation that should have been planned for Bosnia four years earlier, and East Timor got the one that should have been sent to Kosovo. Afghanistan's very different "light footprint" approach draws, in turn, upon the outlines of what Lakhdar Brahimi argued would have been appropriate for East Timor in 1999.

The United Nations may never again be called upon to undertake operations comparable to those in Kosovo and East Timor, where it exercised sovereign powers on a temporary basis. Even so, it is certain that the circumstances that demanded such interventions will recur. Lessons derived from past experiences of transitional administration will be applicable whenever the United Nations or other international actors engage in complex peace operations that include a policing function, civilian administration, development of the rule of law, establishment of a national economy, the staging of elections, or all of the above. Learning from such lessons has not, however, been one of the strengths of the United Nations.

Even more important than learning from past mistakes, however, is learning about future circumstances. Curzon's observations from his 1889 trip to Persia on "the ways of Orientals" were insightful but uncharacteristic. As Viceroy of India, he did not appoint a single Indian to his advisory council; when asked why, he replied, absurdly, that in the entire country there was not an Indian fit for the post. Modern trusteeships demand, above all, trust on the part of local actors. Earning and keeping that trust require a level of understanding, sensitivity and respect for local traditions and political aspirations that has often been lacking in transitional administration. How that trust is managed will, in large part, determine its legacy.

Transitional administration will remain an exceptional activity, performed on an ad hoc basis in a climate of institutional and political uncertainty. But in those rare situations in which the United Nations and other international actors are called upon to exercise state-like functions, they must not lose sight of their limited mandate to hold that sovereign power in trust for the population that will ultimately claim it.

Acknowledgements

The International Peace Academy's Project on Transitional Administrations was funded by the Carnegie Corporation of New York, with additional funding from the Ford Foundation and the John D. and Catherine T. MacArthur Foundation. Many thanks to David M. Malone, Neclâ Tschirgi, Sebastian von Einsiedel, Dino Kritsiotis, Kimberly Marten and Ramesh Thakur for their comments on an earlier version of this text. The views expressed are mine alone.

Notes

1. *Supplement to An Agenda for Peace: Position Paper of the Secretary-General on the Occasion of the Fiftieth Anniversary of the United Nations*, UN Doc. A/50/60-S/1995/1, 3 January 1995, paras. 13–14.
2. Michael Rose, "The Bosnia Experience", in Ramesh Thakur, ed., *Past Imperfect, Future Uncertain: The United Nations at Fifty*, London/New York: Macmillan/St. Martin's Press, 1998, p. 139.
3. See chapter 1 by Sebastian Einsiedel in this volume.
4. For a more nuanced, six-generation model, see Ramesh Thakur and Albrecht Schnabel, "Cascading Generations of Peacekeeping: Across the Mogadishu Line to Kosovo and Timor", in Ramesh Thakur and Albrecht Schnabel, eds, *United Nations Peacekeeping Operations: Ad Hoc Missions, Permanent Engagement*, Tokyo: United Nations University Press, 2001, pp. 3–25.
5. See *Strengthening of the United Nations: An Agenda for Further Change*, UN Doc. A/57/150, 9 September 2002, para. 126: "To strengthen further the Secretariat's work in international peace and security, there is a need to bring a sharper definition to the existing lead department policy, which sets out the relationship between the Department of Political Affairs and the Department of Peacekeeping Operations. The Department of Political Affairs will increase its focus in the fields of preventive diplomacy, conflict prevention and peacemaking. The Department will also intensify its engagement in policy formulation across the full spectrum of the Secretariat's tasks in the domain of international peace and security. It will continue to be the lead department for political and peace-building offices in the field. The Department of Peacekeeping Operations will be the lead department for the planning and management of all peace and security operations in the field, including those in which the majority of personnel are civilians."
6. Jacques Paul Klein, "What Does It Take to Make UN Peacekeeping Operations Succeed? Reflections from the Field", paper presented at 10th Anniversary of the Department of Peacekeeping Operations, New York, 29 October 2002.

7. *Report of the Panel on United Nations Peace Operations* (Brahimi Report), UN Doc. A/55/305-S/2000/809, 21 August 2000, available at ⟨http://www.un.org/peace/reports/peace_operations/⟩, para. 56.

8. International Crisis Group, *Bosnia: Reshaping the International Machinery*, Sarajevo/Brussels: ICG Balkans Report No. 121, 29 November 2001, available at ⟨http://www.crisisweb.org⟩, p. 13.

9. Michael W. Doyle, "War-Making and Peace-Making: The United Nations' Post-Cold War Record", in Chester A. Crocker, Fen Osler Hampson and Pamela Aall, eds, *Turbulent Peace: The Challenges of Managing International Conflict*, Washington, DC: United States Institute of Peace Press, 2001, p. 546.

10. George W. Bush, "President Bush Outlines Iraqi Threat", Cincinnati, Ohio, 7 October 2002, available at ⟨http://www.whitehouse.gov⟩.

11. Paul Krugman, "The Martial Plan", *New York Times*, 21 February 2003; James G. Lakely, "Levin Criticizes Budget for Afghanistan; Says White House Isn't Devoting Enough to Rebuilding", *Washington Times*, 26 February 2003. Aid was later increased further: David Rohde, "US Said to Plan Bigger Afghan Effort, Stepping up Aid", *New York Times*, 25 August 2003.

12. See, for example, International Crisis Group, *Bosnia's Precarious Economy: Still Not Open for Business*, Sarajevo/Brussels: ICG Balkans Report No. 115, 7 August 2001, available at ⟨http://www.crisisweb.org⟩.

13. Brahimi Report, para. 59.

14. International Commission on Intervention and State Sovereignty, *The Responsibility to Protect*, Ottawa: International Development Research Centre, December 2001, available at ⟨http://www.iciss.gc.ca⟩, paras. 2.32, 5.1–5.6.

15. See James Dobbins et al., *America's Role in Nation-Building: From Germany to Iraq*, Santa Monica, CA: RAND, 2003, pp. 160–166.

16. The term "nation-building" sometimes used in this context is broad, vague and often pejorative. Although it continues to be used in this context, "nation-building" has a more specific meaning in the post-colonial context, in which new leaders attempted to rally a population within sometimes arbitrary territorial frontiers. The focus here is on the state (that is, the highest institutions of governance in a territory) rather than the nation (a people who share common customs, origins, history and frequently language) as such.

17. George W. Bush, "Remarks by the President in Roundtable Interview with Foreign Press", Washington, DC, 17 July 2001, available at ⟨http://www.whitehouse.gov⟩.

18. George W. Bush, "Remarks by President Bush and Prime Minister Koizumi of Japan in Photo Opportunity", Washington, DC, 25 September 2001, available at ⟨http://www.whitehouse.gov⟩.

19. Ari Fleischer, "Press Briefing", Washington, DC, 4 October 2001, available at ⟨http://www.whitehouse.gov⟩.

20. George W. Bush, "President Holds Prime Time News Conference", Washington, DC, 11 October 2001, available at ⟨http://www.whitehouse.gov⟩.

21. George W. Bush, "Remarks by the President to United Nations General Assembly", New York, 10 November 2001, available at ⟨http://www.whitehouse.gov⟩.

22. George W. Bush, "State of the Union Address", Washington, DC, 29 January 2002, available at ⟨http://www.whitehouse.gov⟩.

23. *The National Security Strategy of the United States of America*, Washington, DC: President of the United States, September 2002, available at ⟨http://www.whitehouse.gov/nsc/nss.html⟩. See the draft Defense Planning Guidance leaked in 1992: "Excerpts from Pentagon's Plan: 'Prevent the Re-Emergence of a New Rival'", *New York Times*, 8 March 1992. The 1992 document was drafted by Paul D. Wolfowitz, then Under-

Secretary of Defense for Policy and later Deputy Secretary of Defense under President George W. Bush, for approval by Dick Cheney, Secretary of Defense in 1992 and later Vice-President. Criticism of its unilateralist message led to a substantial redrafting.

24. *National Security Strategy*, p. 1.
25. See, for example, Augustine Toure, "Liberia: Why Doing Too Little May Hurt US Long-term Interest", *New Democrat* (Heerlen), 16 July 2003; Elsina Wainwright, *Our Failing Neighbour: Australia and the Future of Solomon Islands*, Canberra: Australian Strategic Policy Institute, June 2003, p. 14.
26. *National Security Strategy*, p. 9.
27. Chris Johnson et al., *Afghanistan's Political and Constitutional Development*, London: Overseas Development Institute, January 2003.
28. See, for example, Richard Perle, "Thank God for the Death of the UN", *Guardian*, 21 March 2003.
29. Michael Ignatieff, *Empire Lite: Nation Building in Bosnia, Kosovo, Afghanistan*, London: Minerva, 2003. See also Niall Ferguson, *Empire: The Rise and Demise of the British World Order and the Lessons for Global Power*, New York: Basic Books, 2003.
30. See, generally, Joseph S. Nye, *The Paradox of American Power: Why the World's Only Superpower Can't Go It Alone*, Oxford: Oxford University Press, 2002.
31. Niccolò Machiavelli, *The Prince and the Discourses* [1531], transl. Christian E. Detmold, New York: Modern Library, 1950, chap. xvii.
32. Stephen Peter Rosen, "An Empire, If You Can Keep It", *The National Interest*, Vol. 71, 2003.
33. George N. Curzon, *Persia and the Persian Question*, Vol. 2, London: Frank Cass, 1966, p. 630.

17

Conclusion: The future of state-building

Simon Chesterman, Michael Ignatieff and Ramesh Thakur

Tolstoy wrote that all happy families are happy alike, whereas every un-happy family is unhappy in its own way.[1] It is tempting to say the same thing of states, as successful states enter an increasingly homogeneous globalized economy and weaker states slip into individualized chaos. As this volume has shown, that would be only partly true. Although all the cases considered here demonstrate the importance of local context – history, culture, individual actors – they still outline some general lessons that may be of assistance in addressing problems confronting states with weak institutions. Put another way, structural problems and root causes are part of the problem of "state failure", but this volume shows that a key question for policy makers is how weak states deal with crisis.

As explained in the Introduction, this volume is the final product of a project that grew out of the work of the International Commission on Intervention and State Sovereignty (ICISS). ICISS acknowledged that state sovereignty is the bedrock principle on which the modern international system – a society of states – is founded. It pointed to the problem of incapacitated and criminalized states, but argued that the best solution is to strengthen and legitimize states rather than overthrow the system of states. A world of capable, efficient and legitimate states will help to achieve the goals of order, stability and predictability and promote national and human security.

The end of the Cold War was not just a defeat of the Soviet Union as the superpower rival of the United States. It also marked the defeat of the ideology of communism and the collapse of the ideology of the command economy by the forces of liberal democracy and market economy. The enterprise of state-making since the end of the Cold War reflects these broader contextual realities. Political correctness aside, the major concerns with regard to state incapacity, failure and criminalization have focused on developing countries and in particular the former colonies. The colonial powers must accept their share of the blame for having ruptured the social development, arrested the political development and retarded the economic development of their wards. But that is history, and by itself does not help us much in pointing the way forward to a better future.

It does, however, attest to an enduring problem. In Western societies, the democratic franchise came after the liberal society and the liberal state were firmly established. In the post-colonial countries, democracy could not be installed as an adjunct of the liberal state, for the latter itself had not been established. In these societies, the rhetoric of democracy often involved, and the logic of the empirical reality occasionally implied, opposition to establishing the liberal capitalist state. Where the traditional culture is little attuned to political competition, the market polity of a competitive political party system may fail to take root and comprise instead just the "top dressing" of a political system.

State nationalism, too, originated in Europe. The state used its institutions and resources to promote national identity in order to consolidate and legitimize itself by manipulating these powerful new symbols. The campaign was so successful that national self-determination became a shorthand for the idea that nationalism requires the creation of a sovereign state for every nation. The nation-state became the focus of cultural identity. Yet the relationship between "nation" and "state" too has been historically contingent rather than logically necessary. The difficulty for most post-colonial societies was that state-building and nation-building had to be embarked on simultaneously. If "post-colonial" is to mean something other than post-independence, then it must entail some enduring legacy of colonial rule for the state that came into being with independence.

In development theory, the state was viewed as autonomous, homogeneous, in control of economic and political power, in charge of foreign economic relations, and possessing the requisite managerial and technical capacity to formulate and implement planned development. In reality, in many developing countries the state was a tool of a narrow family, clique or sect that was fully preoccupied with fighting off internal and external challenges to its closed privileges. In most of the literature, development has meant a strengthening of the material base of a society. A strong state would ensure order, look after national security and intervene actively in the management of the national economy. Yet the consolidation of state power can be used in the name of national security and law and order to suppress individual, group or even majority demands on the government and to plunder the resources of a society.

Three theoretical strands in particular are worth mentioning for explaining the relationship between group struggle and state power. The *pluralist theory of democracy* views democratic public policy as the outcome of a struggle between organized groups for control of the state. Stability is the outcome of cross-cutting cleavages: when individuals belong to multiple groups, the disruptive consequences of group conflict are attenuated; conversely, of course, where groups are homogeneous and individuals belong to mutually exclusive functional associations, social conflict is intensified. The *Marxist theory of the state* holds that two or more classes involved in economic relations of dominance and subordination are necessary for the existence of a state. Threats to the social order and the stability of the state result from an intensification of the class struggle. The dictatorship of the proletariat signifies the capture of social and political power by one class; class antagonisms disappear because there is only one class; and the state as the instrument and embodiment of the rule of one class over another withers away. The third theory of state is that of *the plural society*, a social order in which institutionally segmented groups coexist in one political unit without significant intermingling, and political power is monopolized by one cultural group. In this theory, the most salient feature of the post-colonial state is not its previous history of conquest by an alien culture but the persistence of the cultural incompatibility of its plural parts. This nullifies efforts to forge bonds of common citizenship and instead leads one group to use the state as an instrument of domination over other groups.

As Sebastian von Einsiedel's chapter in this volume emphasized, much discussion of state failure elides a series of definitional problems, most obviously about the nature of the state itself. If the state is understood as the vehicle for fulfilling a social contract, then state failure is the incapacity to deliver on basic public goods. If the state is defined by its capacity to exercise a monopoly over the legitimate use of force in its territory, state failure occurs when authority structures break down. Or, if the state is constituted by its legal capacity, state failure is the incapacity to exercise such powers effectively.

Rather than choosing between these Lockean, Weberian and juridical lines of thought, this volume demonstrates that such definitional questions are misleading: it is not generally the state that "fails", it is the government or individual leaders. In extreme cases, the institutions of governance themselves may be severely undermined. But it is only through a more nuanced understanding of the state as a network of institutions that crises in governance may be properly understood and, perhaps, avoided or remedied. In many situations the remedy will depend upon variables that are political rather than institutional, though the sustainability of any outcome depends precisely upon institutionalizing procedures to remove that dependence on politics and personality.

Not all weakening of state institutions is the same. Across the continuum of strength and weakness of states, the points at which crisis may occur vary. Two broad classes of crisis-prone states highlighted by I. William Zartman are states that are weak and soft and states that are hard and brittle. Weak/soft states lack the capacity to provide internal and external security and are prone to endemic weakness. Hard/brittle states are precisely the opposite, enjoying a strong and often oppressive capacity to maintain stability but organizing that order around a central individual; the displacement of that figure creates a vacuum of leadership that introduces a period of instability or conflict.

The key actors in these situations are, as the foregoing chapters have demonstrated, almost always local. Nevertheless, international actors may also play a critical role, if only in creating the opportunity for local actors to establish legitimate and sustainable governance. This concluding chapter will address these two sets of actors in turn.

Local actors

In efforts to strengthen state capacity, it is necessary to strike a balance between the responsibilities of local and international actors. Sometimes only international actors have the resources to assist with state-building, economic development, conflict prevention and post-conflict reconstruction. But they must take care not to confiscate or monopolize political responsibility, not to foster state dependency on the international community, and not to impede but to facilitate the creation and consolidation of local political competence. In the literature and policy work on failed states, terms such as "legitimacy" and "ownership" are frequently invoked as touchstones for local involvement in building or rebuilding state institutions. Both terms are typically underspecified and their lack of clarity contributes to incoherent policy responses to the practical consequences of the weakening of state institutions. After reviewing the use and abuse of these terms, this section examines how states have sought to institutionalize political structures to protect them from the whims of powerful individuals and the pernicious influence of regional actors.

Legitimacy

"Legitimacy" is sometimes used simultaneously in reference to a government, a regime or a state itself. Its characteristics are sometimes descriptive, akin to "effectiveness", or normative, denoting "good governance". Max Weber's description of different forms of legitimate authority provides a useful departure point for a more rigorous analysis.[2] The obedience of officials and subjects to a legally established impersonal order – Weber's definition of legal authority – may be contrasted with the exercise of power on the basis of coercion or personal affiliation. This is an elaborate way of describing the rule of law. Nevertheless, if governance is also to be effective, it is clear that a broader definition of legitimacy than respect for the rule of law is required.

In significant part, the legitimacy of state institutions may be bound up with the population's historical experience of it. The divergent experience of colonialism, for example, colours post-colonial states in different ways. Costa Rica's relative success is owed, as Abelardo Morales-Gamboa and Stephen Baranyi show in chapter 11, at least in part to a colonial legacy that encouraged liberal democracy and empowered political parties. Pakistan's precariousness, especially in contrast to its neighbour, may be traced to the legacy of a colonial history that differed from India's in a very interesting way. The same British Indian army, with shared social and organizational characteristics and military traditions, took over the reins of government in Pakistan not long after independence, whereas in India it remained under civilian control. In Pakistan, the military and bureaucratic elites joined forces against the politicians. In India, the political and bureaucratic elites joined forces against the military. In India, the repository of nationalism was the Congress Party, which led the struggle for independence; the military stayed out of politics. In Pakistan, the military quickly became the guardian of the national interest in terms of the perceived threat to the new nation from the much bigger and therefore menacing neighbour, and its role is pervasive in the politics and economy of the country.

Singapore, in Patricia Shu Ming Tan and Simon Tay's account in chapter 12, emerges as a rare instance of a colony using the language and institutions of the colonial power against it. For other states, the act of independence – whether from colonial rule or not – may itself be a defining moment for the governance of a state. Some states in periods of crisis may draw on the crisis itself to generate legitimacy. Precisely those conditions that threaten the viability of the state may present opportunities to demonstrate its relevance to the population. This has been done to shore up Singaporean national identity or to mobilize the North Korean population. As chapter 2 on colonialism explained, some foreign elites also saw a vested interest in keeping a population dependent on the beneficence of its leaders.

But how can the positive aspects of nationalism, or a sense of nationhood, be encouraged without trapping a population with an autocratic leader or opening ethnic cleavages? This shared sense of nationhood was an important part of Costa Rica's success. In Afghanistan, the belief in the Afghan state and the absence of secessionist movements are probably the only reasons it has continued to exist through a generation of civil war, foreign occupation, banditry and theocracy.

"Enlightened leadership" – a theme that runs through a number of the previous chapters, Costa Rica and Singapore most obviously – is a partial answer. It is also a challenge to the idea that international assistance is the key to successful state-building. Strong and charismatic leadership may be essential to the success of an independence movement or to seeing a country through the instability that independence can bring, but for every Jawaharlal Nehru (India), Julius Nyerere (Tanzania), Lee Kuan Yew (Singapore) and Nelson Mandela (South Africa), there is a Ne Win (Burma/Myanmar), Idi Amin (Uganda), Mobutu Sese Seko (Congo/ Zaire), Robert Mugabe (Zimbabwe), and many others.

The presence or absence of a strong, capable and honest leader can be a major factor in state-building, but it is not clear what the policy implications of such a finding might be. It is not possible to organize the response to East Timor or Afghanistan on the basis that one has to find a Xanana Gusmão or Hamid Karzai – indeed, it is questionable whether international engagement with a state experiencing a basic crisis in legitimacy should be focused on the elites at all.

A basic question confronting outside actors is whether to engage in top–down or bottom–up policies: to strengthen institutions and leaders, or to foster a functioning civil society in the hope that this will cultivate enlightened leadership in the long term. The sobering assessment that emerges from the chapters in this book is that state-building works best when a population rallies behind an enlightened leader, but very little at all will work if it rallies behind one who is not. Term limits are one way of minimizing this problem, but determined leaders who identify their survival with the survival of the state itself may nevertheless subvert such limits.

There is a surprising dearth of interest in the literature in the best "fit" between type of political system and local circumstances. International policy responses to the financial crises in many parts of the world since the 1990s have drawn criticism for trying to impose a "one-size-fits-all" framework on all troubled states. A similar caution may be warranted with respect to political prescriptions, but less forcefully advanced for fear of being branded a cultural relativist. Yet, in the stable, mature and advanced democracies, there is a comparable commitment to the values and principles of liberal democracy and market economy, but there is no uniformity of pattern in the structures, institutions and processes. Some have presidential government; others are parliamentary republics or constitutional monarchies. Some of the most stable European nations are leading examples of consociational democracy, whereas the United States and Australia are prime examples of robust adversarial politics. There is great diversity of electoral systems, party systems, periodicity of voting and terms of government. All such institutional differences reflect the particular historical patterns of political evolution in the European, American and Australasian settings. Yet the international policy community has been singularly hesitant to explore the connection between differences in institutional arrangements and local variables with a view to maximizing the prospects of liberal democracy and market economy taking root and flourishing.

Ownership

The importance of "ownership" is frequently asserted by international actors in both the political and economic processes of transition, though its meaning is unclear. Often it does not mean control – or even a direct input into decision-making structures. Sometimes qualified by "a sense of", ownership at times bears more psychological than political import. This meaning in English, however, does not always translate well into local languages; in the languages of the Balkans, for example, "ownership" makes sense only in the way that one might own a car.[3]

It is noteworthy that the states included in this volume as relative successes – Mozambique, Costa Rica and Singapore – all enjoyed strong leadership on the part of local elites. Each demonstrates the importance of foreign assistance being tailored to local needs, where possible channelled through local hands. Indeed, not only did Singapore not embrace an externally dictated template for development, some of its policies did not conform to the prevailing international consensus at the time on state-building. In extraordinary circumstances it may be necessary for legitimate international actors to make certain decisions on behalf of a population. As Simon Chesterman argues in chapter 16, such an arrangement should only ever be temporary and there should be clarity about why local control has been suspended and when and how it will be restored.

Such caveats concerning ownership should not be misunderstood as an argument against widespread participation. As chapter 9 by Amin Saikal on Afghanistan shows, social bonds may in some cases be far stronger than institutional ties to the state. The most optimistic aspect of Afghanistan's recent past is that its endemically weak state coincides with a relatively robust society.[4] Tapping into its ethnic, tribal, sectarian and linguistic networks – what Saikal terms "micro-societies" – is an important element of building a stable state.

A key dilemma is how to strike the balance between necessary decentralization (in recognition of the division of power through disparate actors) and the importance of building a centralized state that can itself provide certain basic public goods for the population. Politics is often defined in terms of the struggle for power. Democracy is a means of coming to terms with political power, taming it and making it subservient to popular wishes. Federalism is a means of bifurcating it territorially. A unitary system of government concentrates all legal power in a central government, with subordinate units of government being the creation of and subject to the will of that central government. A federal structure is one solution to the dilemma of the balance between centralizing and centrifugal pressures. But fragile societies such as Afghanistan may resist such an approach because of fears either that it would simply confirm the position of local commanders or warlords, or that it would open the possibility of a federal sub-unit seceding from the whole.

Many countries have had to grapple with the difficult question of maintaining unity amidst considerable diversity through appropriate and adaptable power-sharing arrangements that recognize but are not overwhelmed by the different social groups. States with regionally based ethnic divisions are, as a rule, more stable under federal rather than unitary structures. A curious sub-literature exists on the precise number of sub-units that is desirable: systems with two are highly unstable (as in Pakistan until 1971 and Czechoslovakia until 1992), and systems with four also appear to struggle; five units and above are believed to be about right, with another band of stability around 20–25. The foundation of this esoteric calculus is the ability of federal structures to diffuse decision-making power through different layers of government, increasing the number of arenas for peaceful resolution of political differences.[5] The stability of such power-sharing arrangements, however, relies less on the structures themselves than on the willingness of parties to operate within them. Where elite groups have relatively clear and loyal constituencies organized as political parties, labour unions or other institutions, structured political life will be more stable. These institutions rarely exist in a post-conflict environment, however, and the strategic questions of whether or not to opt into the peace process may be revisited by belligerent groups periodically through the transition. This was the case in Bosnia and Herzegovina: despite powerful international pressure to coerce parties into power-sharing arrangements, parties to the conflict simply refused to cooperate with the new multi-ethnic and inter-entity institutions.[6]

Political parties

The organization of political elites into parties, then, can be a helpful step in moving the exercise of power from individuals to institutions, but it may be a damaging step in infecting the institutions with inter-group conflict. Parties can also help to move power from the military to civilian actors. In Pakistan, as Samina Ahmed shows in chapter 7, the dysfunction of the political elite reinforces the role of the military. Costa Rica offers a radical solution to this problem, having disbanded its military in 1949. Not all countries have such an option, however – and, in any case, the ability to disband the military was evidence of the strength of civilian leadership rather than its cause. In Haiti, for example, disbanding the military in 1995 laid the foundation for state collapse nine years later when the regime was unable to defend itself against well-armed militias. And in Iraq the hasty and comprehensive disbandment of Saddam Hussein's security forces seriously hampered the postwar stabilization effort.

Parties are an important tool for recruiting candidates, organizing constituencies and aggregating public preferences for expression in political forums. Nevertheless, post-conflict elections can serve as a catalyst for the creation of political parties that are primarily – and sometimes solely – vehicles to provide local elites with access to governing power. Such parties may be little more than a repackaging of the armed groups that fought the original conflict.

In some circumstances, international actors may collude in efforts to repackage armed groups as political parties. The decision by the UN Transitional Authority in Cambodia (UNTAC) to treat the Khmer Rouge as a recalcitrant political party rather than an enemy of the peace process was deeply controversial at the time. Including the Khmer Rouge within the process and then isolating it when it withdrew from the elections – while tactically ignoring violence carried out by Hun Sen's State of Cambodia – contributed to the collapse of the Khmer Rouge after the elections, at which point most of its soldiers sought amnesties and abandoned Pol Pot.[7] This might have been an exceptional situation, however. When UNITA withdrew from elections in Angola and the Revolutionary United Front withdrew from the peace process in Sierra Leone, they were ultimately defeated – but only after military confrontations.

Different problems arise when parties coalesce around former liberation movements, such as the Revolutionary Front of Independent East Timor (Fretilin). Support for the party may be cultivated as being identical to nationalism or a national identity, which is an unhealthy basis for multi-party democracy.[8] The temptation to transform an independence movement into the natural party of government is understandable, but the danger is that such a party comes to view itself as the "natural" party of government – and the leader may come to regard himself or herself as indispensable. Nevertheless, this should not be taken as an inevitable consequence. In India, the first great post-colonial state, the Congress Party led the independence movement and held a monopoly of power in New Delhi and in almost all states for two decades after independence; since then, however, alternation of governments by peaceful ballot has been a regular staple of the political diet in the country.

One way of avoiding these problems is to remove political parties from the process. Democracy is commonly assumed to require a party system, although the United States itself did not develop functioning political parties until well into the nineteenth century. Without parties, however, political life is dominated exclusively by the elite personalities involved; this is the danger of a "no-party democracy" such as that embraced in Yoweri Museveni's Uganda, or the "permanent campaigning political movement" that Hazel Smith describes in North Korea in chapter 8. Such a system may be attractive to a population in a country with a history of political violence, where party divisions are seen less as divergent opinions on how the state should be governed than as fault lines that threaten a return to civil war. This was the case in East Timor, where many Timorese questioned the need for parties, an uncertainty born of the belief that divisions between Timorese independence parties had been exploited by Indonesia in 1974–1975. If it is not possible to mobilize political activity around structured arguments for how the state should be governed, however, the issues on which political argument will turn are likely to be the inherently unstable factors of personality or of ethnic or religious affiliation.

Regional influences

An important additional local dynamic that is frequently overlooked in analyses of state failure is how a state's governance problems relate to its regional context. Conflicts – and the economic incentives that foster them – may spill across borders and in some cases international efforts to bring peace may only displace conflict into another area. Andrea Armstrong and Barnett Rubin discuss this in the context of Central Asia and the Great Lakes region of Africa (chapter 4); Mónica Serrano and Paul Kenny outline the regional dynamics affecting Colombia (chapter 5); Benjamin Reilly and Elsina Wainwright examine the South Pacific (chapter 6). These differing accounts demonstrate how a region may impact on the evolution of conflict, the nature of state institutions in a region and the relative interest of external actors to support them.[9]

Adopting a regional analysis of a problem, however, will not always lead to a regional response. Importantly, the regional characteristics of a conflict – and of the proper response to it – may not overlap with regional institutions. The weakening of state institutions may itself give rise to new regional dynamics, often beginning with trade networks that respond to economic demand more than to political form. It became something of a cliché to say of Yugoslavia, for example, that despite its fragmentation it nevertheless continued to form a single black market.[10] South Asia, where political tensions have thwarted all efforts to date of regional integration, may nonetheless form a de facto single market for trafficking in women, exploiting common and persistent weaknesses in state capacity for border control. Trade networks may rely on social networks that extend across borders; these networks may be useful not merely in understanding the flow of resources into a conflict region but also in ensuring that a peace settlement lasts.

In addition to the malevolent policies of neighbouring states – such as South Africa's policy of destabilization in Mozambique[11] – weak institutions in one state may have a direct impact on institutions in those near it. This is clearest when a state becomes a transit point for the illicit flow of money or weapons, as in Afghanistan and the Democratic Republic of Congo, but may also serve a demonstration effect for what is expected in neighbouring states. Colombia, as Serrano and Kenny observe in chapter 5, is far from the weakest state in the Andean region, but it nonetheless has had a corrosive effect on its neighbours.

At the same time, building up the institutions of one state in isolation from its neighbours may not address the causes of conflict. Indeed, insofar as criminal enterprises in some regions see the state as an asset to be captured, state-building without regard to regional dynamics may simply increase the value of a particular prize. Strengthening regional and international governance structures, including formal and informal forums for cooperation and collaboration, may support the emergence of virtuous circles of accountability. More ambitiously, efforts to strengthen institutions in one state may need to be accompanied by efforts to strengthen institutions in key neighbours, perhaps along the lines of Zartman's "early" and "early late" prevention strategies (see chapter 13).

In other situations, regional context may affect the state's capacity even to sustain itself. Chapter 6 by Reilly and Wainwright on the South Pacific points to very different forms of state failure, including environmental collapse. Nauru's exhausted phosphate mines and the impact of rising sea levels on several low-lying atoll states may make these territories literally uninhabitable. These are merely the most extreme examples of a question that is implicit in many discussions of response to state failure – whether a state in a given territory is even viable.

However, the remoteness of these island states has had its own impact, with some otherwise bankrupt states marketing the one commodity they have left: sovereignty. Laundering money and selling passports or flags of convenience have opened the possibility of exploitation by non-state actors, perhaps including terrorists. This has increased the willingness of states in the region – notably Australia – to strengthen regional institutions and use them as the framework for any action in response to threatened state failure. This regional response is in part necessary to avert accusations of neo-colonialism, but it also strengthens regional ties that may provide early warning of trouble in other states and facilitate quick assistance at the political, economic and military level in the event of that trouble evolving into a crisis.

Think local, act global

Though some states are, indeed, islands, dysfunctional or non-existent governance structures can have effects far beyond their shores. Only a decade after the end of the Cold War, the United States redefined its national security strategy, warning that "America is now threatened less by conquering states than we are by failing ones".[12] Strategic interests may at times coincide with humanitarian concerns about the impact of state failure on a population. But, as Michael Ignatieff warns in chapter 3, there are reasons to be wary about the capacity of external action to address internal governance problems. Indeed, much external action either undermines governance structures or puts in place structures that are unsustainable. A first priority when generating policy for such action must therefore be to ensure that it does not undermine the local factors at work.

Diaspora groups, in particular, have generated considerable interest for their potential contribution to state-building – most prominently with the return of large numbers of Afghans to Afghanistan from 2002 onwards. And yet this is an area on which little systematic research has been undertaken. In severely depressed economies, the return of well-educated and motivated exiles could help overcome gaps in the civil service with greater legitimacy than importing large numbers of foreign personnel. That legitimacy is not unlimited, however, and the emergence of the diaspora as a new political elite may itself give rise to more political tensions. In addition, as Saikal points out in chapter 9, a vicious circle may emerge where educated members of the diaspora wait for a stable political and security environment before returning to the homeland, when it is precisely their involvement that is necessary to achieve political stability.

External action

In 1944, Judge Learned Hand spoke at a ceremony in Central Park, New York, to swear in 150,000 naturalized citizens. "Liberty lies in the hearts of men and women," he observed; "when it dies there, no constitution, no law, no court can save it; no constitution, no law, no court can even do much to help it."[13] Building or rebuilding faith in the idea of the state requires a transformation in mentality as much as it requires a change in political structures. The idea that one could generate a rigid template for reconstructing the institutions of law and order in a post-conflict environment is wrongheaded. As Judge Hand recognized, the major transformation required is in the hearts of the general population; any foreign involvement must therefore be sensitive to the particularities of that population at the level both of form and of substance.

The UN Charter is no longer a barrier to international engagement in states with weak institutions. In the past decade, the Security Council has authorized military interventions in states unable to prevent a humanitarian catastrophe (Somalia), following the deposition of the elected head of government (Haiti), and in the wake of economic collapse and social disorder (Albania). This interventionism has not simply been coercive. From the end of the Cold War, electoral assistance has become an accepted feature of the international political landscape, with the Electoral Assistance Division of the UN Department of Political Affairs receiving over 200 requests for assistance from member states. Development actors have a longer history of intrusive engagement in weak states.

This section will consider the motivations for foreign actors becoming involved in state-building, and then turn to the issue of early warnings that indicate that involvement might be required. This is followed by a consideration of the political context within which humanitarian action – typically the first response to a crisis – takes place, before examining the other carrots and sticks that are available to international actors. Finally, the section discusses exit strategies for when the crisis is averted or international attention moves elsewhere.

Responsibility and national interest

Although local actors will typically play the most important role in addressing a crisis in the institutions of governance, this should not be understood as an argument that international actors bear no responsibility for preventing state failure or ameliorating its consequences. In different ways, James Mayall and Michael Ignatieff outline in chapters 2 and 3 the historical and moral arguments for constructive engagement in such states.

There is much to learn from history, but the wrong lessons are frequently the ones most enthusiastically embraced. If the history of colonialism teaches us anything, it is that the imposition of foreign rule can produce widely divergent results. Mayall's chapter examines the lasting effects of grafting state institutions onto pre-existing political structures through colonial expansion; this imposition was often alien in both the form of the state and the manner in which it was imposed upon a population. Nonetheless, it is striking – and rarely commented upon – that the majority of post-colonial states did not, in fact, collapse. How the legacies of anti-colonial nationalism, the territorial settlement accompanying independence, economic development, and the match between political culture and social structure played out depended on local dynamics. But, reinforcing the positive aspects of nationalism, those that encourage the emergence of a state-wide national community and tailor economic development and constitutional structures to the reality of a given society rather than an ideal model seem uncontroversial starting points for external engagement in post-colonial territories.

Ignatieff's chapter outlines the moral argument for greater such engagement – as well as important reasons to be wary of enthusiasm for intervention for motives that are said to be humanitarian. The transformed strategic environment after the 11 September 2001 attacks encouraged some to think that countries led by the United States would be more willing to take on human rights violators if a regime also posed a threat to Western interests. As the war in Iraq came to demonstrate, neither of these factors was essential to some decision makers, and the capacity to follow through on intervention was substantially lacking. Humanitarian arguments in favour of removing the dictator Saddam Hussein were embraced by British Prime Minister Tony Blair in support of the goals of regime change and disarmament advocated by his US counterpart. As the existence of unauthorized weapons of mass destruction remained unproven, the failure to plan for post-conflict operations to reconstruct the country weighed heavily on those who had supported the war not because of any fear that Iraq posed a threat but precisely because the war was supposed to make Iraq a better place. Thus, Ignatieff argues, the use of human rights arguments to rationalize regime change is both intensely problematic and yet unavoidable. If the human rights discourse is to avoid being either idle rhetoric or mere window-dressing on the foreign policy agenda of major states, it needs to reconcile these tensions. This is a prescription for modesty about the capacity of external coercive intervention to make a state work; it is not a recipe for inaction.

Indeed, inaction is peculiarly inappropriate because there is much evidence that the dynamics of certain forms of globalization actively undermine state institutions. The vulnerability of exposed markets to fluctuations in commodity prices may provide a flashpoint for political opposition or a more prolonged decay in support for the state. Even in relatively successful states, such as Mozambique and Costa Rica, the impact of globalization has been ambiguous.

How, then, should action be guided? It would be naïve to expect international efforts to be driven by unvarnished altruism, but there is now some evidence that pursuit of foreign policy objectives in isolation from coherent state-building strategies is at best a waste of resources. Reconstruction in Afghanistan, for example, was driven by the desire to remove that country as a threat to the United States after the 11 September 2001 attacks; on the ground, this military strategy has been pursued in the absence of a similarly clear political strategy. There is a real danger now, as Saikal shows in chapter 9, that the failure to deal with the underlying causes of Afghanistan's weakness could cause it to fail once again. The most perilous aspect of any exit strategy from Afghanistan is the similarity between the current domestic political constellation and the situation in 1992, when the Soviet-backed Najibullah regime collapsed and international interest began to wander from Afghanistan. Then, as now, a weak central government sought to hold the country together: Rashid Dostum wielded power in the north, Ismael Khan held the west, and Gulbuddin Hikmatyar lurked in the wings. The disorder to which this gave rise – and, importantly, the disruption such disorder caused to trade routes – was an important factor in the emergence of the Taliban in 1994. If international attention wanders from Afghanistan again, this downward spiral could be repeated.

Neighbouring Pakistan is being supported far more vigorously, though precisely with a view to supporting the status quo rather than encouraging any form of transformation into a form of government more sustainable than direct military rule. This highlights a paradox of such state-building activities: the very act of supporting them may, when the state is collapsed into the status quo regime, further undermine their legitimacy in the eyes of the general population. It need not be so. As Ahmed argues in chapter 7, ongoing US support for Pakistan's military actively undermines movement towards functioning democracy. If support were conditioned on democratic reforms, this would strengthen the political elite's capacity to shift power from military to civilian hands. Such support is neither sufficient nor, indeed, necessary for such reforms to take place. But it would certainly help.

In Colombia, too, opportunistic military support for a weak state has more to do with the pursuit of a domestic political agenda – the war on drugs, like the war on terror, is waged primarily for the benefit of an American audience – than with the sustainability and legitimacy of the state in question. Taking a longer view on the importance of institutions for regional stability may be inadequate to satisfy such domestic political imperatives, a symptom of the "attention deficit disorder" in foreign policy that afflicts many states.[14]

The record of the United Nations in such situations is far from unblemished, but it does offer two important qualities that unilateral assistance – whether invited or imposed – lacks. These have nothing to do with capacity or experience, but rather concern the political context within which the United Nations operates. First, greater UN involvement may remove accusations of self-interest on the part of the acting country. This was seen most prominently in the elaborate dance performed by the United States and the United Nations through 2003–2004 concerning the latter's role in Iraq. Apart from securing greater international support for post-conflict reconstruction, it was hoped that an increased role for the United Nations in the political process would be a way of distancing incoming Iraqi leaders from the taint of being US puppets. Second, the involvement of the United Nations may help with the "attention deficit disorder" problem. Repeated accelerations of US plans for the transfer of political and security authority in Iraq have been an indication less of the stability of Iraq than of the need to demonstrate achievements in Iraq prior to the November 2004 presidential elections in the United States.

This raises a more general point that runs through the case-studies considered here. Whereas a crisis that thrusts itself onto the international agenda tends to be focused in time, the most important work of building up state institutions takes years or decades:[15] 10 years after a relatively successful operation in Mozambique, that country's own "success" remains uncertain; Singapore remained fragile for decades; and, though Costa Rica experienced moments of crisis, a key factor in its success was the institutional arrangement established after the 1948 civil war. Effective state-building takes time and it is disingenuous to suggest otherwise to domestic publics.

Early warning and analysis

At what point should international actors become concerned about a particular state? The literature on predicting state failure provides a wealth of models, pointing to political, economic and public health indicators that correlate with a high risk of political crisis.[16] These structural variables must, however, be tempered by attention to the local context.

The problem in relation to early warning, as Zartman stresses in chapter 13, is not generally a lack of information. The problem is inadequate analysis and a lack of political will. The need for new early warning systems is far outweighed by the need to use the information already being gathered. In Rwanda, for example, there were a number of warnings prior to the genocide in 1994. The first came from human rights nongovernmental organizations (NGOs). Then the UN human rights system picked up on them, including a report by the Special Rapporteur on Summary and Extra-judicial Executions that raised the spectre of genocide in August 1993. And yet the requisite political will just could not be mustered in the UN Security Council in April 1994 to help stop the killings.[17]

Greater analysis and coordinated dissemination of key information may therefore be more important than access to more information as such. States have nonetheless been reluctant to give the United Nations (or other intergovernmental organizations) any form of independent analytical capacity. This was most evident in the rejection of the Information and Strategic Analysis Secretariat recommended in the Brahimi Report on UN Peace Operations in 2000.[18] For the time being, much reliance is placed on information and analysis provided by states; on the independent capacity of the UN Secretary-General to bring to the attention of the Security Council "any matter which in his opinion may threaten the maintenance of international peace and security";[19] and on the work of NGOs such as the International Crisis Group.

Humanitarian action

When a state enters a period of crisis and its capacity to care for vulnerable populations diminishes or disappears, the first responders are usually humanitarian relief workers. The absence or ineffectiveness of state structures, however, complicate efforts to provide relief. As Thomas Weiss and Peter Hoffman show in chapter 14, the international humanitarian system was designed with an eye to responding to the horrors of inter-state conflict. The new environment in which humanitarians find themselves requires them to interact with a far wider array of actors, and to make decisions about which of those actors would be helpful and which would hinder efforts to restore stability. Key questions surround the actors who may go either way – leaders of political movements, legitimate businesses, individuals seeking employment, and private military companies – and how to engage with them most constructively. This "humanitarian intelligence" requires a change in tactics but also a doctrinal shift in thinking about the role of humanitarians. At the very least, it has triggered a debate on the extent to which humanitarians can remain outside politics.

Donors have an obvious role to play as well. Humanitarian assistance is notoriously supply rather than demand driven, with the result that it is more influenced by donor politics than by the politics of the recipient communities. The fact that donor countries wish to retain control over how their money is spent is not, in itself, controversial. In most cases, this money comes from taxes paid by constituents who hold their government accountable for how tax revenue is spent. Although donor behaviour may be rational from the donor government's perspective, however, the sum total of donor policies rarely presents a rational whole. A particular problem emphasized by Weiss and Hoffman is that short donor time-lines encourage short-term thinking on the part of local actors, often bringing out the worst in those who might otherwise become natural partners. These choices have consequences that go far beyond the emergency phase of humanitarian relief.

There is also a need to be creative about the manner in which humanitarian relief to states in crisis takes place at the intergovernmental level. As Smith shows in chapter 8, the caricature of North Korea as "bad, mad, or sad" is both incorrect and unhelpful. It never functioned as a traditional "Weberian" state because it was not designed to be one. Foreign policy engagement with North Korea currently focuses on its presumed nuclear capacity, but failing to address the weakness of state functions that have begun to disaggregate from the party may foster corruption and further weaken local coping mechanisms for the natural and human-made disasters that have afflicted the country. Security is a key part of this – not least because the fear of invasion is used by Kim Jong Il's regime to justify continued mobilization and the diversion of resources from civilian to military functions.

From persuasion ...

If humanitarian assistance is coming to be seen as political in nature, development assistance has long been regarded as such. Reconstruction aid, in particular, is one of the carrots that may be held out in the course of peace negotiations, with the promise of a pledging conference to come afterwards.

But are such economic levers the most appropriate instruments for driving a state towards success, rather than simply enticing it away from the abyss? And how should success be measured? As Weiss and Hoffman warn in chapter 14, providing assistance in isolation from political strategies runs the risk of extending conflict or reinforcing the structural violence that encourages conflict to return. And, as Michel Cahen argues in chapter 10 in the case of Mozambique, formal criteria for success viewed from the outside – the absence of conflict, the embrace of internationally approved economic models – may not correspond to how success on the ground is likely to be experienced by the local population.

The Marshall Plan, which followed the Second World War, is commonly held out as a model reconstruction programme. Between 1948 and 1951, Europe's aggregate gross national product (GNP) jumped by one-third, agricultural production increased 11 per cent and industrial output increased 40 per cent over pre-war levels. The Plan is variously attributed with laying the foundations of a prosperous European Union and launching the opening salvoes of the Cold War; today it is invoked like a mantra in the response to social and economic problems across the globe.[20]

The Marshall Plan was an act of enlightened self-interest not unvarnished altruism. Marshall himself stressed the impact that Europe's continuing weakness could have on the US economy: an injection of US funds would remedy the "dollar gap" and enable Europe to purchase US raw materials and parts necessary for the continent's reconstruction.[21] And, although Marshall had emphasized that the policy was "directed not against any country or doctrine but against hunger, poverty, desperation and chaos", US officials were deeply concerned about the leftward turn in European politics. Writing in 1947, George Kennan argued that the Marshall Plan would be an effective tool in the strategy of containment.[22] The Soviet blockade of Berlin from 1948 to 1949 actually saved the Plan for West Germany, because it undermined British and French efforts to use US contributions to their respective zones of occupation as a source of funds for war reparations.[23]

Speaking in April 2002, US President George W. Bush likened reconstruction efforts in Afghanistan to Marshall's programme for Europe, though the analogy was criticized for being stronger on rhetoric than on cash.[24] The experience of Bosnia suggests that the success of reconstruction is not dependent on funds alone: far more has been spent per capita there than under the Marshall Plan, yet the economy remains feeble.[25] The scale of the funding was certainly important – Senator Arthur Vandenberg responded to an early report of the proposed figures for Marshall's initiative by suggesting that a mistake must have been made, as Congress would never appropriate that amount of money to save anybody.[26] Equally significant, however, was the multilateral nature of the assistance and the fact that it was channelled through local institutions. It is easy to overstate the level of European ownership; in private, US intervention was said to be "frequent, often insistent". But appearances had to be and were preserved. These appearances were bolstered by a public relations campaign that may represent the largest international propaganda operation in peacetime.[27] This use of local institutions combined with a due regard for propaganda was repeated in the reconstruction component in Afghanistan in 2002. Such genuine and tactical forms of ownership – at least in the area of economic reconstruction – have generally been more effective than mere reliance on its rhetoric.

The scale of the Marshall Plan, its regional focus and the channelling of funds through local institutions certainly bear some lessons for contemporary efforts. But these factors were linked to the circumstances in which the Marshall Plan was formulated and implemented. The very different circumstances in which aid is delivered today suggest the limits of this analogy.

Four themes stand out. First, the resolution of the Second World War provided a clear military and political context for reconstruction. Strategic concerns dominated, ensuring greater resources and a sustained commitment; the clarity of the outcome of the war and the recognition of most borders in Europe also ensured that the legitimacy of recipient governments was, for the most part, uncontested. More recent conflicts have tended to be localized, frequently involving irregular forces and leading to an inconclusive peace. The absence of a common threat and the prominence of actors other than the United States have meant that multiple donors pursue independent objectives, at times inconsistently. Domestic considerations may thus complicate coordination between different governments, with each seeking to finance "pet" projects.

Second, postwar Europe was very different from recipient countries today. The Marshall Plan targeted relatively wealthy democracies with advanced capitalist economies and highly educated populations; the challenge was recovery, not creation. The approach was regional in character and built upon political and military alliances. Recipients now tend to be fragile democracies at best, usually of limited long-term interest to donors. The economies in question are constrained in their capacity to absorb a sudden influx of aid, which tends to be concentrated over a relatively short period. Where state institutions are weak or non-existent, this aid may be largely in the form of emergency humanitarian relief at the expense of development-oriented assistance.[28]

Third, the number of actors has greatly increased, most obviously with the rise of NGOs. This proliferation has fostered niche assistance that contributes targeted assistance in some sectors but further complicates coordination. Many NGOs now function more as service providers for donor agencies rather than as programming agencies in their own right. This encourages some to become "ambulance chasers", deploying to a crisis situation with little or no funding. Though they may bring skills and commitment to the emergency, considerable initial effort is spent raising funds from local donor missions and UN agencies. One Afghan analyst in Kabul wryly observes that "NGOs are cows that drink the milk themselves". Reliance upon multiple sources of funding has also increased the influence of the media, encouraging a focus on crises that are the subject of public attention and sometimes limiting assistance to the duration of that attention. A further consequence is the rise of "flag-waving" activities on the part of donors and NGOs, which seek to gain maximum credit for their activities. This may in turn lead to competition for telegenic projects and a reluctance to engage in mundane or unattractive projects.

Finally, the Marshall Plan took place in an era when the benefits of government intervention were generally uncontested. Donor scepticism today about the appropriate role of government in economic activity at home has, at times, challenged approaches to foreign assistance abroad. The prevailing view in the industrialized world now is that the function of government is to do little more than facilitate a market economy and provide a very few public goods. This is at odds with the widespread view that a strong government often lies at the heart of economic and political reconstruction.

The context within which assistance is delivered to post-conflict territories is therefore quite different from the aftermath of the Second World War. Political considerations continue to play a major part in the decision to provide assistance, but the purposes that assistance is intended to serve are less coherent than the grand strategy envisioned in the Marshall Plan. This is, of course, if the assistance arrives at all. Funds for post-conflict relief may not arrive, or may arrive only very slowly. Actors implementing programmes on the ground must take this into account when they construct budgets, which often requires them to engage in fictional accounting for targets that they know will not be met. This makes responsible financial planning still more difficult.[29]

... to tools of dissuasion

There are not many coercive tools available to international actors to deal with state failure. Zartman provides a catalogue of options in chapter 13 but, if a situation goes beyond the point where words are sufficient, sanctions may be imposed or force may be used (with or without the blessing of the UN Security Council). Both have been the subject of extensive research in their own right,[30] though some lessons concerning the nature of the force deployed bear emphasizing here. Two recent additions to this very limited quiver are international criminal law and transitional administration.

Weber has been mentioned on various occasions through this book and so it is worth stressing that the claim to a monopoly on the legitimate use of force should normally be understood as a requirement for a functioning police capacity. States where that monopoly has been called into question will generally require a robust policing – as opposed to military – response. The South Pacific, where few states face serious external threats from neighbours, is a clear example of this: most states have no real military capacity, but it is the failure of the police forces that has caused problems.[31]

These lessons are not new. When the UN Operation in the Congo (ONUC) was deployed in 1960, the absence of an effective government led it to assume many of the law and order functions of a civilian police force, including the apprehension and detention of criminals, establishing and enforcing curfews, and conducting short- and long-range patrols.[32] These functions were carried out despite the absence of a clear power of arrest, of jails or of functioning courts. It was also unclear what law ONUC was to uphold, because the newly independent state had not had time to codify a Congolese version of the old Belgian law. Such problems were compounded by the inadequacy of troops for such tasks; it became increasingly clear that highly trained riot police would have been more suited to such tasks than military regiments – where civilian police from Ghana and Nigeria operated, they were regarded as worth "twenty times their number of the best fighting infantry".[33] Over 40 years later, the slowness to deploy civilian police continues to afflict UN missions.[34]

By contrast, one area of state-building that has seen an explosion of activity – and, to some extent, learning – is transitional justice. The creation of the International Criminal Tribunals for the Former Yugoslavia and Rwanda and the Special Court for Sierra Leone was, at least in part, designed to address the incapacity of existing institutions to deal with past atrocities. As chapter 15 by Alex Boraine warns, however, it is vital that transitional justice be understood both widely and deeply. It must be understood widely in that it embraces not merely accountability through judicial trials but also truth-seeking and truth-telling, reconciliation, institutional reform, and reparations.[35] Transitional justice must also be seen deeply, for, unless processes and institutions are tailored to address local concerns and draw upon local resources, they are unlikely to be effective or sustainable.

Ideally, all such decisions would be made by local actors. But states with weak institutions are perhaps most prone to undermining faith in the rule of law. A key dilemma, highlighted by Boraine, is how to balance the need for accountability for the past against the need for reconciliation in the future. In the mid-1990s, the widely held view appeared to be that any post-conflict environment should hold war crimes trials today and elections tomorrow. Mozambique provides some evidence that a peace process can work without trials, though perhaps it is too early to make a firm conclusion on this. Spain after Franco is another challenge to the argument that all peace processes must be accompanied by elaborate transitional justice processes. In East Timor there have been public hints of disagreement between the president and the foreign minister over whether to privilege peace and reconciliation or retributive justice in relations with Indonesia. In parts of Latin America we may yet witness transitional justice mechanisms instituted after a delay of over a decade.

How the balance between the past and the future is struck will depend upon local actors. Two general trends can be identified, however. First, if peaceful coexistence is a stated goal of the transition, the transitional government is likely to be restricted in its choices. Second, where such governments are restricted, societies in transition tend to move away from purely retributive models and towards more restorative models of justice. In addition to trials by national, international or hybrid tribunals, Boraine provides an account of the two other major institutional responses to transitional justice issues: truth and reconciliation commissions and vetting.

A more extreme form of international engagement is the one that Chesterman describes in chapter 16: transitional administration. For international actors to assume some or all powers of government is antithetical to many of the lessons discussed here, in particular the need for local input and ownership. But if ownership is not possible in the short term – owing to the inability of local actors to work peacefully together or where institutions simply do not exist – it is better to acknowledge that ownership will be the end rather than the means.

There has been much reluctance to embrace this practice and dignify it with theory. In the case of Iraq, for example, it was sometimes argued that greater involvement of the United Nations would have avoided some of the mistakes made by the Coalition Provisional Authority in its first year of occupation. Three of the most egregious errors in Iraq – failing to provide for emergency law and order, disbanding the Iraqi army, and blanket de-Baathification – ran counter to lessons from previous operations. However, the greatest mistake by US planners may have been the assumption that previous UN state-building efforts have achieved mixed successes because of UN incompetence, rather than owing to the inherent contradictions in building democracy through foreign military intervention.

Exit strategies

In his April 2001 report on the closure or transition of complex peacekeeping operations, UN Secretary-General Kofi Annan warned that the embarrassing withdrawal of peacekeepers from Somalia should not be repeated in future operations. *No Exit without Strategy*, the report was called.[36] For the UN Transitional Administration in East Timor, elections provided the basis for the transfer of power to local authorities; they also set in place political processes that would last well beyond the mission and the development assistance that followed. In Kosovo, where the UN operation was determinedly called an "interim" administration, the absence of an agreed end-state has left the territory in political limbo. Reflection on the absence of an exit strategy from Kosovo, following on the apparently endless operation in Bosnia and Herzegovina, led some ambassadors to the Security Council to turn the Secretary-General's phrase on its head: "No strategy", the rallying cry went, "without an exit".

Singapore's experience of the withdrawal of British troops is an example of the need to manage exit strategies carefully. In chapter 12, Tan and Tay contrast Singapore's efforts to stagger the departure of foreign troops with the popular call in the Philippines for US troops to depart immediately. Domestically popular, the latter strategy left a vacuum of equipment, revenue and skills. The unmanaged withdrawal of foreign security forces may also lead to a resumption of conflict. This fear drives the maintenance of large security presences in Bosnia and Kosovo, and it explains the decision never to send such numbers to Afghanistan.

Elections are frequently cited as the appropriate end-point for international engagement in a crisis. As a medium-term peace-building strategy, there is implicit deference to the "democratic peace" thesis, which holds that democracies are statistically less likely to go to war than are states that are undemocratic.[37] Overemphasis on this empirical argument (which has itself been contested) obscures a secondary finding in the democratic peace literature that an autocratic state in the process of democratization may in fact be *more* likely to descend into conflict, especially internal conflict.[38] More often, however, elections may simply be a short-term tactic that is used to encourage actors to buy into a peace process.[39]

The United Nations and other bodies, notably the Organization for Security and Co-operation in Europe, have developed an outstanding capacity to hold and monitor elections in the most challenging circumstances. Elections in conflict zones such as Cambodia and Bosnia, or in impoverished countries such as East Timor, are rightly regarded as technical triumphs.[40] Technical triumph, however, has only rarely been matched by political success.

In general, the emphasis has been on form at the expense of substance. The transition to democracy requires a transformation in public mentality similar to that underpinning respect for the rule of law. Elections may provide evidence of this transformation, but they are only a small part of what is required to realize it. Building robust market economies and resilient civil societies is just as critical for embedding democracy in larger structures that can survive changes of leaders and parties.

Concluding thoughts

In his book *In My Father's House*, Kwame Anthony Appiah notes that the apparent ease of colonial administration generated an illusion among some of the inheritors of post-colonial nations that control of the state would allow them to pursue their much more ambitious objectives as easily. Once the state was turned to the task of massive developments in infrastructure, however, it was shown wanting: "When the postcolonial rulers inherited the apparatus of the colonial state, they inherited the reins of power; few noticed, at first, that they were not attached to a bit."[41]

Given the fraught history of so many of the world's states, it is not remarkable that some states suffer basic crises in their capacity to protect and provide services for a population; on the contrary, it is remarkable that more do not. This book has sought to examine states in crisis and, in particular, to examine what internal and external factors led some states to avoid altogether going to the precipice, others to go over it, and a third group to return from it. As indicated in the Introduction to this volume, discussion of such institutional crises frequently suggests that, when a state "fails", power is no longer exercised within the territory. In fact, the control of power becomes more important than ever – even though it is exercised in an incoherent fashion.

Engagement with such states requires, first and foremost, understanding the local dynamics of power. The much-cited Weberian definition of the state as claimant to a monopoly of the legitimate use of force is a definition less of what the state *is* than of what it *does*. The legitimacy and sustainability of local power structures depend, ultimately, upon local actors. Certain policies can help – channelling political power through parties rather than individuals, and through civilians rather than the military; imposing term limits on heads of state and government; encouraging and regulating political parties – but their implementation depends on the capacity of local leaders to submit themselves to the rule of law, and of local populations to hold their leaders to that standard.

For international actors, a troubling analogy is to compare engagement with weak states to previous models of trusteeship and empire. Current efforts at state-building attempt – at least in part – to reproduce the better effects of empire (inward investment, pacification and impartial administration) without reproducing its worst features (repression, corruption and confiscation of local capacity). This is not to suggest nostalgia for empire or that such policies should be resurrected. Only two generations ago, one-third of the world's population lived in territory considered non-self-governing; the end of colonialism was one of the most significant transformations in the international order since the emergence of sovereign states. However, it is intended to suggest that a realistic assessment of power is necessary to formulate effective policies rather than effective rhetoric.

States cannot be made to work from the outside. International assistance may be necessary, but it is never sufficient to establish institutions that are legitimate and sustainable. This is not an excuse for inaction, if only to minimize the humanitarian consequences of a state's incapacity to care for its vulnerable population. Beyond that, however, international action should be seen first and foremost as facilitating local processes, providing resources and creating the space for local actors to start a conversation that will define and consolidate their polity by mediating their vision of a good life into responsive, robust and resilient institutions.

Acknowledgements

Many thanks to Sebastian von Einsiedel, Tarun Chhabra and Vanessa Hawkins for their comments on earlier versions of this text.

Notes

1. Leo Tolstoy, *Anna Karenina*, transl. Louise and Aylmer Maude, Oxford: Oxford University Press, 1998.
2. See chapter 1 by Sebastian von Einsiedel in this volume.
3. The peculiarities of conceptual elision in translation are of course a more general phenomenon. In Hindi, for example, there are words for nation (*rashtra*) and kingdom (*rajya*) but not really for state. Thus the President of India is called the Rashtrapati (literally, "the husband or lord and master of the nation"), and the upper house of the federal parliament, the Council of States, is called the Rajya Sabha (literally, "the assembly of kingdoms"). Nor does the word for citizen come anywhere near the rich historical and conceptual connotations of the term in contemporary English theory and practice; rather, *nagarik* is closer to its literal meaning, "inhabitant or resident of", which is closer conceptually to "national" than to citizen.
4. In a similar vein, Ramesh Thakur has argued that: "All agree that India is slow to change. To modernization theorists that was its weakness; to many Indian political scientists that is its strength. Hinduism is distinctive among complex, highly differentiated civilizations for maintaining a cultural identity that is free of a given political frame-

work. This meant that political changes could be implemented without being impeded by religious resistance ... Conversely, the establishment of new political institutions did not pose a threat to the core values of the established social order, and therefore did not unleash general instability" (*The Government and Politics of India*, London: Macmillan, 1995, p. 294).

5. See, e.g., Alfred C. Stepan, "Federalism and Democracy: Beyond the US Model", *Journal of Democracy*, Vol. 10, No. 4, 1999, p. 19; Nancy Bermeo, "The Import of Institutions", *Journal of Democracy*, Vol. 13, No. 2, 2002, p. 96.

6. Terrence Lyons, "The Role of Postsettlement Elections", in Stephen John Stedman, Donald Rothchild and Elizabeth M. Cousens, eds, *Ending Civil Wars: The Implementation of Peace Agreements*, Boulder, CO: Lynne Rienner, 2002, pp. 220–221; Elizabeth M. Cousens, "From Missed Opportunities to Overcompensation: Implementing the Dayton Agreement on Bosnia", in Stedman et al., eds, *Ending Civil Wars*, p. 531.

7. Sorpong Peou, "Implementing Cambodia's Peace Agreement", in Stedman et al., eds, *Ending Civil Wars*, p. 499.

8. Tanja Hohe, "Totem Polls: Indigenous Concepts and 'Free and Fair' Elections in East Timor", *International Peacekeeping*, Vol. 9, No. 4, 2002, pp. 73–74.

9. Such an analysis is, of course, applicable to other regions – most obviously West Africa and the overlapping conflicts of Liberia and Sierra Leone. See, e.g., John Hirsch, *Sierra Leone: Diamonds and the Struggle for Democracy*, Boulder, CO: Lynne Rienner, 2001.

10. See, e.g., "Robertson on Balkans: 'Not a Hopeless Case'; NATO Secretary General Says Allied Successes Overlooked", *Washington Post*, 22 June 2001.

11. See chapter 10 by Michel Cahen in this volume.

12. *The National Security Strategy of the United States of America*, Washington, DC: President of the United States, September 2002, available at ⟨http://www.whitehouse.gov/nsc/nss.html⟩, p. iv.

13. Learned Hand, *The Spirit of Liberty*, 3rd edn, Chicago: University of Chicago Press, 1960, p. 190.

14. See chapter 16 by Simon Chesterman in this volume.

15. See William Maley, Charles Sampford and Ramesh Thakur, eds, *From Civil Strife to Civil Society: Civil and Military Responsibilities in Disrupted States*, Tokyo: United Nations University Press, 2003.

16. See chapter 1 by Sebastian von Einsiedel in this volume.

17. See Colin Keating, "Rwanda: An Insider's Account", in David M. Malone, ed., *The UN Security Council: From the Cold War to the 21st Century*, Boulder, CO: Lynne Rienner, 2004, pp. 500–511; Linda Melvern, *A People Betrayed: The Role of the West in Rwanda's Genocide*, London: Zed Books, 2000; and Samantha Power, *"A Problem from Hell": America and the Age of Genocide*, New York: Perennial, 2003.

18. *Report of the Panel on United Nations Peace Operations* (Brahimi Report), UN Doc. A/55/305-S/2000/809, New York, 21 August 2000, paras. 65–75.

19. UN Charter, Art. 99.

20. See Michael J. Hogan, *The Marshall Plan: America, Britain, and the Reconstruction of Western Europe, 1947–1952*, Cambridge: Cambridge University Press, 1987, p. 431; Walt W. Rostow, "Lessons of the Plan: Looking Forward to the Next Century", *Foreign Affairs*, Vol. 76, No. 3, 1997, p. 205; Peter Grose, "The Marshall Plan – Then and Now", *Foreign Affairs*, Vol. 76, No. 3, 1997, p. 159.

21. See also Scott Jackson, "Prologue to the Marshall Plan: The Origins of the American Commitment for a European Recovery Program", *Journal of American History*, Vol. 65, 1979, p. 1055.

22. "Policy Planning Staff Paper on Aid to Western Europe", 23 May 1947, PPS/1. Kennan,

who directed the State Department's Policy Planning Staff, anonymously published the article that was the intellectual basis for US containment policy through the Cold War: "The Sources of Soviet Conduct", *Foreign Affairs*, Vol. 25, No. 4, 1947, p. 566.

23. Diane B. Kunz, "The Marshall Plan Reconsidered: A Complex of Motives", *Foreign Affairs*, Vol. 76, No. 3, 1997, p. 168.

24. Mike Allen, "Bush Resumes Case against Iraq; Democratic Nations Must Confront 'Axis of Evil,' President Tells VMI Cadets", *Washington Post*, 18 April 2002; "If Afghanistan Goes Down", *Washington Post*, 9 July 2002.

25. Jacques Paul Klein, "What Does It Take to Make UN Peacekeeping Operations Succeed? Reflections from the Field", paper presented at 10th Anniversary of the Department of Peacekeeping Operations, New York, 29 October 2002.

26. Charles P. Kindleberger, "In the Halls of the Capitol", *Foreign Affairs*, Vol. 76, No. 3, 1997, p. 186.

27. David Reynolds, "The European Response: Primacy of Politics", *Foreign Affairs*, Vol. 76, No. 3, 1997, pp. 182–183.

28. See Susan L. Woodward, "Economic Priorities for Successful Peace Implementation", in Stedman et al., eds, *Ending Civil Wars*, p. 183; Joanna Macrae, *Aiding Recovery? The Crisis of Aid in Chronic Political Emergencies*, New York: Zed Books, 2001.

29. See, generally, Shepard Forman and Stewart Patrick, eds, *Good Intentions: Pledges of Aid for Postconflict Recovery*, Boulder, CO: Lynne Rienner, 2000.

30. On sanctions, see especially David Cortright and George A. Lopez, *The Sanctions Decade: Assessing UN Strategies in the 1990s*, Boulder, CO: Lynne Rienner, 2000. On coercive military intervention, see International Commission on Intervention and State Sovereignty, *The Responsibility to Protect*, Ottawa: International Development Research Centre, December 2001, available at ⟨http://www.iciss.gc.ca⟩; Simon Chesterman, *Just War or Just Peace? Humanitarian Intervention and International Law*, Oxford: Oxford University Press, 2001.

31. See chapter 6 by Benjamin Reilly and Elsina Wainwright in this volume.

32. *Second Progress Report to the Secretary General from His Special Representative in the Congo, Mr Rajeshwar Dayal*, UN Doc. S/4557, 2 November 1960.

33. Arthur Lee Burns and Nina Heathcote, *Peacekeeping by UN Forces: From Suez to the Congo*, New York: Praeger, for the Center for International Studies, Princeton, 1963, p. 185; Catherine Hoskyns, *The Congo since Independence: January 1960 to December 1961*, Oxford: Oxford University Press, 1965, p. 295.

34. See Ramesh Thakur and Albrecht Schnabel, eds, *United Nations Peacekeeping Operations: Ad Hoc Missions, Permanent Engagement*, Tokyo: United Nations University Press, 2001.

35. See Ramesh Thakur and Peter Malcontent, eds, *From Sovereign Impunity to International Accountability: The Search for Justice in a World of States*, Tokyo: United Nations University Press, 2004.

36. *No Exit without Strategy: Security Council Decision-Making and the Closure or Transition of United Nations Peacekeeping Operations, Report of the Secretary-General*, UN Doc. S/2001/394, 20 April 2001.

37. See, generally, Michael E. Brown, Sean M. Lynn Jones and Steven E. Miller, eds, *Debating the Democratic Peace*, Cambridge, MA: MIT Press, 1996; Joanne S. Gowa, *Ballots and Bullets: The Elusive Democratic Peace*, Princeton, NJ: Princeton University Press, 1999; Tarak Barkawi and Mark Laffey, eds, *Democracy, Liberalism, and War: Rethinking the Democratic Peace Debate*, Boulder, CO: Lynne Rienner, 2001.

38. Edward D. Mansfield and Jack Snyder, "Democratization and the Danger of War", in Brown et al., eds, *Debating the Democratic Peace*, p. 301.

39. For UN efforts at promoting democracy, see Edward Newman and Roland Rich, eds,

The UN Role in Promoting Democracy: Between Ideals and Reality, Tokyo: United Nations University Press, 2004.

40. See, e.g., *An Agenda for Democratization*, UN Doc. A/51/761, 20 December 1996, para. 13: "Democratization is predominantly a new area for technical assistance."

41. Kwame Anthony Appiah, *In My Father's House: Africa in the Philosophy of Culture*, New York: Oxford University Press, 1992, p. 266. There is a similar saying in India, to the effect that "I've bought the reins, the bit and the saddle; all I need now is the horse".

Index